A RELATIONAL APPROACH
TO REHABILITATION

Brain Injuries Series

Published and distributed by Karnac Books

OTHER TITLES IN THE SERIES

- *Anxiety and Mood Disorders following Traumatic Brain Injury: Clinical Assessment and Psychotherapy* by Rudi Coetzer

Orders:
Tel: +44 (0)20 7431 1075; Fax: +44 (0)20 7435 9076
E-mail: shop@karnacbooks.com
www.karnac books.com

A RELATIONAL APPROACH TO REHABILITATION
Thinking about Relationships after Brain Injury

Ceri Bowen

D Clin Psych, MPhil, BSc. (Hons), C Psychol
Consultant Clinical Psychologist, Defence Clinical
Psychology Service—Joint Medical Command

Giles Yeates

D Clin Psych, MSc, BSc. (Hons), C Psychol
Principal Clinical Neuropsychologist,
Community Head Injury Service, Aylesbury

Síobhán Palmer

Psych D Clin Psych, PgDip, BSc. (Hons), C Psychol
Senior Clinical Psychologist, Brain Injury Rehabilitation Trust

KARNAC

First published in 2010 by
Karnac Books Ltd
118 Finchley Road
London NW3 5HT

British Library Cataloguing in Publication Data

A C.I.P. for this book is available from the British Library

ISBN-13: 978-1-85575-748-6

Typeset by Vikatan Publishing Solutions (P) Ltd., Chennai, India

Printed in Great Britain

www.karnacbooks.com

CONTENTS

FOREWORD

The history of recovery of function has taken a long road from lack of belief in regeneration in the central nervous system to the present stage where it can be scientifically demonstrated that the brain is an organ that is dynamic and capable of dramatic changes following injury or environmental changes (Stein, 1995).

The insight into brain function has been gained from research in the neurosciences, biology, pharmacology, and genetics, and new generations of scanning methods are not only capable of distinguishing damaged tissues but also showing how the functioning of the living brain is changing during the activities of our daily life and during our lifetime. The term "Plasticity" has been coined, and evidence for plasticity has been shown through the whole lifespan (Jones et al., 2006). The belief that brain injury is permanent and cannot be repaired can no longer be held true and neither can the tendency to regard the adult brain as totally rigid (Gazzaniga et al., 2002; Kolb & Wishaw, 2005).

Acceptance of these new findings strengthens the demands for providing more effective rehabilitation. The need for new methods among those working in the field becomes imminent at the same time as new pathways are opened for rehabilitation methods.

The group of three British clinical psychologists, authors of this new book, together with their contributors, all experienced in neurorehabilitation through a number of years, states, that by the term "relational" they wish to emphasize human *relationships* as the most important vehicle for change and they invite their reader to consider broadly in which way relationships make an impact upon the rehabilitation process following acquired brain injury (ABI). The proposal to include the family into the bio-psycho-social perspective is made with the purpose to expand the knowledge available in the team working together during the rehabilitation process.

In this respect, it is further stated that by framing rehabilitation as "relational" and at the same time drawing upon a number of interventionist approaches, new methods and theories will be available: "All the approaches considered for inclusion share a common emphasis on defining brain injury against a backdrop of differing perspectives within social contexts, which will lead to an attempt to reconcile the terms neurology and what is termed social constructionism." The social determinants of identity and the potential therapeutic qualities of socializing together with concerned and committed individuals, groups, and communities will be emphasized.

Reinstating the social influence on brain functioning cannot but bring back to mind the influence of Alexander Luria and his definition of the higher cortical functions as social in origin, mediated through language and conscious in their performance. His demand of the rehabilitation therapist in therapy is to understand the patient's individuality, based on the analysis of syndromes of cognitive function and the patient's socio-cultural background, revealing the social influences in the building up of the functional systems responsible for behaviour and cognition, created in their social contexts. Done properly, a diagnostic proposal illuminating the patient's actual state will be the result on which to choose the right kind of methods and the right kind of feedback in the service of supporting the patient's insight and progress.

Early traditions from Oxford, characterizing the treatment of soldiers after World War II, followed similar lines, where the neuropsychologists Oliver Zangwill and Freda Newcombe collaborated with the neurologist Ritchie Russell, who expressed: "There is an unlimited field for ingenuity to adapt exercise, occupation and entertainment to help the individual to redevelop his/her injured faculties."

Very impressive results of a British outcome study, published by
Freda Newcombe in 1996 showed remarkably good behaviour,
striking presentations in cognitive tests, rare psychiatric illness, and
little difference in self-reports on rating scales between veterans and
controls.

The new book "A Relational Approach to Rehabilitation after
Acquired Brain Injury" resting on methods having proven their
importance opens for new views in an interesting thorough and
convincing discussion in a field of great importance for very many
individuals, their families, and the society of which they are members. A great many case examples are helpful in drawing attention to
the complex interaction characteristic of the field. The book deserves
a wide distribution and a great many readers in the field of neuro-
rehabilitation.

Professor Anne-Lise Christensen

ACKNOWLEDGEMENTS

Ceri Bowen

As editors and authors we each came to this book from different perspectives inspired by each others' new ideas, about the power of creativity when applying therapeutic approaches to address often serious and seemingly intractable issues. My background involved training in Leeds and experiences in taking Clinical Psychology to general hospitals and to problems of chronic illness, which combined with a curiosity for the theory and practice of Family Systems Theory were formative experiences. The area of neuro-rehabilitation and brain injury emerged for me over recent years and in particular, following a period of work as researcher and clinician at the Royal Hospital for Neuro-Disability, Putney, London. It was during this time that I met the co-authors who were quick to join a professional network that we set up and heated discussions soon followed about writing a book.

First of all, I am grateful to my wife Majbritt for bringing a new dimension to my life, for love and support to realize our dreams, also to our daughters Livia and Zara for fun and laughter. Friends and colleagues I wish to thank are: Keith Andrews, Hasan Askari,

Mark Baker, Graham Beaumont, Paula Boston, Sal Connolly, David Cottrell, Tony Coughlan, Sophie Duport, Betts Fetherston, Dorothy Fielding, David Green, Susan Lang, Gary Latchford, Anna Madill, Wendy Magee, Carol Martin, Stephen Morley, Elaine Scott, Roland Self, Patti Simonson, Jose Spring, Peter Stratton, Chris Trepka, and Sheila Youngson. To Oliver Rathbone, Lucy Shirley, and staff at Karnac Books thank you for putting their trust in the project.

It has always been a goal of mine to write books, to follow in my father's footsteps, and I am very grateful to be given this opportunity. Anyone who has written a book knows that to produce one always comes at a price in terms of home-work balance and the fact that we made it to this point has not been without considerable hard work, compromise, and not without tears, but indeed we made it!

Giles Yeates

This book has been a culmination of a wonderful and exciting first 10 years within clinical psychology and neuropsychology. Several people stand out chronologically as marking this journey. First, Gail Leeder for initial encouragement and inspiring supervision in my early days as an assistant psychologist. Fergus Gracey, Jon Evans, and Andrew Bateman, for taking me into the Oliver Zangwill fold and nurturing my chaotic and disparate ideas for my D Clin Psy thesis, and later, through their clinical experience, astute supervision, and flexible open mindedness, developing my clinical neuropsychology skills at OZ, also supporting me to teach and research as core activities within my professional role. Thank you Jon for cementing those skills and experiences in your excellent teaching and organization of the University of Glasgow clinical neuropsychology course.

My interest in systemic family therapy was an unexpected and enchanting fit during my clinical training. I think this was a result of solid teaching by Mark Donovan and Kiki Mastroyannopoulou and good red wine in Italy while reading the Milan team's astounding early work while on holiday at the time. But above all it was down to Mike Luckie, supervisor for my systemic specialist placement and one of the most skilled and inspiring clinicians I have ever had the privilege to see practice. It was he, in response to my 'why don't they work like this in brain injury services?', that put Andy Tyerman on my mental map. It has been an honour in the last few years to work in Andy's service, envisioning brain injury work as it should be done in my view, by working within the web of relationships and contexts that give brain injury form and meaning, Most recently, it has been an exciting new chapter to be supported by the Neuropsy-choanalysis Foundation and mentored by Andrew Balfour and the Tavistock Centre for Couples Relationships, to appreciate the unique contribution of psychoanalytical ideas within ABI clinical work and research.

Finally, this academic and clinical journey has been paralleled by my own personal experiences of love, closeness, and connection. My wife, Natasha has been an enduring source of support, toler-ance, and containment during this time, and has reminded me of the importance of feeling in all aspects of life. The Christmas Eve before the publication of this book saw the arrival of our first child, Sophia. In her tiny cuddles, looks, laughs, and smiles, along with her tears, cries, and struggles, she humbles and moves me each day in a way that unravels a new layer to the mystery of family.

Síobhán Palmer

With thanks to Fergus Gracey, Arlene Vetere, Camilla Herbert, Paul Lewington, and Fiona Ashworth for their refreshing ideas, perspec-tives, and positive energy throughout the years that I have known them. I would also like to acknowledge the clients I have worked with who have each taught me something more about the impor-tance of relationships, and how central they are to the success of our shared rehabilitation efforts. I am especially grateful to those indi-viduals who have been brave enough to allow me to communicate some of this learning and to share their stories here with you. I would like to thank my family and friends for their unremitting enthusiasm, encouragement, and positivity during this project and beyond.

All three authors would like to extend a huge debt of thanks and inspiration to Professor Anne-Lise Christensen, our collective muse for this book. Her forward and private conversations have been a breath of new life for this project in its later phases, providing an encouraging meta-narrative for a relational rehabilitation that has always been present in the brain injury literature, albeit not always visible at times. We also wish to thank colleagues within the Royal Hospital for Neuro-disability (Putney, London), Oliver Zangwill Centre (Ely, Cambridgeshire), Community Head Injury Service (Aylesbury, Buckinghamshire), the Brain Injury Rehabilitation Trust (Kerwin Court, Sussex) and members of the professional special interest group 'TBIFAMILIES', many of whom have influenced the ideas that have emerged in this book.

ABOUT THE AUTHORS

Dr Ceri Bowen is former International Fellow—working with families in the Institute of Neuropalliative Rehabilitation and based at the Royal Hospital for Neuro-disability, London. Trained as Clinical Psychologist and Family Therapy Practitioner, he has previously worked in Community Neuro-rehabilitation and in numerous Family Therapy Clinics. Ceri is also: occasional lecturer at Brunel and Roehampton Universities; founder of a special interest group for rehabilitation professionals working with families in brain injury; and on the advisory board for a major SDO project about the implementation of the NSF for long-term conditions (co-ordinated by the SPRU at York University). His latest completed research, funded by the MS Trust, is entitled "Advanced MS and the Psychosocial Impact on Families".

Dr Giles Yeates is principal clinical neuropsychologist and also a couples psychotherapist at the Community Head Injury Service, Aylesbury. His clinical work involves psychological therapy and cognitive rehabilitation with survivors of brain injury in individual and group formats. In addition he works within the family service to provide couples and family sessions, including work with child relatives. Dr Yeates is also an active researcher and author within the areas of social neuroscience, interpersonal relationships, neuropsychoanalysis, social context, psychological therapies and qualitative research following brain injury.

Dr Síobhán Palmer is a clinical psychologist based at Kerwin Court, West Sussex, part of the Brain Injury Rehabilitation Trust. Having qualified from University of Surrey in 2005, specialising in neuropsychology and systemic approaches to therapy, Síobhán then worked at the Oliver Zangwill Centre for three and a half years where she developed interests of working with adjustment, awareness and cognition within a relational context. She completed the diploma in clinical neuropsychology during 2009, from the University of Glasgow. Her interest in the interplay between emotion, cognition and social context continues in her work at Kerwin Court with adults with acquired brain injury and their families.

CHAPTER ONE

Introduction—the story so far...

A book on "relational approaches to rehabilitation" invites the reader to consider broadly the ways in which relationships with oneself, with others, and within systems, can determine the experience of acquired brain injury (ABI) and impact upon the rehabilitation process following ABI. Although a broad, outward-looking approach, we would like to clarify the specific focus of this book. First, we define a 'relational approach', and the organizing principles behind this way of thinking and working, which will be explored more thoroughly within subsequent chapters. Most readers will be familiar with concepts behind taking a 'psychological' approach to rehabilitation, or incorporating other 'talking therapies', but by the term 'relational' we wish to emphasize relationships as the important vehicle for change. Reasons for giving prominence to relationships and the social environment in our formulation and intervention are three-fold:

1. first, to redress an imbalance in the bio-psycho-social perspective[1] and to bring out the social aspects of brain injury, and to

---

[1] As per the critiques of Engel's biopsychosocial model (Engel, 1980) that warn against an uncritical acknowledgment of social influences among other factors, implicitly

extend this perspective to include bio-psycho-social-*family* dimensions;

2. second, to consider the social determinants of identity, increasingly targeted in interventions (we know that a substantial component of our self-identity, self-esteem, and self-efficacy is derived from our relationships and interactions); and

3. third, to emphasize the potential therapeutic qualities of socializing and conversation with concerned and committed individuals, groups, and communities (i.e., potential qualities within us all!).

The social model of disability proposes that we are all social creatures and we continue to make sense of ourselves and define ourselves by our social interactions, especially after a brain injury.[2] Therefore 'relational' also aims at emphasizing the importance of social interactions and supporting opportunities for people with brain injuries, who might otherwise be vulnerable to a shrinking of their social network. Moreover, the social realm or social context has a large contribution to make to the level of disability that people experience. The importance of the environment has long been acknowledged by brain injury services (i.e., consideration of colour, space, ways that doors open and close, and ways that people can find their way around a building even when they are not oriented) but the importance of the social realm is only beginning to be acknowledged. For people with brain injuries, social interaction is crucial to how they make sense of themselves; for adjustment and finding continuity between pre- and post-injury selves. Conversely, functionally able people may take it for granted, or perhaps automatically prepare and plan events to make success almost inevitable (sometimes without realizing all the preparation work that goes into this). As professionals, it

---

supporting the initial primacy of biological and intrapsychic dimensions (Armstrong, 1987; Yardley, 1996). Approaches espousing biopsychosocial comprehensiveness such as vulnerability-stress frameworks have been described as a 'colonization' of the psychological and social by the biological, rather than integration (Read, 2005).

[2] The World Health Organization's International Classification of Functioning (WHO ICF) has responded to this by asserting that there are different levels of disability and opportunities to intervene at the level of 'activity' (observed behaviour), 'participation' (social positions or roles), 'impairment' (symptoms or signs), and 'pathology' (disease and diagnosis).

is important to take a long-term perspective, as indicated by the UK National Service Framework for neurological long-term conditions (Department of Health, 2005). Family members, as well as survivors, have to make very real and significant adaptations to their identity, and these are crucial to maintaining ongoing well-being and balance in relations to their own needs.

In terms of recognized approaches, one might be left wondering what is new about a relational approach and where does it overlap, or not, with other rehabilitation approaches? This will become clearer as the book progresses, however broadly speaking, by framing rehabilitation as 'relational' we are drawing heavily on a number of interventionist approaches (for example: systemic family therapy, narrative therapy, emotion-focused therapy, the holistic approach to rehabilitation, models of identity reconstruction such as the 'Y-shaped model', behavioural experiments in a social context, therapy that draws on ideas of transference and counter-transference), and so on. Theoretical positions that carry value in this context include: psychoanalytic theory as applied to couple attachments, social psychology, social neuroscience, communication theory, ecological psychology, post-cognitive approaches, personal construct psychology, developmental psychology, attachment theory, and discursive approaches. Theories and bodies of research established outside of brain injury have also influenced discussions found within this book, such as aspects of dementia care (Kitwood, 1997) and mentalizing models of autism (Baron-Cohen, 1997). All the approaches considered for inclusion in this book share a common emphasis on defining brain injury against a backdrop of differing perspectives within social contexts, so another epistemological framework of importance is social constructionism. Given that the epistemologies underpinning 'neurology' and 'social constructionism' approach ideas of structuralism from opposite perspectives, we now consider ways of reconciling these two perspectives, by opening up some of the themes to be further developed in subsequent chapters.

Neurology and social constructionism: Working within the therapeutic space

Historically, brain injury rehabilitation has often taken an individualistic approach, which continues to be a valuable and important aspect of the rehabilitation process (e.g., person-centred care). The work of many disciplines is necessarily individualistic (e.g., physiotherapy, some aspects of occupational therapy). Increasingly, the focus of rehabilitation includes consideration of the psychological aspects of adjustment to injury and identity change. Individual psychological therapy for emotional adjustment often leads into therapeutic identity work that can involve accessing different perspectives on the problem from those in the family and social network, where people may only be aware of incomplete parts of a composite story, see special issue of Neuro-Psychological Rehabilitation (Gracey & Onsworth, 2008). Broadly speaking, such therapy involves helping people to develop a new relationship with their self and update their identity to form a realistic self-representation that includes the impact of the injury as a significant event in their life story, and consideration of their life stories in relation to other people's stories. The social construction of self develops through how people define themselves within relationships, and as such it is helpful to think about brain injury within this context. The process of looking at the social construction of self also opens up flexibility within the therapeutic space and often creates a wider range of possible perspectives on the self, with which to work.

Taking a long-term, whole-life perspective

Rehabilitation is usually required after a sudden one off incident, often unexpected and uncontrollable, has changed the individual's potential to reach their goals and hopes, due to changes in cognitive and often physical abilities. The cognitive, emotional, physical, and communication impairments that can arise after a brain injury will have an impact upon what somebody is able to do, think, feel, and communicate, and these effects influence their ability to maintain roles and relationships. It is inevitable that relationships will be affected, at least in the short term, in ways such as redistribution of roles. It can be hugely challenging to the injured person and their family members to adjust and integrate narratives of life 'before' and life 'after' the injury. People with a brain injury often talk of 'the old me' and the 'new me' as a way of making sense of that, and grieve for the loss of the 'old me' (as often their family do too). Hence a significant component of therapy is in helping people re-establish a coherent identity and life-story, a process that is complicated by cognitive impairments such as memory impairment, so therapy also serves to make large, complex ideas very concrete, clear, and accessible (and thereby smaller). Moreover, within therapy it can be helpful to identify and amplify subjugated stories that date back to positive times and experiences, or by building a helpful narrative about their lives, which brings the before and after discrepancy into a more comprehensive story. This can also be a useful practical tool, to rehearse ways of describing the nature of difficulties to other people. Of course, chronic, long-term difficulties are common to all rehabilitation settings, even within mental health services, although conditions such as depression and anxiety are often not framed in this way and there is not such an obvious before and after comparison.

Flexibility of cognition in social settings

Research stemming from the fields of neurology and neuropsychology has demonstrated precise areas of the brain that contribute to very specific areas of function. Some of the clearest examples of this can be found in research about vision. For example, damage to a very precise area of visual cortex (V5) will mean that an individual cannot see motion, but can perceive still images (Zihl, von Cramon, & Mai, 1983). The reverse is also possible; a condition whereby only moving objects can be perceived. However, lesions to a specific area are more commonly associated with multiple deficits (Mesulam, 1981). For the more recently developed areas of cortex with a multiplicity of connections, such as frontal areas, the functions become increasingly intricate and it is difficult to specify the precise impact of impairment upon function. Variability between neurological injury and functional impairment can be accounted for by a range of factors, and it is fundamental to consider the role of social relationships in this. Clinical examples of variability that is not accountable for by neurological damage include:

- memory impairment that presents when the person is challenged or angry;
- memory retrieval that improves in the context of positive conversations;

- initiation impairments that disappear when the client is in their own environment;
- survivors who can problem solve when presented with complex problems by the people that they know but cannot solve simple problems with people who they do not know;
- behaviour or communication problems that are present with some family members but not with others.

Some of this discrepancy can be understood by the interaction of emotion and cognition and the benefits of familiarity on information processing (reducing complexity, providing subtle cues for initiation and comprehension). Given that differences could be accounted for by the injury but also vary according to social context this will be a focus of the book. However, this suggests that the implications of neurological impairment on functioning are not absolute, rather that an individual can present with their impairments to a greater or lesser extent depending upon who they are with and where they are. In such a case, the relational neuro-rehabilitation clinician might work with the client and family, and other significant people, to educate about the impairment and then spend time thinking about what that means for their relationship with the injured person, rather than treating the impairment directly.

Remembering as developing a shared narrative

Memory rehabilitation targets the most functionally disabling aspects of memory impairment using compensatory approaches (Wilson, 2005) is concerned with strategies to improve and compensate for prospective remembering (e.g., what to buy at the shops, appointments, and remembering to take your keys, phone, and money with you), and with supporting recall or retrieval processes to improve remembering of personally or socially relevant information, or for initiating conversation (i.e., to 'get by' in social and vocational situations). More recently, Goal Management Training (Levine et al., 2000; Robertson, Clare, Carter, Hong, & Wilson, 2000) can be applied to executive aspects of memory: remembering to stay on track with tasks, for example. While these strategies can be applied to social situations, typically it is not routinely done. While assessments have been devised, which attempt to bridge this gap by making them more socially meaningful, there remains a gap, and if we take the relationship between emotion and memory seriously then perhaps there always will be. While we recognize that a test of memory does not need to be valid within a social context in order to be a valid assessment of memory, the extrapolation of findings to social implications could often be made more clearly. Furthermore, memory is a particular skill that is embedded in narrative traditions and, in the past, it was very much at the heart of communities and associated with special skills and virtues (e.g., story-telling and wisdom). It can be useful to think of memory rehabilitation as a process of engaging an individual in a personally and socially meaningful conversation, and constructing a narrative that makes sense to them and that will help them in future situations (the therapy room then becomes a space for rehearsal and role play). This also connects back to ideas about taking a longer-term, whole-life perspective in rehabilitation that comes quite naturally when working in brain injury because people are immediately faced with before and after comparisons of their self and identity.

A problem shared but viewed in many ways

One of the intriguing and often challenging aspects of working with families and other systems following brain injury is gaining a mutual and a 'shared understanding' of the problem (Wilson, Gracey, Malley, Bateman, & Evans, 2009). Given that the injury manifests itself in different ways depending on contextual demands, then the same 'incident' can potentially be viewed differently by each family member. This is really an indication of the complexity of issues that families bring, with differences present within and between families. Deconstructing and normalizing the problem helps the family generate their own questions for future work, as does introducing flexibility into their ideas, through conversation, through which they become increasingly able to see that they each sit at different points on a continuum rather than polarized opposites. Added to this dynamic, can be a pressure on neuro-rehabilitation professionals to be precise and give quantifiable answers to questions about the predicament faced. In turn, some family members may come to expect this from therapists, and this is indeed often important and useful in the acute phase, characterized by confusion and experiences never previously encountered. Yet at other times, or for other families, it may be more useful to see therapy as a chance to take stock and to review where they have got to, or explore new ways of viewing long-standing problems, to be freed up from a stuck position. So expectations can vary about how much relatives want to explore new possibilities. In the following chapters, we highlight this dilemma and others.

Recognizing the potential impact of family break-up and social isolation

Acquired brain injuries may split relationships, and individual members can be scattered in different directions and find it hard to come together again, which is likely to be devastating for couples or for attachment bonds between parents and children. Moreover, it is not always what you might call 'traditional' structures that come under pressure to provide support to the injured person—sometimes it is ongoing contact and support from a neighbour or even a former wife, which proves the key to maintaining motivation and achieving goals by achieving some degree of normality, and managing the difficult transition of living back out in the community. Separations enforced by lengthy hospital stays or periods of residential rehabilitation, and concerns about how children cope can also create a need for therapeutic work around reuniting parents with their children in a graded way where stress is managed.

The role of 'carer' is one that many family members view with some trepidation, and research has shown that some couples just do not identify with the term, and most find it difficult to combine the role of spouse with that of carer, or try out being a carer only to later take a step back (Bowen, MacLehose, & Beaumont, 2010; Bowen & MacLehose, 2010). If the decision to be a carer feels 'forced' then this can be especially damaging for relationships. Of course, not every carer is in a position of being able to choose the tasks they undertake or to perceive that there is a choice, and financial uncertainty and struggle is a reality that many families of people with chronic illnesses face. A further dynamic is the potential for social isolation in families following brain injury that often increases over time (Ergh, Rapport, Coleman, & Hanks, 2002). Specific difficulties in mobility and communication can be seen to exert particular barriers to the creation of new relationships or the maintenance of existing community roles following an injury (Haslam, Holme, Haslam, Lyer, Jetten, & Williams, 2008).

Working with relationships in mind

Services often require that you work individually and can often be set up thus, especially within brain injury services, and consequently cater for individual rather than relational needs. However, even in individual work it is possible to work relationally and or to think relationally (Boscolo & Bertrando, 1996). In some ways, it is more fitting because a survivor is often thinking relationally (e.g., relationship with themselves, with their present or absent memories, with others, with the meaning of disability in society), and many survivors are able to access and describe their narratives about these relationships. Frequently, a survivor's adjustment is intertwined with the family's adjustment and so taking a broad approach that includes working with the family is often a very helpful and intuitive way to help the individual.

Some overarching position statements

Some concepts that will be qualified in greater detail in subsequent chapters, and which may be new to a reader of traditional neuro-rehabilitation literature, include:

- Injured brains are always in interaction with other brains (Firth, 2003; Firth & Wolpert, 2004);
- A shared experience of mind emerges from these interactions (Bateson, 1972; Pearce, 2007);
- The consequences of brain injury are often more apparent when people are with others, than when alone (Yeates, 2009);
- The brain injury can therefore exist in the spaces between people, infiltrating and amplifying distance and disconnection (Bowen, Hall, Newby, Walsh, Weatherhead, & Yeates, 2009);
- Brain injury and its consequences are socially constructed to a degree (Yeates, Gracey, & McGrath, 2008).

Hence, it is equally useful to think of 'brain-injured relationships, families and systems' as it is to think of 'brain-injured individuals', but it is more useful again to conceptualize such alongside resources, talents, skills, and strengths to overcome the challenges that present and are shared within the system. We propose that any neuro-psychological inquiry of the brain and mind has to look outwards (to relationships and context) to arrive at comprehensive enquiry of what lies within the brain.

Chapter outlines

The book begins with two chapters that argue the case for first, a relational neuro-rehabilitation (chapter 2) and second, a relational neuropsychology (chapter 3), giving details of what these might look like. In chapters 4 and 5 entitled "Connections, Closeness and Intimacy" the issues that pertain to couples are considered in some depth, taking a broad definition of intimacy and drawing on recent psychoanalytic theory in relation to couple attachments, before describing suggested interventions. In "Negotiating Contesting Dynamics" (chapter 6) we approach the standard rehabilitation topic of awareness of disability, but do so by presenting theory and approaches to working with difference and conflict within systems, which is then followed with new research and ideas about "Building a Family-Therapist Alliance" (chapter 7) followed by three case descriptions (chapter 8). Applying one body of knowledge to practice then becomes the focus in "Working with Systems" (chapter 9) and "Interdisciplinary Working: a case example" (chapter 10). We finish with "Neglected Sub-Systems" (chapter 11) which focuses on the needs of siblings, work colleagues and community members, and "Relational Rehabilitation Research" (chapter 12); a critique of existing research and suggestions for future research.

CHAPTER TWO

Principles of relational neuro-rehabilitation

What is brain injury?

The first stage of the journey into thinking about brain injury from a relational perspective is to think about what happens when somebody sustains a brain injury (whether traumatic or non-traumatic) and then to step outside of the assumed framework and consider that injured individual within a social context. Implicit within this approach is to identify the important factors of that social context to the individual, and potentially vice versa. This chapter will consider professional and lay discourse about brain injury, also some of the challenges for health and treatment systems, before delineating some of the major dimensions affecting prognosis in brain injury, that is, psychological, social-family, inter-personal factors, and over-arching communication issues. We thereby extend conceptualizations of brain injury by locating family perspectives within bio-psycho-social formulations. Finally, we end the chapter by taking a closer look at the active ingredients of rehabilitation.

Prevalence issues

Estimates of the prevalence of severe brain injury can be difficult to interpret because of the many challenges that surround diagnosis and the varied assessment methods used. In the Western world prevalence figures are thought to vary between 7 and 12 per 100 000 population (Maegele, Engel, Bouillion, Lefering, Fach, Raum et al., 2007; Tate, McDonald, & Lulham, 1998; The Royal College of Physicians and British Society for Rehabilitation, 2003) although some researchers prefer to speak in terms of numbers of disabled survivors, which for instances of traumatic brain injury (TBI) in the United Kingdom, is thought to be about 100–150 per 100 000 of the general population (British Society of Rehabilitation Medicine, 1998).

While no two injuries are the same and hence an assessment of severity poses many challenges, there are further layers of complexity that ABI poses for the system of care:

• assessment difficulties such as detecting severe brain injury versus relatively common mild head injury versus trauma reactions;
• the complexity of difficulties and their invisibility;
• the long-term duration of difficulties;
• the multi-component and labour-intensive nature of rehabilitation;
• culpability and insurance issues.

Hence, in addition to requiring complex and long-term rehabilitation, people who sustain ABI also pose an immense public health issue and the long-term cost of providing care can be tremendous. Good systems of care depend equally on the speed of response and knowledgeable actions taken by professionals attending an accident (or incident) scene, something that varies considerably both within and across different countries (see Winslade, 1998, for a survivor perspective on some of these issues). Moreover, there is a concomitant need to monitor perfusion and intra-cranial pressure (Cowley & da Silva, 2008) in order to prevent secondary injury. These authors warn of the difficulties interpreting severity in cases when ventilation and sedation are used, since sedation removes our most sensitive marker of cerebral function.

The following section examines definitions, patterns, typologies, and categories of brain injury (the professional discourse that surrounds brain injury).

Defining brain injury: Neuroscience and rehabilitation professional perspectives

To suffer a brain injury is to suffer a trauma, yet a brain injury has further repercussions because of the organic or structural changes to the brain, changes that are definite and often permanent, although the process of adaptation will almost certainly vary. It is important to consider the meaning of ABI for the individual and their social and family network and this is affected by how it is defined or measured. These considerations will be important in the later tasks of defining the boundaries of the injury, and how changes in relationships might be understood. The importance of measurement is magnified by the frequent absence of external visual signs of injury. Of course, the long-term nature of brain injury means that preventative approaches that include support for family and friends will almost certainly be also required.

The first task when assessing a person for brain injury is to distinguish between a relatively common head injury (typically a closed injury) and an actual brain injury (either a closed or open injury). This is by no means straightforward, yet brain injuries are thought to typically occur if there is some disturbance to consciousness. A simple scale called The Glasgow Coma Scale, GCS (Teasdale & Jennet, 1974) is often used as a marker of degree of brain injury, for which a score is given for each of the following: eye movements, verbal, and motor responses. This scale has the benefits of being repeatable and can therefore be used to monitor change in a condition. It is also used across different countries and is therefore an appropriate, objective, and brief means of communicating level of consciousness between clinicians.

Unfortunately, there is no uniform assessment procedure for the use of the GCS and consequently it has been suggested one is urgently required, which includes early and repeated assessments at defined intervals, standardized reporting of confounders, and GCS component plus sum scores (Zuercher, Ummenhofer, Baltussen, & Walder, 2009). Cowley and da Silva (2008) also recommend documenting the component scores for the GCS, and to note reasons for an inappropriately low component score (e.g., eye swelling preventing opening or intubation preventing vocalization).

For a brain injury to be considered severe using the GCS, the lowest score must be below 8, also the definition of being in coma.

Severe brain injury is also indicated if there has been a period of loss of consciousness greater than six hours and/or post-traumatic amnesia of 24 hours or more. Nowadays, there are more sophisticated ways of assessing the degree of injury and detecting contusions such as magnetic resonance imaging (MRI) and computed tomography (CT), although the measure that is reported to be most related to functional recovery, at least initially, continues to be the lowest GCS score (Balestreri, Czosnyka, Chatfield, Steiner, Schmidt, Smielewski, Matta, & Pickard, 2004). Limitations to the use of imaging for clinical and prognostic purposes include: that mild injury does not typically result in a significant reduction in brain volume or expansion of the ventricular system; the changing nature of the lesion (a problem for acute or early post-acute phases of treatment) and the fact that atrophy relates more to severity of injury rather than functional outcome; and that as a result of focal anatomical lesions, for example, from gun-shot wounds, further pathology of physiological origin may not be detected including compromised vascular integrity, so functional disruption of cerebral integrity may be considerably in excess of defined areas of damage on MR imaging (Bigler, 2001).

Despite the many drawbacks, imaging research is progressing and exciting new techniques are emerging like functional MRI (fMRI), magnetic resonance spectroscopy (MRS), diffusion, and tensor-weighted MR imaging, along with other forms of metabolic and physiological imaging such as magnetoencephalography (MEG). New research has compared and combined imaging results, for example, Kesler, Adams, and Bigler (2000) examined the relative effectiveness of magnetic resonance (MR) imaging, single photon emission tomography (SPECT) and quantitative magnetic resonance (QMR) imaging in detecting brain abnormalities in 52 traumatically brain-injured patients. Sixty-two per cent of patients had abnormal clinical MR findings, 57% had abnormal SPECT, and 51% had abnormal QMR. Each neuro-imaging modality detected brain abnormalities that the other two did not. Psychological distress was also related to the number of MR abnormalities, particularly in the frontal areas. As a general rule, and to overcome some of the problems associated with the potential unreliability of single indicators of severity and/or incomplete records, Coetzer (2009) in this Book Series has recommended the Mayo Traumatic Brain Injury Severity Classification

System (Malec, Brown, Leibson, Flaada, Mandrekar, Diehl, & Perkins, 2007). This method combines the GCS, post-traumatic amnesia, loss of consciousness, and findings from neuro-imaging, and classifies the brain injury as Moderate-Severe (Definite), Mild (Probable), or Symptomatic (Possible).

From a neuroscience and rehabilitation professional perspective, the process of defining brain injury is fraught with difficulty and is extremely complex. Despite this, the process of defining and quantifying injury presence and severity is mostly a technical exercise involving quantitative scales, and the complexities are not always fully acknowledged. However, the general public have different needs and degrees of understanding and it is to them that we now turn.

Lay understanding

Early studies explored the level of understanding about brain injury among family members and members of the general public, and concluded that in general the public and family members of people who have sustained a brain injury, often lack experience and understanding of ABI and its consequences (Gouvier, Prestholdt, & Warner, 1988; Jacobs, 1991). It has been suggested (Gouvier, Prestholdt, & Warner, 1988) that accurate knowledge could promote adaptation to disability by reducing 'inappropriate levels of expectation on the recovering patient' (p. 341). This was supported by the work of Lezak (Lezak, 1988; 1995) who proposed that family members would be more able to develop realistic expectations of their relative's recovery, if they are given information about cognitive impairment. The discrepancy between realistic expectations of outcome, and client and family expectations of outcome could create a void between families and rehabilitation professionals (see chapter 7). This discrepancy can also create an internal discrepancy within the injured person about what they are able to do, and what it is that they should be able to do (Gracey, Evans, & Malley, 2009). Expectations can be closely linked to knowledge and understanding (Cameron & Leventhal, 2002; Whittaker, Kemp, & House, 2007).

Over the past 20 years, the stories of survivors of brain injury have been increasingly present in the media in forms that are readily accessible to the general public. For example, documentaries (e.g., Shena McDonald, 2004) and written narratives (e.g., Hammond, 2007) about personal experience of brain injury and the BBC One television drama 'Recovery' (2007), newspaper articles documenting recovery and the more subtle but significant impact of brain injury on the lives of those who survive (Vulliamy, 2007) as well as other more regular community awareness campaigns such as the annual brain injury awareness week organized by Headway (www.Headway.com). For this reason, the general public are likely to have greater access to accurate portrayals of the effects of brain injury. However, in a more recent study, 'inaccurate beliefs' about brain injury recovery, and associated disability, continued to be reported. In a qualitative investigation in this area (Swift & Wilson, 2001), which explored knowledge of the general public and non-expert health professionals, 19 people were interviewed (including survivors of ABI, professionals and carers). Interviewees perceived misconceptions were consistent with those identified by Gouvier, Prestholdt, and Warner (1988). For example: beliefs about potential recovery, lack of awareness of cognitive and behavioural sequelae. Other beliefs, not evaluated in previous questionnaires, which have been encountered in our clinical experience with the general public or family members of people with an ABI, include ideas that 'memory is like a muscle, and will recover if exercised sufficiently'; 'writing things down will prevent memory from recovering'; and 'rehabilitation is only useful in the first few months following injury'.

Overall, the limited research in this area indicates that the public (including those with experience of ABI), have a poor understanding of prevention, recovery, and changes following ABI, which is demonstrated in a high percentage of misconceptions. It is important to think about how society's narratives about brain injury, and the potential conflicting information about brain injury, or high expectations of recovery are challenges to the development of helpful narratives about disability for the person with the brain injury. In addition, the stories told in the wider community about disability are likely to have an impact upon the position of the family within the community, in terms of their developing relationship with themselves post-injury, and their capacity to maintain a role in the family 'in spite of' the brain injury (Nochi, 1997; 1998a; 1998b; 2000).

People in low awareness states

Research that focuses on people in low awareness states is a rapidly developing field using techniques at the forefront of the latest technology. Among the pioneers in this area are Schackers and colleagues (2008) who have suggested that the bispectral index is capable of predicting those who leave coma and vegetative state (VS) to enter a minimally conscious state (MCS), and Adrian Owen and colleagues in Cambridge who have taken a neuro-psychological, hierarchical, and task-based fMRI approach to assessing degrees of consciousness in people who are seemingly unresponsive. Interestingly, Owen has summarized how this research applies to disorders of consciousness and described the levels of the hierarchy as: acoustic processing, speech perception, phonological processing, semantic processing, and finally, conscious awareness (Owen, 2008). Owen does acknowledge a number of limitations including that this method of assessment will not be applicable to all vegetative patients, such as those in more 'permanent' states (particularly those of non-traumatic aetiology who are more than 12 months post-injury). Also substantial concerns about a methodology that couples neuronal activity and local haemodynamics are emerging and this suggests that interpreting the results from this kind of research may be much more complex than previously believed (Serotin & Das, 2009). Importantly, it would appear that there may be a degree of activation going on that is completely independent from the demands of the task.

Wilson, Coleman, and Pickard (2008) summarize recent research in the impaired consciousness field by emphasizing that fMRI assessment methods should be used as an adjunct to other methods and they add to the list of limitations the fact that only positive findings on imaging can be interpreted, since false negative results occur in volunteers. Wilson et al. continue by highlighting a continued role for the behavioural assessment of people in low awareness states, recommending their own measure the Wessex Head Injury Matrix (WHIM: Shiel et al., 2000). The WHIM articulates 62 behaviours of graded difficulty that may be of relevance in the recovery process. Janksepp, Fuchs, Garcia, and Lesiak (2007) make further challenges to fMRI research, especially in relation to decisions about withdrawing life-support because, they argue, a variety of primary-process affective states and instinctual emotional actions (e.g., pain "reflexes") can exist without cognitive awareness of those feelings. It may be that there will be a separate category of people who are not in VS, supported by fMRI results, although we cannot be certain what this means functionally, clinically, or ethically.

Case study

Gary's first steps to recovery

(Thank you to Sarah Howley for her conscientious assessment of Gary and wise counsel to the family)

Gary, a gifted computer programmer with Sega, had his whole life ahead of him. Then an unprovoked attack outside a Police Station left him in a coma and fighting for his life. He was a determined and physically fit young man, who soon 'emerged' into a minimally conscious state. We as his rehabilitation team were unsure how much he could comprehend his situation and there were periods when he was obviously confused just wanting to go home or to see his family—calling out 'I want to go home' or 'I want to see my mum', and often at night into the early hours—and all the while his girlfriend visited at weekends. Moreover, when we were unable to understand him (his voice had an unusual prosody), he would shout louder and louder, repeating himself over and again. Things were clearly very frustrating for Gary and the staff. At night he would sometimes crawl out of bed or want to walk before he could really stand.

Over a period of months of intensive rehabilitation, and daily visits from his mother, father, and sister, Gary began to take his first steps walking first with a 'pulpit' frame and then holding onto the arm of his therapist. Because of neglect issues he would usually stoop and veer to one side, at least initially but he was keen to practice each day and with this he improved dramatically. He looked a different person everyday. As psychologists we encouraged him to tell his story and we also assessed his abilities in which he showed marked difficulties remembering details (e.g., when his family last visited) and with executive skills that were because of damage to frontal and temporal lobes. Early conversations would centre on relieving anxieties about his family and future, and reworking the events of the night he was attacked. His family were encouraged to visit in shifts, not all at once, to maintain stamina and also to give Gary space for social purposes, to initiate and practice his conversation skills. I still remember the first time he laughed again and how lovely it was to hear.

Comment from Gary's mother: "I wouldn't wish [our experience] on my worse enemy. To go through so much pain—not physically but mentally—it needs the whole family to commit to helping their loved one. It has been a very stressful time for us all but we can see a light at the end of the tunnel. And Gary being Gary was a fighter from the off. We all talk to each other about our fears and what Gary's future will hold, but we're all positive. We will be satisfied if we get 80% to 90% back of the old Gary. We know it's a long long road but we're all willing to put in the hours to help Gary to become the old Gary"

A relational consideration of accounts of personality change in brain-injured persons

Early reports in the literature often cited the most difficult aspect of brain injury to cope with for family members, as a sense that their injured relative had changed at a deeper, characterological level. A bio-psycho-social deconstruction of this topic has since been described, which proposes that the overlapping fields of social neuroscience, cognitive approaches to self, and identity and psychosocial processes following ABI mount a serious challenge to traditional assumptions of personality change derived from individualistic concepts of personality (Yeates, Gracey, & McGrath, 2008). Interestingly, family descriptions of personality change have been found to be closely associated with the degree of stress or burden present (Weddell & Leggett, 2006), and when this stress is alleviated personality 'repair' can occur (Yeates, Gracey, & McGrath, 2008).

However, damage to specific neural substrates may cause impairment to emotion recognition, thus feelings of 'other' and 'self' can be difficult to access, can be distorted or misrepresented, and these factors could account for the reported sense of 'being different'. Furthermore, dysexecutive problems and a loss of autobiographical memory can devastate narratives about the self (Dewar & Gracey, 2007). In short, survivors may be 'cut off' from a large body of emotional experience and this may mimic personality change. Other questions relate to how much a survivor is willing or able to accept a new identity, and if one's personality has changed, could it have really been a stable aspect of self in the first place? Most probably, these are all questions that the injured person has wondered about. ... Of course, there are certain symptoms that are variations of personality traits that we see in the general public, for example, lethargy and impulsiveness, and so changes better described on a continuum. It is not uncommon to hear the following, 'whereas before he was a bit like that, now he is a lot like that', so perhaps for some people it is more a case of degrees of change along prior trajectories.

Aspects of change for injured persons may have in common components of a generic 'survivor' identity—the effect of shattering assumptions of immunity, impunity, and immortality (Janoff-Bulman, 1992). As well as wondering what has changed and what has stayed the same, identity may appear quite different because of changes to aspects that are determined socially, through our affiliations and the friends and company we keep. Social Identity Theory develops this notion and indeed researchers have found this to be meaningful in the case of an ABI (Haslam et al., 2008). Such feedback gives clues about other people's expectations for recovering skills and abilities, perhaps partly determined by comments made by paramedics at the scene of the accident, or while in a coma.

Prognosis in brain injury

The backdrop to the discussion thus far is the growing body of literature showing the impact of brain injury on relationships, and vice versa (Bowen et al., 2009), particularly studies by Sander and colleagues, which suggest that pre- and post-injury family functioning is associated with later rehabilitation outcome (Sander, Caroselli, High, Becker, Neese, & Scheibel, 2002; Sander, Sherer, Malec, High, Thompson, Moessner et al., 2003). This casts a question over whether severity of injury, assuming this can be assessed with some degree of accuracy, is the determining factor when predicting outcome. Further studies have emphasized the role of social support as a moderator in recovery from brain injury (Ergh, Rapport, Coleman, & Hanks, 2002; Sander, Hibbard, Hannay, & Sherer, 1997). In terms of mediators and moderators, these can be divided up into a number of major categories such as psychological and social-family dimensions to brain injury. All of these play a significant role in prognosis following brain injury.

Psychological dimensions

Psychological issues impacting on the relationship between severity and outcome may include the incidence of depression, anxiety, and other psychological conditions such as post-traumatic stress disorder, psychosis, eating disorders, and so on (Jorge & Robinson, 2002). While no one would argue about the debilitating effects of these conditions for the injured person and/or their close relatives, their aetiology, however, is equivocal and often debated. For example, when conceptualizing depression, especially for cases of organic brain injury, one may need to consider multi-factorial, interactional models in which there is a complex interplay of biological, neuro-psychological, but also individual pre-injury, social, and familial factors (Jorge, Robinson, Moser, Tateno, Crespo-Facorro, & Arndt, 2004; Malec, Brown, & Moessner, 2004). In the case of depression, it is known that people within the general population who show symptoms of depression have reduced dopamine levels, frequently suffer from co-morbid anxiety, while at the same time can be at risk of social isolation and often come from families in which abuse and neglect is common. Following brain injury such individuals may also suffer additionally from neuropathological changes such as deactivation of lateral and dorsal prefrontal cortices, increased activation of ventral limbic and paralimbic structures including the amygdala, along with executive dysfunction and negative affect (Jorge et al., 2004).

Instances of psychological disturbance hinder adjustment to brain injury because it decreases available resources to compensate for the negative effects of brain injury and makes adaptive living more difficult to achieve. Interestingly, recently there has been a move away from interest in solely pathological aspects of psychological health, to a consideration of broader aspects of health and well-being including strengths and virtues. Within the brain injury field this has led to studies investigating instances of, for example, post-traumatic growth (McGrath & Linley, 2006) and more general considerations of the positive aspects of caregiving (Nolan & Lundh, 1999). From a positive psychology perspective, it is equally important to understand individuals and families that show resilience and positive adaptation in the face of adversity as it is to understand those that display 'mental illness'. The impact of psychological factors on outcome following TBI is likely to be mediated by many social factors and it is to this that our discussion now turns.

Social-family dimensions

When it comes to the question of why some people cope better than others there are some factors that go beyond the biological and psychological, some that perhaps even cannot be quantified. Within the depression field, Brown and Harris (1978) found a number of predisposing vulnerability factors in their female sample in a socially deprived borough of London, namely: early maternal loss, lack of a confiding relationship, having three or more children under the age of 14 at home and being unemployed; factors that, it is argued, interact with specific triggers to increase the risk of depression. In an extension of this work, Patten (1991) conducted a meta-analysis suggesting that the lack of a confiding relationship is strongly associated with depression, and that all four of the "vulnerability factors" may be associated with an increased risk of depression. Given the prevalence of co-morbid presentations of depression and brain injury, this work has potential significance when considering adaptation and recovery following brain injury.

Brown and Harris' model is often thought of as a social model of depression, but there are other social factors to consider such as whether returning to work is an incentive to recovery, also level of deprivation and financial security. Further social factors are suggested in the family therapy literature by Burnham (1993) who first proposed the GRRAACCES model as a way of understanding mechanisms of privilege (i.e., gender-race-religion-age-abilities-culture-class-ethnicity-sexual orientation). This is a useful checklist when speculating on the degree of privilege a person may be afforded (or not) in their recovery from a brain injury.

Communication theory also contributes to our understanding of how social processes operate and in particular, the Co-ordinated Management of Meaning model (Pearce & Cronen, 1980; Pearce, 2007) makes explicit the contextual layering of social interactions such that culture influences family script that in turn may influence relationships, the self, right the way down to single episodes of interaction. The force of this influence as one moves down through these layers is called the 'contextual force' but the process is not one way and an upwards force termed the 'implicative force' can also operate so that individual acts can have wider implications. People act on the basis of a composite of their understanding of current and past situations, and so for effective communication in social interactions and effective understanding of social interactions it is important to understand the interplay between the world-views that people bring to an encounter. A match or mismatch between intention and action when communicating can often explain the wider social impact of disability.

Finally, another interesting analysis of the social dimensions to illness has been put forward by Ian Parker, Georgaca, Harper, McLauhlin, and Stowell (1995) who, in their book entitled "Deconstructing Psychopathology," issue further warnings about: positioning effects (again, who are the privileged groups), the ownership of symptoms (whether symptoms are projected onto low-status groups), arbitrary boundaries (whether conditions such as 'depression' are real, that is, what is their basis in science), links to oppression (i.e., social control), and identity influences (the degree to which the pathology is deemed to be a stable trait of the person diagnosed). One needs also to pay particular attention to the language used in the public discourse on pathology, whether there are any implicit assumptions, and also any excluded phenomena. To a degree, all these factors of privilege and entitlement (and challenges to this) can also apply to brain injury, although we are by no means implying that brain injury is entirely a social phenomenon.

Added onto this analysis of the social context in which brain injury is situated is the family context. Again, this can either privilege or disadvantage people in their recovery depending on the level of support that is available. But it is not simply a case 'good' versus 'bad' family relationships. Family factors to consider include the distributions of roles, communication styles, inter-generational attachment patterns, and life-cycle issues (e.g., whether there are dependents and if so, how many; also past experiences of caregiving and multiple caregiving; issues of retirement, etc.). Family factors also interact with social dimensions of control to produce effects at the level of gender particularly in relation to the degree of acceptance of the caregiver role and whether this is expected more of females, but also role flexibility more generally (e.g., in relation to employment issues). As an adjunct to this, medical histories are important sources of information on how poor health has been experienced and managed within the family in the past. Finally, given the increased opportunities for social mobility within society, wider family support cannot be assumed and the degree to which families are mobile and have choices about how and where they live can be a factor aiding or hindering recovery.

The process of adaptation and negotiating impairments

So far we have seen how assessments of brain injury are not an exact science and that different methods of assessment may produce different results. We have also discussed many other factors to consider when conceptualizing brain injury from a relational perspective, often at least as important as the severity of the initial injury in terms of prognosis and recovery. These other factors place limits or privilege the chances of an individual overcoming the negative aspects of brain injury. While some might define these other factors negatively, they can also be viewed as resources, if present and available. In this regard, one could say that the best possible scenario, if one were to suffer a brain injury, would be for this to take place in a country where there are effective and efficient systems of care; and in circumstances where one has good psychological health prior to the injury and access to good social and family support, also to buffer against the effects of any discrimination within communities. This is not to trivialize the issues but to offer a context and framework for the chapters that follow. Each individual considered in this book has suffered a unique injury but also one that is situated in unique social, familial, and cultural circumstances, and this impacts on the subjective meaning the injury has for the individual and family, and their prognosis. We now turn our focus to rehabilitation, and in particular to a review of the defining aspects of rehabilitation from a relational perspective.

Rehabilitation in context: Finding a new relationship with brain injury through others

There are many other factors to consider when thinking about prognosis in brain injury and its impact on relationships and this includes components to rehabilitation services. Medical approaches and other multidisciplinary components each operates either at the individual level or engages with the family-social context, or both, and each impacts separately or in concert with other components.

Working with the sense of self and individual identity of the survivor ("who am I now?") is increasingly recognized as an important aspect of the process of emotional adjustment after brain injury.

Although sense of self is an individual and highly personal experience, it is arguably developed through social relationships and the way that we express ourselves and the stories that we hear about ourselves contributes to the formation of our own identity. Thus, there is a clear link between recovery in rehabilitation and social dimensions of communication (Ylvisaker & Feeney, 2000). As with many sudden changes to one's life plan, the process of adjustment to brain injury involves discovering a way of changing the difficult relationship with the brain injury; in some ways, 'forgiving' the brain injury and accepting the interruption, identifying continuous threads of one's identity from before and after the injury in order to integrate it into one's life story.

Our emphasis in the remainder of this chapter will be on the family-social context, with an acknowledgement of the other factors (e.g., the role of the individual psychological factors and how much treatment and human factors such as motivation, practice, and pacing play in the success of rehabilitation). We also discuss the importance of communication issues and the role rehabilitation therapists have in helping the injured person articulate their experiences.

The challenge of rehabilitation to medical approaches and models

The boundaries of clinical roles are routinely challenged when working in rehabilitation and this is no less the case for medical practitioners or physicians. New concise guidance to good practice entitled "Neurological Long-Term Conditions: Management at the interface between neurology, rehabilitation and palliative care" (The Royal College of Physicians, 2008) details the changing nature of this role and the overlap between these sometimes competing areas of specialty. The report also acknowledges prevailing misunderstanding that rehabilitation is a short-term intervention following a single incident, illness, or injury, but rather that long-term disability management and the prevention of complications forms the majority of work conducted, often in the community and until end-of-life. Moreover, while neurology, rehabilitation, and palliative care overlap in their concern for symptom control, there are also crucial differences in focus that can be summarized as follows:

- Neurology (diagnosis, investigation, disease modification);
- Rehabilitation (physical management, management of cognitive and communication deficits, and profound brain injury);
- Palliative care (end-of-life care, dealing with loss, spiritual support).

Rehabilitation also represents a significant challenge to medicine because of the difficulty translating evidence for specific interventions into clinical practice. To illustrate, most physicians tend to rely on studies using a randomized, controlled intervention design yet the complexities of implementing this approach to produce good quality evidence in the field of rehabilitation are significant. One response to the complexity faced within rehabilitation has been to broaden definitions of quality when assessing research to include *Applicability*, as implemented in the UK National Service Framework (NSF) for Long-Term (Neurological) Conditions (Department of Health, 2005), and to include qualitative and mixed methods designs. This NSF goes further by stating that they value the opinions of service users and their families/carers, as well as the views of professionals. These issues of achieving quality in research trials have also been recently fully addressed and summarized in a succinct manner in an editorial for the Journal *Clinical Rehabilitation*:

> *"When the 'action' is delivery of a specific drug that can be completely isolated, establishing control is easy using an identical preparation that simply lacks the active ingredient. For complex, multifactorial interventions such as surgery or rehabilitation, establishing control is much more difficult, not least because the intervention is rarely a single specific item. Randomization cannot balance non-specific factors associated specifically with an allocated treatment; other aspects of the design need to achieve this as far as possible"*

(Wade, 2009, p. 675).

Wade (2009) continues by arguing that it is impossible to ensure that one group of recipients of care has no rehabilitation intervention whatsoever, particularly when information and emotional support can be incidental but significant in their effects. In short, it is only possible to evaluate a whole package of care or to compare between two such bundles of care.

The role of the multidisciplinary team

Strong evidence has been gathered from Cochrane and other systematic reviews, in support of the combined efforts of a multidisciplinary team for optimum rehabilitation success (Khan, Turner-Stokes, Ng, & Kilpatrick, 2007; Turner-Stokes, 1999; Turner-Stokes, Nair, Disler, & Wade, 2005). The NSF for Long-Term (Neurological) Conditions (Department of Health, 2005) similarly had a strong multidisciplinary emphasis, as reflected in its quality requirements that are as follows:

- a person-centred service;
- early recognition, prompt diagnosis, and treatment;
- emergency and acute management;
- early and specialist rehabilitation;
- community rehabilitation and support;
- vocational rehabilitation;
- providing equipment and accommodation;
- providing personal care and support;
- palliative care;
- supporting family and carers;
- caring for people with neurological conditions in hospital and other health and social care settings.

Increasing dissatisfaction with a purely medical approach to research and clinical interventions with people with chronic conditions, such as acquired brain injury, and recognition of the value of a multidisciplinary team approach has significantly impacted services. Moreover, serious efforts have been made to reverse the trend of the medically dominant approach to diagnosis and treatment that often leaves people unable to access information and support between appointments (which can be up to six months or to a year apart). In particular, the introduction of community multidisciplinary (or interdisciplinary) neurological rehabilitation teams and nurse specialists for particular conditions now offers a myriad of support options that were hitherto not available. This is particularly important given the confusing and often long-drawn out diagnostic process for some conditions (e.g., multiple sclerosis), their impact on major life decisions (e.g., whether to have children or not), set against the potential for rapid deterioration.

Taking a wider perspective

The World Health Organization's International Classification of Functioning (WHO ICF) has been applied to the rehabilitation of cognition (Wade, 2006). In terms of the WHO ICF, rehabilitation therapists might be argued to intervene at the level of 'activity' (observed behaviour) or 'participation' (social positions or roles) whereas medical professionals intervene at the level of 'impairment' (symptoms or signs) or even 'pathology' (disease and diagnosis). In this book, we propose that in some circumstances interventions at the level of 'participation' can impact upon 'impairment' (and vice versa), and therefore alter the frequency, intensity, or quality of signs and symptoms of a brain injury.

There are a number of further reasons for taking a wider perspective, including complications due to the long-term nature of conditions themselves, but also because of a high prevalence of co-morbidity (e.g., between brain injury and depression or brain injury and epilepsy). For acquired and heritable conditions, since the April 2003 reporting on the completion of the Human Genome Project, a new era has been ushered in that is also blurring the boundary between health and chronic illness, and extending the concept of time phases after disease onset to include nonsymptomatic genomic illness time phases (Miller, McDaniel, Rolland, & Feetham, 2006). Taking a broader position reflects the non-medical dominance within the rehabilitation teams, who all potentially have highly relevant roles to play yet operate by using inter-personal skills and techniques to impart knowledge rather than prescribe medications.

Service user choice and treatment preference

Any discussion of the limitations of the medical model as applied to rehabilitation ought to include consideration of issues related

---

Case study

Working side-by-side with the carers

(Special thanks to Claire Morris for her ongoing support before, during and after the transition to long-term care)

Sheila knew there was a chance she would develop the condition that killed her father, a rare form of inherited Creutzfeldt–Jakob Disease or CJD, and 5 years ago her worst fears were confirmed. She was however blessed with devoted husband Stephen who overnight became the best carer she could imagine. The needs of children with a parent with dementia are often underestimated when not only are they witnessing deterioration and living with behaviour as a consequence of dementia that is difficult to understand, but are deprived of both child/parent relationships—with the affected person, and the other parent whose time and attention is taken up by their caring role. As predicted, Stephen increasingly needed to balance the differing needs of wife and 9-year old son Nigel. However, leaving his wife for the first time to take his son on holiday was disastrous, and Sheila became unsettled and began lashing out at carers who provided a sitting service at home. On their return Sheila became particularly insecure and agitated whenever Stephen was out of sight. Eventually respite care had to be withdrawn and Stephen was left to care for his wife alone 24 hours a day.

After approximately four years of increasingly difficult circumstances it became apparent that things could not continue as they were. By this time Sheila had developed severe dyspraxia, would resort to only a few words when communicating, and was unnerved by any new situation or people. It became clear to Stephen that reluctantly he would need to consider full time care but Sheila had very strong feelings about residential care as she had witnessed her father be admitted for respite and never return home.

The first attempt at placing Sheila had broken down after care staff were unable to manage her behaviour so in consultation with Clare, the counsellor for the National Prion Clinic, a highly specialised placement was sought. Clare had counselled Sheila and the family from diagnosis and earning their trust by meeting with them on a regular basis, while supporting carers in ways to validate Sheila and manage denial and other challenging symptoms. A gradual approach and creative partnership between the family, existing carers and new care team allowed the transition to full time care to be initiated at the same time as Sheila became a day patient to see how she settled. Disturbing sensory symptoms and dyspraxia became the key to understanding her challenging behaviour. Attempts to introduce new carers in situations where Sheila was manageable, for example in her wheelchair, was an important component of the transition since carers were not at risk from aggressive outbursts as a result of these symptoms. Trialling a gradual approach allowed new guidelines for care to be developed but we also needed to consult with Stephen who knew the routines that worked when showering and toileting Sheila. It began by taking 2 hours per shower but then became just 30 minutes, and staff soon learned that music and dancing sometimes helped smooth things over! Curiously Sheila would often shake her head when asked, for example, if she wanted a cup of tea, but by this she meant she 'can't' rather than that she did not 'want', as was too easily assumed. Eventually Sheila came to trust the new care team but we never forgot Stephen who increasingly was able to visit and concentrate on fun activities, not just personal care.

to service user choice and treatment preference. To illustrate, once one broadens the focus to include treatments provided by the other allied health professionals then one has to consider the way in which the service user wants these treatments delivered. Physiotherapy, for example, often involves giving advice and demonstrating exercises for the service user to take away and practice. But people with neurological illness and injury often require extra support because of poor memory, concentration, and motivation and so this standard approach really should be adapted for neuro-rehabilitation populations. Similarly, in standard psychological therapy and psychotherapy, therapy operates on the premise that matters discussed within the clinic setting will be generalized to the outside world, which is often supported by practising techniques or carrying out homework outside of sessions, or perhaps by bringing parts of the 'outside world' into therapy. Yet because so many neurological conditions affect one's capacity for abstract thinking, planning, and organization, these service users may need extra support to make these links or it may be necessary for the therapy to be routinely applied in vivo.

Discussions of service user choice and treatment preference include consideration of the Mental Capacity Act 2005, which came into effect in 2007 (Department of Health, 2007). No longer can it be taken on trust that a physician knows what is best for the service user. The reasons for prescribing or withholding drug treatment also need to be justified by medical staff, and this simultaneously offers them appropriate protection from liability. Matters are less clear when informal agreements have been made by the survivor some time ago, when capacity was intact, and these may be considered valid. Hence, the challenge to medical models and approaches ushered in by multidisciplinary teams has been complemented by further initiatives such as the Mental Capacity Act, thereby broadening approaches such that clinical guidelines include both service user and family members as key reference points, in addition to professionals.

The social and family context: Active ingredients of rehabilitation?

A consideration of human factors involved in rehabilitation helps to shed light on the context of rehabilitation and to explore the complex interactions between a specific condition, the individual who is injured or ill, and rehabilitation professionals. In accordance with the WHO ICF framework (Wade, 2006), it might be argued that interventions at the level of activity and participation will have greater relevance to the achievement of social goals. Equally, it could be argued that 'impairment' oriented interventions will have substantial impact on social function. A departure from reductionist perspectives allows for consideration of active ingredients of the social context that enable, for example, the construction and reconstruction of self after brain injury through our relationships with others (Bowen et al., 2009). Impetus for this also stems from studies confirming that relationship functioning can impact positively on rehabilitation outcome (Sander et al., 2002). Additional factors to consider include motivations and incentives to engage in social interaction such as the likelihood of visitors, expectations about discharge, but also to what degree fluency in speech is possible, and if not, will the person accept such a reduced form of communication? Therefore rehabilitation goals not only arise in social settings but social incentives are often necessary before service users will implement practice to improve functioning. It is perhaps for this reason that a number of strands of the literature point to reciprocal, mutual, overlapping, and cumulative influences in terms of psychosocial outcome for family members (Yeates, 2009).

In chapter 9 we discuss how the principles of systemic therapy suggest that there are laws of circular causality in families and that linear cause-and-effect relationships do not exist in a strict sense although this may be how they appear (Burnham, 1986; Stratton, Preston-Shoot, & Hanks, 1990). Yet there are also differences within families in terms of the impact on specific family members and typically what is reported is different impacts for spouses versus parents. Symmetrical and asymmetrical patterning may also be evident (e.g., when one member is depressed, the other is aggressive, etc.), but there are also studies showing more complex interaction effects, for example, between gender, parenting style, as well as depression in the non-injured parent, and the presence of emotional and behavioural problems in the children (e.g., Pessar, Coad, Linn, & Willer, 1993). While much of the available evidence is indirect, it, nevertheless, suggests the relationship between ABI-sequelae and outcomes is non-linear, complex, and circular; in other words, there is a level of complexity and diversity within neuro-rehabilitation that is not explained solely by biological factors but rather the social-family context.

At this point, a case example may help to illustrate some of the ideas we are presenting. Consider a person who has suffered a brain-stem stroke and now shows signs of being 'locked-in', a predicament that has become popularized with the recent film adaptation of the book 'The Diving Bell and the Butterfly' (Bauby, 1997). In this case, the stroke results in a paralysis that prevents speech. The absence of speech has a range of implications, which are primarily pathological (disease impacting on the functioning of the larynx and voice box) and related to participation (the motivation to speak, social opportunities to express oneself with intentionality within these interactions). Speech therapy is often offered to people following strokes to retrain them to communicate effectively, but what in this case when an absence of speech and movement creates a considerable obstruction to social participation? If learning to speak is out of the question are there other possible avenues to help assist this person communicate their needs? Furthermore, how do we conceptualize these alternatives? These days there are many devices and assistive technologies such as switches and sensors that can facilitate communication, even if just to indicate a yes/no response. What a difference this simple technology could make if it enabled someone to choose what clothes they would wear, or what activity to engage in. Given this, the goal of rehabilitation here does not concern rectifying a discrete pathology because the neurological illness has impacted at many levels. Instead, a personally meaningful goal would be to restore some functional capacity to communicate, albeit in a limited sense, by teaching the person to manage a sensor that enables them to give a yes/no response, while at the same time maximizing opportunities to socialize.

Thus far we have argued that from a relational perspective the emphasis of goals is participation, and treating impairment or activity restrictions that arise within a social family context. Therefore, standard therapies addressing pathology, impairment, or participation are all viable but the success of the goal is judged on whether the outcome is an increase in meaningful social participation. The principles of offering dignity and choice, through facilitating communication and increasing opportunities for social interaction have also been emphasized.

Individual psychological factors: The injured person as active participant

In addition to the social-family factors, the injured person is an active participant in rehabilitation, for example, the degree to which they are able to make use of resources available to them to work towards mutually established goals despite their impairments and other constraints. Here we are talking about pertinent issues such as their appraisal of the situation (e.g., motivation, self-efficacy), ability to initiate and sustain effort (e.g., practice, pacing), and awareness and self-reflection (e.g., meaningful goals, acceptance of limitations). In this sense, while the upper threshold for recovery may in part depend on the nature of injury and impairments, it is also open to be influenced by human factors and so may be malleable. Assessing the potential for change involves assessing the possibilities for effective therapeutic bonding with the survivor to work towards personally meaningful goals in a regular and focused way. In other words, a skilled rehabilitation specialist recognizes the injured person as an active part of rehabilitation and the degree of recovery cannot be determined without reference to them. We now discuss ways of fostering in the injured person the most helpful appraisal and the maximum amount of effort and awareness to create a focus on rehabilitation tasks.

Inter-personal factors, social incentives, and scaffolding

From a relational perspective, we are particularly interested in ways of using social incentives to achieve better outcomes in rehabilitation. While increased effort and implementation in the form of practice and pacing are necessary for effective rehabilitation, opportunities to put learning into practice are often constrained socially and environmentally. Hence, the rehabilitation team is required to construct the right kind of social and therapeutic milieu for the person to have such opportunities. Here, a graded approach is helpful whereby the potential for experiencing failure is minimized and success is made more likely by adapting the task and the social and physical environment to make it more conducive and meaningful to the individual; an approach for which, following Vygotsky, Jerome Bruner coined the term 'scaffolding':

> *"Discussions of problem solving or skill acquisition are usually premised on the assumption that the learner is alone and unassisted. If the social context is taken into account, it is usually treated as an instance of modeling and imitation. But the intervention of a tutor may involve much more than this. More often than not, it involves a kind of "scaffolding" process that enables a child or novice to solve a problem, carry out a task or achieve a goal which would be beyond his unassisted efforts. This scaffolding consists essentially of the adult "controlling" those elements of the task that are initially beyond the learner's capacity, thus permitting him to concentrate upon and complete only those elements that are within his range of competence. The task thus proceeds to a successful conclusion. We assume, however, that the process can potentially achieve much more for the learner than an assisted completion of the task. It may result, eventually, in development of task competence by the learner at a pace that would far outstrip his unassisted efforts."*

(Wood, Bruner, & Ross, 1976, p. 2)

The importance of this theory for neuro-rehabilitation was noted long ago by Vygotsky's pupil and contemporary, A.R. Luria, who prioritized the role of scaffolding and verbal mediation within the inter-personal relationship of the carer and survivor (Luria, 1968).

Increasing a person's focus can be achieved by working together with the survivor to clarify meaningful and achievable goals, while concurrently offering psychological support and therapy to help the person accept their new reality and the limitations of their condition. This is something that has been well recognized within holistic approaches to rehabilitation (Ben-Yishay, 1996), which uses a combination of individual and group therapy. This approach also works on the basis that emotional adjustment to injury is facilitated through shared remembering and that scaffolding can be offered to survivors by their peers.

To summarize, the active ingredients of rehabilitation may be biological, in part, but also related to social-family, individual and interpersonal factors, that is, dependent on many aspects of the interaction between professional, service user, and wider social networks. This proposition is not new, but we propose it as a framework for conceptualizing the role of different members of the multidisciplinary team. In addition to these factors, there are environmental factors per se that are more conducive to successful rehabilitation (also environmental barriers), and careful thought needs to be given to how an environment is set up so that the maximum amount of function and activity can be maintained by the person with the injury. In this regard, the profession of occupational therapy plays a vital role by carrying out such assessments, and the relational approach to rehabilitation can be seen to span across a range of disciplines.

Communication between survivor, family members, and rehabilitation team

The theory of Co-ordinated Management of Meaning is helpful for thinking about communication and information giving in rehabilitation because of the distinction it draws between 'transmission' models of communication versus social constructionism (Pearce, 2007). However, as communicators we need to pay particular attention, not to our intended message, but to what is received by the listener, and to continually be checking this out.

In terms of systemic family therapy, we understand that in order for change to occur, some difference (or discrepancy) must be highlighted, although if this difference is too vast then change will be prevented; alternatively, in the words of Gregory Bateson, 'it is the difference that makes the difference' (Bateson, 1972). So the family therapy movement is a strong influence on relational approaches to rehabilitation, particularly the systemic principle that change is achieved by members within a social network giving feedback, both negative and positive, as occurs in the development, maintenance, and resolution of family problems.

In neurological conditions there are likely to be additional complications, for example, when awareness and identity have been altered, there can be a failure on the part of the injured person to truly appreciate the impact of their condition on others. Yeates, Henwood, Gracey, and Evans (2007) clearly showed this in their qualitative study of people with such difficulties, by also interviewing a close relative and comparing their beliefs about the nature of difficulties with those of the injured person. More will be said about how to negotiate differences in awareness and the perception of impairments in later chapters, especially chapter 6. For now we wish to raise the issue of communication as a social process, and to highlight feedback from the listener as key to learning and progress in rehabilitation irrespective of the source (e.g., professional, peer, or family member) or context (e.g., family therapy setting, therapeutic milieu, or individual sessions).

Given the presence of difference within and across families, it is perhaps inevitable that relatives' perceptions of problems following injury often differ significantly from professionals' (Sherer, Boake, Levine et al., 1998; Sunderland, Harris, & Gleave, 1984). This particular dimension of difference is often characterized by frustration for all those involved, and an undermining of collaborative opportunities, and sometimes leads to the identification of 'problem families' (rather than 'family problems') by clinicians. Indeed, it is often complexities within the family-service relationship, which feature in team discussions and more will be said about developing therapeutic relationships with families later in this book.

Summary

In this section, we have outlined the core features of a relational approach to rehabilitation within the social-family context. A brain injury often comes between people and can be destructive to relationships yet by working with the shared reality among members of a network, rehabilitation allows for participation and also improvements to impairments. Human factors are engaged by actively working in the space that opens up between the triad of injured person, professional, and the family and social networks. Skilled rehabilitation teams value the injured person as an active participant in rehabilitation and aim to maximize the positive appraisal, effort, and awareness they give to rehabilitation, but social incentives and scaffolding can also be helpful to the process. Creating a social herapeutic milieu gives survivors the opportunity to receive positive, regular, and insightful feedback, whether from professional, peer, or family member. In this way, identity reconstruction is an integral component of a relational approach to rehabilitation.

CHAPTER THREE

Towards a relational neuropsychology

Defining mind and brain

Mainstream neuropsychology is not typically associated with relational thinking. Indeed, it has been the opposite for the most part, with a common definition being the study of mind-brain-behaviour relationships (e.g., Heilman, 2003), with 'mind' being very firmly rooted in an individual's cranium. This seems conceptually far away from 'ecologies' of mind or similar epistemologies (social constructionist, post-modernist, discursive, narrative, etc.) spanning and extending beyond multiple craniums. Indeed, Dominic Abrams, the chair of the British Psychological Society's research board in 2004, marked out these two traditions to define diversity within the profession:

> "Psychology itself is a very disparate discipline. For example, methodological and theoretical differences between neuropsychology and discourse analysis are far greater than differences between most branches of sociology and anthropology" (p. 260).

However, away from the lecture rooms a pragmatic dilemma confronts the neuro-rehabilitation clinician. A connection to the material parameters of an altered neurobiological substrate is necessary. Applying relational perspectives without considering how, say, the system or socially constructive processes have been in part influenced by the brain injury would be incomplete. In this book, we take the position that the ultimate reality of a brain injury is structured, organized, and imbued with meaning at the social/relational level. However, we would be naïve if we did not acknowledge this level has changed as a function of the injury occurring (and its many diverse consequences). One useful metaphor may be to the movement of ripples through a lake following the drop of a boulder—a physical event but which is formed by the spreading, generative action through the water (social relationships) itself.

As neuro-rehabilitation has relied on neuroscience and neuropsychology to improve its efficacy as one of its multiple tools (Wilson, 2005), several family therapists and/or systemic-orientated clinicians have argued for the need to include neuropsychology within the toolbox of family work (Bowen, 2007; Johnson & McCown, 1997; Laroi, 2003; Yeates, Henwood, Gracey, & Evans, 2007). Johnson and McCown (1997) have argued for the birth of a new profession, skilled in both neuropsychology and family therapy, while others would identify both skill sets within core neuro-rehabilitation professions such as clinical psychology (Wilson, 2005; Yeates, Henwood, Gracey, & Evans, 2007). There seems at least to be a shared assumption that unmodified psychological therapy of any kind, notably family work, will have limited efficacy if not adapted to respond to neuro-psychological changes post-injury (Bowen, 2007; Johnson & McCown, 1997; Laroi, 2001; 2003; Yeates, Henwood, Gracey, & Evans, 2007).

There may be several roads to this integration. At first this may seem to require a constant pendulum swing between two differing ontologies, epistemologies, or methods. This swing may actually be quite a dynamic, creative, and generative process. However, we can also look for relational thinking that already exists within neuropsychology, in some cases existing before social constructionists and family therapists started to poke their noses around this neighbourhood. There are indeed a range of intellectual traditions within neuropsychology, and although cognitive neuropsychology has remained a dominant paradigm until recent times, relational, ecological, and post-cognitive orientations are there to be found.

Here, we will tackle the traditional cognitive domains that most commonly feature in neuro-psychological assessment reports or compartmentalize neuro-rehabilitation literature: *language, memory, visuo-spatial perception and praxis, attention,* and *executive functioning.* We hope to present to the reader lesser known, perhaps marginalized perspectives, studies and findings within these core domains that all serve to locate such functions within relationships, not isolated skulls. We will illustrate the very practical advantages of applying these traditions through brief case vignettes throughout. In addition, the new fields of affective and social neuroscience are noteworthy for our aims in this chapter. We will outline in this chapter some of the early conceptual challenges that have already been highlighted in this literature when thinking about *social communication.* We will then explore the social neuroscience literature in more detail in the following two chapters as we consider intimacy and couples' relationships.

Language

This domain may seem too obvious to include let alone start a review of emerging relational neuro-psychological perspectives. As discussed in previous chapters, the appreciation of language as the central mechanism for social construction and relational influence has remained a core conviction of post-modernist thinkers and is complementary to second-order cybernetics (e.g., Bertrando, 2000). However within neuro-rehabilitation, changes in language following brain injury were one of the first invitations towards the interior of the survivor, when Broca (1865) published a case-study on aphasia and postulated an area of damage in the left frontal cortex. As Freud's (1891) early study of aphasia sowed the seeds for the structural model of the mind within psychoanalysis, aphasiology and speech and language therapy has now evolved into a relational consideration of the social context in both assessment and rehabilitation.

In a special issue of Aphasiology (McDonald, 2000), communication disorders were firmly put back within the social contexts in which they are manifested. That is, the socio-cultural background of individuals with aphasia, the communicative conditions in which aphasic errors occur or are ameliorated, the ability of survivors to moderate their communication across differing communicative contexts, and the broad and complicated social aims for communicative acts that are pertinent in differing contexts. In more controlled conditions, Jorgensen and Togher (2009) have shown how mono-logical narratives by individual survivors that appear to deviate from normal convention, appear indistinguishable from controls when the narrative is elicited in a group, relational context. Beyond the injury and neuro-psychological impairment itself, some authors have shown how expressive difficulties lead to malignant communicative practices by others such as conversational repair and talking over survivors or in the third person (Sabat & Harre, 1992). These can serve to threaten the continuity of social identity and agency for the survivor (also see section on memory below).

Furthermore, an emphasis on the social context of communication will be sensitive to the new demands that are created as this context radically changes, as is currently happening in our society. There is a progressive emphasis on remote, non-face to face communication using a variety of media via the internet and social networking sites. Existing research by UK CONNECT (Elman, Parr, & Moss, 2003; Moss, Parr, Byng, & Petheram, 2004; Parr, Watson, & Woods, 2006) see www.ukconnect.org/research_221.aspx) has shown that while social and community access is potentially offered by the internet, survivors of ABI who have language difficulties are undermined by the vast quantity of unstructured and non-signposted information on the web.

Relational language rehabilitation

There is a whole movement of functional communication within speech and language therapy, which emphasizes the context as the level of intervention, not the impairment in isolation. In accordance with the WHO ICF model (Wade, 2006), this can be seen as targeting the level of impairment through intervention at the level of social participation. Specifically communicative acts are supported by specific re-organization of interactional conditions, and use of varied communicative tools. These intervention approaches often use group session formats, prioritizing social interactions and social relationships as core mechanisms and outcomes. Combinations of speech and language therapists and family therapists may make potentially excellent co-therapy teams in responding to changed communication following ABI and its relational impact. The use of systemic questioning techniques that have been useful for people with learning disabilities and dementia may offer potential, as would non-verbal techniques such as drawing or spatial sculpting (Minuchin, 1974). Elsewhere in the family therapy literature, emotion-focused couples therapy (EFT) has been described (Stiell, Naaman, & Lee, 2007) where one person has aphasia (in a wider consideration of couples and chronic illness). This model emphasizes disruptions to active connection and attachment processes through the disruption to communication and EFT therapists seek to facilitate re-connection and secure couple attachments through supporting communication within the couple.

Organizations such as UK CONNECT (www.ukconnect.org) have explicitly drawn on narrative therapy and community psychology models to prioritize the creation of new relationships and strengthening of social group membership as key outcomes for aphasia sufferers. They create community gatherings and road shows in remote or rural areas, bringing people together and facilitating communication and formation of community. They are also interested in website design and advocacy, using both an impairment-based knowledge of both aphasia and the actual experiences of survivors in navigating the net.

Case study

Aphasia and family organization

Following a left middle communicating artery ischaemic stroke, a 45-year-old man, Bill, was left with a range of receptive and expressive language difficulties, in addition to verbal memory and verbal abstract reasoning deficits, plus difficulties conceptualizing grammatical inter-relationships (Luria's pseudo-spatial relationships). Prior to his stroke, he was very busy with a range of small businesses and spent little time with his wife and 10-year-old child. During this time the wife and child developed their own mutual routines and interests. Following the stroke and unemployment, Bill was keen to re-invest in family relationships, particularly to be closer to his son. However, he found that he was often unintentionally ignored as the rest of the family 'just got on with it', and did not expect him to be interested in their activities. He became increasingly hopeless and would often be heard saying "what is the point?!," trying less and less over time to create conversational opportunities for connection with others. He was left spending most of his time outside, tending to their chickens, who, he acknowledged, were not the best of company.

> The family work had two simultaneous foci, (a) to renegotiate who does what with whom in the family, and (b) to find mediums and forms of representation that would assist Bill in understanding the dynamics of the family and the vicious cycles that were maintaining the sense of distance within relationships. With regards to the former, opportunities were sought for father and son time together that could occur in contexts where there was not too much cross-talking between large groups of people and lots of general stimulation. This necessarily involved Bill accepting that he would have to broaden his own repertoire of interests to connect with his growing son in new ways. The family session discussions were often very hard for Bill to follow, with frequent reference to abstract concepts and arrangements of relationships around different issues. Visual diagrams such as venn diagrams, basic pictorial representations, pre-injury metaphors, and spatial sculpting in session were used to develop a shared formulation of the presenting problems.

Memory

When you think of memory, what comes to mind?

- Do personal memories, events, and experiences, being recalled 'within' you, feature right now?

Take a closer look at those events.

- Does anyone else feature in these, either directly or indirectly?
- If you met up with those people now, would the sharing of those memories be important or significant?
- Would the act of sharing have any kind of influence on how these memories may subsequently be remembered?

Think of times when you have jointly remembered or retold an experience with someone close, perhaps to others who have had no previous connection with that memory (e.g., telling others about an awful meal in a restaurant or a wonderful holiday).

- Was that re-telling a parallel, completely consistent process between you and your 'co-rememberer'? Or was there an interaction, adding in bits here or there, a relay process that contributed to the overall story, or even a dispute or contesting process about what actually happened or who did what?

Think about the word remember: *Re*-member, *Re*new *member*ship. This framing, perhaps less visible behind dominant images of an individual act of list learning in a neuropsychologist's testing session or the inner experience of a solitary being, is nonetheless, central to every experiences and uses of memory. The contrast between the two scenarios is actually very significant in terms of output/what is remembered. Harré (2002) highlights a study by Dixon (1996), comparing the remembering of older and younger persons. When isolated, individual older people performed more poorly on laboratory tests of memory than younger people. However, Dixon showed that when older people were allowed to participate in conversations about their past, their remembering was comparable to group recall by younger persons. Although we might explain this difference in terms of cognitive approaches to neuropsychology, where we identify impairments in specific aspects of memory and remembering, this comparison by Dixon raises a question; which demonstration of memory ability in the older group is the veridical, *real* picture of memory here? Unphased by such epistemological dilemmas, Neely, Vikström and Josephsson (2009) have advocated the use of caregivers alongside people with neuro-disability to facilitate the emergence of memories with relational contexts.

Collective remembering

Social psychologists have drawn attention to this 'collective remembering' (Edwards, 1990; Edwards & Middleton, 1986; Harré, 2002; Middleton & Edwards, 1990) and the psychological and relational work that is achieved through it. When a memory features in mental life, people are always involved in either the memory and/or the remembering of it. So connections are formed, and people are brought together through the process of remembering. Social identities and group membership are often made possible through shared cultural, family, friendship, or intimate memories, constructing a historical dimension and often structured through a narrative (Bruner, 1990; Sarbin, 1986) . Therapists have developed a specific approach re-membering work that aims for increased meaning and inclusion within contested and forgotten stories (Myerhoff, 1982). The act of remembering also involves a process of certification and negotiation within a group of interested parties (Kreckel, 1981), this process being evident when certain memories are judged to be false or confabulations by others. Jacoby (1997) has constructed the notion of 'social amnesia', where certain traditions, views, or narratives become forgotten within or across generations due to a lack of re-propagation and sustenance through communication practices. Jacoby notes that this loss can be motivated, and focuses on episodes and perspectives in history that become forgotten by nations. Social amnesia can also be seen in academic practices, as a function of wider socio-cultural trends. Examples include some of the psychological traditions outlined in this chapter, which have become decoupled from neuro-rehabilitation formulation over the last three decades.

Semantization

Complementary to this is a collection of perspectives that have been grouped together under the banner of 'semantization' in the representation of long-term memories (Cermak, 1984; Meeter & Murre, 2004). The two dominant models of long-term memory organization is the standard consolidation model approach, including the Trace-Link model (Meeter & Murre, 2004; Murre, 1996), and in contrast the Multiple Trace Theory (MTT, Nadel, & Moscovitch, 1997). The former postulates that initial memories of experience rely on hippocampal involvement to establish distributed representations within a neocortical substrate. Over time, traces between nodes within the neocortical distributions become strengthened, such that hippocampal involvement is progressively less required in their activation/ retrieval. In contrast, the MTT model maintains a role for the hippocampus as long as the memories exist, acting as an indexical pointer for neocortical representations.

Both these models incorporate a conceptualized transformative process over time (Rosenbaum, Winocur, & Moscovitch, 2001; Winocur, Moscovitch, & Sekeres, 2007), where initial episodic memories that include rich details of sensory, temporal, and environmental surroundings (achieved via hippocampal involvement) become independent from the immediate environmental circumstances, as they are organized within neocortical representations. Where both hippocampal and extra-hippocampal neocortical structures are intact, both generalities and specifics can be recalled, although there is a progressive loss of detail in recall over time.

Still echoing the experience-dependent-independent distinction, others have drawn attention to the semantic nature of remote human memories versus episodic representations (Cermak, 1984; Cermak & O'Connor, 1983), suggesting that memories become more 'fact-like' and less 'event-like' over time. Meeter and Murre (2004) described this theoretical position as 'semantization'.

Evidence supporting neuro-imaging is provided by Reed (2005), who highlights a trend of para-hippocampal cortical and white-matter involvement in remote memories. In contrast, hippocampal involvement is restricted to recent memories. Similarly, neuro-psychological evidence supports a temporal dimension of semantization, progressively involving neocortical as opposed to hippocampal structures. There is a contrast between memory impairments characteristic of Alzheimer's disease and Semantic Dementia, where the latter is characterized by preservation of recent episodic memories and loss of remote (inferred as semanticized) representations (Graham, 1999; Graham, Becker, & Hodges, 1997; Meeter & Murre, 2004; Murre, Graham, & Hodges, 2001; Snowden, Griffiths, & Neary, 1996). The remote memories of amnesic patients with hippocampal damage, while superficially intact, have been described as being semantic, inflexible stories rather than episodic memories, or to lack sensory detail or vividness when compared to controls (Kinsbourne & Wood, 1975; Rosenbaum, Priselac, Köhler, Black, Gao, Nadel, & Moscovitch, 2000; Viskontas, McAndrews, & Moscovitch, 2000).

The progressive involvement of cortical representations resulting in semantic, event-independent remote memories has face validity. However, debate exists within the long-term memory neuroscientific field on how this transformation/semantization may occur. Rosenbaum and colleagues (2001) describe a process of the 'relational context' of learning (here meaning the temporal, spatial, and feature characteristics of the learning environment) becoming progressively less important, while a generalized schematic of the object of learning (e.g., a food preference in rats) is emphasized. Meeter and Murre (2004) infer this account as a description of rich episodic memories "falling apart" (p. 852), leaving behind an abstract semantic frame. They also infer that a process of repetition and over-learning is necessary for this transformation to be achieved. While they describe the central role of both conscious mental rehearsal and re-exposure to memory cues, in addition to memory representations within dreaming, they cite animal learning experimental evidence that contradicts the need for over-learning for remote representations to be formed.

This debate reveals both the potential of neuroscientific findings for relational thinking following ABI and also the limitations of individualist, reductive discourse inherent to this field. As the reader may have noticed, the term 'relational context' is even used in this literature, but only to describe the physical environment and the relationship between this and an animal subject. Two conceptual omissions are evident: the social context/dimension of human remembering and a sense of purposeful agency in the memory process. The descriptions above refer to a non-agentic process determined by biological parameters and the learning process, unfolding over time. An alternative level of description has been provided in an unpublished doctoral thesis by Gingell (2005), who briefly suggests that the recall strategy of the subject may contribute to the semantization of memory. She suggests that remote memories are lacking in detail, guessed at, but then searched for and (significantly) evaluated with reference to personal semantic information (Odegard & Lampinen, 2004), thereby semanticizing those traces recalled. While an active, agentic subject now emerges in the semantization account, they are still isolated from context.

Judgements about whether a memory is 'real' or 'imagined' are said to be the function 'source monitoring systems' (Johnson, 1997). Many neuro-psychological explanations have been offered to account for the phenomenon of 'confabulation' ('false remembering'), which include deficits in reality monitoring, among other theories, including impairment of aspects of executive systems and memory functioning (DeLuca, 2000; Schnider, 2003). In addition to impairments with source and temporality monitoring, motivational and emotional factors are also said to be important (Fotopoulou, Conway, & Solms, 2007). For example, in the case of OP (Conway & Tacchi, 1996), confabulation occurred in the context of explaining others' seemingly 'odd' behaviour towards her (in the absence of her own awareness of her brain injury). Researchers have found that the content of confabulations is not emotionally neutral, but is likely to create a narrative about the world that is more positive for that individual (Fotopoulou, Solms, & Turnbull, 2004). Here we have an interesting example of interacting emotional, social, and neural processes indicating that the social context of the person with ABI will again be a significant influence on the presence of their symptoms.

Semantization and collective remembering

If human remembering is constructed as a socio-linguistic, active process, then the process of narration and its social dynamics (Bruner, 1991; Sarbin, 1986) becomes a highly relevant level of description for semantization. Original episodes will be remembered and retold within relationships and communities, constructed and progressively re-constructed through socio-linguistic meanings and conventions, with new socio-relational influences at each retelling. Here we finally arrive at a relational neuro-psychological account of memory, which can be useful in a relational approach to memory problems following ABI.

If we re-emphasize remembering as a collective, socially connecting process, we are in the same territory as for language rehabilitation mentioned above, and can begin to see how this social dimension unfolds following neuro-disability. If people can no longer retrieve specific details from the past as part of a conversational process, particularly if these details were significantly meaningful for a set of relationships (wedding day, birth of a child, the day of the injury itself), then distance will be the result: relationships will be partitioned, not cemented. If this becomes a progressively more frequent occurrence, with survivor's being able to participate, remember and 'be' in fewer and fewer remembering conversations, than this is nothing less than a growing threat to self and relationships, a socially isolating experience.

This clinical consideration has been developed within the dementia literature, inspired by the work of Tom Kitwood (1997). Although Kitwood's approach has been criticized on some levels (Baldwin & Capstick, 2007; Dewing, 2008), it provides a valuable contribution to understanding of neuro-psychological symptoms within a social context. Writers have drawn attention to 'malignant social psychological processes' that involve people with dementia being progressively objectified, talked over, ignored, and excluded from opportunities to meaningfully express agency and personhood. Importantly, Sabat and Harre (1992) have shown how specific neuro-psychological difficulties in recall of information and ability to express oneself eloquently, can make people with dementia more vulnerable to conversational repair (having the beginning of memories and sentences being conversationally 'filled in' by others without the opportunity to correct or disagree), being talked over/ignored or constructed solely in the third person.

Relational memory interventions

In the 1980s Barbara Wilson initiated a paradigm shift in memory rehabilitation (Wilson, 1987). She achieved this via an ontological reframing of memory—before it was an unalterable loss, a tragic consequence of injury. Using her behavioural background, Wilson drew attention to memory following ABI as a learning process. As such it is amenable to changes in learning and retrieval conditions, including the use of external memory aids. This behaviourist perspective linked individual survivors with their environment, partially extending memory beyond damaged brains. In doing so, new options for memory rehabilitation were created.

Similarly, Wilson's repositioning of memory can be extended further, as a process existing between people, connecting and defining relationships post-injury. In doing so, perhaps a new, conversational technology of memory rehabilitation can be facilitated. Within couples, family, and community work, the neuro-psychological intervention would be to identify the conversational and interactional conditions that produce the relational failures of a particular memory difficulty, and to determine the psychosocial consequences of this. This could be the identification of particular types of remembering or particular types of material, or particular questions that make it more or less difficult to retrieve and contribute. This inquiry would occur in parallel with the mapping out of specific relationships that are compromised by these failures and the idiosyncratic meanings of such. In response, conversational conditions could be re-arranged, perhaps with the use of specific conversational/memory aids, to facilitate the 're-entry' of persons back into dialogue and enable relational connections to be reformed.

This may be the prioritization of visual over verbal mediums in remembering interactions, or in the case of working memory difficulties or those influenced by attention or executive difficulties, the identification of key cues, words, or phrases that more reliably elicit the desired memory or anecdote. One example would be specific narrative therapy (White & Epston, 1990) questions that have inspired use within qualitative ABI research (Patterson & Scott-Finlay, 2002). Instead of promoting questions that invite direct experience, others could be chosen, which access salient scripts, themes, or narratives: "What usually happens when that occurs? ... "What would you generally advise other survivors of ABI on this matter?" This would be accessing the semanticized neocortical representations highlighted by neuroscientists (Rosenbaum, Winocur, & Moscovitch, 2001; Winocur, Moscovitch, & Sekeres, 2007), while retaining an invitation and continuation of personal agency and identity.

Case study

Remembering the 'New Us' in couples work

(We acknowledge the intuitive input of co-therapist, Sandra Barton)
A couple, Tony and Mary, requested couples sessions to explore changes in their relationship following post-encephalitic cognitive difficulties experienced by the husband. He contracted the virus soon after retiring and they and their two adult children had not yet re-organized themselves around the retirement, let alone the brain injury. Mary was struggling with her son who had returned to live with them after his business had folded, but was now trying to run the business from home, primarily using the family kitchen. Mary felt that the son was not considering their needs as parents following retirement, wanting a quieter life, less hassle and to have friends over in a presentable house. At the same time Mary felt a growing sense of distance between her and Tony, who seemed to her to be less by her side in family matters. Since his injury he found it very difficult to remember new information.
    When discussing their perspective as a couple privately, Tony and Mary would agree on how to respond to their son's inconsiderate behaviour. However when Mary would confront her son, Tony could not remember the preceding conversation to support his wife. Mary felt that the son would manipulate this memory loss to his advantage, and cue Tony into an earlier, but now outdated narrative about the 'boys in the house sticking together within entrepreneurial spirit against all the odds'. The son's point of view was that he had not heard his father say anything different post-retirement, and had only known his father as someone who was a successful businessman, building up a company from grass-roots and having nothing, a pattern the son was trying to

emulate now. Tony was left feeling confused and impotent during these clashes, and would suddenly leave the situation feeling he had let everyone down.

We spent the first few sessions of couples work facilitating a conversation around post-retirement life and preferred identities within this. We would use narrative questions around 'typical' and 'usual' scenarios for retirement, rather than quiz Tony directly on his recollection since the injury. He did have access to an anticipated retirement life, dreamt up with Mary several decades ago. We cross-referenced this with the 'usual' scenarios previously discussed and derived a meaningful new narrative as a result, careful to facilitate a mutual involvement for both Tony and Mary in this emerging new story. These details were documented as a summary letter sent to the couple at the end of each session, who were instructed to spend some time alone reading and sharing responses to each other between-sessions. We made rich use of metaphors and tropes that constituted the couple's retirement dream from the decades previously (e.g., "us as suburban hedonists") in these letters to graphically strengthen this emergent narrative.

The last stage of therapy was to orchestrate a meeting between the parents and both their children, for the latter to witness the unveiling of the former's new life narrative. We programmed some phone alerts with Tony to deliver some discussion points at the time of the scheduled meeting. Tony began to fill in a daily diary chronicling their new hedonistic life post-retirement, to which he would add small pieces of artwork within a newly found creative side. When points of disagreement would arise with the son and his business plans, the couple would discuss together first and Tony would set some phone alerts to remind him of his intended message to the son when they would later meet to talk about these issues.

Finally, specific family or social network members may be collaboratively identified, considering who would be most supportive of social identity continuity in their facilitation of the survivor's narration and remembering. Such considerations should promote empowerment for the survivor of ABI, in terms of their ability to influence what is spoken about, what is jointly remembered, and what meanings and explanations for things are offered and prioritized. From a cybernetics perspective, increased agency in the survivor's remembering within context would then influence broader family responses and create new social and conversational conditions for joint remembering and connection.

Visuo-spatial perception and praxis

The field of visuo-spatial perception and praxis mirrors some of the paradoxical twists and turns of theory that have been described in the memory neuroscientific literature, sometimes asserting a reductionist neural position, yet later or even at the same time unwittingly providing a neuro-psychological link to relational thinking. A core dilemma to researchers within these fields is to conceptualize the inter-relationship of perception, action, and context, to make sense of often contradictory findings across experiments and pathological presentations.

For the last two decades, a dominant conceptual scheme has been provided by Ungerleider and Mishkin (1982) and then refined by Milner and Goodale (1995), who discriminate two parallel visual processing streams. These were a ventral occipito-temporal stream, which processed object features to enable recognition and comprehension—the 'what' stream. Its counterpart, a dorsal occipito-parietal stream was initially considered to be the 'where' stream (Ungerleider & Mishkin, 1982), processing the spatial relationship of targets in relation to the individual (egocentric coordinates), to permit visual guided action such as reaching and grasping.

However, the study of both streams was plagued by unusual findings that have emerged more recently. The 'what' stream seems to dissociate into separable prehension elements for living versus non-living things, with one category being preserved over the other in differing neurological conditions (Laws, 2005; Turnball & Laws, 2000; Warrington & Shallice, 1984). Concurrently, the function of the 'where' stream seems to be exponentially transformed by the process of action itself. For example, survivors with visual hemi-neglect seem to exhibit this only in peri-personal space—their acts of line bisections do not exhibit neglect when using a laser pointer for extra-personal targets beyond reaching space. When given a long stick to bisect these same targets however, the neglect re-appears (Berti & Frassinetti, 2000; Rizzolatti, Berti & Gallese, 2000). The act of purposeful tool use does seem to fundamentally change perception. Animal studies have shown that a monkey's visual field will expand to include the entirety of a large rake when held (Iriki, Tanaka, & Iwamura, 1996; Iriki, Tanaka, Obayashi et al., 2001).

At the same time, the study of skilful, intentional movement (praxis) has tied itself into knots trying to develop a comprehensive typology of disorders of praxis following neurological damage. Traditional schemes have included ideational versus ideomotor apraxia (the work of Liepmann, 1900–1920), pantomiming versus copying versus instrumental use, limb versus orobuccal, dressing versus combing, etc., all noted to be frequently used inconsistently (Greene, 2005). These static typologies have struggled to cope with the fact that the pattern of praxis difficulty would vary remarkably depending on the action, the tool that was being used, and the context in which the action occurred (Greene, 2005).

Collectively, this literature provides multiple indications that earlier notions of visual and praxis neural systems as autonomous, isolated, sequential processors and programmers are not viable. We have critical dimensions of environment/context and action structuring and transforming the range of possible perceptual operations. This literature has begun to respond to these dimensions in its theory-building. The dorsal and ventral streams of visual cognition have since been reconceptualized as a 'how to' and 'what for' systems (e.g., Buxbaum, 2007). This scheme emphasizes these systems' role in facilitating meaningful, interactions between the subject and their environment, which is both goal-directed and constrained by the context in which they occur. This approach was co-developed with findings that the dorsal stream further breaks down into a grasping, prehension system that guides movement to gain more information about an object, and a 'use' system for skilled, purposeful action (Buxbaum, 2001; Frey, 2007; Rizzolatti & Matelli, 2003). These two dimensions do not exist in separation.

With regards to the ventral stream and its living and non-living categories, there has been a move away from assuming a separate, pre-determined neurological specialization. Some authors have suggested that this split emerges from a history of a subject interacting within their environment. This could be the increased familiarity of one category over the other within an individual's lifetime of experiences (Funnell & Sheridan, 1992). For example, men have been shown to be better at recognizing tools where women are better at recognizing living things (Laws, 2004). An alternative view is that non-living things are more structurally diverse, have been engineered for function within a historical relationship with humans and so 'afford' a greater requirement for structural encoding, recognition, and use (Turnball et al., 2000).

These new schemes therefore emphasize the intimate and constructive mutual relationship between brain and environment, with action being at least in part environmentally cued, itself transforming the perceptual and prehensive experience. These recent trends have led to the renewed interest in ecological psychology and the work of J.J. Gibson (1977; 1979). For a long-time, this tradition has been marginalized as a separate psychological movement away from mainstream disinterest in how brains interact with environments (e.g., see http://www.trincoll.edu/depts/ecopsyc/isep). This approach rejected both behaviourism and cognitivism, adapting a direct realist philosophy. This is that there is no constructed intermediary mental representation that deviates from physical reality to guide organisms within the world. Instead, indeterminate structural and other physical properties of the world 'afford' a limited number of interactions and uses. Over time, interactions between the organism and the affordances of the physical world produce relevant meaning and guides to action, although this is always constrained by physical properties of the environment.

Paradoxically, this philosophy both is the antithesis of constructionist frameworks that dominate this book, yet it emphasizes the organizing power of context, as per social constructionism and cybernetics. The most significant objects within a person's environment to be perceived and which stimulate action are often other people. The cumulative affordances for social action and meaning, which are generated within successive person-to-person interactions, have been considered in a second-order cybernetics consideration of Gibsonian ideas (Maturana & Poerksen, 2004).

The beginnings of reparation between mainstream neuropsychology and ecological psychology have brought back in an interest on how the context organizes mental life and neuro-psychological functions. More recently, the importance of agency and goal-directed behaviour has been brought into dialogue with the influences of ecological affordances. Findings have shown that object affordances are attended to and responded to differently, depending on the intentions and plans of the actor (Gold & Park , 2009; Pavese & Buxbaum, 2002) and the integrity of their executive and praxis neural systems to support these operations (Bickerton et al., 2007; 2009). At the same time, such intentions are inseparable from the environment in which the organism is situated—studies of canonical neurons in the frontal cortex have shown these to activate in response to the sight of objects/tools that would later activate these neurons during the use of such objects (Rizzolatti, Berti, & Gallese, 2000).

Similarly, the links between semantic knowledge and action have been emphasized as more intimate and reciprocal than previously thought (Hodges et al., 2000). An interesting dove-tail has recently emerged between social psychology and neuroscience. Discursive approaches to language and conceptualisations of the world have viewed it as primarily a form of (social) action rather than consti-tuted through abstract representations independent from its use. Researchers of mirror neurons and somato-sensory/motor circuits have suggested that neural systems for motor action may be suita-ble as a foundation for the emergence and ongoing manifestation of language (Gallese, 2006; Gallese & Lakoff, 2005), with mirror neu-ron activity been recorded during language use. These researchers also suggest language use as a prominent arena for intersubjectiv-ity and attentional attunement between persons (see below). The cross-dialogue between mainstream neuropsychology and ecologi-cal approaches is useful in that it begins to shift a view of a physi-cal, realist context structuring neuro-psychological function, to a relative, changing and constructive context of meaning that will evolve to generate new affordances of human-environment interac-tion over time.

Relational visuo-spatial rehabilitation

Instead of a post-hoc search of strategies that will be useful to a con-textually isolated damage visual-perceptual system, the concept of affordances opens up a whole ergonomic science of environmental adaptation to achieve function and activity. Indeed, this approach has been pragmatically and empirically developed in the absence of the above theory, includes the work of James Purdon-Martin's (1961) with parkinsonian patients, and modern use of smart houses or cueing technology to facilitate sequencing, praxis, and skills use (e.g., O'Neill et al., 2007). Rehabilitation studies of post-ABI ideomotor apraxia have used an ecological emphasis to successfully train actions that are highly compatible with (afforded by) objects (Barde et al., 2007).

Indeed, the studies of Bickerton and colleagues (2007; 2009) are evolving a sophisticated science of the dynamics between top-down (goal-driven) and bottom-up (object-afforded) processes as part of the subject's interaction with context. These studies, building on the work of others (Cooper & Shallice, 2000; Forde & Humphreys, 2002; Humphreys & Riddoch, 2001; Pavese & Buxbaum, 2002) show how certain forms of ABI (involving frontal and basal ganglia damage) lead to a specific difficulty in enacting goal-driven intentions in the face of discrepant environmentally afforded cues (traditionally referred to as 'utilization behaviour'). This science, not permitted through a more reductionist agenda, would suggest that the focus should be on structuring environmental affordances for certain groups to permit socially valued action and participation.

Case study

Affording a preferred self within the social spotlight

(With many thanks to the lead therapist in this work, Rob Jobe)

Aidan, a 19 year old survivor of a RTA, was left with attentional and working memory difficulties in addition to parkinsonian-like movement difficulties that made getting started and maintaining a smooth gait very problematic when walking. His main rehabilitation goal was to get a girlfriend. He often would go out in his local city centre with his friends, which involved walking down busy pedestrian areas to access his favourite bars and clubs. He described these particular walks as 'running the gauntlet'. He was very self-conscious of his walking as it might appear to others, especially girls. Social anxiety has been shown to be a common experience following ABI (Newton & Johnson, 1985; Johnson & Newton, 1987). He was sure that he was constructed as nothing more than a "cabbage, disgusting to others". In this relational position he experienced himself as even more disabled. His physiotherapist was sure that his level of mobility would be improved were it not for this incapacitating psychological process.

It was clear that his walking down this 'pedestrian gauntlet' would become progressively more incapacitating as he caught the eyes of those people walking in the opposite direction, triggering off this more debilitating mode of experience. Psychological models of social anxiety (Butler, 1998) posit an increasingly attentionally-demanding mode of 'self-as-social-object' processing. For Aidan, this was a vicious cycle depriving him of scarce available attentional and praxis control resources. However his praxis response was afforded to a debilitating position by the gaze of others, mediated and constructed through his relational history post-injury to signify incapacitating disability, otherness and disgust.

After some early experiments with Aidan to identify the role of self-focused attention, psychological support aimed to free up attentional and automatic praxis control through attentional training (Clark & Wells, 1995; Wells & Clark, 1997) involving the refocusing away from the gaze of others to the shop windows on either side of him. In these he could see the latest clothes fashions, clothes he enthusiastically bought and was proud to wear. Sometimes he would catch his own reflection blending in with the shop displays. These stimuli afforded a different sense of self, a discerning dresser, young, charming. Cued into this different perceptual-action relationship, Aidan's initiation and gait during walking notably improved, became more fluid. His outcome of this piece of work was a beautiful girlfriend.

Attention

Without much controversy attention is considered by most to be an active neuro-psychological process engaged by organisms in their management of and interactions with information from the environment. Traditional neuro-psychological typologies of attention (e.g., Posner & Peterson, 1990) specify a vigilance/sustained attention system (involving right dorso-lateral pre-frontal cortex, sometimes also incorporating divided attention), a selection system (involving the anterior cingulate), and an orientation system (involving the bilateral posterior parietal cortex in addition to the superior colliculus and the lateral pulvinar nucleus of the posterolateral thalamus). Difficulties in these domains will have social consequences when it is people who are not attended to as they might once have been pre-injury. Clinical experience of the authors suggests that difficulties in disengaging attention and switching can be socially disastrous, with survivors being captured by some aspect of either their environment or personal concerns and in so doing making major social transgressions (e.g., intruding on others' personal space, cutting over or ignoring others in conversation, or failing to attend to social feedback that their behaviour is problematic).

Recent research has focused on a social specialization for at least a form of attention, shared social attention and orientating to the eye gaze of others. This has been linked to the superior temporal sulcus (STS, Langton, Watt & Bruce, 2000; Perrett, Mistlin, Hietanen, Benson,

Bevan, Thomas et al., 1990; Perrett, Smith, Potter, Mistlin, Head, Milner et al., 1985) and has been identified as a necessary precursor for more sophisticated theory of mind/mentalizing abilities (e.g., see Baron-Cohen's shared attention monitor, SAM, 1997). For a subgroup of people on the autistic spectrum this ability is indeed absent, as are mentalizing abilities (Baron-Cohen, 1997). In adult ABI, difficulties have been reported in both shared attention (Campbell, Haywood, Cowey, Regard, & Landis, 1990) and voluntary shifting attention towards others' eye gaze (Vecera & Rizzo, 2006). This is discussed further in chapters 4 and 5. Returning to traditionally non-social areas of attentional investigation, Solms and Kaplan-Solms (2000) note that neuropathology of the right peri-sylvian area (where frontal, temporal, and parietal areas meet) is known to involve a disruption to both spatial and attentional functions. However, they note that while the emotional or relational dimension of these patients is not traditionally studied in Anglo-Saxon neuropsychology, there may be neuro-psychological alteration here too (see also the links between attention and emotion in Heilman's attention-arousal loop framework, 1991). They note a change in the emotional valence of self-other representations as a function of injury, with inter-personal consequences. While not rigorously supported with empirical evidence (see chapter 10 for a more detailed discussion), this is a fascinating suggestion, synthesizing emotional, attentional, and spatial-relational dimensions. An equally intriguing observation has been provided by a French neuropsychologist, noting that people with left-sided spatial inattention following right hemispheric injuries are often referred to by care-staff as 'la gauche'—the left. This denotes an uncanny inter-personal quality (Morin, 2004), as does the compounded meanings within the Latin *sinistra*.

Beyond individual brains, family therapist and other post-modern thinkers frequently use the term 'attending to' as a description of social mechanisms, whereby certain meanings, constructions, narratives, or possibilities are minimized, emphasized, or kept in shared mind. The systemic practices of mapping the problem-determined system (Anderson, Goolishian, & Winderman, 1986) or reflecting on conceptual lenses and problem invitations (Hoffman, 1990) within consultations with families are examples of 'attending to'. Reflective attention to hegemonic and subjugated meanings is an essential component of post-modern deconstruction. Here we have a dynamic social equivalent of the aforementioned organismic mechanisms, to be used to manage and interact with linguistic, conversational, and social landscapes.

Relational rehabilitation of attention

In addition to a sensitivity to social processes of attention, neglect, and prioritization within families and professional systems as described above, a relational neuro-psychological consideration of attentional rehabilitation is key. The principle of cues and alerts to facilitate monitoring and arousal has remained central to both attention and executive rehabilitation. However, this has been linked into an uncritical assumption of survivor as information processor, with incomplete feedback and feed-forward monitoring systems. This has led many rehabilitation clinicians to suggest that relatives be the cues, alerting factors and monitors to complete the survivor's information processing system. Although these interventions have documented success in improving information processing, this cognitive position is naïve to the dimension of relational meaning and context, the power differences within differing configurations of family relationships and the history in which these have evolved (e.g., what it means for an adult survivor to be 'nagged' by their mother to remember appointments, as they did when they were a child). Survivors are sensitive to this dimension, experiencing this arrangement as a series of disempowering, patronizing acts. The relatives themselves may feel uncomfortable too, and these interactions change the arrangement and meaning of their relationship. For more on this, see the case example in the next section and chapter 6.

One approach would be to carefully select the family member who would prompt or alert, based on a careful assessment of relational meanings within a given family and a collaborative identification of empowering supportive family relationships. Recent use of technology in alerting and cueing following ABI may be more context-friendly, and actually achieve the social neutrality expected within the naïve information processing models. Manly and colleagues (2002; 2004; Fish, Manly, & Wilson, 2008) have provided both experimental and real-world evidence of the effectiveness of electronic, content-free cues delivered via a pager or mobile phone, in sustaining the attention of survivors to a significant task goal, achieved through increasing right frontal cortical activation (O'Connor, Manly, Robertson,

Hevenor, & Levine, 2004). Set up by the survivor and delivered from beyond the immediacy of the family interactions and relationship structure, these alerts are less likely to re-organise family relationships and communication in unhelpful ways. For this reason, the use of electronic cues and alerts has been advocated within both interpersonally focused individual therapy (Yeates, Hamill, Sutton, Psaila, Gracey, Mohamed & O'Dell, 2008) and family work (Yeates, 2009). The use of pagers and alerts has been associated with relationship and caregiver positive gains (Yeates et al., 2008).

Case study

Simultagnosia for family experience

(With thanks for the collaboration of Annie Sheldrake in supporting this family)

Simultagnosia, a perceptual-attentional style that is piecemeal and misses whole gestalts or the overall context, is often produced from bilateral parietal lesions, often part of Balint's Syndrome. Family therapy assessment of one stroke survivor, Derek, who experienced these difficulties revealed not only functional difficulties, but a progressive alienation from the rest of the family. In the same way that he could not attend to/perceive the overall gestalt of a visual array, shared constructed meanings within dynamic family interactions could not be attended to, mapped and held together as a whole. His relational experience was consequently one of isolation and distance from others, who had access to a larger, unknown picture. The apparently hidden meanings that bound others in the family together were inaccessible to him and left him with a mildly persecutory relational experience with those that were for the most part very close to him before his injury (his wife and daughter). He had a strained relationship with an adult son pre-injury, and possibilities for post-injury reconciliation were consistently thwarted by Derek being unable to see his son's point of view, constructed as it was with referents to broader family gestalts.

Visual diagrams such as mind-maps with highlighted markers and computerized interactive, dynamic flow charts were used to guide Derek around the inter-related meanings employed by the whole family. This allowed to a certain extent opportunities for Derek to see his connection to others in the family around important issues. However, his piecemeal perceptual style was a constant barrier to social connection in a way that is not dissimilar from the hypothesized local-feature processing and systematizing styles articulated within the autism literature (Baron-Cohen et al., 2005; Frith & Happé, 1994).

Executive functioning

Here we will mainly consider those contributions typically associated with the dorso-lateral pre-frontal cortex: goal-directed behaviour, planning, organization, working memory, higher controls of
attention, cognitive flexibility, and meta-cognition (e.g., Duncan,
1986; Shallice & Burgess, 1996). The roles of orbito-frontal and ventro-
mesial frontal substrates are considered mainly in chapters 4 and 5.

This collection of higher abilities has come to be known as executive functions, and has been intimately associated with frontal cortical areas. However, the distributed neural circuitry that connects
frontal to other areas has been emphasized in case studies of executive dysfunction following posterior, cerebellar damage (Schweizer
et al., 2008). The complexity of executive functions has encouraged
both a reductionist agenda to understand the sophistication of the
neural substrate (e.g., Stuss, 2007) and an ecological approach to
assessment and rehabilitation, given that executive problems are
only manifest in unstructured, novel, and complex environments
(Shallice & Burgess, 1996). The research identifying the social consequences of executive impairments is reviewed in chapter 4. It is
worth noting here that such studies have emerged secondary to a
focus on functional consequences for individuals.

A glance back to the first account of executive functioning rehabilitation following ABI finds a rather different perspective. A.R. Luria
was a co-investigator of Vygotsky within social and cultural psychological research, in addition to being a rehabilitation researcher.
As such, his view of executive functions such as the regulation and
programming of behaviour was that they were socially mediated in
development. That is, they were initially provided externally by the
interactional influence of the primary caregiver (within the shared
zone of proximal development, Vygotsky, 1979) and progressively
internalized by the child (Luria, 1961; 1968; 1976). This Vygotskian
perspective will be familiar to many social constructionist readers,
in that it prioritizes language and the cultural use and transmission
of tools to facilitate psychological functions. Within his adult neuro-
rehabilitative work, Luria (1968) took this approach to re-creating
a socially mediating context to support executive functions post-
injury, even if these functions could no longer be internalized on
their own.

Luria's focus on language and social context may have been lost in Western neuro-rehabilitation's adoption of his ideas. Yeates and colleagues (2008) have noted the value of a socio-linguistic dimension of executive functioning for therapeutic work on inter-personal relationships following ABI. The theoretical and rehabilitative perspectives on goal-directed action by Duncan (1986) and Shallice and Burgess (1996) are linked by these authors to inter-personal formulations of goal-directed sequences within dialogical psychotherapy models (e.g., Cognitive-Analytic Therapy, Ryle et al., 1990), permitting a re-conceptualization close to Luria's orientation.

However, some constructs associated with executive function have radically differing ontologies if they are couched within a reductionist-biological perspective or a social-action linguistic framework. Meta-cognition and mentalizing refer to knowledge and awareness of mental states, be it ones own (meta-cognition) or those of others (mentalizing). For this former the cognitive construction is of thinking about thinking, be this an individual's monitoring, self-reflection, or empathic connection to others. Meta-cognitive abilities have been linked to Brodmann's area 10 in the most anterior part of the frontal lobe, with both dorsal and orbital aspects (Burgess, Quayle, & Frith, 2001; Stuss, 2007) and naturally have become an increasingly prominent concept in brain injury rehabilitation (e.g., Ownsworth & Fleming, 2005). Outside of brain injury literature, meta-cognitive processes and deficits have been heavily implicated in the aetiology of anxiety, depression (Wells, 2008), and psychosis (Moritz & Woodward, 2007).

Dennett (1978; 1987) suggested that a key evolutionary stepping stone was homo-sapiens newly acquired ability to introspect on oneself via a specialist module, and then to use that to understand the mental states of others for social and survival gain (see review in Baron-Cohen, 1997). However, a direct mental-biological translation of a meta-cognitive process runs the risk of an infinite regress: how about thinking about thinking about thinking? Each time a further layer of reflection is added, is a new area 10 required? We will hit the material barrier of skull too quickly! An alternative viewpoint is that meta-cognitive perspectives are socio-linguistic constructions, derived from a particular vocabulary of meta-cognitive referents, with its own grammar and invited through certain conversational trends (e.g., Antaki & Lewis, 1986). Meta-cognition is thus a discursive process and not directly dependent on a neuro-anatomical module or substrate. This also suggests that following ABI, meta-cognitive functions can be facilitated through conversational and linguistic interventions (see the Murray and Yeates study described below).

Relational executive rehabilitation

As noted above, alerting technology can be used within a relational perspective for social gains. Both psychotherapeutic intervention and functional rehabilitation of executive functions using Vygotskian ideas have demonstrated important clinical gains (O'Neill et al., 2005; Yeates et al., 2008).

Experimental neuro-psychological evidence shows that where some people with neuro-disability are not able to access an awareness of a first-person perspective, they are able to access the same information if it is constructed in third-person terms (McGlynn & Kaszniak, 1991; Reisberg, Gordon, McCarthy, & Ferris, 1985). This has led to a rationale for using narrative therapy techniques of externalizing, for both awareness issues (Yeates, Henwood, Gracey, & Evans, 2007; chapter 6 in this book), and post-injury adjustment, identity and connection, and intimacy within couples work (Murray & Yeates, in preparation). Sessions were held with a survivor of an anterior communicating artery stroke and his wife. In this intervention that produced gains in meta-cognition for the survivor and closer connection for the couple, no extra layers of Brodman's area 10 were synthetically manufactured and implanted into the survivor's cortex. Instead, a conversational-linguistic repositioning was facilitated, which allowed an introspective, self-reflexive function to be achieved and maintained by the survivor. This repositioning was first invited by the therapists but subsequently evolved to a different and idiosyncratic set of subject positions. First the stroke, typified by angry outbursts and problems with goal-directed behaviour, was to be kept in the kitchen. This was to allow the couple to have brief holidays from the stroke for defined periods of time. This then evolved to a construction of the stroke as 'Chucky', to keep an eye on, kept on a metaphorical lead, in case he sneaks off the radar and causes havoc in the relationship. This therapeutic construction was consistent with the theories of executive dysfunction noted above—if we had suggested that a permanent departure from Chucky could have been achieved, this work would have been destined for failure. By keeping Chucky on the lead, the supervisory attentional systems relationally shared by survivor, partner, and therapists could be employed in effortful control to generate and maintain novel solutions. Letting Chucky slip off the lead, off the radar of everyone's awareness would be equivalent to a switch back to contention scheduling, automatic, habitual processes that had insidiously maintained distance within the couple relationship. We all know that Chucky gets up to most mischief when no one is looking or underestimates him.

Case study

Beyond nagging and violence in goal management training

(We acknowledge the creative input of co-therapist, Kate Psaila)

Couple work was undertaken with a survivor, Phil, and his girlfriend, Jackie, who asked for help with anger management. Through a relational deconstruction of the moments of violence (Goldner, 1990; Vetere & Cooper, 2001), a simultaneous neuro-cognitive and historical-inter-personal dimension was revealed. The couple reported that acts of verbal and occasionally physical aggression, enacted by both, occurred follow-ing repeating triggers. These were often moments that required online, reactive, or responsive problem-solving to arrive at a decision important for them both. This included coping with a burst water pipe in their new home, and responding to the crises of another family member. On two occasions the trigger was cruelly the couple being at a loose end and attempting to decide how to spend a precious day together when Jackie was not at work (she now holds down two jobs to make ends meet for them as a couple following Phil's post-injury unemployment).

They had previously co-constructed their relationship as one of mutu-ality and equality, a team, everything being decided together in part-nership. At moments of essential decision-making post-injury, which had previously always signified 'them as team', Phil was left unable to contribute due to dysexecutive problems with planning, set-shifting, anticipatory reasoning, and responding to change. Subjectively Phil felt frustrated, fuzzy-headed, and panicky in these moments. Jackie would try to help to support Phil, suggesting ideas. However, these served only to confuse Phil more, being filled up with mental content that did not con-nect too well together. Over time, Jackie's suggestive helping, now sig-nifying her powerful competency in relation to Phil's disability, became constructed as nagging, intrusive, disempowering. Phil would lash out in words or action, Jackie would be horrified at these new occurrences, and would sometimes fight back, both feeling confused and so unlike the team they once were before, distanced through the negation of this relational meaning.

Our dilemma as therapists was the wish to introduce a cognitive rehabilitation strategy to support Phil's problem-solving and goal-directed functions, Goal Management Framework, GMF (Evans & Miotto, 2006; Robertson, 1996; Wilson et al., 2009). However doing this would be one more relational enactment of disempowerment and disablement in the particular context of this couples relationship (flagging up Phil's need and difference, also risking the positioning of Jackie as the helpful, able prompter of the strategy use). Our solution was to present this strategy as a need for them as a couple, to be used at points of difficult decision. However, we introduced the GMF to Phil first, asking him to pass on to Jackie as the temporary expert, and to report back to us how he felt, in his honest opinion, the GMF served them as a couple and a team.

Social communication: Early dilemmas and controversies

An application of social neuroscientific concepts within ABI is presented in chapters 4 and 5. Here we will briefly document early dilemmas and controversies that are present in the new field of social neuroscience, and we will be interested to see how these are managed in subsequent years.

The first is the issue of intersubjectivity. Do researchers frame the neuro-psychological study of individuals interacting with others as bridges between compartmentalized, contained organisms, with interactions between processes and representations occurring inside heads? Or is this area the very study of processes and phenomenon, which transcend individual brains, which are emergent properties that cannot be reduced to component nervous systems? A significant development within this area, probably familiar as a sound-bite to many readers now, has been the discovery of 'mirror neurons' within the inferior parietal and frontal cortices (Gallese, 1999; Gallese, Keysers, & Rizzolatti, 2004; Rizzolati et al., 1997), which code social stimuli such as mouths, hands, and actions involving these in both self and others. The alignment and attunement of mirror systems in multiple brains may be better served by more dyadic conceptual frameworks focused on process (e.g., Frith & Wolpert, 2004; Hatfield, Cacioppo, & Rapson, 1994) than those that posit inputs and outputs of contained, 'boxed' individuals (e.g., Tonks, Williams, Frampton, & Yates, 2007).

The next dilemma is a view of static disabilities versus context-dependent, variable action. A striking finding exemplifies this. Selective emotion recognition deficits have been demonstrated in ABI populations (e.g., Adolphs et al., 1994, see chapter 4), in studies using static picture stimuli of facial expressions. However several investigations (Adolphs, Tranel & Damasio, 2003; Humphrey, Donnelly & Riddoch, 1993; McDonald & Saunders, 2005) have demonstrated that a survivor of ABI is who are unable to recognise static emotion expression stimuli, can recognise these when in motion. Dynamic-based emotion recognition is hypothesised to additionally recruit intact parietal cortices (Adolphs et al., 2003). Emotion recognition in ABI groups can be compromised however when both video and audio-speech stimuli are present, creating multi-tasking demands for participants (McDonald & Saunders, 2005). Moving video stimuli are also arguably a more naturalistic dynamic context for interpreting social meaning, however rudimentary. Discursive psychologists have similarly turned to mentalising from a perspective of social action, accessing and reproducing certain trends of talk. As with meta-cognition, Harré (2002) and Hutto (2004) have argued against a representational framing of an individual's comprehension of other people's intentions, goals, and beliefs. They emphasize conversational conventions for mentalizing talk/vocabulary, in contrast to a cognitive assertion of a theory of mind (Premack & Woodruff, 1978). Humphrey (1984) has noted that all world languages have a vocabulary of mental states, and Wellman (1990) describes the grammar of belief/desire referents. Discursive approaches have definitely mapped out the conversational socialization of children into mentalizing talk (Dunn, Brown, & Beardsall, 1991; Fivush & Fromhoff, 1988), which may reflect a simultaneous social and neuro-psychological developmental process from a Vygotskian process.

As clinicians working with survivors where there is a change to mentalizing talk and process post-injury (e.g., a loss or a skewing, see next two chapters), these discursive accounts require some effort to apply. There are clear cases of a pathology of mentalizing following injury alongside intact vocabulary and grammar use for all other categories of psychosocial life (e.g., Channon & Crawford, 1999), which seems to support a modularized, representational cognitivist account. If we do not assume that there is an acquired loss of the capacity to create internal representations of other's mental states, we must conclude that there is a selective loss of mentalizing talk and grammar conversational convention, either through a barrier to access and/or reproduction. This leaves us in a similar position to the neuropsychologists who are confronted with selective semantic loss of living versus non-living categories following acquired neuropathology (e.g., Laws, 2004), or other semantic specific category loss in semantic dementia (Hodges et al., 2000).

If we follow the aforementioned contemporary ecological response to selective dissociations such as these, we would be invited to attend to the way in which certain propensities to be organized around social cues may be diminished post-injury, resulting in a different affordance trajectory. Of relevance here is the challenge mounted by mirror neuron theorists to mentalizing, who instead focus on role of both language trends and the ecological affordances of action constrains within social interactions, in the automatic movement of one person's intentions into an observer's mind (Gallese, 2006). Part of this trajectory may be reflected in an unconventional use of mentalizing vocabulary and grammar, maintained through altered interactional patterns with others. This relational framing of complex, dynamic processes may be fitting for the complex and distributed neural circuit substrates that have been identified as crucial for mentalizing activity (Frith & Frith, 2003; 2004). It may be useful for the orientation developed within this book. Within systemic practice, the vocabulary of empathy has been explored as therapeutic intervention, to facilitation of connection between people that had hitherto been precluded through distancing conversational conventions and dynamics within a system (Wilkinson, 1992).

An additional point of debate in neuroscience generally, and in particular for social neuroscience, is an affective turn to the role of feeling, emotion, and embodiment for core neuro-psychological processes. This seems to be a wider development in the social sciences, as a similar turn has been noted in psychosocial studies and critical social psychology (e.g., Cromby, 2007; Redman, 2009), indicating its significance for relational thinking of all kinds. Whereas the clinical theorists of mentalization, executive function, and social problem-solving (see above; Grafman, 1994) posit cold representations and logical processes, others draw attention to the embodied, affect-driven dimensions of emotion recognition (Gallese, 1999), empathy-related processes (Watt, 2007), and social decision making (Damasio, 1994). This affective turn constructs a bodily, quicker, less rationalist account of intersubjectivity. Some contrasts of cognitive versus affectively orientated theoretical accounts relevant to clinical accounts of personality change following ABI have been provided by Yeates, Gracey, and Collicutt-McGrath (2008).

Finally, the field of social neuroscience and its application presents pertinent moral dilemmas. There is an increased danger through this field to present a decontextualized account that pathologizes all deviation of social interaction from an arbitary (or white, middle-class Anglo-Saxon) norm (Yeates, 2007). Tests used to mark change post-injury could be used to legitimize the discrimination of social diversity in general. It is necessary therefore, to advocate socially relative and sensitive formulations that situate acquired social neuro-psychological difficulties in the varying social contexts in which they occur (Brothers, 1997). We aim to apply this orientation in the following two chapters.

Conclusions

A review of traditional neuro-psychological domains has been presented, which summarizes perspectives both from within and outside the mainstream neuroscience, which invite relational thinking and application (e.g., social-functional approaches to language, collective remembering, semantization, ecological psychology, social attention, Vygoskian social mediation of higher psychological functions and discursive approaches to meta-cognitive and mentalizing phenomena). Specific connections are made to neuro-rehabilitative and systemic practice and new approaches suggested, guided by this literature.

The purpose of this chapter has been to facilitate the 'reaching out' of neuropsychology to the relational thinking outlined elsewhere in this book, and to reciprocally inform relational therapeutic work using helpful neuro-psychological principles. In doing so, a traditional partition of perspectives is aimed to be avoided. However, we are mindful of the use of neuropsychology and its traditional biological determinism within reductionist agendas.

Neuropsychology is an important component to our thinking and practice, particularly when it is framed relationally. However, the core assumption of a position orientation to social context is that this is the ultimate reality of any psychological phenomenon, and that social contextual processes will exert the most significant influence on the lives of survivors, families, and communities. It is from this stance that we continue our exploration of the relational dimension of ABI.

CHAPTER FOUR

Connections, closeness, and intimacy in couples relationships: Theory

In chapters 1 and 2 we introduced some novel relational framings of brain injury, taking it out of individual persons and skulls and locating it between people. We described brain injury as a relationship, an organization of relationships, or perhaps existing in the spaces between people. In this chapter, we want to explore how spaces between romantic partners can be widened following injury so people who were previously close become distanced, or how inter-subjective space is intruded upon in a way that is experienced as challenging or even disturbing. We will present a theoretical unpacking of strained relationship and challenges to intimacy in this chapter. We continue to use a combination of systemic and neuroscientific ideas, while also bringing in ideas from psychoanalysis. This application seems appropriate for the quality of experiences reported by those in couples relationships and the striking language used. We will use the term 'intimacy' in its widest sense—an inter-personal, psychological connection between two people, which may include personal sharing and inter-connection of mental life. This may or may not involve a sexual relationship.

ABI and couple outcomes

Outcomes for couples following ABI are marked by both pessimism and complexity. Divorce, separation, and marital breakdown have been one group of trajectories studied by researchers, with the other two predominant clusters of research focusing on disruption to sexual relationships, together with strain, burden and mental health difficulties experienced by partners.

With regards to separation and divorce, initial studies using small samples painted the most pessimistic picture, with rates reported as high as 79% of ABI samples (Thomsen, 1974). However, larger samples (n ≥ 100) have been studied by groups in the USA and UK more recently, and both have reported rates that are much lower. Divorce rates of 15% and 17% for divorce were respectively reported by Kreutzer and colleagues (2007) and Wood and Yurdakul (1997), with the latter authors noting a 49% of marital breakdown (Wood & Yurdakul, 1997). These authors note that such rates are comparable with national figures of divorce in the general population for both USA and UK.

However, while couples may be staying together, they report high levels of marital dissatisfaction (Blais & Boisvert, 2005; Gosling & Oddy, 1999; Wood, 2005), dyadic maladjustment (Peters, Stambrook, Moore, & Esses, 1990; Peters, Stambrook, Moore et al., 1992), and disruptions to sexual relationships (Gosling & Oddy, 1999; Oddy, 2001; Ponsford, 2003). Both members of the couple are more likely to become progressively socially isolated over time (Bond, Brooks, & McKinlay, 1979; Brooks, Campsie, Symington, Beattie, & McKinlay, 1987; Elsass & Kinsella, 1987; Prigatano, 1986). For the partner themselves, increased burden, strain, stress (Thomsen, 1984), and clinical levels of anxiety and depression (e.g., Carnwath & Johnson, 1987; Perlesz, Kinsella, & Crowe, 2000) are likely outcomes. While there are mixed findings as to whether partners experience more strain than other relatives, such as parents (Gervasio & Kreutzer, 1997; Ponsford, Olver, Ponsford, & Nelms, 2003), outcomes for partners are agreed as being unique (Brooks, Campsie, Symington, & Beattie, 1986).

Subjective reports of altered intimacy following ABI

There is something unique about couples' experiences following neurological injuries: comparisons with orthopaedic, spinal injury, and progressive (non-neurological) illness samples have revealed lower levels of negative outcomes in the relationship domain for these groups (Rosenbaum & Najenson, 1976). Partners' subjective experiences of intimate connections with their brain-injured loved one reveal a notable quality of disturbance. Those published are dominated by female partners' descriptions of male survivors. Descriptions include references to "living with a monster," analogous to "living with Jekyll and Hyde" (Wood, 2005). Others describe being "married to a stranger" (Wood, 2005), "married without a husband" (Mauss & Ryan, 1981), wanting their real husband back (Wood, 2005). The emotional side and intimacy "feels wrong" to some partners (Gosling & Oddy, 1999), with the emotional side feeling "badly damaged" (Oddy, 2001), and partners reporting a greater dislike for physical contact of any kind (Rosenbaum & Najenson, 1976).

These intimate accounts contain themes of both an absence but also a presence of something deeply disturbing within relational life post-injury. Gregory (Gregory, 1998) notes that an everyday language is lacking to describe or structure such experiences. Insufficient research has been conducted on partner's experience of intimate connection with survivors, and none have reported the intimate experiences of both partner and survivor side by side.

The other source of subjective information of relevance can be found in therapists' accounts of their clinical work with survivors. The closeness of psychotherapeutic relationships, connections made within these sessions, personal knowledge, and experiences shared, can approach some qualities of couples relationships. Writers have noted that therapeutic alliances are often emotive, 'roller-coaster' relationships. The intensity and rapidly oscillating quality of these has been highlighted (Lewis, 1999): the therapist or rehabilitation clinician can be put on a pedestal/being admired by the survivor, and then attacked or denigrated. A similar pattern of splitting and fragmented relating in a collection of patients with ventro-mesial frontal damage has been identified (Kaplan-Solms & Solms, 2000), with a frequent confusion of self and other, fantasy and reality in the relationship with the therapist. Lewis (1999) describes in response to a patient's idealization or devaluation of the therapist, a reciprocal therapist's experience of pride or uneasiness.

Injured brains to injured intimacy

The key question that follows from these finding is what specific links exist between a damaged brain, pre-injury and post-injury experiences and processes, and these striking experiences of intimacy within couples' relationships? We propose that these associations are complex and multi-layered, and any therapeutic response to altered intimacy needs to be orientated to this complexity. A by no means exhaustive organization of common threats to intimacy post-injury is presented below: threats to intimacy from the wider context (including services), from the process of caring itself, from anger and violence within couple relationships, and finally our current understanding of the role of neuropathology and neuro-psychological impairment within this.

Threats to intimacy from wider context

Any consideration of specific links between neuropathology and altered intimacy must situate such within a broader tapestry of social contextual influences that have demonstrated across studies to predict couples outcomes post-injury, in addition to brain-injury-related factors such as severity of injury and associated sequelae. These are reviewed in full in chapter 12 but include the age and gender of each partner, duration and nature of pre-injury relationship, level of financial strain, work status of survivor, presence of children in the family, and progressive social isolation over time for the couple as a whole. Culture has been shown to be an extremely relevant dimension (Vanderploeg, Curtiss, Duchnick, & Luis, 2003), with the physical and psychosocial dependence of male survivors on the one hand producing greater burden in American partners (Rosenbaum & Najenson, 1976) while on the other liberating Israeli wives and reducing their fears of abandonment (Kravetz, Gross, Weiler, Ben-Yakar, Tadir, & Stern, 1995).

Threats to intimacy from services?

The emergence of second-order cybernetics and post-modernism in the 1980s and 1990s within family therapy has stimulated a key point of reflection for services. No longer are families or couples who attend clinics there to be observed and formulated. Instead, clinicians prioritize a reflection of their powerful influence on what is brought to the session, what is talked about, and who comes at all. Services are intertwined with families in an 'observing system' (e.g., Boscolo, Cecchin, Hoffman, & Papp, 1987; Cecchin, 1987; Von Foerster, 1982), with all of the power differences that this entails. For ABI services, Yeates (Yeates, 2007; Yeates, Luckie, DeBeer, & Khela, 2010) has noted the ways in which services unwittingly serve to add to the range of challenges that face families and couples post-injury. Through the common service priority of the injury survivor and their damaged brain (the 'skull seduction', Yeates, 2007) and recip-rocal positioning of relatives' needs as an adjunctive afterthought, a partition is created between survivor and partner experiences (e.g., the 'awareness/insight' problems of survivors and the (unre-lated?) 'adjustment' needs of relatives). This draws curiosity away from how issues such as adjustment, depression, and trauma are shared within a couple post-injury. Even within one session, such as an initial assessment, a common practice is to interview survi-vors and partner separately. While this may highlight important dis-crepancies in accounts and may allow one or both partners to share important confidential information, the telling of the shared couple story and shared witnessing of each other's story is prevented. This may follow a number of existing prior cognitive, emotional, and social factors, which have also prevented shared sense-making (see chapters 2 and 6).

A further way in which services and professional involvement can threaten intimacy is to inadvertently pathologize couple coping. The ABI literature has often proceeded from an assumption of a homog-enous family and a normal model of (white middle class) family functioning, despite the evident diversity within and across families in problem perception and coping (Yeates, 2007; Yeates, Henwood, Gracey, & Evans, 2007). Any pre-injury couple diversity in shared social rules and styles of coping that deviate from this norm may be pathologized as maladaptive post-injury, with rehabilitation teams unwittingly becoming policing forces of family normality. Couples' unique resources may not be fully exploited as a result of services' blindspots or even prohibition of their value.

Threats to intimacy from caring

The development of a caregiving relationship between survivor and romantic partner during the acute phase is often necessary and over a long period of time may be organized by the physical self-care needs of the survivor (washing, toileting, dressing, feeding). This may occur alongside the survivor's acute disorientation and aggressive communication during the acute phase. When this phase passes, authors have noted that it is not easy for couples to resume an equal, physically intimate relationship. Gosling and Oddy (1999) have drawn attention to the 'ambiguous position' of the partner, where resuming a role as a lover can be incompatible with the previous duties as toileter, mother-figure, or surrogate nurse (Gosling & Oddy, 1999; Wood, 2005). While predominantly referring to the experience of female partners, this relational position and its barriers to intimacy has been anecdotally reported also for a male partner of a female survivor (Clarici & Guiliani, 2008). A number of authors have identified a common discourse from relatives, which constructs the survivor as like a 'child growing up again', to be looked after and cared for (Wood, 2005; Yeates, Henwood, Gracey, & Evans, 2007). Some authors (Gervasio & Kreutzer, 1997; Hall, Karzmark, Stevens, Englander, O'Hare, & Wright, 1994; Kreutzer, Gervasio, & Camplair, 1994b) have suggested that the over-dependency of survivor in reciprocation to the parentified relative role, is more congruent and manageable for actual parents than for spouses. Yeates and colleagues (2007) have also shown that these child-like positionings by relatives are often accompanied by subjective claims of a threat to self in the survivors (see chapter 12 for more on this). Together these patterns of meaning-making can be seen to progressively divide and distance couples following injury.

As the months and years progress post-injury, there may be significant and permanent role change within a couple's relationship in terms of vocational status, financial management, and parenting responsibilities (Maitz & Sachs, 1995). This may significantly alter closeness within the relationship (in terms of who is in the house and who is away working or with children, and how each person feels about the roles they have lost to the other). The pressures of caring for the survivor may indirectly increase psychosocial demands for the couple by draining financial and time resources while preventing both partners from resuming work and increasing household income. Often necessity dictates that a job and parenting responsibilities have to be juggled alongside the caring activities.

Finally, the act of caring has been shown to involve circular patterns of influence for the mental health of both survivor and partner. In stroke research authors have found that caregivers (including partners) are more likely to be depressed if the survivor is depressed or psychologically distressed (Carnwath & Johnson, 1987; Dennis, O'Rourke, Lewis, Sharp, & Warlow, 1998; Draper et al., 1992; Wade, Legh-Smith, & Hewer, 1986). Others have found the reverse direction: the presence of depression for the survivor of stroke is associated with depressed caregivers (Carnwath & Johnson, 1987; Kotila, Numminen, Waltimo, & Kaste, 1998). In the systemic therapy literature, Elsa Jones and Eia Asen (Jones & Asen, 2000) construct depression as the process of being 'de-pressed'— pushed down by the weight of something bigger or more powerful. Jones' framing invites us to think about depression not as something residing biologically within individuals, but as a state of organization and meaning that has been created by things bigger than individuals: loss, power and socio-economic inequalities, abuse, and disability (including ABI). Viewing depression as a particular organization of relationships allows us to think about how those around the 'depressed individual' are connected to that individual and how these connections are structured within the language of depression and related assumptions of care and recovery. These organizations perhaps create contextual conditions that maintain 'depression' and its associated myths within a family, including the process of caring itself.

Threats to intimacy from anger and violence

The associations between anger and violence exhibited by the survivors of ABI and reduced psychological well-being of relatives have been known for a while. Increased anger and behavioural difficulties in survivors have been associated with increased likelihood of partner's low mood (Gillen, Tennen, Affleck, & Steinpreis, 1998), anxiety and depression (Perlesz, Kinsella, & Crowe, 2000), and strain or burden (Brooks, Campsie, Symington, Beattie, & McKinlay, 1987).

The presence of anger in a relationship post-ABI has been associated with increased likelihood of divorce (Kreutzer, Marwitz, Hsu, Williams, & Riddick, 2007).

Traditionally within the ABI literature, anger and aggression have been framed and studied as a main effect of ABI, either directly (using the concept of episodic dyscontrol syndrome, Eames, 2001) or as learned patterns of behaviour (e.g., Alderman, 2003). These constructions limit our curiosity about the relational dimension of anger following ABI. In contrast, there is a rich systemic literature on domestic violence (DV), focusing on relational patterns associated with this. A literature search on DV and brain injury yields few results. Those DV studies that do not focus on ABI specifically have shown that over half of perpetrators have a history of TBI (53%, Rosenbaum, Hoge, Adelman et al., 1994; 62% Rosenbaum & Hoge, 1989). One of the few ABI studies that focus on DV highlights the complexity of this phenomenon post-injury: difficulties in executive functioning, low self-esteem, and high alcohol use collectively predicted increased rate of DV (Marsh & Martinovich, 2006). The other appearance of the term 'brain injury' in the DV literature is as an unrecognized consequence suffered by the victim (Monahan & O'Leary, 1999). The connection of DV and brain injury seems to be intimate and potentially circular.

Within the systemic literature, authors have noted how the presence of violence in a relationship can constantly organize the whole relationship and its constituent inter-personal interactions, even when an act of violence has not occurred for some time (Goldner, Penn, Sheinberg, & Walker, 1990; Vetere & Cooper, 2001; Vetere & Cooper, 2003; Walker & Goldner, 1995). These authors have focused on rigid gender dichotomies and binds common to violent relationships. The perpetrator's sense of autonomy and self-resilience are felt to be intruded upon by the partner being too close or through the process of care and affection. This intrusion can be a trigger for violence. Paradoxically, messages or threats from the partner that they will leave can also be triggers, signalling abandonment and/or betrayal. This can be paralleled by a victim's options for refuge being negated under their sense of duty to care and feeling of closeness within this. All of these themes, not written about ABI, are still very relevant.

Case study

The relational context of anger management

Jon had been seeing a clinical psychologist for anger management strategies to cope with increased anger and irritability following his TBI. The psychologist used a CBT model, focusing on identifying triggering situations, anger-related thoughts and coping strategies, supported by cognitive rehabilitation techniques. However, this work involved the survivor only. Jon's increased anger had a particular meaning for Kelly, his wife. She had grown up with an abusive father and had chosen Jon on the basis of his difference from her father, to bring up their two young children in a world free of intimidation and threat. They had enjoyed such a world for the first four years of their marriage, until the TBI. Now the rare points of connection and tenderness that did occur in their relationship post-injury were in tearful but sincere making up following a huge argument. At other times, Kelly rarely felt loved or thought about.

The critical incident arrived when, following a heated and escalating argument, Jon left their small flat using a time out strategy. He took his pent up anger out on the garage door, kicking it until his feelings subsided. He felt calmer and proud for preventing an actual moment of violence between them. He returned to the flat to find Kelly packing a suitcase and ushering the two children towards the front door. Kelly had heard the banging on the garage door, which took her vividly back to the bangs of her father around the house that would reliably signal an impending beating. Thinking that she and the children were in imminent danger, her present priority was to keep them safe. Jon was astounded and tearfully confused at why everything was suddenly going wrong even though his own coping strategy had worked for him personally. Sensing that he was about to lose everything, he lost control and lashed out, hitting Kelly in front of the children.

The intertwined nature of violence and intimacy is suggested further by these authors. They have pointed to secret moments of redemption and alliance within cycles of violence, rarely disclosed to helping professions. Between episodes of violence there may be apologies, promises that this will never happen again, tenderness, bonding, and closeness. These can act as points of reconnection, acting as a 'photo negative' of the distance and severing of bonds created by the violence. In the context of ABI that may be a barren wasteland for tenderness and closeness, these rare moments of connection may be cherished, despite the partner's knowledge that the violence will occur again. For others around the couple, including professionals these moments are often viewed with suspicion and so these are kept as a secret between the couple, providing a binding force within the violence.

Threats to intimacy from neuropathology

As noted above, there is something unique about neurological injuries that jeopardize couple relationships, connection, and intimacy. Within the psychosocial complexity previously discussed, there is also a very deep sense for partners that things 'feel' different and wrong now. Social and affective neuroscience has begun to permit a very intimate neuro-psychological exploration of how social communication and attachment patterns can be compromised following very specific neurological damage, perhaps resulting in the subject accounts described above.

Earlier psychosocial outcome investigators identified emotional, personality, and behavioural changes as greater predictors of partner burden or stress in comparison with cognitive or physical changes (Brooks, Campsie, Symington, Beattie, & McKinlay, 1987; McKinlay, Brooks, Bond, Martinage, & Marshall, 1981; Oddy, Humphrey, & Uttley, 1978; Thomsen, 1974; 1992). Within the emotional and personality change categories, these authors identified problems such as aspontaneity, stubbornness, increased irritability, emotional modulation and lability, and temper outbursts as the greatest predictors (Weddell, Oddy, & Jenkins, 1980). The cognitive deficits identified in these studies were restricted to memory, speed, concentration, and some language difficulties.

Within the last decade, neuro-psychological concepts have been sharpened and extended, permitting a re-examination of the separation of cognitive and personality/emotional/behavioural in these outcome studies. Difficulties that may now be attributed to executive cognitive deficits are discernible from the behavioural indicators (aspontaneity, stubbornness, difficulties responding to changes in routine, disinhibition) in the studies by Brooks and colleagues (1987). More recently, executive difficulties demonstrated through neuro-psychological assessment have indeed been shown to be associated with reduced social participation (Nybo, Sainio, & Müller, 2004; Vilkki et al., 1994), strained social relationships, and inter-personal difficulties (Mazaux, Masson, Levin, Alaoui, Maurette, & Barat, 1997; Yeates et al., 2008) alongside other psychosocial outcomes (Tate, 1999; Villki, Ahola, Holst, Ohman, Servo, & Heiskanen, 1994). Executive and memory dysfunction has been shown to be varying sub-components of some survivors' unawareness of disability (McGlynn & Schacter, 1989), which in turn has been shown to be predictive of negative outcomes in relatives in the aforementioned outcome studies (e.g., Brooks, Campsie, Symington, Beattie, & McKinlay, 1987; Thomsen, 1974; 1984).

The categories of personality and emotional change in the partner burden and stress studies also require greater specificity and neuropsychological formulation (Yeates, Gracey, & Colicutt-McGrath, 2008). Descriptions of childishness, irritability, emotional lability, and poor impulse control were included in these broad categories, as were referents to social interactional problems (losing track of social conversation, withdrawing from social interaction, behaving in a socially embarrassing way). These difficulties are now studied within the contemporary field of social neuroscience, which acknowledges cognitive, affective, and relational dimensions of such. This literature has been used by Obonsawin and colleagues (2007) and Weddell and Leggett (2006) to specify social neuro-psychological deficits as one set of predictors, alongside more influential mental health and relational predictors of relatives' personality change judgements.

The social neuroscience literature began as disparate studies each emphasizing either cognitive or affective aspects of social cognition in individuals artificially isolated from social interactional sequences. However, calls for the study of these phenomena within social context (Brothers, 1997) and in social interaction have started to be acknowledged, and the first social interactional and communicational meta-framework has been forwarded by Frith (2003) and Frith and Wolpert (2004). These accounts of 'neural hermeneutics' focus on brains interacting with other minds. These frameworks and the perspectives of Gallese (2006) inform the organising framework below, used to review studies of relevance to the neuropathology of intimacy and connection.

'Perspectival intersubjective space'—Decoding others' mental states

Often a social communicational sequence is not immediate or face to face, is marked by ambiguity or complexity or is a removed anecdote or narrative of a social exchange. In such situations the observer/listener is confronted with an interpretive dilemma. For the observer's brain, a 'cold' cognitive process begins of decoding and inferring mental states in the speaker through analysis of available information, which may include their biological movement, eye gaze, predictive computations, alongside the application of contextually-relevant information (Baron-Cohen, 1997; Frith & Frith, 2006). From this information, predictions and hypotheses are formed of others' intentions, goals, beliefs and desires. Subsequent information reveals any error in these hypotheses, which are then updated.

Decoding others' mental states is often referred to as mentalizing or 'Theory of Mind' (ToM), and following traumatic brain injury, stroke or neurosurgical lesions, damage to anterior cortices, temporal poles, and superior-temporal sulcus, has been shown to disrupt this ability (Baird, Dewar, Critchley, Dolan, Shallice, & Cipolotti, 2006; Channon, 2004; Channon & Crawford, 1999; Channon & Crawford, 2000; Happé, Brownell & Winnder, 1999; McDonald & Flanagan, 2004; Rowe, Bullock, Polkey, & Morris, 2001; Stone, Baron-Cohen, & Knight, 1998; Stuss, Gallup, & Alexander, 2001). These difficulties have been shown to be functionally separate from executive functioning problems (Rowe, Bullock, Polkey, & Morris, 2001). Both mentalising theorists and their challengers, the mirror neuron theorists, agree that mentalising may both be more automatic than previously thought but also independently necessary for intentional decoding in situations of ambiguity or complexity, where intentions are not easily communicable (Frith & Frith, 2006; Rizzolatti, Fabbri-Destro, & Cattaneo, 2009). This system also appears to be necessary for the demarcation of self-perspective from the perspective of the other (Frith & Frith, 2006).

This form of intersubjectivity, which allows for a sharing and contrast of mentalised perspectives within a given social encounter, is derived partly from the analysis and attentional prioritisation of eye gaze in others. This process has been shown to involve the superior temple sulcus or STS (Perrett et al., 1985; 1990), and lesions to this area have been shown to produce deficits in this ability (Campbell, Haywood, Cowey, Regard, & Landis, 1990). Baron-Cohen (1997) notes that beyond basic detection of eye gaze direction, there is the encoding of others' gaze perspective from this information (i.e., they and I are looking at the same thing). Sophisticated mentalizing abilities are developmentally dependent on this shared attention and the assumptions that underlie this ability. Shared attention can be exercised via visual and other modalities (e.g., touch), but Baron-Cohen argues that the visual modality is the quickest and most efficient route. In patient EVR, a well-known case of social communication impairment following ABI, emotional recognition was preceded by an impairment in voluntary shifting attention towards others' eye gaze (Vecera & Rizzo, 2006). Social face encoding via the STS has also been dissociated from facial identity recognition, involving the lateral fusiform gyrus (Haxby, Hoffman, & Gobbini, 2000). However, the consequences of prosopagnosia arising from damage to the latter are equally socially devastating (Haxby, Hoffman, & Gobbini, 2002).

'We-centric intersubjective space'—Aligning and attuning to others

Additional dynamic processes of socio-emotional communication occur alongside mentalizing, which are stimulated by actual face-to face social contact and action. These have been argued to be more prominent forms of everyday social cognition than mentalizing (Gallese, 2006; Hutto, 2004) and serve to effectively align the 'felt' subjectivities of those engaged in interaction with each other, in a 'shared manifold' (Gallese, Keysers, & Rizzolatti, 2004).

One 'we-centric' process involves imitation and embodied simulation, involving both mirror neuron systems in the posterior prefrontal and inferior parietal cortices and connecting para-limbic cortical areas, including the anterior insula and anterior cingulate (Gallese, 1999; see Watt, 2007 for review). These have been shown to work in tandem with mentalizing operations (Schulte-Ruther, Markowitsch, Fink, & Piefke, 2007). This embodied simulation principal is that the same groups of neurons dedicated to recognition of acts/communication from others also fire when the individual is performing/expressing those actions themselves (Gallese, 1999). This seems to hold for both intentional matching of motor movements (Rizolatti et al., 1996) and the recognition of emotional experience (confirmed for pain and disgust; Calder, Keane, Manes, Antoun, & Young, 2000; Singer, Seymour, O'Doherty, Kaube, Dolan, & Frith, 2004). These findings have been developed to conceptualize the coding for inner/embodied, felt subjective experience as also a core mechanism of imitation and emotion recognition (Gallese, 1999) in the expressions of others. This simulation is considered by Frith (2003) and Frith and Wolpert (2004) to be the central mechanism in the observer of a social dyad aligning themselves to the subjectivity and goals of the speaker, much more effective than a purely mentalizing operation.

Other researchers point to an even quicker affective socio-communicative process. Known as contagion (Hatfield, Cacioppa, & Rapson, 1994), this is the automatic 'passing around' of emotional experience from one person to another as emotions are expressed through the face, body, and verbal communication. This is understood to require no conscious or intentional cognitive action, and to be mediated solely through brainstem-limbic-para-limbic cortical systems, without neocortical involvement (Watt, 2007). There is some debate about the independence of this process from embodied simulation in the social alignment process, intersubjectivity, and empathy (see Watt, 2007, plus commentaries in the same journal issue). However the emergent result of these processes is a shared intersubjective field and attuned resonance of felt experience between social agents, where shifts in emotion can be quickly and at times intimately attended to.

In the case of brain injury, several studies have highlighted how different combinations of cognitive and affective alignment processes can be disrupted following injury. There is an increasingly frequent observation that a deficit post-injury in emotion recognition is simultaneous with a difficulty accessing subjective information about that specific emotion in oneself (Blair & Cipolotti, 2000; Calder, Keane, Manes, Antoun, & Young, 2000; Damasio, 1994; Hornak, Rolls, & Wade 1996). Reduced recognition of emotions in facial and vocal information following TBI (McDonald & Flanagan, 2004), and specifically ventral frontal damage has been identified by several authors (Hornak, Rolls, & Wade, 1996; Milders, Fuchs, & Crawford, 2003), as has emotional recognition from faces and body postures (Jackson & Moffat, 1987) and recognizing some emotions in faces while also attributing emotions to story protagonists (Blair & Cipolotti, 2000).

Selective disruptions to the experience and perception of negative emotions such as anger and fear associated with damage to (predominantly right) medial-frontal and somato-sensory cortices, amygdala, and connecting circuits (Adolphs, Tranel, Damasio, & Damasio, 1994; Baird et al., 2006; Blair & Cipolotti, 2000; Park, Conrod, Rewilak, Kwon, Gao, & Black, 2001). Selective impairments in the recognition and experience of disgust have been found following insula damage (Calder, Keane, Manes, Antoun, & Young, 2000), and a specific deficit in sadness recognition has been reported following frontal ABI by Blair and Cipolotti (2000). These latter authors have also suggested that emotional recognition may be independent from mentalizing ability, demonstrating impairments in the former and competency in the latter following a different case of ventro-medial frontal damage.

The recognition of basic emotions from the direct expression of others occurs within a rich, multi-modal process of social communication. Following ABI, other deficits in social communication are evident, such as the comprehension or production of social pragmatics and prosody, and the social inference of sarcasm, deceit, and irony (Cicerone & Tanenbaum, 1997; Martin & MacDonald, 2003; Milders, Fuchs, & Crawford, 2003).

Those investigators studying empathy following brain injury have converged in thinking with the aforementioned social neuroscientists in conceptualizing empathy as a heterogeneous capacity involving both cognitive and affective components (Eslinger, 1998; Hynes, Baird, & Grafton, 2006). A deficit in empathy following stroke or TBI has been observed as a final pathway for a range of cognitive and affective deficits (Eslinger, 1998; Grattan & Eslinger, 1989; Shamay-Tsoory, Tomer, Berger, & Aharon-Peretz, 2003).

Closing the communication loop

The dyadic social sequence is completed as the predictive coding, emotion recognition, and embodied simulation/contagion information are used by the observer to form a response, such that the original speaker's communicative behaviour is concluded (as the speaker feels understood, acknowledged, etc.). This stage may be quite diverse in nature, with the information used from previous stages guiding a number of social cognitive activities (decision-making, problem-solving, social judgement, and of course new emotional communication from the original observer).

In a TBI sample, Milders and colleagues (2003) found difficulties in detection of social norms (also found by Blair & Cipolotti, 2000, together with social judgement problems in a case of orbito-frontal damage), social problem-solving (Channon, 2004; Channon & Crawford, 1999) together with relatives ratings in difficulties in pragmatics of communication. Pullen, Morris, Kerr, Bullock, and Selway (2006; Morris, Pullen, Kerr, Bullock, & Selway, 2006) have used a virtual reality paradigm to highlight a failure of social proxemics in an orbito-frontal damage sample that is respecting and responding to others' personal space. A further difficulty affects regulation and frustration tolerance within social situations (Burgess & Wood, 1990). In some cases of frontal damage, survivors have been unable to access social schema knowledge during both mentalizing (Channon & Crawford, 2000) and social problem-solving, normally used to inhibit aberrant behaviour (Dimitrov, Grafman, & Hollnagel, 1996; Grafman, 1994; Grafman, Schwab, Warden, Pridgen, Brown, & Salazar, 1996). This access may in part be mediated by temporal pole mnemonic and semantic codes (Firth & Frith, 2004).

However, Saver and Damasio (1991) reported intact access to social knowledge in their famous case of ventro-medial frontal damage, EVR. The Iowa group used this finding to develop a model of somatic marker deficits restricting an ABI survivor's access to visceral/emotional signals during social decision-making, resulting in impaired reversal learning across differing contingencies or an impaired sense of future costs and benefits in this activity (Bechara, Damasio, Damasio, & Anderson, 1994; Damasio, 1994). While the methodology of this group has been challenged on several grounds (e.g., Maia & McClelland, 2004), the principle of interoceptive processes having a central role in social decision-making is acquiring increasing support (Dunn, Dalgleish, & Lawrence, 2006).

Park and colleagues (2001) have found that damage to amygdala prevents both the normal recognition and experience of emotion, and the ability to generate social responses (without overt external cues) congruent with a display of such emotion within the individual's social field. While these investigators have noted the central role of emotions in social behaviour, dorso-lateral frontal executive (Blair & Cipolotti, 2000), working memory, and attentional (Damasio, 1994) cognitive processes have been identified as working in interaction/tandem/synthesis with emotional signals, with cognitive content perhaps being biased and directed within social goal-driven behaviour (Damasio, 1994).

Interacting Dyadic Processes, Attachment, and Intimacy

Taken together, these impairments within this latter stage can be seen not to close the communication loop, either following misalignment through other socio-emotional communicative problems, or from maladaptive behaviour using aligned perspectives. On the completion of this three-component framework (decoding of mental states, aligning to others' emotive communication, and closing the communication loop), new interactions are cumulatively opened up in a circular process familiar to systemic readers. Damasio (2003) has termed emotionally competent stimuli (ECS) as those environmental aspects that have a triggering effect on emoting neural areas that trigger the evolution of emotional experience and the generation of social responses within an organism. For the ventro-medial frontal areas, ECS are social in nature, and include expressions and/or experiences of others' violation of social norms, others' suffering, others' contribution to social co-operation, embarrassment, guilt, and despair (Damasio, 2003).

Within this, core interpersonal processes of emotional communication are central to the inter-subjective experience of intimacy. Watt (2007) has emphasized the role of attachment neural systems in the contagion/affective aspect of empathy, with a socially motivated response to alleviate the distress of another being inseparable from empathic communication. He draws on Panksepp's (1998) typology of affective neural systems on the mammalian brain, separating out seeking, nurturance/care, separation distress/social bonding and social affection systems, among others. These specific socio-affective systems are highly relevant for studying intimacy and its pathologies following ABI.

Panksepp has identified the neuro-anatomical and neuro-chemical bases for these systems, with the anterior cingulate, diencephalon, mid-brain, and brainstem commonly involved along the routes of these circuits. Neuro-imaging studies have shown that for both romantic and maternal love there is an activation of Panksepp's systems alongside a deactivation of the cortical areas associated with mentalizing and perspective-taking (Bartels & Zeki, 2000; 2004). These findings suggest that for deeper connecting processes of intimacy, affective/contagion processes have primacy over any engagement of more cognitive social communication processes.

What would it be like for two people, lovers and mutual attachment figures pre-injury, when these neural socio-affective systems are damaged in one brain? How would that be experienced by both minds during moments that used to be characteristically intimate? For the non-injured partner, are the disturbing descriptions of "damaged" and "wrong" relationships that were described at the beginning of this chapter the inter-subjective experience of the neurological lesion in the other?

A study of ABI from an explicit attachment framework remains absent. However in the dementia literature, a small number of publications (Browne & Shlosberg, 2005; Miesen, 1992; 1993; 1999; Miesen & Jones, 1997) have highlighted particular proto-typical attachment behaviours within this group, including parent-fixation and attachment-seeking behaviours (crying, calling out, seeking reassurance, and proximity to others). These behaviours seem to interact with level of cognitive ability although there is debate about change in attachment behaviour as a function of disease progression. Pre-morbid attachment style has not been shown to have a significant influence on the specific post-diagnosis attachment behaviour exhibited (Browne & Shlosberg, 2005). Although the malignant social milieu (Kitwood, 1997) of many dementia care settings comes to mind as a causative factor, this finding may also suggest a direct effect of damaged neuro-affective circuits on attachment process. However, Browne and Shlosberg caution that their negative finding may reflect methodological limitations of the study.

One TBI study explored predictors of the affective qualities of post-injury inter-personal and self-other relationships (these are collectively referred to as object relations within psychodynamic theory). These were associated with pre-injury pre-morbid inter-personal difficulties (Gagnon, Bouchard, Rainville, Lecours, & St Amand, 2006), commensurate with similar comparisons of personality style pre- and post-injury (Tate, 1999; 2003). Neuropsychoanalytic investigators have conceptualized altered self-other relating following right peri-sylvian damage (Kaplan-Solms & Solms, 2000), with all good qualities retained for self and all negative attributes directed externally to the world and others. They claim this pattern results from primitive, regressed forms of object relating as spatial, attentional, and affective representations are undermined by neurological damage. While these insights were based on a small number of clinical cases, subsequent group and other empirical studies have supported this finding (Fotopoulou, Solms, & Turnbull, 2003; Turnbull, Evans, & Owen, 2005). These are intriguing claims for a self-other relational pattern as a direct consequence of acquired neurological damage. However, neuropsychoanalytical investigators will need to provide stronger controls for pre-morbid inter-personal influences in future studies.

In all of these studies, the focus is on the person with neuro-disability and significant others around them are not studied. Elsewhere in the ABI literature, studies have demonstrated empirical associations between clearly defined social cognitive impairments and psychosocial outcomes. Using self-report questionnaire measures of socio-emotional impairment, associations have been demonstrated with spousal relationship satisfaction (Burridge, Williams, Yates, Harris, & Ward, 2007) and survivor and relative judgements of personality change (Obonsawin, Jefferis, Lowe, Crawford, Fernandes, Holland, Woldt, Worthington, & Bowie, 2007). Indirect measures of orbito-frontal function have been used to demonstrate associations with relatives' judgement of personality change (Weddell & Leggett, 2006). Neuro-psychological measures of social cognition have discriminated participants described anecdotally by significant others as exhibiting socio-emotional difficulties in everyday life (Blair & Cipolotti, 2000; Cicerone & Tanenbaum, 2007).

Only four ABI studies to date have explored empirical relationships between social neuro-psychological tests and significant others' ratings on standardized questionnaires of social and affective behaviour. The first was actually within a child head injury group (Pettersen, 1991), demonstrating a link between impaired recognition of facial emotion expression and parental ratings of socially inappropriate behaviour. This association was also noted in adult brain injury samples: Hornak and co-workers (1996) found a relationship between failures on tests of facial and voice expression recognition by 8 of 11 ventro-medial frontal injury participants, and rehabilitation team members' ratings on a social behaviour questionnaire. However, neither study reported an actual quantification of these associations. Milders and colleagues (2003) explored the relationships between relatives' questionnaire ratings of TBI survivor social-emotional behaviour, social activity, and both social cognition and executive functioning tests (emotion recognition, mentalizing, and cognitive flexibility). This study failed to find any significant associations, but with a relationship between mentalizing and a total socio-emotional behaviour scale score approaching significance. A recent study by this group using a larger sample (Milders, Letswaart, Crawford, & Currie, 2008) failed to demonstrate any associations between these measures.

Partners' responses to socio-emotional communication impairments may be complex. An observational study by Godfrey, Knight, and Bishara (1991) noted that relatives of severe brain injury survivors who demonstrated poor social skills actually demonstrated higher levels of facilitative behaviour and positive affect than relatives of a good social skills brain injury group. The authors suggest that relatives actually invest more in maintaining social interactions with a socially unresponsive person. To date, no study has explored the associations of objective measures of social communication post-injury and dimensions of couple relationships (i.e., shared experience rather than another's rating of some aspect of survivor social functioning). The application of relevant neuro-psychological literature to therapeutic work with couples post-injury must therefore proceed with flexibility, drawing on multiple non-unified sources, but also with caution.

Case study

Knots and eggshells

Following viral limbic encephalitis Sean was left with noise sensitivity, heightened irritability, difficulties in mentalizing, and problematic recognition of anger and anxiety. He and his wife Michelle were in their early sixties and had planned to spend their retired life together in a greater degree of closeness and connection, now that busy work schedules no longer existed. However their free time was now experienced as tense, unnatural for how they used to be as a couple and on a knife edge. Sean would spend most of his time on the computer, while trying to minimize his environmental stimulation each day. Michelle knew the importance of not making too much noise—this would lead to outbursts from Sean—but the worry of making noise left her 'treading on eggshells'. In trying to be quieter than a mouse she would become clumsy through heightened anxiety and drop plates in the kitchen, etc.

Over time their relationship began to deteriorate. Sean progressively experienced Michelle as an increasingly persecutory figure, making loud noises on purpose, making his post-injury life a torment (which he secretly felt was some kind of revenge for his neglect of her needs during his busy working life). He would also misinterpret much of her communication and behaviour as intentionally malevolent. For example, he came home early one day and tried to have a nap. Not expecting him to be in, she strolled in 30 minutes later singing at the top of her voice. Sean's mentalizing difficulties prevented him from adopting her perspective and lack of knowledge about his earlier arrival, leaving him with the conclusion that she woke him up in such a harsh way on purpose.

He was often rude and abrupt to her. Michelle would grit her teeth until she reached breaking point and then would scream at him. Sean would be unable to pick up any of the early signs of her increasing agitation, so was left confused for the sudden and dramatic response. This would be one further source of evidence to him for her malevolent campaign against him.

Conclusion

We have outlined several domains where the couple relationship is infiltrated by an acquired brain injury, and closeness is replaced by a sense of damage and otherness, with increasing distance and strain over time. While this chapter culminated in a neuro-psychological account, we see this as situated and shaped by the broader spheres of influence outlined earlier, including reductionist and partitioning trends within service responses. However, conceptualizing the inter-relationship of these factors in a clinically useful manner requires subtlety and an attendance to the quality of reported couples' experiences. We hope to approach these standards in the next chapter. The subject of intimacy for couples after ABI is an under-researched area, and this chapter represents an early attempt to gather relevant and potentially useful ideas. Research data on this topic are being collected by one of the authors and will be presented in a future book within this series (Yeates, in preparation). For now, we offer a counterpart chapter in the pages that follow, which takes these theoretical ideas and epistemological observations and generates a range of therapeutic applications within couples work.

CHAPTER FIVE

Connections, closeness, and intimacy in couples relationships: Intervention

A large range of literature has been presented in the preceding chapter, all relating to couples' experiences of intimacy post-injury. This has not been an exclusive selection, but an amalgamation of studies that have spoken out to the authors in different ways as intimacy has been considered. Other studies and ways of thinking about intimacy may be immediately apparent to readers, and a rich eclectic approach to the topic is welcome. The coverage of studies above has spanned from damaged neurobiology to social context and all these levels have a place in formulating interventions.

At the point of referral, a choice confronts the clinician: does a particular framing of neuro-psychological deficit that may impact on relationship invite the clinician towards the 'interiority' of the survivor's recovery (Newnes, 2006), so creating a service-led partitioning of the couple's experience? Or does an all-embracing conceptualization of the couple-as-situated-within-social-context risk missing an engagement with the disturbing peculiarities of close intimate experience following certain forms of neurological injury? This in turn could alienate the couple from a potentially unique conversation about confusing inter-subjective experience that may not be easily captured within everyday discourse and language. It is suggested here that an engagement with meaning and complexity, plus contextual comprehensiveness, key tenets of systemic work, would support the use of all the knowledge reviewed above. While these various levels would be a target for engagement, a flip-flop between levels would be required to maintain sensitivity to both the unique qualities of couples' inter-subjectivities post-injury and the inter-personal and contextual complexities in which these are situated.

Working with context

Couples often bring their story of closeness and intimacy since the time of injury, which may be difficult to discern from a story of problems in the individual survivor post-injury and/or a story of identities or the partner's misunderstanding of the survivor. Pre-injury narratives of relationship or even earlier transgenerational narratives may have a structuring or meaning-making in couples' accounts of post-injury life. One story strand that is glaringly missing from the literature above is the subjectivity of the survivor, as partners are describing a damaged relationship or personality change. This is one half of the coin and needs to be mapped out in relation to partners' stories.

It may be likely therefore that clinicians are required to engender curiosity about how post-injury problems 'in the survivor', the past and current caring of the partner, and wider sources of support or hardship are all inter-related. Social isolation is a current concern of community approaches to brain injury services and voluntary sector organizations (Tyerman & King, 2008; Yates, 2003), noting the value of increasing social networks and multiple social group membership (Haslam et al., 2008). Taking a conversational journey away from a damaged brain to allow a hearing of economic hardship and social isolation for both partners may be a very powerful gesture by 'brain professionals', respectfully recognizing how an ABI can 'de-press' (Jones & Asen, 2000) the couple in very global ways.

The paradoxical dynamics of caring may be explored along the way. Watzlawick and Coyne (1980) described an elegant intervention with a 'depressed' survivor of stroke and his wife, using ideas from strategic and systemic family therapy. The husband was becoming increasingly depressed, feeling misunderstood and unsupported as the wife and the wider family frustratingly tried to encourage him to recover. The therapists needed to respond both to the disempowered position of the husband within the family caring dynamic, but also respect the courageous and role-defining sacrifices that the wife and others were making in the process. The therapists delivered the following message "you must encourage him by discouraging him... but I'm probably asking too much of you." They directed the devotion of the wife and family to being 'cared for' by the husband, while keeping a vigilant watch for signs of recovery. The wife was supported to begin to prepare the husband's breakfast but then to leave it half finished, feeling 'ill'. No more recovery pep talks were initiated by the family, the husband was no longer continually called downstairs for things, he was left to provide his own encouragement to go for walks. This creating space for him to re-acquire responsibilities and a provider identity within the family once again (see chapter 5 for ideas on how to re-structure roles and relationships where the survivor has initiation or other executive difficulties).

Yeates, Luckie, DeBeer, & Khela (2010) have described a post-Milan systemic intervention with two women who both sustained post-concussive difficulties following a road-traffic accident. The mother and adult daughter hit the windscreen in a head-on collision. The daughter initially experienced a tumultuous year of depression and oscillating mood, cared for by her mother, who was also holding down a job as a professional carer and managing her own post-concussive cognitive, emotional, and physical symptoms. The authors worked together with the two women and their grandparents to understand how following this year, the daughter progressed to full recovery while the mother simultaneously declined to a daily experience of depression and persisting cognitive difficulties. During this time, clear role and material opportunities that were afforded to the daughter, contrasted with those progressively lost by the mother.

However, the key to the formulation was the historical family positionings around care and support versus self-resilience. Using the Co-ordinated Management of Meaning Model (CMM, Pearce, & Cronen, 1980), the authors considered how every other family member's recovery from adversity had been constructed within a dominant discourse of 'inner self-resilience'. However, from the mother's perspective, everyone's personal triumphs of inner resilience had secretly benefited from being 'shored-up' behind the scenes, by her caring (cuddling, soft words of encouragement, providing moments of sanctuary and protection). The mother's own experience of depression and incapacity left her without the support of being 'secretly shored-up' by others in the family (it was only her who did this in the family) and the simultaneous loss of her role as 'shorer-upper' as she struggled more, unable to help others. The mother's experience of post-concussive depression was synonymous with loss of close care and nurturance with others in the family and the inter-personal identities derived within this.

The intervention that followed was to create room for the shoring up marginalized discourse within the family, while emphasizing the family's collective noticing of the mother's pre-injury identity returning again within this new relational arrangement. This work places an emphasis on how intimacy between any family member can be structured within pre-injury caring roles and interactions, and changes to such post-injury may be associated with distancing and perceived loss/changes in self. As recommended by Maitz and Sachs (1995), family or couples interventions focused on role re-negotiation post-injury (when sensitive to the nuances and idiosyncrasies of family relational meanings), can be powerful resources for fostering intimacy and connection.

Specific mental health issues

A range of emotions and a diverse palette of mental health experience may be pertinent to couples' exploration of intimacy. We have already outlined the relationally organizing power of depression. The judgement of personality change (with its organic determinism and implied hopelessness, Yeates, Gracey, & Collicutt-McGrath, 2008) in couples has been shown to be associated with anxiety and depression in both survivors and relatives (Obonsawin et al., 2007; Weddell & Leggett, 2006). Post-traumatic stress symptomatology in survivors such as social withdrawal, hyper-arousal, and blunted affect has been shown to be constructed by relatives as personality change and individual psychological treatment of these difficulties can result in the relative witnessing a return of their loved one's personality (McGrath, 1997). There is a moral imperative therefore to identify mental health issues within the couples' post-injury experience that may be amenable to psychological intervention (Yeates, Gracey, & Collicutt-McGrath, 2008).

With regards to mental health issues, anger and violence are a common reason for referral to rehabilitation or couples therapy post-injury. Considering anger and violence, the work of systemic authors described above would suggest a comprehensive assessment of contextual triggering and organizational influences (see chapter 9 for overview), and also to make explicit the secret moments of alliance and redemption (Goldner, Penn, Sheinberg, & Walker, 1990). By openly discussing the role of these intimate moments within cycles of violence, the binding power of this secret can be negated. Also, a standard individualist therapeutic approach to anger for survivors will never address the unique historical meanings of anger in relationships post-injury and how this relates to intimacy. A partner may have witnessed or been a victim of DV within their childhood and had chosen the survivor based on their difference from their parents. Only then to lose that person/way of life away from their past to an injury and find themselves back in a relationship to a perpetrator of violence.

Working with neuropsychology

The range of socially orientated executive functioning and memory rehabilitation interventions described in chapter 3 are all relevant here, with the use of electronic alerts and paging having been recently showed to reduce caregiver stress (Teasdale, Emslie, Quirk, Evans, Fish, & Wilson, 2009). The specific use of alerting as part of a psychotherapy intervention for anger in an intimate couples relationship has been reported by Yeates and colleagues (2008).

Furthermore, the literature on the neuropathology of social communication has suggested a small range of interventions that may be useful in circumventing the aforementioned deficits. These have emerged from a tradition of social skills training (Boake, 1991), more recently developed by Skye McDonald and colleagues to involve multi-component packages and techniques that aim to re-teach essential facets of social comprehension and behaviour. Social skills approaches for ABI have themselves been evaluated using controlled group trial methodologies (McDonald, Tate, Togher, Bornhofen,

Long, Gertler, & Bowen, 2008). The relational context has been considered as a parameter of this work, as one evaluation has shown the increased efficacy of a 'communication partner' over the solo acquisition of social skills by an isolated survivor (Togher, McDonald, Tate, Power, & Rietdijk, 2009).

This group of clinician-researchers has tried to tease out the most effective components and influential target areas for these types of intervention (Bornhofen & McDonald, 2008a; 2008b), using both experimental and intervention evaluation studies. Croker and McDonald (2005), McDonald and Flanagan (2004), and Saunders, McDonald, and Richardson (2006) have demonstrated in TBI groups theory of mind deficits, loss of emotional experience, difficulties in emotion labelling and matching. However, abilities in these areas did improve when contextual information was provided. One strand of intervention is to improve social encoding, using intact social knowledge, available mediums of information and structured, directed cues to facial processing. McDonald, Bornhofen, and Hunt (2009) compared the role of focused attention versus mimicry for emotion recognition in a TBI sample, but did not find persuasive results for either technique. Elsewhere, training to identify emotional expression from facial, bodily, and conversational cues is now a common component in neuro-rehabilitation.

Training packages developed within the field of autistic spectrum disorders include components on recognizing and accessing emotional states in self and others (using external scaling procedures), practising emotional expression and eye contact, perspective-taking, and mentalizing (Solomon, Goodlin-Jones, & Anders, 2004). Similar training has since been provided in TBI groups, focusing on improving knowledge of emotion in common contexts, judgement of both static and dynamic emotion cues and social inference from dynamic cues (Bornhofen & McDonald, 2008a). These authors report improvement on a variety of social communication measures in a treatment group versus controls within an RCT design. In terms of responding to others, social problem-solving frameworks, addressing executive problems, emotional regulation, and related social processes have been proven efficacious within ABI samples (Rath, Hennessey, & Diller, 2003). Within experimental studies, Anderson and Phelps (2000) and Park and colleagues (2001) report an ability of ABI survivors with bilateral amygdala damage to produce explicit information relating to negative emotions when overtly cued to do so, despite their inability to process such information automatically. This suggests that external cues may have a role as an intervention to facilitate socially congruent experience and discourse. The recent work on interoception in social decision-making has not been formally applied to treatment approaches. However, the problem of subjective access to affective-somatic experience has been reconceptualized from an absence of such signals to a continuum of dampened to intense signal post-injury.

As such, experimental procedures to increase the intensity of these signals in healthy subjects have been described by Damasio, Grabowoski, Bechara, Damasio, Ponto, Parvizi et al. (2000). In the assessment of interoception during decision-making by survivors of ABI, scaling and biofeedback paradigms are used to gather more detailed information (Dunn, Dalgleish, & Lawrence, 2006; Turnbull, 2004, personal communication). Future studies are required to see if intensity modulation, scaling, and feedback protocols can be used as interventions to improve ABI survivors' access to interoceptive signals in emotional experience and social decision-making, thereby effecting resultant social responses comparative with that pre-injury.

Case study
Different wavelengths, loving & being needed (With special thanks to Nicola Creamer and Dr Clara Murray as co-therapists in this work) Adam and Deidre had been struggling in their relationship since Adam's ABI, a haemorrhagic rupture of his right middle cerebral artery during neurosurgery that left him with right-frontal cortical damage. Socioemotional communication deficits evident on testing included difficulties mentalizing, comprehension of sarcasm and recognition of disgust (alongside attentional and verbal abstract reasoning impairments).   During their working lives they had been separated by mutual business and geographical distance (Adam commuted long distances). Both were keen to enjoy their time together and become closer now they had retired and their three children had grown up. Deidre's own childhood had been emotionally turbulent. Her mother did not express any positive emotion or physical affection towards her, and a younger sister became a rival for her mother's thoughts. In contrast Deidre would spend summer holidays with an aunt who would constantly hug and comfort her, a

precious time that would always come to an end and was threatened by constant disapproval by her mother. Adam was always a very practical man, and in this way the couple often had to negotiate throughout their marriage, common gender differences in response to distress. However before the ABI Adam usually was able to 'tune in' during important moments and comfort his wife when necessary.

Following the ABI Deidre complained of daily experiences where she would be emotionally pushed away by Adam, made to feel unwanted and undeserving of existing alongside him. Adam would in turn say that in these moments he is trying to avoid any arguments by pulling back, trying to avoid putting his foot in it. However this would become a vicious cycle whereby Deidre would respond to Adam's silence, experienced as rejecting, by pursuing, trying harder to get an acknowledgement of her needs. In sessions the therapists would experience a strong sense of panic and urgency being passed into us, strong pulls to be recruited to validate Deidre's point of view in response to brief contributions by Adam. His own attempts to respond to the issues that Deidre raised would be based on misunderstandings, thereby becoming further triggers for Deidre's alienated position. There was a huge sense of frustration, a knotting-up of feelings and hopelessness in the room at these times.

We applied the metaphor of different bandwidths in radio broadcasts (from Aston, 2009—a great resource for this kind of work) to positively connote how both styles of communication in the couple were well intentioned but out of synch from each other. In later sessions we would focus on only one piece of content brought by the couple and spend the whole session deconstructing it in terms of attachment cycles and positions, then applying directed social comprehension strategies with Adam to facilitate his tuning in to the affective level of Deidre's communication. This would be at times very powerful and emotive and lead to dramatic points of reconnection. The remaining sessions of the therapy aimed to maximise the re-occurrence of these moments of reconnection.

Static versus dynamic; thinking versus feeling

While social communication interventions such as those above are a promising new direction for cognitive rehabilitation, they seem insufficient for couples intimacy work. As the reader will recall from chapter 3, an individualist, mechanistic orientation to social communication would organize the development of interventions that would manipulate inputs and outputs. If the assessment of a core ability such as emotion recognition following injury is dependent on the use of static versus dynamic cues (Atkinson, Heberlein, & Adolphs, 2007), then interventions in this area will surely be similarly affected by the presence or absence of a dynamic focus.

To make these useful adjuncts to couples therapy a more interactional perspective is required. In terms of formulation, aforementioned components of social communication can be readily linked to conceptualize cumulative, problematic, circular sequences between partners. This may involve a partner expressing distress to an ABI survivor, perhaps as a result of an existing faux pas or social comprehension failure. In turn, the survivor would then be unable to gather, access, and/or use the partner's expressive information to respond in a way that will alleviate their distress. This would be a further instance of social failure, perpetuating a cycle of social disability with increasingly grave consequences for the relationship.

At the same time, a technology of socio-emotional rehabilitation in the service of couples' connection should be informed by the neuroscience and phenomenology of love (Odent, 2001). As we have seen in the Bartels and Zeki studies (2000; 2004) mentioned in the previous chapter, this is primarily an affective neuroscience— the deep connection involved in intense love is characterized neurologically by de-activation of cortical (thinking) processes and a centrality of medial, affective processes. A technology responding to socio-emotional communication impairments within a couples therapy session would need to be sensitive and responsive to micro-shifts in the dance of affective interaction and meaning negotiation. In terms of therapy itself, the dynamics of emotional rupture or insecure attachment responses has begun to feature prominently in both the formulation and interventions of family therapists (e.g., Dallos & Vetere, 2009; Johnson, 2004).

A well-evaluated and evidence-based approach is EFT pioneered by Sue Johnson (e.g., 2004), which is based on systemic and humanistic practice, fused with attachment theory. This has been used with aphasic stroke survivors and their partners (Stiell, Naaman, & Lee, 2007). The approach is characterized by the following components:

- Creating an alliance
- Identifying negative attachment cycles (e.g., pursuing/blaming-withdrawing)
- Accessing emotions underlying positions

- Reframing the problem (in terms of negative cycles, underlying feelings, and attachment needs)
- Engaging each partner in an intense, affective exploration of experience (fears and attachment needs). Expressing these experiences to a partner
- Promoting acceptance of partner's experience and new interactional patterns
- Creating emotional engagement: asking for needs and wants to be met
- Facilitating new solutions to old issues
- Consolidating new cycles of attachment.

These components overlap considerably with the techniques and foci that we suggest for general systemic practice in neuro-rehabilitation (chapter 9), so is an important approach to consider. For our current consideration, this approach does provide a useful level of focus to formulate how acquired socio-emotional impairments can steer a couples' reciprocal attachment pattern in new, distancing directions. This can be done as they are manifest in the room during sessions, following the EFT process. A central technique of EFT is the use of enactment within couples' sessions, to allow secure attachment interactions to occur in response to triggers and reconfigure the couples' inter-subjective experience of attachment, closeness, and intimacy. This technique is highly emotive and should be used critically and cautiously with couples. However, this approach can provide the arena where some of the social skills strategies can be sensitively introduced to a couple to see if reparatory interactions can be instigated in response to attachment ruptures (see case study).

One final intriguing future area of intervention may be the use of oxytocin. This neuro-peptide has been implicated in Panksepp's (1998) nurturance/care, separation distress/social bonding, and social affection systems. It is sometimes called the 'cuddle hormone', heavily influencing post-coital bonding. It has been associated with a range of attachment and nurturing behaviours in both maternal and romantic love. Its role in multiple aspects of social cognition has been emphasized, including social memory and recognition, emotion recognition, reduced amygdala activation, and social approach behaviour (Domes, Heinrichs, Michel, Berger, & Herperz, 2007; Kirsch, Esslinger, Chen, Mier, Lis, Siddhanti et al., 2005).

Recent research has focused on the potential of oxytocin as a social communication intervention, administered as a nasal spray. In normal humans it has been shown to increase feelings of trust (Kosfeld et al., 2005), mentalizing (Domes, Heinrichs, Gläscher, Büchel, Braus, & Herperz, 2007), and gaze to the eye regions of others (Guastella, Mitchell, & Dadds, 2008). The only neurological population to have received this spray are people with autism, who have been found to have sustained improvements in their affective comprehension abilities (Hollander, Bartz, Chaplin, Phillips, Sumner, Soorya et al., 2007) and reduced repetitive behaviours (Hollander, Novotny, Hanratty, Yaffe, DeCaria, Aronowitz et al., 2003). In non-clinical samples of couples attempting stress-inducing and potentially divisive tasks, this spray increased positive communication while reducing cortisol levels, a biomarker of stress (Ditzen, Schaer, Gabriel, Bodenmann, Ehlert, & Heinrichs, 2009). While this intervention raised huge numbers of questions from a context-focus perspective, its role as an adjunct/component of couples therapy with an emotional focus is plausible. A future randomized control trial evaluating couples therapy in ABI services with and without oxytocin nasal spray would be welcome.

A unifying concept? Projective identification

All of the above factors may influence a couples' inter-subjective experience, following ABI. The reader will recall from the previous chapter that the act of caregiving often involves a repositioning of two romantic partners to a parent-child pattern, rendering each other unrecognizable to each other and precluding intimate connection. Yet, compared to other long-term conditions that necessitate similar role change, there is a unique set of factors relating to neuro-disability that lead to comparatively more problematic couples outcomes and a dark, disturbing language of damage, intrusion, and alienation.

For the couples therapist, it is the shared discourse of the couple, organized by the therapeutic encounter and the responses of the therapists, together with the nuances of interactional patterns within the therapy room that allows all of these factors to be thought about. These meetings are points in time that intersect the historical dimension of meaning that is brought to bear on post-injury experiences.

How then, to make the complex links between altered neurology, couples interactions, and wider social and historical context during the course of clinical work? Furthermore, how to use these conceptual links responsively within a given session? How also to remain close to that quality of damage and disturbance that seems central to at least the partner's experience?

One set of ideas that may be well suited as both a theoretical bridge and an in-session epistemological lens can be drawn from the psychoanalytic literature. The unique language of psychoanalysis can approach these counter-intuitive intimate disturbances, locating socio-emotional communication deficits within social and interactional context. In terms of inter-subjective quality, Freud's (1919) notion of *Das Umheimliche*, 'the uncanny', seems to have an intuitive fit with a disturbing presence in partners' experiences. This description of moments in subjective experience refers to a sense of a presence of 'alieness' and otherness overlapping with a point of familiarity, hidden from others, unexpected and intruding into intimate inter-subjectivity. Fiegelson (1993) provides a comprehensive account of this phenomenon in relation to TBI, noting how the mental functioning and subjective experience of the partner is undermined in their connection with the survivor that is both familiar and strikingly alien to them. Similar connections are provided by Lacan's (1949; 1953; 1958; 1977) notion of *objet a* (see Morin, Thibierge, Bruguiere, Pradat-Diehl, & Mazavet, 2005 for a further application of this Lacanian concept within ABI samples) and Bion's (1962) *Beta Elements* within the lack of a containing function.

Of most relevance is how such experiences come to be shared between people. The process of knowing others in a felt, intimate sense, and also experiencing a personal sense and idea of one's own self through these interactions is referred to as *identification* by psychoanalysts. In this view, such a felt sense of closeness and knowing of a person in an intimate and familiar way is actually dependent on the recognition and interactions of the other (Freud, 1957/1917; 1961/1923; Lacan, 1949; 1953). Any change to a survivor's ability to recognize and respond to a partner will result in both the partner's historical, continuous sense of the survivor being disrupted with an intrusive sense of alienness regarding the survivor. Furthermore, the partner's own sense of self, dependent on the continuity in interactions and in relation to the survivor will also be altered, resulting in the very deep and personal sense of 'parasitic' alteration from an externally intruding force.

Melanie Klein and psychoanalysts influenced by her ideas have developed the concept of identification to its most interactional potential and also its most disturbing sense. Her construct of *projective identification* refers to the process of projecting unwanted parts of the self to another and then experiencing/identifying with the other as defined only by those unwanted parts. The emphasis and thinking about projective identification has progressed in its own right, and is currently used in different ways within the psychoanalytical literature. A good review is provided within several chapters of Ruszcynski and Fisher's book (1995).

Klein's (1946) original conceptualization of projective identification was of an evacuative process that exists solely within an individual's unconscious phantasy. However, her followers have progressively emphasized that this may be a feature of all interpersonal communication and interaction (Bion, 1959; Rosenfeld, 1971). Some have thought about the unidirectional enactment of an individual's projective identification on another (Feldman, 1994). Others, including Bion, have considered how it is impossible not to feel the effects of another's projective identification, being pushed and nudged by it into fulfilling and reciprocating the representations in phantasy (Bion, 1990; Spillius, 1994). Joseph (1987) draws attention to the simultaneous communicative and controlling quality of the projective identification process.

The communicative and inter-personal emphasis has been applied by couples psychoanalytic psychotherapists working within a post-Kleinian and object relations orientation (Ruszcynski & Fisher, 1995; Scharff & Savege-Scharff, 1991). These authors are interested in how the projective identifications of both partners interact in reciprocal and cumulative ways and also in the particular intersubjective quality of these processes in both 'pockets' of common couple experience and also where couples are experiencing prolonged difficulties. Stanley Ruszcunski (1995) builds on earlier work by Rosenfeld (1964) to think about particular patterns of identification and object relating between couples, where mental contents from one partner colonizes the other in intrusive, possessive, and omnipotent ways, denying any separateness of the other. Good qualities in the other partner are attacked by these colonizing contents. Morgan (1995) extends this to a picture of this happening in both directions within a couple's relationship, which she refers to as 'projective gridlock'. Here the couple is organized in a very anxiously fragile way through mutually rigid projective identification. Any implication of the other's separateness or difference is intolerable, experienced as persecutory and intrusive, and projective identification is subsequently intensified to minimize or deny this difference.

In both formulations the developmental links are emphasized between projective identification and Klein's (1946) paranoid-schizoid position. A developmentally primitive organization of object relations that re-appears constantly within adult life, the subject relates to its self and others through part-objects (affective-cognitive-relational mental contents). That is split, disparate qualities, with which the subject forms separate, rigid, and contradictory relations. A unified whole object, a person, with a mixture of good and bad qualities that can be loved and for which can be shown concern (the depressive position), is not possible within this organization. Splitting and projective identification are key defences that are used by the subject to ward off persecutory and destructive anxieties, where entirely good or bad objects are projected into others and related to on that basis. The reader is invited at this point to return to the description of right peri-sylvian damaged patients and their inter-personal qualities as described by Kaplan-Solms and Solms (2000) in chapter 4.

Socio-emotional communication impairments and projective identification after ABI

How would the changes to couples relationships following ABI be manifest as altered projective identificatory process? Gross behavioural changes and the definitive emergence of anger in relationships post-injury may be characterized inter-subjectively by both an intrusiveness and increased fear of separateness by both partners. This was noted above as central to many patterns of violence within relationships. This may be new to the couple relationship and so foreign, and alien, or this may represent an extreme and more rigid form of object relations that existed pre-injury (e.g., see Gagnon, Bouchard, Rainville, Lecours, & St Amand, 2006; Yeates et al., 2008).

In any case, particular historical relational meanings and subject positioning may be a part of this—the partner's horrified recognition of the re-emergence of a violent figure from her past, now in the shoes of her former nurturing lover who had once defined her break from 'those kind of relationships'.

Absence of invested, emotive relating to another may feature as an inter-personal quality where depression or anxiety is central to a couple's relationship. Klein (1946) notes that absence of a former good relation can be experienced as a presence of a persecutory attacking object within a paranoid-schizoid organization. Klein's whole approach was initiated by Freud's (1915) paper on mourning and loss, where aspects of the person who is no longer present are taken in by another (introjected). This synthesis of both absence of good and presence of something intrusive seems relevant to partner's experiences reported above.

However, the aforementioned social communication impairments may have a particular and subtle presence within couples' inter-subjective processes. Several authors (Greatrex, 2002; Roeckerath, 2002; Schore, 2002; Watt, 1986; 2007) have begun to demystify the concept of projective identification and related phenomena. They first validate its plausibility and importance, and second specify the neural mechanisms that are likely to be involved. Importantly, these authors assume that projective identification is a necessary feature of human inter-subjective life and central to intimate relationships, but also that it can take adaptive and rigidly defensive and colonizing, maladaptive forms (Schore, 2002). Within this communicative framing, the aforementioned neuro-psychological processes such as mirroring and embodied simulation, affective attunement and contagion become central constructs (Watt, 2007). Similarly, their acquired dysfunction can be conceptualized to alter the pattern of projective identification within a couple.

Memory and executive difficulties can obviously alter any identificatory process, as aspects of selves and connections between selves are lost (e.g., Dewar & Gracey, 2007) or actions of a loved one become more contradictory, chaotic, and alien (see Yeates et al., 2008 for an example). Alterations to shared attention, loss, or change in eye contact as reported by Vecera and Rizzo (2006) could be experienced by the partner as a lost intimate connection or new presence of something unwanted.

Difficulties in mentalizing and social inference could create a huge range of inter-subjective consequences, with strands of shared identities and continuous nuances being lost or replaced with error-ful or rigid representations of the partner. These would be experienced as alien intrusions for that partner. Pre-existing connections within inter-subjective experiences may be withdrawn or eliminated as a result of some social communicative impairments, with perhaps a simultaneous absence/malign presence inter-subjective quality. The split relating in patients described by Kaplan-Solms and Solms (2000) or Lewis (1999) can be conceptually completed by the couples psychoanalytic thinking on projective identification. It can be seen how being the changing recipient of all things good and then all things bad, and to be defined as such by someone who used to love and support all of your human, changing imperfections, would be both an intrusive colonization and potentially a threat to self. Partners' responses to these patterns must then be all the more confusing for survivors to comprehend within their reduced palette of mental representations of others.

Watt (2007) notes how relevant the social neuroscience concept of contagion may be for considering inter-subjectivity and projective identification. Having a known neural correlate of affects automatically passing between people makes the communicative, inter-personal version of projective identification, easy to appreciate. This also suggests the striking possibility that in an intimate attachment relationship, the uninjured partner will experience, inter-subjectively, the lesion in the anterior cingulate, insula, or other structure of the survivor, with possible subjective properties of discontinuity and otherness. Here we arrive once more within this book at conceiving a real diffusion and mobility of a brain injury within a shared landscape or ecology of mind (Bateson, 1972), between people. Finally, the dramatic changes in survivors' social and affective decision-making, impulse control, or other social behaviour are often experienced as cruel, thoughtless, or child like by others (Oddy, Coughlan, Tyerman, & Jenkins, 1985), even termed as 'acquired sociopathy' by Damasio and colleagues (Bechara, Damasio, Damasio, & Anderson, 1994; Damasio, 1994). Here we return to the intimate loss of personhood and presence of something/someone altogether unwanted and explicitly attacking.

An emerging formulation, based on research data, and which links these levels of analysis will be reported in full in a future publication within this book series (Yeates, in preparation). For now, an early idea based on pilot data is that prior to an ABI, each couple's relationship has its own unique relational arrangement and forms of projective communication and identification. Each arrangement has a point of inter-subjective vulnerability where the idiosyncratic conditions conducive to closeness, intimacy, and recognition of each other have to be maintained and worked at by the couple. For example, an assertive husband may act as a container for his partner's vulnerability (this containing simultaneously being a containing identity for himself). This structures a sense of closeness within their containment, but only as long as the assertion is part of 'who' the husband is in relation to his wife. Acquired socio-emotional impairments serve to produce de-synchrony within the couple's interactions and thinking about one another. These de-synchronies 'open-up' like wounds the historical vulnerabilities within each couple's arrangement, producing an intrusion of something unwanted and unrecognizable 'within' each partner's experience of the other. To return to the example, the husband may lose his assertion at critical points in his interaction with his partner due to initiation problems, or his protection is implicated as less certain through social faux pas and/or misinterpretation between them. Inter-subjectively, the feared vulnerability that both previously warded off through their respective roles suddenly manifests between them, at the heart of the couple. The reader is cautioned that these are ideas in progress and subject to further refinement or refutation as the research progresses.

Couples psychotherapy technique

Combining systemic, neuro-psychological, and psychoanalytical perspectives with a lens on projective identification would seem to necessitate an exploration of the rich contextualized meanings that are brought to bear by the couple in narrating changes to their intimacy and connection, but also to attend to where such discourse fails or struggles to give meaning to something altogether more unfamiliar and disturbing. Qualities of loss, absence, presence, intrusion, damage, disruption, and disturbance should be attended to by therapists, and the location and punctuation of these meanings within broader relational and conversational patterns understood. Couples psychoanalytic psychotherapists have noted the close fit of their described phenomena and attachment-orientated couples work (e.g., Clulow, 2001). Alongside those integrating attachment ideas with systemic practice (Dallos & Vetere, 2009; Johnson, 2004), an emphasis is placed on creating a secure base within the therapy session so that more anxiety-provoking and disturbing states of mind can be explored.

Douglas Watt (2007) makes some excellent points on how visceral, automatic contagion, and attachment responses are adaptively and seamlessly linked with intentional simulating, perspective-taking, elaborating, abstracting, and creative cognitive responses within skilled empathy, sympathy, and compassion. The feeling of others' emotional states is necessary for immediate connection and emotive responding. Conversely, the failure of mentalizing or perspective-taking skills in ABI survivors may invite clinicians to see if in contrast affective communication skills are intact and to be used. However, these same automatic mechanisms can lead to unhelpful emotional/ attachment responses (e.g., through amygdala activation), which can also close down connections (also emphasized in Johnson's work). Both connecting and distancing automatic affective processing are characterized by deactivation of cortical areas. Watt suggests that it is the subsequent engagement of the more cognitive abilities, which allows two or more people to reflect on their inter-subjective experience and 'do differently' in the moment if needs be. Both dimensions of response are essential within the right combination, emphases here on a neuroscientific basis and elsewhere within systemic explorations of empathy (e.g., Wilkinson, 1992).

This combination is highlighted within the therapeutic approaches described above. Use of affective contagion and attachment within inter-subjectivity alongside careful thought to effect change is evident in the combination of recognition and enactment techniques of Sue Johnson (2004), and in the skilled use of therapists' own emotive responses (counter-transference) to couples as advocated by couples psychoanalytical psychotherapists (Clulow, 2001; Ruszcynski & Fisher, 1995; Scharff & Savege-Scharff, 1991). Systemic skills in elaboration and creating new connection and relationships within language and meaning could be said to be a very sophisticated use of more cortical-based mirroring, social inferential and mentalizing systems. As intimate moments of felt disturbance will be narrated and constructed within a rich discourse of historical, and relational meaning, core systemic techniques of circular questioning, deconstruction, and relational curiosity are all relevant to both enquiry and supportive change. However, the timing of these interventions will still reside within an effective alignment process between therapists and couple to resonate and inspire, desired affective responses.

While the recent discovery of mirror neurons has been seized by theorists and promoters of empathy in most schools of psychological therapy, clinicians should not be seduced by an isolated view of this neural system alone and make use of the diversity of social communication operations (Yeates, in preparation b). In couples work following ABI, the neuro-rehabilitation approaches to social cognition deficits may be useful in assessing what dimensions and facets of inter-subjective connection are retained or can be meaningfully resurrected through a compensatory excursion through other modalities of communication (thinking about and knowing versus feeling, hearing versus seeing, connecting through broader structures of meaning such as pre-injury or new social roles or narratives of diversity in togetherness).

Psychosexual therapy

This is a core profession in itself and a range of techniques and adaptations for disability from this field have been successfully introduced into ABI work (e.g., Blackerby, 1990; Simpson, 2001). A common evidence-based approach is sensate focus (Masters & Johnson, 1976), the graded increase in sexual activity (e.g., holding hands, cuddling, non-sensual massage, naked massage, genital stimulation, oral sex, penetration with the person who will be penetrated having full control, initially for a few minutes only and then building up time and diversifying technique, position, etc). However, the transition and pace through these stages is informed by the therapist's attention to the shared experience of the couple, alert to themes of anxiety or rejection. This work would undoubtedly be organized by the physical, sensory, and cognitive abilities and needs of the survivor, including the exploration of any other influencing factors, such as side-effects of anti-epilepsy medication, etc.

Psychotherapeutic approaches to sexual work (Gambescia & Weeks, 2006; Hawton, 1985) have noted how dominant discourses of sexuality in modern society tend to construct a monolithic picture of heterosexual, male-instigated, penetrative sex in a missionary position only. The systemic practice of drawing a 'sexual genogram' to map sexual beliefs and narratives across and within family generations is recommended (Hof & Berman, 1986), to see how relationships and access to sexual connection is organized within these meanings. For any couple who deviate from this picture, these cultural patterns result in potentially alienating and limiting access to helpful thinking. This is particularly true where one or both partner has a cognitive or physical disability, and penetrative sex in a missionary position is not possible (or even preferred!). The figure 1 below shows that as the construction of sexual connection moves away from this dominant discourse, diversity increases and so potential access for couples to sexuality increases. The disability rights movement continuous to generate useful resources for these endeavours, as do disability-orientated sexuality websites such as www.beecourse.com or www.maryclegg.com.

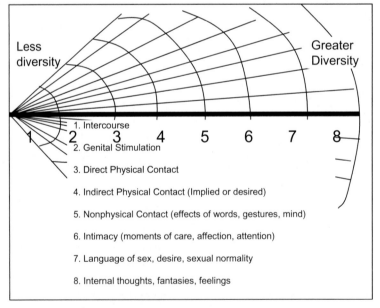

Figure 1. Visual Representation of the Relationship between Sexual Expression & Diversity (IFT, 2005).

Finally, any technical or context-focus psychosexual intervention will also have to negotiate the complexities of altered intimacy and attachment as discussed above, and beyond ABI, conceptual and therapeutic links have been made in this regard (Clulow, 2001). Jennie Ponsford's (2003) survey of sexual changes in TBI survivors noted the greatest influence of psychosocial factors on post-injury reduction is sexual activity, including anxiety, depression, low self-confidence, feeling unattractive, behaviour problems, and relationship difficulties. While increasing or making more mutually satisfying the sexual contact between the couple is a key dimension of relational connection, the wider threats to intimacy may have to be negotiated first, to make sexuality an emotionally safer and connecting experience.

Conclusions

It is hoped that throughout these last two chapters, two aims have been achieved: first the concept of intimacy has hopefully been expanded beyond the bed sheets to the diversity of inter-personal connection and meaning, and of course the multiplicity of ways and levels in which this can be threatened. Second, the need to move between a contextualized orientation to capture such complexity has been advocated, as per the general orientation of this book. However, in this chapter we emphasize the need to flip-flop between this approach and the intimate quality of disturbance within the inter-subjective space of the couple, which may be unique to neurological injuries. The communicative process of projective identification, conceived by Melanie Klein and used as an essential epistemological tool by couples psychoanalytical psychotherapists, is offered as a bridging idea that will permit such a flip-flop. These ideas and the attachment-influenced systemic approaches, such as Johnson (2004), form useful in-session micro-level approaches to attend to the influence of altered neurobiology within the historical and interactional meanings of affective couples' communication. In addition, neuro-rehabilitative strategies for social cognition impairment may be complementary to these couples therapy approaches, if used in contextually and dynamically sensitive ways.

CHAPTER SIX

Negotiating contesting dynamics: A relational approach to awareness of disability after brain injury

"If a tree falls in the woods without anyone to hear it, does it make a sound?"

"If a survivor has a differing account of their disability from others but no-one is there to judge this as different, do they lack insight?"

"If everyone within a family has a different account of problems since the injury, and all of these differ from the account of clinicians, who is aware of what? What is the problem to be addressed, one or more of these perspectives, or the disagreement itself?"

If this was a traditional neurological or neuro-psychological text book, this chapter would be about awareness of deficits. Words like insight and maybe denial might also be used. The focus will generally be on the individual survivor, be it a description of a core neuro-cognitive deficit compromising awareness (McGlynn & Schacter, 1989), or a psychological defensive reaction to minimize the distressing impact of injury and disability (Goldstein, 1939; 1942). There may be a greater degree of sophistication and a formulation of interacting neuro-cognitive and psychological factors, perhaps with a sensitivity to the meaning and subjectivity of the survivor within this (e.g., Kaplan-Solms & Solms, 2000; Prigatano, 1991; Weinstein & Kahn, 1955).

A common approach to assessment (and so epistemology, the way of 'coming to know' about awareness after injury) will be the identification of a true, veridical account of the survivor's disability (perhaps an objective measure of cognitive or functional performance, or an observational rating provided by a clinician, perhaps by a relative, only if they satisfactorily agree with professionals). This 'true' or 'more accurate' account is then used as a benchmark from which the deviation of the survivor's account can be assessed and quantified. In practice this is as a quantified discrepancy between ratings on the same questionnaire or scale of a particular domain of functioning. Interestingly, this approach appears to have become something of a grail quest, with differing discrepancy measures of 'awareness' not satisfactorily correlating with each other (Sherer, Boake, Levine et al., 1998). Sensitivities to the social context, also demand characteristics are likely to play a role. For the injured person, they may be suffering from extreme confusion and fluctuating accounts or recall of events; and the relatives can hardly be considered neutral or unbiased when clearly they want the best care for their loved one, and/or may have considerable anxiety about the shared abilities within the family to cope with a very uncertain future.

In addition, the reliable divergence of ratings from those not having sustained the injury, be this a difference between family members (e.g., Kreutzer, Serio, & Bergquist, 1994) or significant differences in problem ratings between relatives and clinicians (e.g., Sunderland, Harris, & Gleave, 1984) remains as a thorn in the side of the search for the reliable and valid measure of 'awareness' or 'insight' in brain injury rehabilitation. In outcome research too, increased involvement of multiple relationships restricts the predictive power of awareness factors based on discrepancy ratings. This trend is perhaps exemplified in the findings of one study, by Trudel, Tyron, and Purdum (1998). These authors found that a predictive equation of an awareness discrepancy rating, behavioural disturbance, neurological severity post-traumatic amnesia (PTA), and disability measures showed a trend of less predictive value as the outcome measure represented increasingly more inter-personal contexts. Specifically, whereas the equation accounted for 76% of the variance in terms of participants' eventual level of independence, 66% was accounted for in terms of residential support, and 56% of variance was predicted in a measure of vocational status.

Systemic awareness work as peace-keeping?

Let's take a step back for a minute. We have a configuration of persons with differing accounts (with perhaps some accounts being more commonly held and persuasive to more people than others), with this difference and disagreement causing distress and conflict for all concerned. This scenario is actually familiar to us in modernity—a political and diplomatic dilemma to be managed and solutions to be sought. How would a peace-keeping or corporate or even a family mediation service approach this? Initially, perhaps to view a certain degree of ripeness for change—a 'constant crisis' (Lederach, 2003) or even 'hurting stalemate' (Mitchell, 2003)—as a pre-requisite. Outside of these specialized fields, we might have a vague notion that the key ingredients to such a response would be a respect for all the respective views and positions, not a privileging of one over the other. This position would not just be an uncritical ideal to show respect, but an acknowledgement of the inherent truth held in each account, given their unique history and interests. Here also we need to be mindful of people's self-esteem needs and their sometimes emotional attachment to their perception of events. Hence, an emotional reformulation of conflict resolution would involve helping parties see the benefit of entering into a dialogue, that this would not signify a threat to their sense of reality (or self-esteem), that their view can co-exist with another's in a non-competitive way. In other words, to move from a zero-sum perspective (each competing view is a threat to the validity of each individual perspective) to a non-zero-sum, 'win-win' re-conceptualization of the situation (each party has reason to gain from voicing their opinion). This not only directly addresses the issue of self-esteem needs but can also act as a catalyst for transforming and shedding new light on conflicting relationships in a helpful way. It is naïve to believe in a 'one-size' solution and to assume more persuasive powers are needed, but individuals will only abandon their defensive stance if they see an advantage to adopting a new strategy. Once at the table, there may be an attention to the process of negotiation and argument, an identification of flash points, and a steering towards more accessible areas of discussion, where mutually agreed. What understanding would a mediators bring to awareness issues in families following ABI? What would be the 'road map' to family-survivor-clinician collaboration following the raising of an awareness judgement (see also chapter 7).

If we take the combined heritage of Batsonian, cybernetics, and social constructionist perspectives outlined earlier in this book and apply this to issues of awareness of deficit/relational disagreement following injury, we may have more in common with a mediator's position. Here we would be interested in the landscape or ecology of ideas and accounts around disability and change, who is involved in these ideas and what are the implications for the relationships concerned? Finally, how are differences in ideas and accounts managed, what part does the brain injury have in this management and how does this difference reciprocally influence the content of the accounts that are put forward or held on to in the face of opposition? As advocated elsewhere in this book, the neuro-psychological perspective is relevant, but only as it is situated within a complex, dynamic social context.

As we will show, if you apply a relational curiosity to the dilemmas raised by neuro-psychological studies on awareness of disability, new 'insights' may emerge. Finally, this whole endeavour is very much an appropriate focus for a second-order cybernetics, reflexive clinical framework. That is, we are approaching a vivid dynamic of meaning negotiation and contestation (whose account of disability and change is maintained as valid and useful), with a power differential (who and how many subscribe to a particular account), and where the narratives concerned are drawn from broader, historical socio-cultural discourses of meaning. However, our involvement as clinicians will also fundamentally re-organize this system of meaning (the neuro/'head'-experts validating an interior-pathological explanation of the difference in one person's account, or even a construction of family denial, so further defining parameters of authenticity and value within this system). This entry of systemic thinking will be shown to be of significant value for this work, perhaps an approach sorely missed. However, it will lead us to an unexpected reconciliation of neuro-psychological findings in a beautiful circularity.

Neuro-psychological dilemmas and relational responses

Dominant accounts of awareness of disability following ABI have always included those that focus exclusively on the psychodynamics of an emotionally driven, DD (e.g., Goldstein, 1939; 1942; Guthrie & Grossman, 1952; Rosenthal, 1983). However, these formulations did not sufficiently address earlier, paradigmatic studies of anosognosia—unawareness of left hemiplegia following right hemisphere lesions (Babinski, 1914). This finding remains constant—right-sided and frontal lesions are associated with more marked differences in a survivor's account of disability (including the classic complete denial of a paralysed limb exhibited in anosognosia), than left-sided or posterior lesions (Feinberg & Roane, 1997). Therefore there *must* be a link to an altered neurological, material substrate. Neuropsychologists have since documented a variety of unawareness phenomena, with differing neuropathologies and differing aspects of cognitive or physical malfunctioning being negated (see reviews by McGlynn & Schacter, 1989; Vuilleumier, 2004). This has led cognitive neuropsychologists to propose a modularize account of awareness difficulties, separating out general monitoring mechanisms with feed-forward and feedback connections to different cognitive modules (memory, somato-sensory function, etc.), plus an executive component to take this information and make appropriate plans around this (Goldberg & Barr, 1991; Heilman, 1991; McGlynn & Schacter 1989).

These two conceptualizations have sat alongside each other within a partitioned organization. Clinicians and researchers have acknowledged the validity of both a reactive emotional process and a specific neurological substrate, and have proceeded by attempting to differentiate those awareness presentations post-injury, which are the result of either impaired self awareness (ISA) from neurological damage or defensive denial (DD). Initial empirical validation was provided for this distinction (Ownsworth, McFarland & Young, 2002; Prigatano, 1991; 1999; Prigatano & Weinstein, 1996). Differentiations of presentation have been suggested (Havet-Thomassin et al., 2004;

Prigatano, 1999). Also clinical as well as assessment methods have been suggested based on this partition (Prigatano & Klonoff, 1998). Prigatano (1999) subsequently refined this dichotomy to partial and complete sub-categories for ISA and DD. Other authors have provided accounts of how differing neuro-psychological deficits interact with varied defensive emotional processes (Langer, 1992; 1994; 1999; Langer & Padrone, 1992; Lewis, 1989; 1991; Lewis & Rosenberg, 1990; Prigatano, 1991; 1999; Prigatano & Weinstein, 1996; Weinstein & Kahn, 1955).

However, other findings have questioned the validity of the ISA/DD partition and therefore created a conceptual dilemma for neuropsychologists. Ramachandran (1994) reported a series of studies where vestibular stimulation was applied to the ipsi-lesional hemisphere of classic anosognosic patients, following previous reported interventions of this kind (Cappa et al., 1987; Rode et al., 1992). That is, warm water was injected into the right-sided ear of patients who had not been acknowledging their hemi-paretic left-sided limb. During the stimulation, patients suddenly began acknowledging their impairment to the investigator, *and* also acknowledged that they had been denying this when previously asked, before stimulation. However, this effect was only transitory, as after a few minutes patients returned to their initial stance (reality?) that nothing was wrong, and did not acknowledge that they had said anything contrary in the interim. So here we have definite lesions, but a pattern of disability talk (or not) that seems to fit within a dynamic denial picture, but which is controlled by a physical intervention!

Prigatano and Johnson (2003) responded to these findings by a further re-organization of earlier typologies, this time suggesting both organic ISA and organic DD. They stick to their previous association of damaged right frontal and somato-sensory cortices with ISA. In addition, they offer subcortical damage as responsible for DD, drawing on other observations of a denial presentation where such damage has occurred (House & Hodges, 1988; Prigatano, 2002; Vuilleumier, Chicherio, Assal, Schwartz, Slosman, & Landis, 2001). However, Ramachandran's anosognosic patients who received vestibular stimulation would have had neuropathology more fitting with the ISA grouping, suggesting that this neuropathological distinction is not sufficient. Perhaps then, further conceptual work needs to be done. Neuro-psychoanalytic authors suggest that the subjective quality of altered awareness of disability following injury, regardless of aetiology, still follows the same profile and psychic defensive role of denial (Clarici & Giuliani, 2008; Kaplan-Solms & Solms, 2000; Turnbull, 2002). Clinicians have noted that ISA and DD are in most cases actually indistinguishable (Ownsworth, 2005) and even neuroscientists have acknowledged that a motivated element may be a universal factor for any specific neuropathology (Vuilleurmier, 2004).

The hidden inter-personal dimension

But is something missing here? Is this pursuit of emotional versus neuro-cognitive unawareness missing another dimension entirely? In all of these studies, the patient reported on their disability status to *another*. An investigator, researcher, or clinician, asking specific questions and directing attention to certain aspects of experience. The development of second-order cybernetics in systemic family therapy drew attention to 'observing systems', clinicians, and researchers influencing and existing as part of the social phenomena they observe (e.g., Boscolo, Cecchin, Hoffman, & Papp, 1987; Cecchin, 1987; Von Foerster, 1982). This inter-personal dimension cannot even be separated from the vestibular stimulation studies. It is unclear how anosognosic patients would behave on their own in the absence of an observational presence. However, from a dialogical perspective (e.g., Bakhtin & Holquist, 1982), even physical solitude will be an inner conversation of past beliefs/voices/witnessing and current experience.

In fact, the nature of questions posed by another has been shown to be a pivotal influence on the resultant account of disability provided by survivors. Concise questioning resulted in more concordance in the ratings between people with ABI and their relatives, compared with open-ended questions (Gasquoine, 1992; Gasquoine & Gibbons, 1994; Sherer, Boake, Levine et al., 1998; Sohlberg, Mateer, Penman, Ginny, & Todis, 1998; Steel, Kreutzer, & Sander, 1997). Marcel, Tegnér, and Nimmo-Smith (2004) observed that anosognosic patients are more likely to acknowledge their deficit if this is discussed in third-person form as opposed to first-person form, and if the question refers to a specific episode as opposed to a generic fact. In addition, there is an effect on occasion if the emotional tone of the questions is altered, asking questions to a survivor in a hushed, whispered, conspiratorial tone! Jaffe and Slote (1958) describe further inter-personal influences with these patients, and Ramachandran (2004) has recently identified a striking influence on anosognosic patients' disclosure of disability when he 'forewarns' them in advance that they will soon be hemiparetic on one side following an injection (of what is in reality a saline solution). Fotopoulou and colleagues (2009) have used videos and mirrors, conceptualized as creating a third-person perspective in an 'outside' relationship to the self, to effect permanent changes in a patient's awareness of hemiplegia. In asking ABI respondents to rate their level of physical disability in terms of 'present self', 'past self', 'future self', 'typical person', and 'head-injured person', Tyerman and Humphrey (1984) found that while participants rated present and future selves unrealistically, they reported numerous changes in their present versus past selves. Finally, experimental studies have demonstrated that people with neuro-disability who will deny their own deficits will recognize and acknowledge those deficits are externalized onto another person, such as a carer or described in a vignette (McGlynn & Kaszniak, 1991; Reisberg, Gordon, McCarthy, & Ferris, 1985).

Psychoanalytic observers have reported on the fluctuations of disability accounts during psychotherapy sessions with this clinical group (Clarici & Giuliani, 2008; Kaplan-Solms & Solms, 2000; Turnbull et al., 2002). They note that momentary acknowledgements of disability and loss, and associated experiences of intense sadness are produced by questions, interpretations, or conversational content that centre on loss, within the developed psychotherapeutic relationship. However, these moments quickly revert back to indifference, lack of affect, minimization, or unacknowledgement of disability, noted to be similar to the temporary effect of vestibular stimulation (Kaplan-Solms & Solms, 2000). An interesting comparison was provided by Clarici and Giuliani (2008) who reported on parallel psychotherapies of a female survivor of ABI and her daughter, both organized within the mother's lack of awareness of her deficits (see below for details). Whereas the psychotherapist's interpretations/constructions allowed the developmentally immature daughter (in terms of age) to work through her feelings of loss and progress across sessions, the mother's momentary glimpses of awareness were never sustainable in response to the same therapeutic intervention.

One of the authors of this book (GY) developed an interest in a relational understanding of awareness phenomena following ABI, after observing how within a neuro-rehabilitation unit the organic, biological accounts of awareness dominated all thinking regarding certain clients ("he's got no insight because of his brain injury"). As we have seen, there is an intimate connection between brain injury and account of disability, but not in an interactional vacuum. Rehabilitation staff, in their focus on the interiority of the survivor's brain, were less interested in the conversational patterns between them and the survivor, which prompted the awareness judgement (Staff: "you have a memory problem" … Survivor: "no I haven't, get off my case". … Staff: "yes you have, why can't you see?". … Survivor: "f*** off!"). This amounts to a direct confrontation of defensive posturing, an accusatory stance that does not acknowledge the power differential of professionals making value judgements about intimate attributes at the core of one's identity/self. At the same time, it is his or her own reality while in a state of extreme confusion.

These interactions definitely have a part to play, and the aforementioned literature point to conversation and relationship as important parameters for awareness of disability.

As noted already, isolated survivors are always within a relationship with themselves, which may be more or less influenced by relationships with others. Feinberg and Roane (2003a; 2003b) consider anosognosia to feature as alterations to a continuum of personal relatedness or significance. That is, an alteration to a relationship between the self and a part of the body. In this sense, anosognosia can be compared to misoplegia and somatoparaphrenia, where hemi-paretic limbs are experienced as alien, or babies, often existing within quite hated and persecutory relationships (e.g., Morin, Thibierge, Bruguiere, Pradat-Diehl, & Mazavet, 2005; Moss & Turnbull, 1996).

Finally, in addition to relatedness, meaning and agency are further dimensions of accounting of disability. A passive lack of input or content implied in some purely neuro-cognitive accounts, and even specified as producing a lack of eventual 'discovery' regarding one's deficits and their impact. While passivity may be a feature in some presentations, other authors have placed an emphasis on the survivor's agentic, purposeful search for meaning, regardless of how accurate their account is judged by others (Clare, 2003; 2004). Neuro-psychoanalytic authors have agreed with this focus, with a caveat that this agency is mediated by a need to avoid the distress of the disability, hence the split or fragmented nature of survivor's accounts (Clarici & Giuliani, 2008; Kaplan-Solms & Solms 2000; Moss & Turnbull, 1996; Turnbull, 2002; Weinstein & Kahn, 1955).

But how does a survivor's search for meaning sit alongside a similar process for relatives? There has traditionally been a partitioning of literature and phenomenology for the sense-making/adjustment of survivors and their significant others (Yeates, 2007). That is, the neuro-psychological anosognosia literature for survivors and briefer, separate considerations of denial and staged adjustment of relatives, with little attempt to identify inter-relationships between these. As with the presence of other persons in the observations noted above, the wider interactional and social context of sense-making needs to be identified to fully appreciate the significance of this for awareness.

The wider socio-cultural context of sense-making following ABI

The importance of the wider social context for awareness of disability following neurological damage has been graphically illustrated by a collection of cross-cultural studies of awareness. Prigatano and Leathem (1993) compared New Zealand TBI participants with either English or Maori ancestry on a discrepancy rating measure of awareness (Patient Competency Rating Scale [PCRS]), Prigatano, Altman, & O'Brien, 1990). Those participants from English ancestry typically overestimated their competencies in social and emotional functioning, consistent with previous studies using American participants (Prigatano, Altman, & O'Brien, 1990). Interestingly, Maori participants responded differently, reporting a level of competency far below that of either their English-New Zealand counterparts or their relatives. However, a confounding variable was identified in this study, as the Maori participants had a higher incidence of left hemisphere dysfunction, limiting cultural interpretation.

To further explore cultural influences, a second study was conducted with Japanese TBI participants, again using the PCRS (Prigatano, Ogano, & Akamusa, 1997). In contrast to American TBI participants, Japanese respondents did not overestimate their competencies in social and emotional functioning, but did overestimate their abilities to perform self-care activities. The authors interpreted this trend as indicating the greater social cost of disclosing dependence in terms of self-care. The influence of culture has also been demonstrated in participants with dementia (Gianotti, 1975). In this study, Northern Italian dementia patients from a Roman Catholic background exhibited less denial of illness than Swiss dementia patients from Calvanistic Protestant heritage. It would appear that culture determines the degree to which people are willing or able to disclose their problems, and also that individuals self-report on the basis of the information they have to hand, which may be in part due to their cultural lens. The CMM, (Pearce & Cronen, 1980; Pearce, 2007) mentioned in chapter 2 acknowledges that in order to understand discrepancies which arise, it is helpful to unpick the layers of meaning that surround a social event (remembering the content of each speech act can also be viewed as a specific episode, located within a relationship, and within a cultural context, see case example below). These communication theorists provide an extension to Bateson's (1972) seminal application of Logical Type theory to familial constructed meanings. These authors have specifically applied this framework to analysing the process of Milan systemic therapy (Cronen, Johnson, & Lannamann, 1982).

While these cross-cultural studies powerfully draw clinician's awareness to the social dimension, more micro-level contexts such as family-level interactions are influential (Yeates, Henwood, Gracey, & Evans, 2007). Availability and presentation of clear information was found to be one of the most important perceived needs of families after TBI (Hayes & Coetzer, 2003; Yeates, Henwood, Gracey, & Evans, 2007). However, evidence suggests that there are few basic socio-cultural sense-making resources outside of TBI specialist professional frameworks to aid any person's understanding of the physical and cognitive changes associated with brain injury. As described in chapter 2, a study by Swift and Wilson (2001) indicates that both general public and non-specialist health professionals have inaccurate beliefs concerning the recovery and diversity of problems experienced by survivors. Gregory (1998) even notes a lack of basic language appropriate to describe the experience of TBI.

This would suggest that it is unsurprising that the accounts of change from both people with TBI and relatives differ from the specialist discourse of neuro-rehabilitation professionals (Elliot & Remenyi, 1982; Fordyce & Roueche, 1986; Lanham, Weissenburger, Schwab, & Rosner, 2000; Malec, Machulda, & Moessner, 1997; Sunderland, Harris, & Gleave, 1984). The consistent finding that both people with TBI and relatives are aware of physical TBI seque-lae (Fischer, Trexler, & Gauggel, 2004; Levine & Zigler, 1975; Malia, 1997; Sherer, Boake, Levine et al., 1998) is also understandable, as in contrast to subtle cognitive deficits, physical difficulties are more recognizable within lay frameworks.

A qualitative inquiry of changing awareness in people with TBI by Dirette (2002) showed that the key points of transition commonly resulted from comparisons between current and pre-morbid performances on a meaningful, salient aspect of functioning. The importance of a meaningful dimension of comparison has been acknowledged in a doctor's own-account of denial following TBI (La Baw, 1966; 1967; 1968a; 1968b; 1969), who used aspects from both professional and personal contexts to eventually make sense of changes. The comparison of self and other people with greater impairment has been identified as influential for awareness in the dementia literature (Clare, 2002; Hutchinson, Leger-Krall, & Skodol Wilson, 1997).

The relevance for pre-morbid discourse and meaning, including those pertaining to the self, to structure embodied experience in relation to others after ABI has been noted by several authors (Clare, 2004; Prigatano & Weinstein, 1996; Weinstein, 1991; Weinstein, Cole, Mitchell, & Lyerly, 1964; Weinstein, Friedland, & Wagner, 1994; Weinstein & Khan, 1955; Yeates, Henwood, Gracey, & Evans, 2006; Yeates, Henwood, Gracey, & Evans, 2007). Nochi has noted how such sense-making and self re-construction is dependent on others and relationships (1997; 1998a; 1998b; 2000). It is through the re-negotiation of old roles, forging of new relationships that people with TBI develop a sense of identity once more, and a coherent narrative to account for their experiences.

These studies suggest that sense-making resources are embedded within social relationships, if it is not the social relationships themselves that may be the most important sense-making resource. Haslam and colleagues (2008) have shown how multiple group membership strengthens social identity after stroke and seems to offer a number of neuro-psychological and mental health protective functions. Collectively, these studies suggest that awareness of change in both people with ABI and their relatives, while dependent on psycho-education from professionals, is also dependent on pre-morbid sense-making resources within social contexts and relationships, and the active dimension of sense making is inherently a social one.

The differing sense-making resources used by people with ABI and families to understand the changes following injury occurs in parallel with the social act of defining awareness and its associated deviations. Professional definitions, which form the ontological basis for scientific inquiry into awareness phenomena and associated clinical interventions, have recently received a deconstructive analysis in both psychosis and dementia research. Specifically, authors have drawn attention to the socially situated nature of professional awareness definitions, identifying cultural differences (Kirmayer & Corin, 1998), and have even located Western psychiatric constructions of awareness within a specific historical lineage of ontology (Berrios & Marková, 1998).

A reflection of the definition of awareness in professional discourse is desirable for clinicians working in brain injury. It is evident that the use of the term *anosognosia* beyond a description of unawareness of hemiplegia (e.g., Kihlstrom & Tobias, 1991) serves the rhetorical purpose of maintaining an intrapsychic construction, even when discussing a person's awareness of behaviours subject to subtle social judgements (e.g., unconventional behaviours). This linking of the latter to the more extreme, less controversial unawareness of hemiplegia negates the relative uncertainty of the latter phenomenon. A content analysis of the use of the term 'insight' or a synonym in psychiatric and psychological texts highlighted the lack of clarity in the terms' definition and operationalization (Bond, Corner, Lilley, & Ellwood, 2002).

It can be seen that the social context influences and gives form to the resultant accounts of disability drawn upon by survivors, and also structures the practices (differentially by relatives and clinicians) by which these accounts are judged to be evidence of a lack of awareness. Authors have tried to make closer links between contextual parameters and altered neurology. Prigatano (1999) has speculated that following damage to frontal and anterior temporal cortices, there is a deficit in personal awareness of socially relevant conventions for a given cultural background. Morin and colleagues (2005) note how following right ABI the relationship between a survivor and their hemi-paretic limb is structured through axes of gender and culture (feminine, maternal relations). Similarly, in their study of anosognosia for plegia, Marcel and colleagues (2004) observed that male participants were more likely to overestimate driving abilities than female participants, implicating the gendered nature of the social cost of such deficits (Vuilleurmier, 2004).

Weinstein and colleagues have shown that the way in which these pre-injury contextual meanings will be drawn upon by the survivor can in itself be altered by certain cognitive deficits (Prigatano & Weinstein, 1996; Weinstein, 1991; Weinstein, Cole, Mitchell, & Lyerly, 1964; Weinstein, Friedland, & Wagner, 1994; Weinstein & Khan, 1955). Others have provided comprehensive biopsychosocial frameworks of awareness of disability following neuro-disability, which identify neuro-psychological, psychological, and contextual factors (Clare, 2004; Ownsworth, Clare, & Morris, 2006; Toglia & Kirk, 2000).

These accounts are important in situating altered neurology within social context. However they remain rather static, and require an integration within those studies above that identify the immediate inter-personal conditions that influence the particular content of survivor's accounts. In addition, we are left wondering how those accounts of change and disability from relatives and significant others sit alongside those by survivors. As described in the CMM model (Pearce, 2007), speech acts are embedded within social and cultural contexts and within a time frame, so understanding past events is crucial to understanding current interactions.

Dynamics of sense-making: Organization, negotiation, and contestation

Few studies have actually looked at how accounts of disability actually come to be held within a given system. A few studies have described shared denial, or 'anosognosia by proxy' (Butler & Light, 2003), where several people around a person with neuro-disability come to provide similar accounts of disability, all of which may seem incongruous with 'bare facts' about a disease or condition. This trend has been shown to organize family members *and* the professionals working with them (Butler & Light, 2003; Glaser & Straus, 1965; Hutchinson, Leger-Krall, & Skodol Wilson, 1997).

In a study of dementia, Hutchinson, Leger-Krall, and Skodol Wilson (1997) demonstrated that in some cases, despite their own suspicions/knowledge of the pathological origins of dementia-related problems, the person with dementia, family and the general practitioner maintained what Glaser and Strauss (1965) called 'closed awareness contexts'. That is, family members actively engaged in concealing their knowledge from each other. In other families, the authors found that all members maintained a 'mutual pretence awareness context', where all concerned strove to reconstruct the problems as indicative of a non-pathological origins, despite all actually believing the contrary. Similar findings have recently been reported in the context of couple conversations about a diagnosis of dementia (Clare 2002; 2003).

Butler and Light (2003) present cases of parents denying the obvious deficits of their neuro-cognitively disabled children (each with progressive conditions). They wonder if the intimacy of the parent-child relationship is more closely associated with the degree of anosognosia by proxy, although they also note that patient-professional relationships were similarly organized. The hypothesized correlation of denial and relational closeness was taken up by Clarici and Giuliani (2008), in their report of anosognosia by proxy in a nine-year-old daughter, organized by her mother's impaired self-awareness following a TBI. They note that the daughter and grandparents most closely shared the survivor's minimization of hemiparesis and dysarthria, whereas the sisters of the survivor and her ex-husband disputed this account.

While others may dispute how these authors prioritized each relationship along a continuum of closeness, the account of the daughter's minimization of physically obvious motor and speech difficulties is fascinating. Her mother only acknowledged changes in her vision as a result of the accident while minimizing all other motor and somatosensory deficits. Similarly, the daughter would also note that her mother "didn't see too well out of one eye," which she felt was the reason that "mummy sometimes bumps into things." However, she would point out to the therapist, when both walking behind the mother, how normal the mother looked, at the very moment that a pronounced limp was evident. This account stands as a useful contrast to those previously mentioned as this focuses on a static, not deteriorating neuro-disability, without the terminal implications.

Others have highlighted how a survivor's account is far from accepted by others in a family, with this difference being a source of significant distress (Yeates, Henwood, Gracey, & Evans, 2006; Yeates, Henwood, Gracey, & Evans, 2007). Light and colleagues (1995) have shown how initial agreement between survivor and relatives' ratings changed over a year, with relatives' rating moving closer to those of clinicians. Clarici and Giuliani (2008) described in their paper the disputation of a female survivor's account of disability, by her sister and ex-husband from the beginning. In addition, these authors note how the shared denial of the daughter was eventually worked through to a point of loss and mourning in psychotherapy, leaving the brain-injured mother's ongoing minimization of her deficits behind in isolation. From this new point of acceptance of the loss of her once intact mother, the daughter could describe the hopelessness and her frustration regarding her mother's confused account of needs ("mummy's nonsense").

Yeates and colleagues (2006; 2007) draw attention to the micro-detail of contestation in accounts within family contexts. Wider meanings are drawn upon by the survivor and their relatives to make sense of change post-injury. This may be a discourse of personhood, the kind of person the survivor was/continues to be, which the survivors tended to use exclusively to construct their accounts of change. While relatives also drew upon such meanings, they would also use a language of both brain damage ("it's because of the brain injury") and childhood naivety ("he's like a child growing up again") to mark out changes in the survivor's ability and even personhood. These latter meanings had rather different implications for the survivor's agency and responsibility, but were necessary to relatives to manage and explain the unusual and sometimes hurtful actions of the survivor (e.g., a husband's tendency to be mildly sexually inappropriate to waitresses).

It was this difference in meanings used by relatives versus survivors that created both dilemmas and anxieties for all concerned. For survivors, this could be experienced as a very threat to self ("I could have just disappeared"... "they were talking over me rather than with me"), depending on the historical meaning of that particular relationship. In response, this stimulated an effort to orientate relatives to their perspective, to show how they were returning to the person they were before. For the relatives, this orientation was a source of anxiety (worries that the survivor will attempt a facet of independent living before they had sufficient ability to do so), and a further indication of their naivety and was actually used to make an explicit judgement that the survivor lacks awareness. See chapter 7 for a discussion of cases illustrating these dilemmas.

Krefting (1990) uses communication theory and Bateson's framework to explore the inter-relationship between the sense-making of survivors, relatives, and clinicians. She draws attention to the points of intersection and communication between these parties and notes that difference is experienced as threatening, undermining, and prohibitive of further communication. In particular, relatives are positioned in a 'double-bind' of paradoxical communication, where their identities as supportive of the survivor (and by implication their account of change) may not fit with their own differing account. Furthermore, their perspective may also be incongruent. with the narratives of disability from clinicians, and the expectations of support associated with this (see also chapter 4). A collective result is that the pre-injury identities of both survivors and relatives, in relation to each other, are rendered unavailable through the paradoxes within these communicational patterns.

This is significant as others have shown that pre-injury personal and family identities are often needed, romanticized, and idealized in relation to how life actually was before the injury (McGrath, 2004). Yeates and colleagues (2006) noted that when there is an experienced threat to self within the contesting of accounts within families following ABI, pre-injury identities provide much necessary stability and meaning, and perhaps are resultantly drawn upon in much less flexible ways compared with that pre-injury. Shared stories of the minimization of difficulties may be more indicative of the presence of a shared culture with a degree of pull or power over its members. Stories of disputes over accounts of difficulties often have personal significance in terms of people's identities and it is for this reason that they sometimes become ongoing loops of contestation.

Intervention: Mediation, truce talks, and building uneasy alliances?

Current interventions within the awareness literature have not produced satisfying results. The main application of the neuro-psychological frameworks is the view that the unaware person is an 'information processor' with a faulty monitoring mechanism. The suggested remedial action is to provide the missing feedback exter-nally when the deficit occurs, normally from rehabilitation staff and family members. This widely used approach varies in its format, encompassing feedback provided verbally (Coetzer & Corney, 2001; Fordyce & Roueche, 1986; Prigatano & Fordyce, 1986), reviewing video recordings (Ylvisaker & Szekeres, 1989; Youngjohn & Altman, 1989), based on predicted/actual performance data (McGlynn, Schacter, & Glisky, 1989), given situationally, in post-hoc review sessions, as part of a behavioural program (Bieman-Copeland & Bywan, 2000), and in supervised functional, work, or community settings (Ben-Yishay, Silver, Piasetsky, & Rattock, 1987), individu-ally or in groups (Deaton, 1986; Wachter, Fawber, & Scott, 1987). Feedback is often provided following psychoeducation regarding consequences of brain injury (Prigatano & Fordyce, 1986; Szekeres, Ylvisaker, & Cohen, 1987; Ylvisaker, Szekeres, Henry, Sullivan, & Wheeler, 1987).

The provision of feedback has also been modified in several ways to address limitations in traditional formats. To address defensive responses, an approach of couching negative feedback regarding problems between positive feedback has been suggested (Sherer, Boake, Levine, et al., 1998). It has been noted that a subtle changing of the way the feedback is worded can result in greater acceptance by people with awareness problems (Feher, Mahurin, & Pirozzolo, 1990). This is interesting in itself, but not unexpected given the insights of the CMM model. A further problem is that verbal feedback is often ineffective for more severely injured people, especially if they have comprehension problems. In response to this barrier, Alderman and colleagues (Alderman & Burgess, 1994; Alderman, Fry, & Youngson, 1995; Alderman & Ward, 1991) advocate the more efficacious use of adjunctive behavioural methods such as response cost procedures, which are considered to utilize intact implicit memory abilities (Knight, Rutterford, Alderman, & Swan, 2002).

Despite these modifications to the feedback procedure, the evidence for the effectiveness of these interventions remains limited to single-case studies (e.g., Bieman-Copeland & Bywan, 2000), which some authors feel is inadequate (Fleming & Strong, 1995). Other authors question the generalizability of these approaches outside the rehabilitation setting (Butters, Glisky, & Schacter, 1993; Schacter, 1991; Youngjohn & Altman, 1989), and even the efficacy of many of the interventions in any context (Bieman-Copeland & Bywan, 2000). Some authors argue against more confrontational feedback approaches (Moore, Stambrook, & Peters, 1989; Novack, Berquist, Bennet, & Gouvier, 1991; Ylvisaker & Feeney, 1998; Ylvisaker & Szekeres, 1989), noting that such approaches can have a negative effect on self-esteem, and recursively maintain unawareness (see Toglia & Kirk's model, 2000). A confrontational feedback approach is arguably against the ethos of working within the person with ABI's 'phenomenological field', a key principle of neuro-psychological rehabilitation advocated by Prigatano (1999).

In contrast, psychoanalytical authors have described intricate therapeutic work seeking to respond to the changing microfluctuations of awareness, using the therapeutic relationship as a vehicle to enable access to feelings of loss and sadness and facilitate acceptance and working through. While contributing to our understanding of the inter-personal conditions for changing accounts of disability, these pieces of work are aimed at individual survivors (Kaplan-Soms & Solms, 2000), or parallel separate therapy sessions for survivors and relatives (Clarici & Guilani, 2008). All report disappointing results, with moments of acknowledgement of disability not being sustained beyond periods of minutes. Other authors have used the questionable ISA/DD partition to specify differing interventions for differing forms of unawareness following ABI, with the latter being suited to conventional psychotherapy and the former benefiting from psychoeducation, group rehabilitation, and graded activity participation with systematic feedback (Ownsworth & Clare, 2006).

Clarici and Giuliani (2008) question this technical separation, noting that all of these techniques represent the building of a relationship with survivors one way or another. It can be argued that individual-focused interventions of any kind do nothing to respond to the disconnections within families as a result of disagreement and differing accounts of disability. Findings from rehabilitation outcome research also point to the interplay of awareness difficulties for clients, reduced working alliance with clinicians, and poorer rehabilitation outcome (Schoenberger et al., 2006a; 2006b; 2006c). These and other findings have collectively prompted clinicians to propose whole organizational structures of interdisciplinary rehabilitation programmes based on a process of increasing awareness and adjustment (Wilson, Bateman, & Evans, 2009; see chapter 7 for this and adjunct model for relatives-clinicians sense-making).

If it is indeed the quality of relationships that is important for sense-making in both rehabilitation and family contexts, perhaps then, a mediator's or peace-keeper's approach to this work *would* be welcomed, bringing all aggrieved groups to the table? A systemic approach would definitely suggest some novel ways forward. Through this approach, the goal is never to 'persuade' the injured person of how they are different and 'changed for the worse' since the injury, but rather the goal is for the family or relational system to find a way of talking about what they each see as different in themselves and in each other. Thus, opening up a new conversation where people can feel safer to talk and explore their perception because the 'truth' is not being pursued. This can be beneficial because although the non-injured relatives or professionals might be 'technically correct' that the injured person is more at risk in some way since the injury, their repeated highlighting of this risk and attempts to recruit others (e.g., other professionals or relatives) into this 'lesson' is not successful in reducing risk; creating a safe way of exploring change without an 'ultimate truth' bares more hope for potential resolution.

As per recommendations elsewhere in this book, an initial step would be to map out all of the meanings and beliefs within a given 'awareness context', their socio-historical origins, and importantly who is involved in these ideas and how are relationships and communication organized by these differences (Anderson, Goolishian, & Winderman, 1986). Circular questions of degree and difference (Cecchin, 1987; Penn, 1982; 1985; Tomm, 1987; 1988) would be useful in developing curiosity with a family (and other clinicians) about the static or changing nature of this difference: "Who agrees most with this (e.g., the survivor's) story of change? Who agrees least? What is it like for those not in agreement, what dilemmas does this create for you as a family? Are these positions always taken by those concerned?" The neuro-cognitive expectation of family members as neutral providers of feedback (Cotrell, 1997) must be carefully evaluated in the light of a systemic formulation, with the meaning of such feedback markedly different depending on who in the family it is and the history of their relationship (see also chapter 5).

To open up any initial divides between the stories of change from a family and those of professionals, reflecting team conversations (Andersen, 1987) and/or the use of narrative therapy's (White & Epston, 1990) community witnessing techniques from community user accounts of ABI could be used to explore multiple perspectives within all groups. This is a very different approach to that taken traditionally. Instead of increasing feedback and expecting convergence, access to feedback from a multi-verse of perspectives illuminates divergence. However, the timing of such approaches will need to be considered here, with psycho-education and the communication of certainties perhaps more necessary sooner to the onset of the injury and the loosening up of rigid narratives more important when these outlive their usefulness.

However, narrative therapy may offer something else of extreme value for building peace and reconnection in the context of disagreement and difference in sense-making within a family following ABI, which is the technique of 'externalizing'. This involves the conversational repositioning of the problem outside of particular persons, constructed as a source of difficulty affecting people collectively. The result of this reconstruction is that two or more people who were initially divided by the location of the problem in one person can then collaborate in unison against something external to themselves.

Case study
Using CMM to formulate family contestation and an awareness impasse *1. Background:* Paolo sustained a diffuse severe injury at the age of 19 after falling from some scaffolding, although there was a right frontal and parietal focus. His mother is English and father, who

passed away when Paolo was 10, was Spanish. Throughout all of his teenage and early adult life Paolo had occupied the role of man of the house, looking after his mother following the father's death. He held down 2 part-time jobs and took driving lessons while studying for A-Levels and left school at 18 to work as a builder, to earn some hard cash, create some future financial security and eventually run his own construction company. His mother has always been proud of her son's independent and driven spirit, seeing so much of her husband in him. The injury left him with several enduring problems: altered gait and mobility, together with executive, attentional and memory problems.

2. Points of contestation:

Five years post-injury Paolo was keen to return to driving and work. His motto was to 'get on with it'. He did not see or acknowledge that he had any residual difficulties, apart from 'forgetting things now and again like we all do'. When his difficulties in walking, planning, attending and memory were brought to his attention, often in an exasperated way by his concerned mother, Paolo would become angry and disengage from brain injury services all together.

3. Dynamics of contestation:

There were clear neuro-cognitive error monitoring difficulties and a very passionate emotionally-driven process for Paolo that served to ward of difficult thoughts, images and experiences of a disabled self. However these were situated and structured within a virulent dynamic perpetuated between mother, son and services. The CMM model was used to formulate the clash of relational meanings at the core of this dynamic:

Cultural pattern: Western autonomy & productivity; gender roles

Family myth: Immigration narrative, building up from grass roots ?

Life script: Getting on with it, it's up to Paolo to provide ?

Relationship: Mother as vulnerable to Paolo as protector ?

Episode: Mother being looked after by Paolo, heir apparent ?

Speech act: Vulnerable Paolo being supported by mother ?

Cognitive Difficulties   ABI team invited to improve awareness

Content: Mother trying to support Paolo to see his new limitations

The example of Paolo's mother not reciprocating his 'unaware' efforts to return to driving and work can be seen to contradict higher order levels of meaning within the family which have previously been exerting a downward influence. The result, represented as a bottom-up set of influences, is Paolo's experience of not being recognised meaningfully for whom he still feels he is. Equally his mother is positioned in an unfamiliar role, caring and not being cared for. This completes the 'strange loop' (Pearce and Cronen, 1980) where-upon the meaning of an episode of support with reference to both discourses is violated, unable to be sustained through bottom-up constitutive communication.

4. Meaning of possible rehabilitation interventions given (3):

As a service we had to align ourselves within Paolo's discourse of self to not be seen as a mechanism of disempowerment or betrayal by the mother. We also had to respect her genuine anxieties for Paolo over-stepping his competencies. Our solution was to use a professional language of contracting with Paolo, getting him to pick good people to take care of some key tasks in the family week or support him to do so (both maintaining his responsible role), to free him up for quality time with his mother.

The use of externalizing following ABI is described elsewhere in this book and beyond (Murray & Yeates, in preparation). However, externalizing conversations may have specific value for a family locked into a contesting dynamic about who holds the most accurate account and who are left stuck by the implications of such difference. Instead, family members can be invited to collaboratively respond to the externalized threat of 'disagreement' and its influence of family communication (Yeates, Henwood, Gracey, & Evans, 2007), even if this is initially an uneasy, shaky alliance in the shadow of the former disagreement. From the studies reviewed above, the reader may notice an interesting dovetail of family therapy and neuroscience. A similar conversational framing is used by experimental neuropsychologists to show people with awareness difficulties to be more able to identify a problem if it is framed as external to themselves, such as in the third person, in a vignette, or with reference to another person (Marcel, Tegner, & Nimmo-Smith, 2004; McGlynn & Kasniak, 1991; Reisberg et al., 1990).

Conclusions

As promised in the introduction, we have completed a circular journey from neurology to dyadic interactions to wider social contexts, notably that of the family, and back to a reconnection with neuropsychological findings. The link between neurology and context seems to be around the creation of relationships within conversation and sense-making. Relationships between observing self and observed experience (with and without the direction of others), relationships with at times painful feelings that are evoked as part of this, relationships with others in the accounts that are made public, the difference that emerges in relation to the accounts of those others, and the dynamics of proxy agreements or contestations that are the stuff of this difference. If one takes an epistemological and therapeutic orientation that engages with the level of relationship (involving all parties concerned), then several new therapeutic options are created, addressing an area of clinical need. These ideas are provisional and require further studies to substantiate what kind of conversational repositionings are more or less fruitful for contesting family interactions.

CHAPTER SEVEN

Building a family-therapist alliance

Introduction

ABI can result in a multitude of changes to the injured individual, which impact upon individual and family functioning. The impact of ABI on the family has been researched extensively since seminal papers raised awareness of this area of need (Panting & Merry, 1972; Romano, 1974; Walker, 1972). Subsequent studies also report significant changes in family functioning after ABI (Curtiss, Klemz, & Vanderploeg, 2001; Ergh, Rapport, Coleman, & Hanks, 2002; Jacobs, 1991; Perlesz, Kinsella, & Crowe, 1999; Testa, Malec, Moessner, & Brown, 2006). A majority of investigations report a negative impact of ABI on the injured person's family members (Brooks & McKinlay, 1983; Gervasio & Kreutzer, 1997; Kreutzer, Gervasio, & Camplair, 1994a; Livingston & Brooks, 1988), especially spouses and partners (Blais & Boisvert, 2005; Burridge, Williams, Yates, Harris, & Ward, 2007; Perlesz, Kinsella, & Crowe, 1999) However, in their critical review of psychological and marital adjustment, Blais and Boisvert (2005) suggest that there are differential effects on the family, depending on the severity of injury, stage of recovery, and type of relationship to the injured person (e.g., partner vs. parent). It would appear that while this distinction has the potential to clarify matters, the most consistent finding appears to be the third of these variables—that partners uniformly show greater distress than parents, who may be considered as resorting back to old familiar protective roles, particularly for injured young adults. In contrast, couples are challenged by a particular set of problems, largely due to increased responsibilities within the family for one partner and a general loss of intimacy, as well as cognitive-behavioural sequelae such as an increased level of mood swings in the injured partner (Woods, 2005). The level and quality of strain can also depend on the localization and extent of the injury, and on the prognosis of the condition. For example, levels of strain and ability to cope are influenced by whether the condition is seen as non-degenerative (such as after TBI), relapsing-remitting (such as MS) or progressive (such as Alzheimer's disease or Huntington's disease). Rolland (1994) has developed these ideas further into an integrative model, arguing that the way chronic illness affects the family depends on a number of factors such as the:

1. Psychosocial dimensions (onset, course or progression, outcome, incapacitation, level of uncertainty);
2. Time-related stages or factors (crisis or diagnosis, chronic, terminal, also aspects of transition and adaptation);
3. Key family life-cycle issues (e.g., if children are involved, are they living at home or do they live close by?).

Moreover, in the case of a life-threatening illness or injury, the process of family adaptation to has been likened to "navigating uncharted territory" (Steele, 2005). In a very graphic illustration, Moore, Stanbrook, and Peters (1993) describe the effects of an ABI in terms of centripetal forces bringing the family together (family coping style, marital adjustment, number of years married) and centrifugal forces forcing them apart (number of children, age of oldest child, amount of perceived financial strain). Overall, a key task for any therapist is to map out the incidence of predisposing vulnerability factors and heightened risk (Rolland & Williams 2006), and for this a bio-psycho-social-family framework is useful.

Emotional adjustment of family members

Rates of family dysfunction after ABI are reported as occurring in 25–74% of families affected (Testa, Malec, Moessner, & Brown, 2006) depending upon the measures, samples, and definitions of dysfunction used. Negative emotional responses and adjustment reactions of family members are commonly described and measured as anxiety, depression, and caregiver burden (Perlesz, Kinsella, & Crowe, 1999). Although sample sizes, methodologies, and some bias in interpretation of measures prevents clear conclusions about prevalence and severity of distress among family and caregivers (Perlesz, Kinsella, & Crowe, 1999), the literature does draw attention to the significant need among some (but not all) of this population. A recent investigation by Rivera and colleagues (Rivera, Elliott, Berry, Grant, & Oswald, 2007) investigated factors predictive of depression in carers of people with a TBI. In a sample of 60 carers, they identified 29 care-givers who met criteria for depression and reported that ineffective problem-solving, negative, avoidant, and impulsive response styles were predictive of depression, in addition to whether the caregiver reported physical symptoms of depression. These factors were not associated with length of time caregiving, perceived burden, or other demographic variables.

Research indicates that the well-being of family members, and the family functioning as a unit, is not separate from the rehabilitation of the individual with ABI. Rather than being separate, studies indicate that improved family functioning is associated with reductions in disability and increased employability of the person with the injury (Horwitz, Horwitz, Orsini, Antoine, & Hill, 1998; Sander et al., 2002). Gan and colleagues (Gan, Campbell, Gemeinhardt, & McFadden, 2006) report significantly higher distress in families effected by brain injury compared to normative samples and concluded that high levels of caregiver strain related to poorer system functioning as measured using the Family Assessment Measure-III (FAM-III) (Skinner, Steinhauer, & Santa-Barbara, 1984), and they also reported that poor-problem-solving (a specific subscale of the FAM-III) by the family as a unit was also related to poor family adjustment and system functioning.

While couples and children have the biggest adjustment to make, it should be noted that brain injury typically impacts on every member of the family. Family adjustment to ABI is an emotional journey, and in psychological terms makes demands on individuals that require an understanding of one's own psychological make-up and the ability not to react to what are likely to be intense emotions. Among the emotions commonly reported are guilt, frustration, relief, 'utter sadness', loss, despair, and empathetic pain due to the contrast between one's own subjective quality of life and that of the injured individual. Love is really pushed to its limits.

The complexity of emotions that accompanies severe brain injury is seen both in their range and their multi-faceted nature. The multi-faceted nature of emotions can be illustrated in terms of a dialectical model (Bowen, Madill, & Stratton, 2002). In this sense, emotions of guilt may be acted upon because the underlying components are not recognized, such as anxiety; anxiety may be due to not knowing exactly what caused the injury or as a result of feeling out-of-control with respect to what happens in the life of another person. As we have noted in earlier chapters, misunderstandings can also result from a limited knowledge of the brain and processes of rehabilitation, which again may be acted upon. By its very nature, the outcome of a brain injury is difficult to predict, making it difficult for professionals to give an accurate prognosis (Lefebvre & Levert, 2006; Lefebvre, Pelchat, & Levert, 2007; Lefebvre, Pelchat, Swaine, Gelinas, & Levert, 2005). So relatives may be frustrated in their attempts to seek out information, and instead people can be prone to attack others who are seen as the holders of that knowledge.

The emotions that people go through following ABI are often likened to a bereavement; generally thought to proceed via denial, yearning, protest, or anger, and finally, adjustment to the new situation (Chwalisz, 1998; Lezak, 1986). It is often noted that there is no typical bereavement process and that everyone is unique. For the family members of people after ABI, the experience of grieving can be likened to 'disenfranchised grief' (Doka, 1989) as losses for them and their family are multiple, yet the injured person is alive and so grief is often left unrecognized by society. In many ways, the stage is set for people not to identify their experience as grief, and to resign themselves to be 'in it for the long-haul', instead viewing the brain injury as a test of character, commitment or faith.[1] In addition, the

---

[1] There are other situations in which humans become accustomed to uncertain, albeit time-limited waiting in the service of life, as seen for example, in pregnancy.

dynamic of time is at play in that individuals can appear 'frozen' or 'stuck' in time, which is a recognized reaction to trauma as a person relives the events that led up to the injury, to find an alternative ending. There is no guarantee that family members will move forward at the same rate or even reach a similar 'place'. The ability of the system to move beyond this status, relates to their shared resources, resilience, and coping styles.

Families also maintain their hope long into recovery, and sometimes such hope, is contrary to medical opinion. Although often labelled as 'denial' and failure to accept the medical information, hope can be seen as adaptive and sometimes necessary for family coping (DePompei & Williams, 1994) and for future-oriented action. For example, in a series of interviews with family members after ABI (Palmer, Herbert, & Vetere, *in prep*) one interviewee explained that even after eight years *"… I suppose in the back of my mind I know [she won't get completely better] … but I just hope some miracle will happen."*

In terms of studies of carers and relatives, there has been a general bias towards the assumption that ABI will bring about negative (or pathological) emotions in family members, for example, when sadness becomes depression. Research samples have often been selected from support groups, so the sample will be biased in favour of people seeking support; those who are coping are unlikely to be members of such groups. Furthermore, Perlesz, Kinsella, and Crowe (1999) note in their review of papers prior to 1999 that researchers have often simplified the adjustment process or quantification of distress and re-analysis of the data indicates that there is likely to be many family members whose resilience has not been documented. They note the lack of literature investigating the families who have adjusted and coped well; resilience among relatives of people with ABI is generally an under-researched area.

This bias is the focus of a new 'Positive Psychology' movement (Seligman & Csikszentmihalyi, 2000), and in the field of brain injury this has stimulated new studies, for example, examining when post-traumatic stress disorder becomes post-traumatic growth (McGrath & Linley, 2006). Blais and Boisvert (2005) summarized that problem-solving skills, positive reinterpretation of problems, low avoidance, and low levels of magical thinking are associated with higher adjustment (p. 1231) for the individual with the injury and their caregivers. Evidence emerging from other studies challenges the stereotype that brain injury will naturally lead to separation and divorce in the family (e.g., Kreutzer, Marwitz, Hsu, Williams, & Riddick, 2007; Wood & Yurdakul, 1997). A qualitative study by Karpman, Wolfe, and Vargo (1986) began to identify themes relating to needs among parents caring for adult children with ABI including themes associated with positive adaptation. Their themes identified co-operation and cohesion within the family, and although the focus of their investigation was not family alliance with professionals, their findings could arguably suggest that co-operation and cohesion with professionals would also relate to positive adaptation.

The relationship between coping and outcome

It has been suggested that the adjustment of the family system influences the outcome of the injured individual (Sander et al., 2002). Of particular importance to relational outcome, is the ability of the injured individual to empathize (Burridge, Williams, Yates, Harris, & Ward, 2007) and the ability of the family system to problem solve and to work together (Leach, Frank, Bouman, & Farmer, 1994; Rivera, Elliott, Berry, & Grant, 2008; Wade, Carey, & Wolfe, 2006). Problems with empathy and poor family problem-solving may be understood by a common impairment in executive functioning; notably in abstract reasoning and flexibility (McDonald, Bornhofen, & Hunt, 2009). Other case study evidence comes from a paper describing the exceptional recovery of a patient with encephalomyelitis (in MCS):

> *"The role of Kate's family and friends in her emotional recovery must not be underestimated. In the context of a highly supportive and understanding family, Kate was given chance to adjust. Without this support, it is unlikely that Kate could have recovered to the extent that she has"*

> (MacNiven et al., 2003, p. 531).

Ability to empathize and ability to problem solve are two skills crucial to coping, according to the original model of coping proposed by Lazarus and Folkman. This model proposes two distinct styles of coping; problem-focused and emotion-focused (Lazarus & Folkman, 1984). *Problem-focused* coping strategies alter or eliminate the source of stress through approaches such as problem-solving. *Emotion-focused* strategies regulate or reduce emotional distress caused by the source of stress, possibly through seeking emotional support or seeking a different perspective of the situation (Avero, Corace, Endler, & Calvo, 2003). In stressful situations people are said to predominantly adopt one style of coping, although most people employ a combination of problem-focused and emotion-focused strategies. A more recent model proposed that coping comprises three factors; task, emotion, and avoidance (Endler & Parker, 1994). Their model incorporated the new dimension of 'avoidance' coping in addition to task-oriented and emotion-oriented style dimensions. In this measure, task-orientation involves problem-solving, but can also involve cognitive restructuring if it is purposeful in finding a solution. Since supporting the use of rehabilitation strategies is purposeful in finding a solution, it is arguably a task-oriented strategy. Information-seeking is also included in this category. The emotion-oriented coping style includes 'emotional responses, self pre-occupation and fantasising' p. 35 (Endler & Parker, 1999). It is orientated towards the individual and intended to reduce stress. Avoidant-oriented coping encompasses attempts to avoid the stressful event, either through activity or thought. Avero, Corace, Endler, and Calvo (2003) comment that avoidant styles are adaptive only for short-term uncontrollable situations and are maladaptive long-term. This could be because individuals do not cognitively process (and thereby experience) the event but maintain high anxiety and psychological arousal, but mechanisms for this process require further investigation.

Different styles have been demonstrated as more or less adaptive depending on whether the stressor is long- or short-term. Literature suggests that perceived control over a situation also mediates the relationship between coping strategy and psychological distress (Avero, Corace, Endler, & Calvo, 2003). When a situation is perceived as changeable, a task-oriented approach is most adaptive because it reduces levels of anxiety and depression, and is related to positive well-being. In support of this, previous studies show an emotion-focused coping style is associated with greater psychological distress than the problem-focused style (Kausar & Powell, 1999). Conversely, when a situation is perceived as unchangeable and out of one's control, an emotion-focused (emotion-oriented) style is more adaptive (Collins, Baum, & Singer, 1983). In an interview study, relatives living with people after ABI talked of a variety of useful coping strategies, depending on available support, the specific nature of the stressor, and the time since injury (Palmer, 2005).

Owing to the variety of challenges that brain injury presents, some of which are controllable and some of which cannot be changed, coping will require a variety of strategies, including use of emotion-oriented strategies, some information-seeking and task-oriented strategies, and even some avoidance (e.g., hope), which may be adaptive in the short term, as described above. Overall, the research in this area is quite advanced and it has been demonstrated that coping style may account for more of the variability in caregivers' psychological health than patient level of functioning (Sander, High, Hannay, & Sherer, 1997). Further research has demonstrated the added value of "collaborative" tasks in memory rehabilitation for dementia patients (e.g., by giving instruction about how to prompt), and also that dimensions of manageability and meaningfulness are predictive of family adaptation to brain injury (Kosciulek, 1997a). This may support task-oriented coping, in that families often gain relief if they can find new priorities and goals to focus on and develop a sense of meaning from caregiving.

Family members as co-therapists?

Clinicians are increasingly aware that optimum outcomes in rehabilitation are achieved when good working relations are maintained with carers and the family and attempts to involve the family have generally been subsumed under the banner of "working collaboratively with families" (Sohlberg, McLaughlin, Todis, Larsen, & Glang, 2001) and the potential benefits of including families in the rehabilitation process are numerous. Included in this is a role for service providers and individual clinicians in supporting families to make sense of and cope with challenges. Using relatives as co-therapists can be useful in terms of consistency of support, and furthermore, families may be the first to observe significant signs of recovery, and interpret early communications or idiosyncratic behaviours in the case of very severe brain injury. While there are reasons to safeguard family members and avoid situations where relatives are seen as replacements for rehabilitation specialists, in some countries rehabilitation relies upon the involvement of relatives and one should not underestimate the potential for families to augment rehabilitation given the frequency of their visits (Judd, 1999).

Along these lines, a range of individual and group interventions, from education to family therapy have been supported in the literature (Andrews & Andrews, 1993; Boschen, Gargaro, Gan, & Gerber, 2007; Christensen, Skaggs, & Kleist, 1997; Lefebvre, Pelchat, & Levert, 2007; Mazzucchi, Cattelani, Cavatorta, Parma, Veneri, et al. 2000; Oddy & Herbert, 2003). In a discussion of service design and outcome measurement (Tyerman, 1999), the need for post-acute, community-based ABI services is highlighted and three forms of family liaison are outlined:

• Collaborating with families in relation to rehabilitative intervention.
• Family information provision and ABI education.
• Family support and if necessary formal family therapy.

Despite this plethora of research documenting the need, a number of small and qualitative intervention studies and numerous anecdotal accounts of positive intervention, the absence of a clear theoretical framework for family interventions after brain injury has been noted (Boschen, Gargaro, Gan, & Gerber, 2007).

Critical components of family interventions in brain injury

There is no strong research evidence supporting any intervention for working with families after brain injury (Boschen, Gargaro, Gan, & Gerber, 2007). This may be because the range of needs is so broad that one approach cannot address the complexity of presenting problems potentially found in this group of families. In the absence of a clear theoretical template for conceptualizing family engagement with services, a range of interventions are described in the literature, for which there is varying empirical support (Boschen, Gargaro, Gan, & Gerber, 2007; Kay & Cavallo, 1994; Kreutzer, Kolakowsky-Hayner, Demm, & Meade, 2002; Lefebvre, Pelchat, & Levert, 2007; Oddy & Herbert, 2003; Rotondi, Sinkule, & Spring, 2005; Serio, Kreutzer, & Gervasio, 1995; Zarski, West, DePompei, & Hall, 1988). Education and support for families of people living with ABI is promoted widely in the literature (Oddy & Herbert, 2003) and is often requested by family members whose relatives are working with rehabilitation professionals. Information alone, whether delivered in written or workshop format, is necessary but not sufficient for clinical and statistical changes to be observed in carers (Morris, 2001; Sinnakaruppan,

Downey, & Morrison, 2005). The timing of information provision, method of delivery and amount of 'jargon' are all important factors in how 'useful' information is perceived to be by receiving family members (Palmer, 2005). The Social Services Inspectorate (1997) recognized the importance of addressing information and support needs, in addition to those of the injured person. The Health Select Committee (2001) also recommended provision of information for family members and recommended greater involvement of families in their relative's recovery and rehabilitation, in addition to separate caregiver support as a means of beginning to address their own adjustment and coping.

In terms of specific therapy models, in New Zealand, Smith and Godfrey (1995) were among the first to describe family interventions based on cognitive-behavioural approaches, whereas in the United States, Padrone (1999) adopted an individual psychotherapeutic approach sensitive to the unique impact that brain injury can have on different family members (depending on variables such as the stage in the patient's life cycle and pre-existing relationships within the family). A more comprehensive programme has been developed in Virginia (USA), described by Kreutzer, Kolakowsky-Hayner, Demm, and Meade (2002). These authors propose five levels of intervention:

1. Family therapy,
2. Marital therapy,
3. Individual therapy,
4. Group therapy, and
5. Bibliotherapy.

The interventions are all underpinned and informed by what they called the 'Brain Injury Family Intervention Curriculum' (Kreutzer, Kolakowsky-Hayner, Demm, & Meade, 2002). Other components of family interventions have been suggested from critical reviews and studies, including: problem-solving with cognitive restructuring (Blais & Boisvert, 2005); positive reappraisal and family tension management (Kosciulek, 1997b); inter-personal empathy skills (Burridge, Williams, Yates, Harris, & Ward, 2007). Taken together, relational interventions applied to a brain injury population need to address particular issues related to problem-solving, positive reappraisal, communication, and intimacy.

Involving relatives and families

From a pragmatic perspective, it is crucial that relatives are involved with the rehabilitation process because their injured relative's recovery is unlikely to be complete and it is probable that family members will assist with care, strategy implementation, prompting, and other tasks post-rehabilitation and be the primary long-term support system for the injured individual (Gan & Schuller, 2002). Therefore, contact with relatives and carers is an essential component of assessment and rehabilitation, and should form part of ongoing support to maintain gains (Department of Health, 2005a; Department of Health, 2007; Gainotti, 1993; Prigatano, 1986; Wilson, 2002). Changes to the physical environment and styles of interaction with their relative may be required (Perlesz, Kinsella, & Crowe, 1999). During rehabilitation, clinicians will offer suggestions about strategies that may help the injured person adapt to disability (Proulx, 1999). Strategies include restorative, compensatory, and behavioural approaches. These strategies are usually recommended for continued use during home visits and after discharge. Proulx relates the extent to which relatives continue to support strategies, to the alliance held between relatives and clinicians during rehabilitation.

Contact with relatives has a range of purposes, such as outlined by Tyerman (1999, above). The inclusion of relatives and carers as co-therapists and adjuncts to individual client rehabilitation, might include collaboration about mechanisms of feedback to support developing awareness (Bieman-Copeland & Bywan, 2000), collaboration with reinforcement schedules (Wood, 1987) and in training the use of 'cognitive strategies' (Prigatano, 1999). While the involvement of relatives and carers is a necessary and valuable component of neuro-psychological rehabilitation, both the family adjustment process and reciprocal patterns of influence between clients and relatives warrant careful formulation as a precursor to clinical decisions about the level of family involvement (see chapters 6, 8, and 9 for further discussion of formulation). To enable a successful re-integration of the injured person into the family system, the need to work together is greatest when family coping is most challenged. In such circumstances, it can be especially difficult for families to engage with 'the reality' of their loved-one's disabilities and family members may be less available or able to engage with rehabilitation.

Therefore, some attempts to work alongside family members and endeavour to include them in rehabilitation, present challenges and dilemmas for the family and the clinician. Challenges are sometimes practical (e.g., finding times to meet) or relate to dynamic, emotional processes (e.g., negotiating a shared understanding or a new way of communicating). Reponses to such challenges occasionally result in descriptions of families, whether present or absent, as 'difficult', 'reluctant' or 'in denial' by people outside of the family, including professionals.

When the family member is completely absent from rehabilitation services, this clinical dilemma can be managed through working individually, or working relationally through other systems around the client, or perhaps by working with the narratives that the client holds about their place within their particular systems and hypothesizing together about their relative's points of view. It is important to include the voices/perspectives of a range of members of the system, in terms of the process of collaborative enquiry and endeavour to develop hypotheses about the identified problem (Dallos & Draper, 2007). Families can also be included using other mediums, such as telephone, letter, written reports, or webcam conversation. Anecdotally, these situations are likely to pose a challenge to clinicians because when communication is limited it is more difficult to pick up on subtleties of communication and fully listen to the family members' stories. There are important for establishing a working alliance and developing the 'shared understanding' (Wilson, Gracey, Malley, Bateman, & Evans, 2009). It might be suggested that, just as a systemic family therapist might use 'curiosity' to develop an understanding of the 'theory of constraint' (Breunlin, 1999), which underpins reluctance, rehabilitation clinicians could similarly bring curiosity into their thinking about the different family points of view, and positively connote the intentions of those who are finding it difficult to engage with rehabilitation. In so doing, this could develop an understanding of the 'logic of their reluctance' (Hardham, 2006) for each individual, and potentially increase their involvement with rehabilitation teams.

This chapter discusses how curiosity was used in research to understand more about the perspectives of family members, and develop ideas about possible obstacles to development of a working alliance with families, as well as considering potential approaches to the repair of ruptures in relationships, when/if they occur. We now consider issues of terminology and identification of the types of dilemmas that we refer to in this chapter.

Collaboration and alliance

The documents cited here appear to use the terms 'collaboration' and 'working alliance' to indicate a relationship between the relatives and the service providers that enables them to work together towards a shared goal. For the purpose of this chapter, it is assumed that these terms can be used interchangeably. This relationship will be conceptualized as similar in the process of formation and disruption as the therapeutic alliance.

Professionals and family members are individually limited because each lacks the expertise of the other; families have limited knowledge of ABI and professionals have limited knowledge of the individual prior to injury. DePompei and Willams (1994) propose that when the two perspectives are combined, a collaborative and fruitful relationship can be created. This relationship can be framed in terms of a 'working alliance' (DePompei & Willams, 1994). This idea of 'working alliance' is also used in the UK Social Services Inspectorate report of the TBI project (1997). The concept of therapeutic alliance was first developed by Greenson (1971) as the ability of the people in the relationship to work together towards a common purpose. It is characterized by an open and trusting relationship (Sexton & Whiston, 1994). The alliance has consistently been shown to be one of the most effective predictors of outcome from psychological therapy, regardless if the orientation of the therapist (Blow, Sprenkle, & Davis, 2007). Although it is generally used in the context of therapeutic relationships in mental health settings, it has been explored in the context of clients with ABI and their relationship with their therapist (Schonberger, Humle, & Teasdale, 2006a,b) and there may be further scope for thinking about therapeutic alliance in the context of collaboration and working alliance with families in rehabilitation settings.

Literature discussing or investigating the working alliance between relatives and staff members in ABI settings is scarce in relation to brain injury rehabilitation, but useful parallels can be drawn from child and family and mental health literature. Briggs (1997) identified three important clinician characteristics for development of a collaborative relationship between relatives and service providers:

- expertise,
- role replacement, and
- inter-personal communication skills.

'Role replacement' is the ability to relinquish control to the family member and involve them in care, which allows them to share the position of 'expert'. Perhaps illustrating the importance of 'expertise', Dinnebeil and Rule's (1994) investigation of factors that influenced collaboration between parents and service coordinators, found that clinicians who are self-confident and appear to be well informed were also regarded positively by family members (Dinnebeil & Rule, 1994).

Sohlberg and colleagues (2001) developed a model of collaborative practise for ABI rehabilitation settings in America, which was based on a two-year study using participatory action research with eight relatives of people with ABI. The model suggests that collaborative practice is achieved through three intervention phases with services, which are summarized in Figure 1. The phases within Sohlberg et al's model (2001) and the factors identified by Briggs are consistent with the dimensions that form a therapeutic alliance, as identified by Gaston (1990). In particular, Gaston emphasised that of 'empathy' and 'agreement of goals' are crucial factors in the formation of an alliance. Within the ethos of rehabilitation centres nationally, there is an increasing endeavour to include family members and address components of the alliance by involving family members in goal planning and review meetings. This is identified as a necessary aspect of rehabilitation in the National Service Frameworks for Long-Term Conditions

1. Learning the family's background, needs, and issues
2. Helping families determine their priorities
3. Teaching families to systematically observe events in their environment relevant to the issues of concern
4. Providing feedback on trends noted in family observations
5. Offering suggestions for strategies and helping families generate methods to monitor strategy success
6. Revisiting goals and monitoring issues of concern on an ongoing basis.

Figure 1. Stages of intervention, taken from Sohlberg et al. (2001).

(Department of Health, 2005). Despite this, it is sometimes difficult to develop or maintain an alliance with family members, and the clinician is likely to be presented with a variety of dilemmas about how to involve family (Levack, Siegert, Dean, & McPherson, 2009).

In clinical practice, it is not always possible to consistently develop a collaborative working alliance with family members (DePompei & Willams, 1994; Sohlberg, McLaughlin, Todis, Larsen, & Glang, 2001). Therefore, it can be difficult to actualize intentions to involve family members in care-planning, education, or support groups and so it can make it a challenge to find a means of collaborating and sharing knowledge and understanding with family members in a way that makes the most of each side's skills and resources. This means that often it is not possible to intervene effectively to support families in managing the tensions or coping with their own adjustment processes. If support from a service influences rehabilitation outcome, it follows that tensions in the relationship, or dysfluencies in communication between clinicians and family members could be to the detriment of the injured person's rehabilitation outcomes. It follows that it is crucial that we understand how best to engage the family members, while also recognizing individual differences and the likelihood that different people will benefit from different levels and approaches of intervention and support.

Dilemmas

In clinical practice, the clinician, family, and client are likely to find themselves in dilemmas. Once the need for a family meeting is established, initial dilemmas can be around:

- When to initiate family work;
- Who to invite; and
- What to offer when developing a session plan (managing competing objectives of client, family, clinician, and organization).

Once the session is arranged, subsequent dilemmas arise for the clinician. For example:

- Establishing who is the client (individual client or family group) and therefore, whether sessions will have an individual focus (e.g., making a shared plan to keep the injured person safe) or a relational/family focus (e.g., spending more time looking at family patterns of interaction and considering systemic adjustment issues).

- Related to the above, there is a dilemma about establishing whether (in the context of an individualistic rehabilitation programme) will the goal of family sessions be for the individual, the family, or the funding organization.

Finally, during the work, observed dilemmas might include:

- Sharing and confidentiality; what is shared with whom and when.
- When the therapist also works with the client in individual sessions there can be an unhelpful imbalance of information. However, the amount of information held by the therapist can enable greater understanding and helpful formulation.
- While exploring and defining the problem with the family, family members may each describe their point of view and 'present their evidence' that something or somebody needs to change. When these views are conflicting or polarized (as often they will among distressed families) the therapist can have the sense of being 'pulled' into different positions and alliances. Dilemmas arise around whether to intervene and advise or whether to listen and reflect

Each family presentation needs to be conceptualized individually according to the dilemmas and the different family members. Despite this, the journey of emergency treatment and acute care after ABI and the process of adjustment to rehabilitation and acceptance of a different future is common to many families. Some suggestions for considering practicalities of working with families are outlined at the end of this chapter, which are based on the authors' clinical experiences of negotiating integration of family members into the rehabilitation process. However, the authors advise that family interventions, including meetings, discussions, and goal planning would ideally be based on individual formulations of family process. Frameworks to assist conceptualization of the family presentation are described below, and a range of 'tactics and techniques' are described in chapter 9. Two fictional cases are described below, to illustrate potential dilemmas for the clinician.

Example 1

Nigel has returned to live with his mother since his brain injury, and is attending a rehabilitation programme where the primary goal is to manage his anger through learning arousal reduction skills, increasing his self-confidence and his assertiveness. Nigel's mother is understandably concerned that if he becomes frustrated or upset, there is a significant risk he will lose his temper and disengage with rehabilitation services or that he will have an angry outburst in the community and the Police might become involved again. She there-fore telephones the centre on a regular basis to talk to the staff about their work with Nigel. She explains that Nigel continues to become agitated on his home visits and that the staff do not see the extent of the difficulties. The formulation developed with Nigel is about his sense of control and choice in his life, that he believes he is not a 'dif-ferent person' since the injury and therefore he needs to explore his ADL and social skills in order to identify for himself where differ-ences lie, and so develop his awareness of changes since the injury. The staff would like to collaborate in this experiment with Nigel, but his mother and Case Manager would prefer that the staff find a way of persuading Nigel of their viewpoint regarding difference and risk in order to keep him safe and reduce frequency of argu-ments at home.

In this example, the members of the system each recognize that there is a problem, but each may have different conceptualizations of the reasons behind the problem and therefore the potential solu-tions. In this dilemma, it is likely that the clinician can feel 'drawn' into different perspectives and it is their task to help the system to negotiate these different perspectives, including that of the treating team, towards a more helpful position. A more helpful position is not always a shared position.

Example 2

John's wife, Elizabeth, is currently attending a rehabilitation pro-gramme as a day patient. Elizabeth has discussed her emotional reaction to her injury with the psychologist, and the formulation is that her adjustment is maintained by the limitations imposed on her role at home. Her role is limited because John's efforts to take care of Elizabeth and show that he is a good husband (despite the catastrophic impact of the injury on their marriage) include doing all the cooking and domestic tasks and telling Elizabeth to "rest and get better" when she is at home. Unfortunately, Elizabeth has begun to question her "usefulness" at home and whether she belongs to John because she does not wish to be a "burden" and these thoughts maintain her depression. To offer Elizabeth the maximum chance of a successful discharge home, it is necessary that the couple begin to renegotiate distribution of roles. However, John says that he is unable to come to the Centre because he is unable to take time away from work; he explains that he is unable to work from home to make up the time, because he has so much to do in looking after Elizabeth. The team formulates that John would benefit from working on his adjustment process but cannot find a way to open the conversation with him or arrange a meeting.

Interviews with family members

An investigation into the perspectives of family members with regard to their relationships with rehabilitation professionals was conducted, and is described by Palmer, Herbert, and Vetere (in prep). In this study, interviews with family members explored factors that inhibited a positive working relationship and factors that enabled this to develop.

Research design

In this study, 32 family members in daily contact with people who sustained an ABI between 10 months and 7 years previously, were interviewed about their experiences of developing strategies in collaboration with professionals, and about what made it easier or more difficult to work alongside the professionals. The research questions were as follows:

1. How did family members discover the strategies they have used for managing changes since the injury?
2. How have family members coped with their relative's injury?

3. What do family members perceive to have been helpful and less helpful about the professionals they have met during their relative's treatment and rehabilitation?

A range of relationships and perspectives were represented, including parents, partners, and adult children. The semi-structured interviews sometimes involved more than one member of the same family. Using the GCS (Teasdale & Jennett, 1974), all participants' relatives had sustained a moderate (31%) or severe/very severe brain injury (69%) from TBI (67%), stroke (25%), and other causes such as operative complications causing secondary anoxic injury (8%). Participants ranged in age from 23 to 76 years with a mean age of 53 years at the time of the interview.

The interview transcripts were all analysed using a Top-Down Theme Analysis (Dallos & Vetere, 2005) in accordance with each of the research questions. Four transcripts were selected for more detailed interpretative phenomological analysis (Smith, 1996) about the dynamic relationship with professionals. Each was selected on the basis of representing exemplars of the third research question.

Results

The narratives that emerged from analysis of the transcripts (see Table 1) indicated that family members come into contact with rehabilitation services already feeling disconnected with many aspects of their lives as they knew them pre-injury. They are likely to have a limited understanding of brain injury, by experiencing emotional sequalae of their own in addition to role change and potential financial strain. At this time, family members have some expectations about what will happen during their involvement with the rehabilitation service, which is in part based on their experiences of acute care, which were often upsetting and highly concerning to them. These narratives often continue and can be 'played out' in post-acute rehabilitation services, proving to be an obstacle to collaboration between family and therapist, and preventing the family member from trusting the clinician with their own emotional response. Expectations of family members might subsequently be low (e.g., 'there is nothing that can be done') or high (e.g., 'this service will be the answer') and

Table 1. Themes emergent from analysis (Palmer, Herbert, & Vetere, in preparation).

Emergent themes	Superordinate theme	Master theme
Importance of family support Anxiety Grief reaction Physical illness Sleep disturbance	Emotional and physical impact	Personal impact: disconnection
Future plans Relative's personality Changes in role and family life	Loss	
Ongoing difficulties Ongoing lack of understanding Professionals failing to meet expectations	Frustration and hopelessness	
Friends and social support services Impact on family	Misunderstanding of others	Understanding and knowledge
Visibility of disability Information Explanation	Mismatch in expectations	
Acknowledgement Involvement Answering questions	Listening and personal interest	Professional communication style
Honesty Competence Power	Necessary characteristics of professionals	
Personal interest Calm Friendly	Likeable characteristics of professionals	

transcripts highlight the pitch of expectations as the point of tension in the alliance. Consistent with Watson and Greenburg (1995), the mismatch in expectations can trigger a rupture of two types: either, the relationship does not develop, or the relationship breaks down. This investigation included conversations with family members who described both forms of rupture. Among these participants, the following factors can help to re-negotiate the working alliance:

- Honesty of clinicians (acknowledging limitations and saying "I don't know").
- Respect, listening and an interest in the individual.
- Clinician is informed, and shares information in an understandable way (so as to include the family).
- Clinician demonstrates competence (shown by openness to questioning).
- Clinician is responsive (by offering a perspective or directing to appropriate resource) .

We will now look at how to incorporate this understanding into our formulation of individual families and their responses to rehabilitation and how clinicians might then respond to the family member's dilemmas as expressed through their anger, anxiety, or withdrawal.

Formulating the dilemmas

It is proposed that the emotional reactions of family members to rehabilitation and their expectations of rehabilitation can influence the ability of family members and rehabilitation teams to build a working alliance together. A tentative model of this process, developed through interviews with family members, is summarized in a diagram in Figure 2. The process is consistent with findings of other researchers; for example, Dinnebeil and Rule also identified that clinicians who are self-confident and appear to be well informed were also regarded positively by family members in their study (Dinnebeil & Rule, 1994). Further, Llewellyn and colleagues identified a mismatch between expectations and experiences, which could be influenced by provision of information (Llewellyn, McGurk, & Weinman, 2005). This supports the themes identified in this research; expectations of rehabilitation are influenced by information and were crucial to establishing collaboration. Although many practitioners are addressing education and information in daily practice, it was the authors' interpretations from the transcripts that a basic understanding of brain function and how Health and Social services function organizationally is assumed by professionals in their explanations.

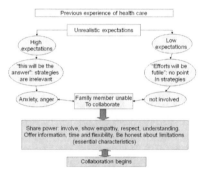

Figure 2. A tentative model of collaboration between family members and professionals in post-acute rehabilitation.

The transcripts highlight the importance of the process of how clinicians share their knowledge of ABI in a clear and accessible manner, which is also respectful and helpful. The process of how information is conveyed appears to be of equal importance to the content of the information. In relation to the collaboration model proposed by Sohlberg and colleagues (2001), the transcripts highlight a need to attend in more detail to the first stage of collaboration "learning the family's background, needs and issues" in order to create a foundation for the later phases. There is considerable overlap between the themes emerging from this research, and concepts described within models of illness perception and adherence to medical advice (Cameron & Leventhal, 2002; Whittaker, Kemp, & House, 2007).

This analysis lends itself to the positive connation that family members do generally have the intention to collaborate but that disappointed expectations or sense that professionals do not have time to include their opinion into the interventions, which results in a separation of intention and action (a rupture). This model suggests that in order to move towards a more helpful level of engagement, family members benefit from the opportunity to:

1. discuss their experiences prior to rehabilitation;
2. discuss and negotiate their expectations for rehabilitation;
3. hear about the role and limitations of rehabilitation; and
4. receive information about brain injury in general, and additional opportunities to discuss the rationale for interventions that they need to be aware of.

The points outlined are proposed as opportunities for family members to feel listened to and to potentially become more involved in the rehabilitation programme, such that they can gradually develop a shared understanding of rehabilitation and brain injury. According to the four points raised above, if ruptures occur in the alliance, the points can be redressed. Some of these points have also been highlighted in other works, such as the Brain Injury Family Intervention curriculum (Kreutzer, Kolakowsky-Hayner, Demm, & Meade, 2002), which is proposed as an approach to reducing the likelihood of commonly encountered problems.

1. Understand the typical consequences of brain injury.
2. Recognize ambivalent feelings and develop strategies for positive coping.
3. Recognize the brain injury happens to the whole family.
4. Recognize the detrimental affects of guilt and the need to care for one's self.
5. Appreciate the natural limits of rehabilitation.
6. Help to extend improvement well beyond the first six months.
7. Avoid giving inconsistent or contradictory advice.
8. Understand the differences between physical and emotional recovery.
9. Manage stress more effectively.
10. Learn effective ways to judge success.
11. Avoid working on too many things at one time.
12. Expand support systems.
13. Recognize and address gaps in the system of care.
14. Encourage communication and asking questions.
15. Politely address disagreements.
16. Resolve conflicting advice and information.

(taken from Kreutzer, Kolakowsky-Hayner, Demm, & Meade, 2002, p. 353)

Resolution of ruptures

Situations in which the relationship between family members and healthcare professionals deteriorates can be framed in terms of the ruptured therapeutic alliance (Watson & Greenburg, 1995).

There are two main subtypes of therapeutic rupture; confrontation and withdrawal (Safran & Muran, 2000), which result from perceived vulnerability and anxiety or anger. This is in keeping with a division of two subtypes of rupture, Watson and Greenburg (1995) postulate that problems in the alliance result from either 'goal related' or from 'relational' factors. Ruptures were similarly described in association with a theme of 'sense of vulnerability/loss of control' which emerged from transcripts in the study described above. Therefore, clarification about the purpose of, and thinking behind a proposed rehabilitation intervention (or strategy) is likely to help re-establish a positive alliance. Understanding the rationale for a strategy will increase the likelihood of successful implementation. This concept was also supported by the transcripts in the study described above. Other suggestions for restoration of a ruptured alliance are outlined by Safran and Muran (2000) in their review. These include: asking the family member about what prevented them using the strategies, increasing information provision in order to clarify misunderstandings and suggesting achievable tasks, clearly planned, in order to increase success experiences and build on hope.

This literature implies that resolution of ruptures is through negotiation of a more equal negotiation of power between families and clinicians. To achieve this equality within an ABI setting is potentially challenging, due to the necessary specialist nature of professionals and the historically medical model approach to treatment. When using reflective approaches to listen to the family member's point of view, the clinician sensitively balances empathy and neuro-psychological expertise by reflecting on the family member's story from a position of strength (see chapter 10 or further comment on technique). When considering the development of an alliance between families and therapists, it is crucial to consider the influence of context on beliefs held and the lens through which individuals perceive the problem. Divergence of relatives' problem perceptions from clinician's problem perceptions is described elsewhere (Sunderland, Harris, & Gleave, 1984). For example, multiple systems are usually involved with any one individual, who holds different agendas, assumptions about best practise and there are different requirements and restrictions within each system (Palmer, Psaila, & Yeates, 2009).

The model proposed above offers a means of understanding the perspective of some family members, but it does not offer a means of understanding the multi-directional interactions between clinicians, family members, other organizations and the client themselves. Although it has some clinical utility, it is insufficient for formulation of complex relational dynamics. However, it does provide a formulation of the dilemma for the family member and how this might lead them to hold a certain position with respect to rehabilitation. An additional model will be described below, which develops from an individually focused model of adjustment and the rehabilitation process, and extends to include the family and wider systems.

A Y-shaped model of adjustment and safety seeking

Emotional adjustment after TBI is suggested to relate to both internal self-discrepancies (Nochi, 1998a) and inter-personal discrepancies (Nochi, 1998b). The maintenance of such discrepancies can be appropriately formulated within systemic models of family functioning and may alternatively be referred to as 'contesting dynamics' between members of the system (Yeates, Henwood, Gracey, & Evans, 2007). Cognitive behavioural models can also be used to formulate discrepancy (Dewar & Gracey, 2007). We propose that these notions of threat and discrepancy offer a description of the starting point of rehabilitation for the client, family, and therapist. Themes of inter- and intra-personal discrepancies are referred to in the literature using terms such as conflict, discrepancy, and dissonance. Within this chapter, the term 'discrepancy' has been selected to represent the difference between how people think they should be and how they think they are. This is in keeping with self-discrepancy theory as investigated post-TBI (Cantor et al., 2005).

A model depicting the process of rehabilitation for individuals is illustrated in Figure 3, which will later be used to understand the process of family adjustment and interacting dynamics; an understanding that can provide a framework for clinicians to make sense of patterns of communication within families, which forms the foundations of their alliance and potential collaboration. First, the model will be described as it relates to individual adjustment.

The Y-shaped model (Gracey, Evans, & Malley, 2009) proposes that after brain injury, the injured person identifies a discrepancy in their sense of self, often on an 'implicational' level. This is consistent with the sense that they are fundamentally 'under threat'; their interactions with their environment lead them to conclude that they are somehow 'different' or 'disabled' since the injury, and this change means they are unable to participate in society in the way that previously defined their identity. This model is known as the Y-shaped model because at the beginning of rehabilitation, the individual starts at a point of discrepancy (for example, between "how I think things should be" and "how I feel things are now") and the injured person experiences distress and threat regarding their perceived discrepant identity. The discrepancy is represented in the two sides of the top of the letter Y.

After brain injury, people attempt to achieve safety using their coping strategies that were well established prior to the injury (e.g., work harder, withdraw from social contact, or plan to do things that make me feel 'more like myself'). Unfortunately, these coping strategies are not always helpful or possible after brain injury and can serve to maintain the sense of discrepancy and threat.

Through the process of interdisciplinary behavioural experiments to link 'doing' and 'meaning' at an implicational level (Bennett-Levy, Westbrook, Fennell, Cooper, Rouf, & Hackman, 2004), which are set up within the 'safe' context of a rehabilitation programme, the discrepancy begins to reduce and the sense of threat lessens. The injured person is gradually able to update their self-identity to develop a more realistic self-representation. This reduces the sense

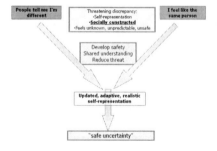

Figure 3. The Y-shaped model of neuro-psychological rehabilitation (Gracey, Evans, & Malley, 2009).

of discrepancy, increases safety, and thereby brings together the two sides of the Y into a single point, as illustrated below.

In summary, the main stages of the Y-shaped process are:

- Establishing a sense of trust and safety in the therapeutic milieu.
- Developing a 'shared understanding' or formulation of problems, incorporating issues relating to threat and discrepancy, with the injured person and their relatives.
- Testing out discrepant beliefs.
- Developing a 'positive formulation' of how things might or could be based on pre-injury and post-injury positive or alternative experiences.
- Supporting maintenance of gains and further consolidation.

The Y-shaped model can be applied to systemic interactions, as described below.

The Y-shaped cone

The Y-shaped process described above can be extended to include the wider family by conceptualizing the identity of the family as discrepant. The 'threatening discrepancy' can be understood as developing from interactions with other people. Further, it is probable that other family members will hold their own discrepancies (e.g., about being a 'good enough' parent or partner) that they cope with by attempts to lessen the discrepancy through their behaviour, what they say or what they think. See Figure 4 for an illustration of this. Family interactions are proposed as a factor in maintaining discrepancy or developing safety for the injured person and for the wider family identity. Attempts are made by different people within the system to increase a sense of safety, cohesion, family identity, and family purpose (e.g., explain to the other family members or professionals, what the problem is and what needs to be done in order to resolve it). However, sometimes these attempts can have the opposite effect; through reducing sense of threat to one person (e.g., a mother deciding to prevent her daughter going to a party, in order to maintain her safety) can highlight discrepancy for another (e.g., the daughter perceives that she is 'treated like a child' and must therefore assert her independence more strongly). In this way, attempts to increase safety can paradoxically increase the discrepancy, especially when the attempts are made from one perspective trying to "convince the other" of their chosen solution to the current dilemmas faced by the family.

Imagining that each person within the system is aware, on some level, of a discrepancy, and they are seeking to reduce their anxiety or concern about themselves or another family member. Their attempts to reduce uncertainty and increase safety create a discordant pattern of interacting discrepancies and safety seeking from multiple overlapping perspectives (and can result in a 'contesting dynamic' such as described in chapter 6). This discordant pattern can be conceptualized as dynamic circle formed from the top of multiple 'Ys' (discrepancies held by each family member). Through incorporating the range of perspectives into the scenario, the top of the Y can be visualized as circular and becomes the Y- shaped 'cone' model of family adjustment as the discrepancies for each person become smaller and the Ys move/funnel closer together. This model (illustrated in Figure 5) can contribute to thinking about the dynamics between families, services, and professionals.

The concept that emotional adjustment, coping style, and reactions of the family can maintain low awareness and emotional adjustment difficulties for the person with the injury is supported by qualitative research studies (Yeates, Henwood, Gracey, & Evans, 2007) and case description (Dewar & Gracey, 2007). See also chapter 6 for further

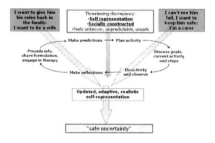

Figure 4. Y-shaped model of neuro-psychological rehabilitation representing relational perspectives at the top of the Y (adapted from Gracey, Evans, & Malley, 2009).

discussion of 'contesting dynamics' within families after ABI and chapter 8 for a clinical case example.

In accordance with the Y-shaped cone, the purpose of family sessions would be to support family members to look 'outwards' from their position, and invite them to learn more about the dilemmas and motivations of other people within their system. The aim of intervention with a family group would therefore be to create awareness within the system that each person is holding a different internal dilemma/discrepancy that they are trying to resolve. In so doing, we are inviting the family members to really get to know the different levels of the problem, to broaden their knowledge of how other people see it, and to spend some time together hypothetically 'walking around in the problem' to slowly begin to consider new 'possibilities for making it less of a problem' (Mason, 1993) than it currently is. Creating a safe context to begin sharing something of each individual's discrepancy, which positively reframes their actions as their best attempt to improve the situation for the family, enables a shared understanding to emerge. A true 'shared understanding' is the joining of all in a helpful new narrative that opens new opportunities and possibilities, and not the convincing of others by one. Systemic family therapy offers approaches for addressing such work with families, such as described in the next two chapters ('case descriptions' and 'working with families').

Summary

This chapter has outlined some of the current thinking with regard to building and maintaining relationships with family members

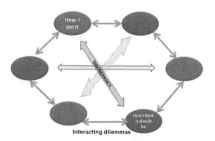

Figure 5. The Y-shaped 'cone' of interacting discrepancies within a system (Palmer & Gracey, 2008).

during rehabilitation, drawing on models of collaboration, and alliance from other areas of psychology as well as the limited research from within neuropsychology. The literature suggests that ruptures in the alliance need not be catastrophic but can be clinically useful if used as an opportunity to stop and think about the positions and needs of each person within the system. The tentative model of collaboration described highlights the importance of recognizing the individual's previous experiences and expectations for rehabilitation outcome, when attempting to develop a working relationship. This provides a framework for conceptualizing and exploring the perspectives of individuals within the system. The interaction of these different perspectives can then be formulated using the Y-shaped cone of emotional adjustment after brain injury, and from here the interacting dilemmas can be gradually mapped out. This latter model incorporates the importance of considering safety and challenging efforts to achieve safety that may inadvertently reduce flexibility within the system or maintain the problem. This concept is akin to the concept from within family therapy described as when the 'solution becomes the problem'.

The exact nature of family and carer support provision is contingent on a team formulation of each family, including the client with ABI, and the relationship between the family and the service. The literature strongly suggests that clinicians need to respond to family members' need to be listened to, and to be given information as relevant to their questions at the time that they need it, which is often idiosyncratic. However, sometimes it may be crucial to invite the family to slow down, take a step back, and explore how their own reactions might be influencing the reactions of others, and there is a role for the relational neuropsychologist in helping the family understand how this can exacerbate ABI sequalae. While clinicians may offer their time, it is important that services provide the resources that enable and support clinicians to do this. In this sense, the service needs sufficient flexibility to listen to family members and respond to what they need (through offering information, intervention, explanation, or directing to the appropriate service or resource). This need not be time-consuming but may require careful planning and is likely to require a flexible family-centred approach.

Table 2. Who, what, where why, how of working with families:
Considerations when designing a service for supporting family members.

Question	Considerations	
WHO... to include?	• Child or young adult relatives • Carers	• Adult relatives or close friends • Which team members?
	Consider who is significant to your client, discuss involvement with your client, and consider which of the family support services are appropriate (i.e., therapeutic sessions might include different people to those involved in information sessions.)	
WHAT... are the aims	Current literature suggests that family members need an opportunity to: • discuss experiences prior to rehabilitation • discuss expectations for rehabilitation • understand the role and limitations of rehabilitation • received information about ABI and specifically about the rationale for interventions (as appropriate) *If ruptures occur in the alliance, these points can be redressed.*	
WHERE... to meet?	Phone calls Monitoring forms Family home or rehabilitation centre	Webcam Letters, Questionnaires
	Family work can take place in a range of settings depending on type of work, provided it is a safe context (i.e., confidential and free from interruptions)	
WHY... we work with families?	**Emotional reasons** • Confusion, uncertainty, need for information, and sense-making • Strain, burden, sub-clinical, and clinical emotional difficulties	

(continued)

Table 2. Continued

Question	Considerations
	• Isolation from wider sources of support • Changes, tensions, and breakdown within family relationships • Tensions or mismatched expectations between themselves and others (client/ professional) about rehabilitation **Service-related reasons** Collaboration, Education, Emotional Support
WHEN ... to offer intervention or support?	The opportunity to have helpful conversations is provided by • Keyworker contact • rehabilitation meetings • relative's groups • education days/sessions *Family members need an opportunity to have the conversations with professionals or other family members, to learn about ABI and for their stories to be heard. Therefore, it is not necessary that they engage with all the above interventions. The timing of information and support is very individual.*
HOW ... to involve family members?	• Information seeking • Collaboration • Support • Involvement in clinical sessions

CHAPTER EIGHT

Case descriptions

This chapter offers three examples of relational thinking and intervention, which have been conducted within the context of a multi- or interdisciplinary rehabilitation; two illustrations are taken from work done within a holistic neuro-psychological rehabilitation programme, and one within a neurobehavioural residential programme. These are presented below. We start by briefly introducing the case of Grace and Steve.

Grace and Steve

Grace a 63 year old British woman, married to Steve for 27 years with no children, sustained ABI as the result of viral encephalitis 6 weeks prior to rehabilitation. Prior to the injury, Grace's role at home was in domestic tasks, managing finances, linking family together and working full time. Steve described himself as a 'sounding board' and a 'support' for Grace. After 4 months in rehabilitation, her disorientation gradually subsided and her most significant impairment was in the domain of memory, particularly with both encoding and retrieval of verbal information. This meant it was difficult for her to organise and keep track of her daily activities; a key skill in her 'organising' role at homes.

During rehabilitation, Grace made significant physical improvements but continued to experience significant memory impairment, was disoriented when she visited home and could not retrieve the names of previously familiar places. She developed memory strategies that increased ability to live independent of Steve, but she had difficulty remembering to use them without support. Steve was worried that she would not cope on discharge and he expressed his worries in conversation with Grace. He worked hard to ensure finances and housekeeping tasks were kept up to date so Grace did not need to worry. Despite his efforts, Grace continued to be very worried about her memory, so Steve also remained worried and continued to do all the tasks at home. Grace and Steve were supported to talk about what was on their mind and what they were feeling. They talked through their thoughts about discharge plans and what they were each looking forward to or concerned about. It was noticed that in these sessions, Grace was very quiet and Steve would talk for most of the time. Whilst Grace had some difficulty with initiation of speech, she initiated significantly more in groups with peers or in individual sessions than in sessions with Steve.

Initial formulation

Since her injury, Grace had received a diagnosis of anxiety and depression, for which she was receiving pharmacological treatment. Her depression was believed to be secondary to anxiety and worry, and therefore the service was able to provide Grace and Steve with four clinical psychology sessions to focus on managing shared worry about memory. During these sessions, it became apparent that both Grace and Steve had been so shocked and upset by Grace's illness, and also by being physically separated from one another for the first time in many years, that they had coped by "just getting on with" the things that needed to be done (adopting a 'task-oriented' coping style when together) and did not talk about their emotions together (absence of 'emotion-oriented' coping). In contrast to their usual roles, Grace would allow Steve to take the lead in conversations, while she remained silent. She had become focused on her health and Steve had adopted all the household tasks, and this was described by Steve as 'role reversal'. Further formulation and intervention with this couple are briefly described.

Grace's subjective experience and the meaning of silence

As Grace recovered, she explained that she saw Steve's increased competence with household tasks and interpreted this as a sign that "he does not need me anymore." Subsequently, any sign of memory or other difficulty since the injury was a trigger for her to think about how "useless" she felt and how she couldn't contribute to their marriage any longer. Grace was, of course, unable to talk with Steve about this for fear that he might confirm it so whenever she had this thought, she remained silent. The worry made it more difficult for Grace to problem solve, think through, and apply her attention to a task, which resulted in less success than she was capable of, which perpetuated her fear of being "ruined" and reluctance to express her feelings. In other words, the worry had brought silence to their relationship, and the silence meant they were unable to connect and problem solve together as they had previously done.

Helping each other so much that we came to a standstill

Over the course of two sessions, they were supported to identify the following cycle: "Steve worries about Grace, so he expresses what the problem is to professionals (in order to look after Grace and obtain help for her), but Grace interprets this as evidence that she is 'ruined' and 'very badly damaged' and begins to worry about their future as a couple. This leads her mind to wander so she does not follow the conversation, and then when she is asked to contribute she is 'lost', which provides further evidence for "I'm ruined and useless" and further compounds her fears about their marriage, creating more 'silent worrying'. When Grace was quiet, Steve would attempt to 'test' her memory (asking her questions about what she can remember) in order to generate evidence and prove to Grace that her memory was not as damaged as she feared. Unfortunately, this amplified the difficulties that Grace believed she had. This cycle was drawn out on a large piece of paper with Grace and Steve while it was happening.

Interrupting and introducing a new pattern

Work involved the therapists earning the right to interrupt Grace and Steve's conversations when they were observed to be in the cycle identified above, and asking them both to 'stop and think' about one another's emotions and intentions in that moment. Grace responded well to questions that were not directly about problems, but were instead about how she feels and what she thinks about specific activities she had done (e.g., asking "what did you do this morning ... what did you enjoy about it ... that sounds interesting ..."). Through this experiment, we learned that Grace was able to access more detail from her memories when she was relaxed, and when she felt Steve was not 'testing' her recall. The latter intervention was accompanied by development of strategies for Steve to use to support Grace to remember: rather than his previous strategies of pointing out the problem, he was encouraged to slow down and ask Grace what she thought and how she was feeling, and to ask clear, specific questions. Grace and Steve drew out the 'new cycle' that 'felt more natural' and drew out the questions that Steve would ask Grace on the telephone.

A team approach

In addition to this intervention, the multidisciplinary interventions also emphasized errorless learning strategies to support Grace to learn to use memory compensation strategies (e.g., using a diary), and specific educational interventions included working with Grace and Steve together to understand how memory could be effected by worry. At the end of the rehabilitation programme, Grace was discharged home. She was consistently using her memory strategies and Steve was consistently using the questions that they had developed together in the couple's sessions. Both Grace and Steve said that telephone (and other) conversations were more enjoyable and comfortable now, and they had started to feel "connected" again. Steve described how Grace had become increasingly more confident and competent with her strategies, that they were able to talk together about how they both felt about the memory difficulty, and Steve told the rehabilitation team that "I've got my Grace back."

The development of a working formulation, and how it guided a relational intervention within the context of a residential rehabilitation programme was described. This intervention successfully enabled Grace and Steve to find ways of talking to each other again that opened up a conversation about how they were each feeling, and a two-way conversation about how they would like to be supported. Grace was discharged to her home shortly after this was achieved.

Should additional time have been available, further consideration or application of the concepts described elsewhere within this book would have been an appropriate next stage.

A second case has been chosen, which illustrates a relational intervention conducted primarily with an injured man using systemic ideas to consider his wife's perspective and develop a shared language for talking about their difficulty talking. The couple found it difficult to talk about their emotions after the accident, which created emotional distance between them. Brief therapeutic work enabled them to 'unlock' their shared problem-solving resources again. This is illustrated in the case of Ron and Mandy (below).

Case example: Sketching out a shared language

Ron and Mandy had been married for 17 years before he was involved in a car accident in which he sustained a severe brain injury (diffuse axonal injury and frontal contusions) but no orthopaedic injuries. Ron's duration of PTA was recorded as three weeks. After the injury, he returned to work in a different capacity, but it proved increasingly difficult for him to meet the demands of his employers, and despite their attempts to support him, he became increasingly stressed at work and unable to meet deadlines. His distress was expressed at home through irritability with the family and his young children. He was referred to rehabilitation with the aim of exploring strategies to support work re-integration. Neuro-psychological assessment at this stage (five years post-injury) indicated significant difficulties with executive functioning, in particular the skills of goal management and impulsivity. In addition to exploring cognition, the rehabilitation assessment included discussion with him and his wife together.

Ron and Mandy described their shared dilemma at home since the injury:

- They had changed roles and responsibilities within the home.
- Both Ron and Mandy described feeling stressed, and each said that they felt misunderstood by the other, and unsupported.
- However, the primary presenting problem was Ron's anger towards Mandy and occasionally towards their children.
- Anger had come as a surprise to both of them, and they had stopped talking about the feelings with one another, as they had before.

Overall, both agreed that their intimate moments of understanding one another, intuitively sharing the strain of parenting young children and maintaining professional jobs, and shared moments of emotional closeness occurred less frequently. They explained that the potential for such conversations was also less because of the 'threat' of anger or criticism that was the source of some avoidance for both. They described feeling lonely because they had each lost the support of one another, at a time when they needed it most.

Ron engaged in weekly sessions with a clinical psychologist to reflect on the impact of the injury on himself and on his family. Mandy had wanted to be closely involved with the rehabilitation programme but was restricted in her availability due to work commitments. Therefore, much of the 'couples' interventions were done with Ron, who took the work home to Mandy and continued the conversation with her. Ron described his family, which was mapped in a genogram (see Figure 1).

Using the genogram served as a means of scaffolding conversation about relationships within the family, and Ron shared his experience of how his relationship and interactions between himself and Mandy were changed. As he did this, we started to sketch out an illustration (Figure 2) of what he was describing, which helped him to keep track of his thought process (thereby serving as a strategy for compensating for difficulties with working memory and tangential conversation).

Through this drawing process, Ron described that he and Mandy were both feeling 'churned up inside'. Prior to the accident, and in the early years after the accident this is something that they would have talked to one another about (and in so doing, using their attachment relationship to 'soothe' insecurities, 'calm' autonomic responses and support problem-solving). However, over recent times, they were less able to talk to one another about the 'churned up' feelings; leading neither to feel 'soothed' but instead Ron was coping with his emotions by attempting to resume his old roles, but failing (due to poor problem-solving and impulsive responses, that is, 'jumping in without thinking'). This disappointed Mandy who was hoping he would succeed. She would tell him that he could have approached the situation differently, and his response was then to become agitated and verbally aggressive (which he illustrated by arrows coming 'outwards' from himself) and her response, in turn, was to

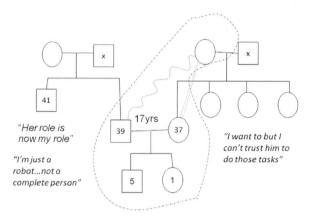

Figure 1. A simple genogram illustrates that Ron and Mandy had been married for 17 years. They lived with their two young children and also with Mandy's mother with whom Mandy had a close relationship, but Ron had a difficult relationship with her. Ron had needed to surrender some family organization tasks to Mandy, and felt that her role in the home was now what his used to be. Mandy said she would like to be able to trust Ron to do those tasks again, but continued difficulties with organization and planning made this impossible. Ron concluded that he was "just a robot" and "no longer a complete person." Ron identified his older brother as a confidant, although unfortunately, he lived in a different country so contact was infrequent.

'shut down' and 'go in on herself'. Mandy was then seen by Ron as somebody who held responsibility for everything in the family, such as organizing the children and management of the house and she delegated tasks to Ron that she thought he could cope with. Unable to problem solve independently, or contribute his own ideas to the planning of family activities, Ron described himself as a "Robot." Ron said the result of this process between him and Mandy was that his son and daughter were closer to Mandy and her mother looked at him with 'disapproval'. He valued the support of his brother, who he could confide in.

    The next thing that Ron explained was that although he and Mandy found it difficult to communicate, he believed that they both desired a more open communication because of their love for

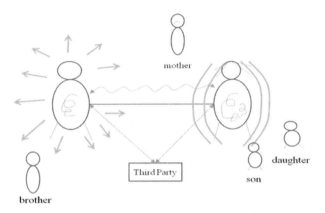

Figure 2. A computerized format of sketch made by Ron while describing the challenges of communication between himself and Mandy, within the context of their broader family relationships and alliances.

each other (illustrated in the solid line between them), and they sought the help of the 'third party' to find a way to talk again which felt safe.

Ron's illustration describes the 'attachment injury' experienced since the accident by both people, triggered by role change. This description also can be seen to characterize the "ambiguous position" (Gosling et al., 1999) that Mandy was in, in relation to wanting to be a wife but frequently needing to be Ron's support and carer. Ron took the diagram home to talk through with Mandy, and when he returned the following week he described sharing the diagram with Mandy while sitting together on a Sunday morning. Ron described how the diagram had provided a structure for his thoughts so that he was able to explain his feelings to Mandy without becoming 'lost' or confused, which he was vulnerable to when describing complex ideas, especially regarding emotive topics. He also said he felt that having the diagram on paper meant that it served as a 'third party' and enabled them to begin to talk about their emotional experiences. Ron talked about how they had cried together (and in doing so, begun to re-discover safety in their emotional communication) about how the unwanted injury had come into their lives and altered ('stolen') their connection.

The diagram, alongside education about the cognitive sequalae of Ron's brain injury, provided a common non-blaming language for the couple. At the same time, Ron participated in an intensive rehabilitation programme where he developed strategies to enable him to problem solve and plan more effectively and approach tasks more systematically. The strategies included goal management training (Levine et al., 2000; Robertson, 1996) especially self-prompting to "slow down … stop and think" and ask himself "what am I trying to achieve … what is my main goal?" Regular use of relaxation strategies enhanced his goal management. Teaching Mandy about these strategies, and supporting them to negotiate how he can find the time to do his relaxation at home, or how she might help him think through his goal management tasks, enabled them to structure their communication, and learn how to enable him to find ways around the executive impairments and to ultimately regain responsibility for more tasks at home, as well as unlocking their previously good communication styles that they had been unable to access at the start of rehabilitation. Other therapeutic 'tactics' that contributed to the work with Ron and Mandy included: (1) supporting them to clearly articulate their thought processes underlying their emotions, over the course of multiple sessions using sketches and metaphor to help keep track of the conversations. The tactic of drawing the picture of the family was then used as a basis to discuss how he and Mandy would like things to be, and has similarities with the technique of 'sculpting' (Minuchin, 1974); (2) normalization of their reactions in terms of their pre-injury relationship; (3) facilitating conversations about their joint hopes for the future, and identifying specific joint aspirations (Gosling et al., 1999); and (4) facilitating them to use their unsolvable problems (e.g., having a house too small for their growing family) as a vehicle to establish greater closeness (Jacobson, Christensen, Prince, Cordova, & Eldridge, 2000) while also using the rare but important sessions with Ron and Mandy together to model the skill of "treating … with respect and warmth, whilst taking their cognitive and behavioural limitations into account p. 794" (Gosling et al., 1999).

Case description: Developing awareness without 'taking sides'

We will introduce a clinical case and highlight the challenges of building an alliance with the family as a whole, dilemmas faced by the clinicians, the response of clinicians to these, and the impact of responses on perceived alliance with the client (Gaynor) and her family.

Background

Gaynor was 24 years old when she began her rehabilitation programme. This was two and a half years after she was the passenger in a car involved in an RTA, in which she sustained numerous orthopaedic injuries and a severe brain injury. Her GCS was 7/15 at the scene and recorded as being 11/15 four weeks post-injury. PTA persisted for more than 10 weeks. Gaynor reported no memory for the event or the acute treatment subsequently. She described patchy memory for the three years preceding the accident, which encompassed the majority of her time at university. Assessment indicated difficulties with attention and executive skills of planning, organizing, and impulse control. When Gaynor began rehabilitation, she described herself as "impatient, adventurous and independent." She said that she had always been these things, and that although some people say she has changed, she minimized any possibility of change and explained to the rehabilitation team that she is "the same girl."

Changes and disputes

The most notable change, in terms of their family impact on relationships, was the disputes about how Gaynor was now "different" and "at risk," and discussion was organized around Gaynor's low awareness of changes since the injury.

Gaynor's mother (Mrs B) caringly said to Gaynor that "you just need to accept that you're different now." In response, Gaynor would clearly insist that "I'm the same girl" and "I'd be fine if you would leave me alone ..." she specified that people should allow her to live independently and refrain from scrutinizing all her decisions. She said that other people would realize that she has no long-term problems if she were allowed to live independently, spend time with her friends, and return to work as she would like to. Consequently, there were frequent disputes within the family about Gaynor's level of independence, "impulsive decision making" and risk taking. Gaynor said she felt trapped and treated like a "baby" and a "little girl" by her parents and she said she would like to "just go" and prove that she can be independent. By the time Gaynor began rehabilitation, Mrs B had secretly phoned and cancelled at least two flights abroad, which Gaynor had booked "to escape the situation." The issue identified by the family as the problem was 'negotiating independence'. Despite this, Gaynor could only identify one problem: impatience.

Alliance dilemmas

Working with Gaynor posed the rehabilitation staff with dilemmas about how to position themselves with the family and with Gaynor because Mrs B often telephoned the rehabilitation centre explaining how difficult things were at home and offered details of situations that Gaynor had not shared with the team at that time, explaining her anxieties that Gaynor would not "make the most out of rehab" and asking the staff to 'stop being so nice' and to begin to 'point things out' so that Gaynor could start to get better. This can be understood as Mrs B's attempts to recruit the team as additional voices in telling Gaynor what her problems are. In terms of alliance, this can also be understood as Mrs B's attempt to assess her expectations of rehabilitation and whether it would be 'another disappointment' or 'the answer'; thereby setting up an impossible task for the rehabilitation team that would struggle to gain an alliance if they could not join forces with the family in persuading Gaynor that she has changed. However, if they did the latter, they would be unable to maintain the alliance with Gaynor because they would be 'joining her mother's side', and in accordance with the Y-shaped cone, such a decision would probably exacerbate Gaynor's discrepancy and lessen further her sense of safety; thereby polarizing positions and making change even less likely.

Therefore, while acknowledging the difficulties experienced at home, the rehabilitation team faced the challenge of maintaining an alliance with Gaynor and her parents while containing their discordant perspectives, and creating a safe environment for Gaynor to begin to slowly explore her identity and skills post-injury. Provision of information about the possible consequences of brain injury, was likely to further polarize this family's positions, and they had already been provided with such information by previous services.

Many of the important factors in building an alliance: listening, competence, responding, and honesty, were compromised in this case. For example, when Mrs B phoned to express her concerns but ask that this is not shared with Gaynor, the clinician's alliance with Gaynor was challenged through having knowledge of the 'secret call'. Further, the clinician is less able to respond actively to the information provided in the call because of its 'secretive' nature. The competent clinician may not be viewed as such by the family members because they seem unable to 'get it' and use their power to react as each family member would hope in order to convince the other of the 'true solution'. In this example, the rehabilitation team is holding the dilemma of a family who is 'stuck' in their interactions, unable to progress beyond their contesting dynamics based on the definition of the problem and the appropriate responses.

Formulation and interventions

Initial work focused around hearing Gaynor's individual story, and the 'Impatience' was a good starting point to work with because it afforded the opportunity for narrative questioning (see chapter 9) about 'the impatience' and how it had a 'good side' and a 'tricky side'. We were able to use it as a basis to explore her thinking about before and after the injury: Gaynor said it was a problem she had "always" had. We asked her to richly describe the impatience and what the effects of being impatient on her life are, and are there times when she manages the impatience? Who else is impatient in her family? When does it work well? Gaynor noted that she cannot spend her life being impatient but sometimes it can be helpful. So we asked: when is it a problem? When is it important to be the most patient? And what happens to your body when you're being impatient? During this time, when Mrs B called the unit, she was asked not to share information with the team that she would be uncomfortable with Gaynor knowing. The team reminded her of their position with regard to confidentiality of information regarding Gaynor, inviting her to consider ways in which she might like the rehabilitation team to support her to share her concerns or with Gaynor. Conversations with Gaynor about 'the impatience' generated curiosity about her parent's perspectives and how they might be the same or different to her own.

Family sessions were then offered and initially, building an individual alliance with Gaynor and each of her parents did not present a challenge as each saw the clinician as 'the judge'; the root to resolution of their individual discrepancy (i.e., 'this is the professional who can persuade my daughter/mother/father of the true resolution to this problem'). Although, it was not possible to maintain the position of clinician as 'the judge' this was formulated as an initial position that provided sufficient hope within the system to engage the family in a meeting together, in which they might have a different conversation.

Over the initial family assessment sessions, Mrs B described her position as one of attempting to keep her daughter safe; protecting her from making plans that do not take account of her vulnerability post-injury, while also being the 'peace maker' and protecting Gaynor from arguing with her father. She indicated that these were attempts to reduce her own sense of discrepancy between feeling that she is either a "good mother who does her best" or a "bad mother who did not protect her daughter." Unfortunately, her efforts have the opposite effect and inadvertently increase the discrepancy that Gaynor feels, who then attempts to be even more "like her old self" (making spontaneous decisions and refusing to share her plan with her parents), which temporarily reduced her own sense of threat. In turn, this inadvertently increases her mother's anxiety ("my daughter is unsafe and I need to do something to make her safe"), making her more likely to state her solution again with increasing force, and so on. Her attempts to protect her daughter by 'teaching' her about her disabilities, were triggering disputes, and were inadvertently reinforcing Gaynor's position of 'no awareness'. Gaynor's father described his position as wanting there to be less arguments at home, not really understanding why they were happening, and torn between whether to support his wife or his daughter. This family were understood as being 'at the top of the Y' where each person's attempts to reduce their discrepancies were magnifying the sense of threat (discrepancy) for another.

Once the family had agreed to meet together, the therapists were able to gently but clearly take the relational risk of then explaining that they were not going to provide 'the solution' in that session (illustrating 'honesty' and 'recognition of limitations' while maintaining their hope of finding new possibilities for the family, and reducing conflict). It would not be possible to preserve the dynamics while maintaining the position of 'judge'. Therefore, the therapist's task was to share the family dilemma (previously held by the team) with the family themselves, and invite them to use their family resources and resilience to consider possibilities for making it less of a dilemma.

Therefore, they invited the family to get to know their shared dilemma by 'walking around in the problem' (Vetere, 2007) at the top of the Y, and posed a question to the family: "what does Gaynor's independence mean to you and what would independence be like if Gaynor were to be independent?" Taking time to deconstruct the problem and normalize individual responses to it, the family was helped to generate their own questions for future work. They spoke about viewing the ABI in the context of adolescence, which provided a helpful framework for conversation. We reflected that the parent's experiences were different in degree but not necessarily in kind, and were also unexpected in terms of family life-cycle stages (McGoldrick, Gerson, & Petry, 2008), which identified the differences in each family member's dilemma. That is to say that Gaynor's parents had been expecting to soon begin their retirement, but this plan had been changed by the accident and instead, they returned to an active parenting role.

The deconstruction of independence took place over two to three sessions, after which the family had started to tentatively have different conversations with one another. The family reported noticing their opinions were not vastly different from one another but that what they meant by the term 'independence' was different in each case, despite using the same word. They were then supported to identify what they would like to learn about next, and develop some plans to work on together. Although the family wanted to rush towards major solutions (e.g., Gaynor suggesting her parents should allow her to go abroad on holiday), the therapists' role was to encourage them to continue to 'go slowly' and really spend time getting to know the problem, before making major decisions. Deconstructing the problem and supporting the family to take it further than their linear or blaming explanation by externalizing and witnessing the alternative story was a means of introducing curiosity and flexibility into their narratives, and identifying negative cycles between people's interactions. The family meetings became a place where continuums were explored together, rather than a place where fixed truths were outlined. For example: that there is a 'middle ground' between 'free-range' and 'strict' parenting in terms of who holds the responsibility. Rather than placing the problem entirely in the blame of the brain injury, or entirely in the blame of Gaynor's behaviour as 'childlike' (two narratives that closed down curiosity) the reframe of 'adolescence' was used to help the family conceptualize Gaynor's striving for independence in the context of their wish to protect her and keep her close. Through conversation about independence, the reframe of 'impulsivity' emerged, highlighting how much Gaynor's parents had enjoyed and now missed Gaynor's social 'spontaneity' (i.e., bringing friends around at short notice or going to events 'at the drop of a hat') and so they agreed that complete elimination of impulsive decisions was no longer their goal, which provided leeway for Gaynor to negotiate.

Review

The task of the therapist was to provide a safe environment in which the family members could be supported to map out their different opinions in a way that they each recognized their contribution and felt listened to by the therapist and their family members. The task was also to create a space where the family members each began to notice each other's positive intent behind their actions, which were previously viewed as destructive. This approach was 'respectful' through acknowledging the complexity of the situation. In short, slowing the conversation down (Vetere, 2007) enabled this family to remove the pressure to solve the problem or convince the other of their perspective. Instead, they were able to better get to know and understand their own dilemma, which offered the opportunity to introduce curiosity and subsequently flexibility into their stories. Introducing flexibility into their ideas enabled people to see that they each sit at different points on a continuum rather than on entirely different planets. Taking the time to explore the different perspectives (the discrepancies and individual suggestions for resolution) provided the bridge between holding a somewhat fragile alliance with individuals within the family, to developing collaboration with the family as a group with a shared understanding of the work that might be ahead.

Summary

Three cases have been described to illustrate the application and integration of ideas described throughout this book where the injured relative was concurrently participating in an intensive rehabilitation programme. This chapter aims to provide examples of clinical work that demonstrate relational interventions as a feasible component of intensive rehabilitation programmes, and provide a framework for considering creative mediums of engaging clients in conversation about their family, or intervening in a manner that is respectful of cognitive impairment, and which can also be linked back to individual rehabilitation aspirations or goals.

Special thanks to Fergus Gracey, Paul Lewington, and Anna Healey for their contributions to these cases.

CHAPTER NINE

Working with family systems:
Tactics and techniques in practice

In this chapter, we outline a model for working with family systems after brain injury, which in particular draws on methods obtained from the family therapy literature. We are aware that brain injury services are varied in their organization and in the resources available to meet needs beyond the immediate needs of the injured individual. However, we would like to share some of our work conducted where we have been fortunate to work in services allowing opportunities for broader inclusion and consideration of relational approaches. We also appreciate that clients are individual and that the impact of brain injury upon a client and their context is unique, and that for some the level of disability and alteration in behaviour is profound. In spite of this, we believe relational thinking can be applied to the understanding and formulation of a broad range of presentations, although interventions will be tailored to be sensitive and understood by clients and their system.

A general note is needed at the outset, about the departure from biomedical and person-centred approaches to rehabilitation, and a refocusing on 'system-centred' thinking in rehabilitation, research and new clinical practices emphasizing the family-therapist alliance. This we emphasize because on many occasions, traditional approaches invite a curiosity about the impact of brain injury that rests solely on the person and their isolated psychology, moving the 'torch-beam' away from relational meanings and processes, and leading to other system members being routinely absent from the formulation-intervention process (see also chapter 11). Alternatively, here we invite formulations that are contextualized with the 'couple/family as the client'. This brings into sharp focus any contesting dynamics, alliances, and ruptures between members of the system (see also chapters 6 and 7). A holistic formulation that includes all members of the system also invites consideration of circularity; a cornerstone of family systems theory and therapy (Palazzoli, Boscolo, Cecchin, & Prata, 1980) and when this is recognized it is possible to see the dramatic way relationships organize around a brain injury, via a system of mutual influence and feedback loops (Bowen et al., 2009). The circular processes at work mean that the impact of brain injury is felt by all members of a system.

Understanding the family system

Over the course of the last 50 or so years since its inception, the field of family therapy has undergone many changes to the distinct models that exist in the literature. For the purposes of this discussion, we distinguish four types of family therapy: strategic, structural, systemic (associated with the Milan school), and narrative. There are some assumptions that underlie all family therapy approaches:

- Families consist of individuals but also relationships, boundaries, and hierarchies;
- Parts of a family are inter-related (one part of the family cannot be understood in isolation from the rest of the system);
- Family members are governed by communication patterns (we are constantly in communication with each other even when we choose not to communicate);
- People act on the basis of their beliefs;
- Even problematic behaviours may have a positive intention;
- The causality of problems as defined by the family is often 'circular'; that is to say, the origins and maintenance of a family problem are distributed across family members.

The strategic school of family therapy has evolved over the past 50 years, in association with the Mental Research Institute in California, as documented in the early paper on 'double-bind' and schizophrenia (Bateson, Jackson, Haley, & Weakland, 1956). Key pioneers of this approach have been Jay Haley (1978), Chloe Madanes (1981), Steve de Shazer (1982), Insoo Kim Berg (de Jong & Berg, 2002), and Bill O'Hanlon (O'Hanlon & Bertolino, 1999); there was also close collaboration with Milton Erickson initially (Haley, 1978). A founding belief of this school of thought was that 'the problem is the solution'; that is to say that the family's solutions to problems have now become the problems, that is, well-intentioned but maladaptive attempts to find resolution. Unsurprisingly, strategic or brief therapists tend to focus on the process of therapy and work in the here-and-now. They can also be quite provocative in their interventions, for example, using paradoxical intention or the miracle question to provoke a change in the families who consult with them. In this sense, notions of 'resistance' are routinely questioned (de Shazer, 1982). When adopting this approach in neuro-rehabilitation settings, it would be important to ask about and to monitor times and situations when the problem is not present (the idea of 'problem-free talk').

Structural family therapy is most often associated with Salvadore Minuchin, who pioneered work using ideas of boundaries, sub-systems, and hierarchies (Minuchin, 1974). Central to this theory is the idea that, to be 'healthy', families need clear boundaries, particularly around the parental and child sub-systems. In this sense, it is important to monitor for coalitions between a child and a parent, against another parent (so-called 'triangulation'), so extreme closeness across generations and sub-systems would be hypothesized to be inappropriate. While often criticized as being too traditional and prescriptive, a helpful example of a structural intervention is the technique of enactment, to challenge unhelpful patterns of communication and redefine role relations. Within neuro-rehabilitation this may be used to address the problems of dependency and to intervene into situations where children or spouses become carers. Therapists using this model pay close attention to non-verbal behaviour (e.g., how people are seated) and would be very active when intervening to change.

It is interesting to note that the term 'systemic' has been adopted as a generic term for family therapy and perhaps this reflects the impact of this founding group of therapists from Milan,[1] following their re-reading of Bateson's (1972) "Steps to an Ecology of Mind." Key components to the systemic model, as set out in a series of guidelines, are: hypothesizing, circularity, and neutrality—later redefined as curiosity (Cecchin, 1987; Palazzoli, Boscolo, Cecchin, & Prata, 1980). Systemic therapists are often associated with seeking to find 'the difference that makes the difference'. The meaning behind this quote is the notion that families are constrained by their beliefs, and that it is only by introducing flexibility into belief systems, that change can occur. However, change will not occur if the 'new belief' or 'new idea' is *too* different from their previous beliefs and behaviours, or if it is *not different enough* from these. Therefore, the therapist seeks the right balance or size of difference to make the difference to family beliefs and behaviour.

The Milan model is also known for making a distinction between first- and second-order change, the latter of which is thought to reflect a deeper and more long-lasting change that goes beyond symptomatic relief. This became a focus in treatment because it was often observed that one symptom would often be replaced by another, or that the problem would move between family members. Linked to these ideas is the notion that families will often act in accordance with the principle of homeostasis, that is, that certain behaviours have the effect of maintaining members' proximity to other members of the system. Influenced by broader movements within social constructionism and the critique of Feminism, this group progressed from a first- to second-order cybernetics (Von Foerster, 1982) theoretical base during the late 1980s to consider how they as 'observing systems' were powerful influences on the families they consulted (Cecchin, 1987). Indeed, how this plane of influence became a source for inspiration for the two men within the Milan group to develop new approaches to practice and consultation.

The narrative movement of family therapy and community work changed the landscape of therapeutic approaches in part because of the deconstructionist philosophy that underpinned it. Beginning in 1990, with the seminal work "Narrative Means to Therapeutic

---

[1] The Milan model of family therapy can be dated back to the ground-breaking book "Paradox and Counterparadox" in 1978, by Mara Selvini-Palazzoli, Luigi Boscolo, Gianfranco Cecchin, and Giuliana Prata.

Ends" (co-authored with David Epston), and ending with "Maps of Narrative Practice" in 2007 shortly before his death, Michael White challenged the therapeutic community to rethink many of its grounding assumptions. Externalization is one of the strategies, which features heavily in narrative therapy works. By external-izing problems, a 'problem' is personalized and delineated and thereby given boundaries, making it appear more manageable, and thereby emphasizing the distinction between problem and person. Externalization also enables members of the family and social net-work who may previously have been divided by the problem to unite against it (an important element within neuro-rehabilitation). Within relational rehabilitation the strategy of externalization can be used to encourage the individual to relate in a new way to their brain injury, by investigating its properties and the ways in which it has impacted on one's former and current life. As rehabilitation therapists, we need to pick up the cues and be sensitive to exactly how the survivor describes their brain injury (remember chapter 2 and the fact that no brain injury is alike), after all the injured person is the most informed individual about their brain injury and how it has changed their life.

As will be detailed in further sections of this chapter, elements of all these models can be usefully applied to neuro-rehabilitation settings, whether it is 'problem-free talk', working with sub-systems, introducing ideas of difference, or helping a family unite against the brain injury that currently divides the family system.

A relational approach to formulation in neuro-rehabilitation

"In effect a primary aspect of formulation is the juggling of ... competing definitions or constructions regarding problems in families."

(Vetere & Dallos, 2003, p. 66/7)

In their book, Vetere and Dallos (2003) present a composite family model that has five components. These are:

1. deconstruction of the problem from all perspectives;
2. description of problem-maintaining systems;
3. beliefs and expectations;

4. emotions and attachments; and
5. contextual factors.

Taking this as a framework, we now present a case using these domains to bring into the foreground the defining aspects of the model. We will return to the case later in the chapter when we discuss intervention strategies. This method of formulation is further described in later work "Attachment Narrative Therapy" (Dallos, 2006) and "Systemic Therapy and Attachment Narratives" (Vetere & Dallos, 2009).

The first part of the model (deconstruction) is important within neuro-rehabilitation work because of the 'contesting dynamics' that exist within the family as each member in turn manages their own adjustment to the injury. This we have already seen in the earlier chapters, particularly in relation to couples work, but we now extend this to include the perspective of children, who also have the added layer of complexity that each is simultaneously developing, cognitively and emotionally. The implications of this are that the family picture is constantly shifting and so not static. This added layer of complexity can be a factor in problem-maintaining systems and feedback loops, for example, if initially children are at an age when they are unable to understand the full implications of the injury to their parent. This in turn sets up beliefs and expectations about the problem that may have to be directly addressed. Further details of specific issues for children when adapting to a parent's brain injury are given in Daisley and Webster (2008).

Family 1

At time of referral to the community neuro-rehabilitation team, Julie was being seen solely as an outpatient by both Consultants in Neurology and Neuro-Rehabilitation, every few months. The community team began visiting Julie and were immediately struck by the close atmosphere between the children and within the house generally. Psychological support was offered to both Julie and to her children, who would initially each have separate appointments, but with their mother present. Two therapists visited on occasions because of the complex issues that arose for this family, as evident in ongoing family discussions. Breaking the issues down into the five

Julie

Julie was a 47 years old British woman and mother of two, a son aged 11 and a teenage daughter aged 18. Prior to contact with our service, Julie was rushed to hospital for emergency clipping of an aneurysm and neu-ro-surgical removal of a haematoma. There were remaining smaller and intact aneurysms and this was a considerable source of anxiety for Julie. Her main complaints were of subtle changes to her attention, memory, and concentration, and as an avid reader this was having a significant impact on her quality of life. She had also had to give up work. As a woman who had prided herself in her independence and her ability to be a single-mother to her children, she had substantial difficulty accepting help and support from other people.

components of the model, Figure 1 (overleaf) describes the defining features of the case.

In terms of deconstructing the problem, different members of the family were preoccupied with different aspects of the situational dynamics. For Julie, there were significant but subtle cognitive changes and lapses in her autobiographical memory for events, also impacting on her everyday memory. The children, in contrast, had been thrust into premature responsibilities when mum was in hospital and one sensed they were acutely aware of the fragility of their mother's condition and what might happen should there be a recurrence of a rupture to an aneurysm. For the elder of the two children, the punctuation in the family life cycle was having significant repercussions for her aspirations in life given she had deferred going to University but instead taken a job locally. She clearly felt the need to monitor her mother and stay in constant touch, keeping the whole family in mind at a stage in her development that would usually have been characterized by increased independence. The younger of the two children was losing his sense of being the 'special one', and instead having to support his mother. Reports from school indicated he was more irritable than previously he had been and was getting into fights with his peers and this was unheard of. Both children seemed to be feeling the loss of their mother's executive skills, managing all the competing demands that fall on a family these days. For the rehabilitation team, there were concerns about support for Julie and for the children, so

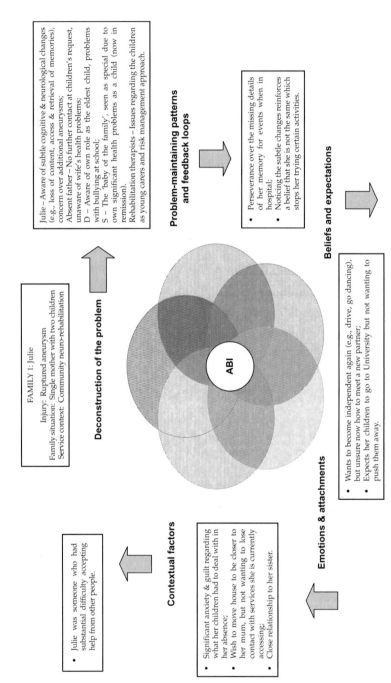

Deconstruction of the problem

FAMILY 1: Julie
Injury: Ruptured aneurysm
Family situation: Single mother with two children
Service context: Community neuro-rehabilitation

Problem-maintaining patterns and feedback loops

Julie – Aware of subtle cognitive & neurological changes (e.g., loss of content, access & retrieval of memories), concern over additional aneurysms;
Absent father – No further contact at children's request, unaware of wife's health problems;
D – Aware of own role as the eldest child, problems with bullying at school;
S – The 'baby of the family', seen as special due to own significant health problems as a child (now in remission).
Rehabilitation therapists – Issues regarding the children as young carers and risk management approach.

Beliefs and expectations

• Perseverance over the missing details of her memory for events when in hospital;
• Noticing the subtle changes reinforces a belief that she is not the same which stops her trying certain activities.

Emotions & attachments

• Wants to become independent again (e.g., drive, go dancing), but unsure now how to meet a new partner;
• Expects her children to go to University but not wanting to push them away.

Contextual factors

• Julie was someone who had substantial difficulty accepting help from other people.

• Significant anxiety & guilt regarding what her children had to deal with in her absence;
• Wish to move house to be closer to her mum, but not wanting to lose contact with services she is currently accessing;
• Close relationship to her sister.

Figure 1. A systemic formulation of family 1.

for the family as a whole. In terms of the Y- (or cone) shaped model (described in chapter 7), all parties were in a different place; life was not as it was supposed to be. For the mother, she was independent and singly responsible for her children, yet was struggling to read and write. The contrast could not be starker. For the children, they were taking on responsibilities for their mother and for themselves, when life should have been about having fun.

With regard to problem-maintaining patterns, Julie seemed in a perpetual state of perseverance and rumination about the state of her health and about what difficulties she might encounter in the future. She was very much focused on the detail of her exact injury, while her children were concerned about who would be there for them should their mother be taken ill again. This rumination was having a slowing down effect on Julie and causing her to be very cautious in all her activities, again reinforcing the belief that something was seriously wrong.

Julie's beliefs and expectations centred on how she would be able to recover her independence, for example, when would be the right time to drive was a question that perplexed her, and the fact that after 'a year' she may be able to do this amused her but also unnerved her. She was also conscious that perhaps now she depended on her children more than they depended on her and this was a novel and unsettling experience for her. The fact there were remaining aneurysms was also disconcerting and added to her anxiety and fear about making future decisions.

Julie's emotions and attachments were heavily weighted towards feelings of anxiety and undeserved guilt. She clearly felt she had failed her children in some way, yet this was from the perspective of an outdated self-concept, an identity that did not reflect the person she now was. The attachments she felt for her children had therefore come under considerable strain and required support from external sources to weather this. She was also very conscious of the importance of her attachment to her own mother and sister, for her own personal support but also because of the important role they might again have to play for the children.

In terms of wider context, Julie remained constrained by her independent self, and there was a felt sense of this discrepancy, a discrepancy between her self-identity now and previously.

Following formulation of the issues, we now describe the techniques and tactics that we have found to work with considerable success in the field of neuro-rehabilitation. Later in the chapter we return to this first case, before presenting other cases to illustrate different aspects of the model.

Gaining a mutual and shared understanding of the problem: Sustaining hope

One of the intriguing aspects of working with families follow-ing brain injury is gaining a mutual and 'shared understanding' (Wilson, Gracey, Malley, Bateman, & Evans, 2009) of the problem (see also chapter 7). Family members often bring this dilemma with them, but they may be looking for ways to resolve it, or they may be making sense of it in unhelpful ways such as using blame or linear ways of thinking about it (e.g., she can behave because she never loses her temper at the rehabilitation centre). Sometimes the most helpful thing to do is to provide a space where the family can open up this discussion between themselves facilitated by staff, thereby perceiving more circular connections between events. Opening up the space to do this can be tricky, because it depends on how much time you have. Some services are so restricted for time that they do not have much opportunity to offer treatment in addition to assessment. However, when resources are available, it may be useful to set up a situation where you have one or two clinicians and ask the family to invite who they think is important and set out chairs for those people whether or not they attend (Burnham, 1986). Then set the scene that the problem cannot be solved in that specific hour, but that the first step is in identifying the problem as they each see it. Supporting them to discover it for themselves but in the presence of an independent person—the 'professionals', can be very helpful. We can then also help them continue to explore any variability in their accounts beyond linear or blaming explanations. These are the points at which narrative ideas can be extremely helpful for finding the alternative or untold stories, the stories that move away from complexity. Ideas of witnessing and externalizing can also be helpful here because they take ownership of the problem away to a certain extent. For example, reflecting with family members that from what they are saying sometimes the brain injury really comes between them and stops them from talking clearly to one another yet other times it is as if it was not there at all may lead to further clarification about what is it about these moments, which makes them happen and how can we encourage more of them?

Of course, a further issue to be grappled with is how the injury manifests itself in different ways depending on contextual demands, and so there are real reasons for different sides of the problem being apparent at different times and to different people, in such case which descriptions do family members find more empowering? As well as the answer to this being the ones that confer with their views, family members may also show a preference for the descriptions that indicate a better prognosis. Indeed, all of us will be familiar with the not uncommon phenomenon of the family that 'shops' around, asking different team members the same question until they find the answer they seek. Given this possibly, are there better and less good ways of conveying a professional opinion to families? Definitely conveying a message that does not take away the family's hope is helpful and one way of doing this with integrity, would be to highlight cases where the survivor has progressed against the odds and against the predictions of the doctors. Giving this as an example of what could happen fosters a feeling of togetherness that may be priceless for the survivor and family's continued motivation. In addition, it is important to give a description that references each family members' view (is multi-faceted) and that highlights flexibility of cognition, because if there is a contesting dynamic within the family, then one reason for this is most likely that the consequences of the injury appear variable to the family, and acknowledging this is a way of engaging with their perception of reality. Over time one becomes more and more aware of the complexity of working with families, and the complexity of issues that they bring; all families are so very different.

Finally, an additional issue that comes up in this work is that part of the experience of neuro-rehabilitation services is about precision and there being a quantifiable answer so where some family members may come to expect this from therapists, others may seek an opportunity to stop and think about where they have got to so far. To reiterate, it is important to convey a description of the problem that is hopeful, is multi-faceted, and accurate but reflects any variable presentation of the survivor and hence, has the effect of "opening space" for family members to consider new possibilities.

*Applications and adaptations of family therapy
to brain injury contexts*

In this section, we wish to elaborate on the tactics and techniques that have been found to be helpful within mainstream family therapy and relate these approaches to the emotional adjustment of families after brain injury, while also being mindful of the components of family interventions that are known to be important to this population (see also chapter 7). This section offers a platform from which therapists are invited to think creatively about which tactics or techniques are appropriate for their situation, and trial-selected approaches to their own formulated interventions.

In a recent randomized controlled trial in which systemic couple therapy was demonstrated to be a proven treatment for depression (Leff, Vearnals, Brewin, Wolff, Alexander, Asen et al., 2000), therapists found a number of generic intervention strategies to be helpful (Jones & Asen, 2000), namely: hypothesizing, joining, and engagement, circular interviewing, enactment, focusing on strengths, problem-solving, challenging, family life-space techniques (e.g., genograms, mapping), reframing, inter-session tasks (e.g., homework), and non-couple sessions interspersed with couple sessions. Similarly in their model, Vetere and Dallos (2003) highlight the beneficial effects of hypothesizing, circular questions, reframing, genograms, problem-solving, and solution-focused approaches.

Many families affected by brain injury have functioned effectively as a system prior to the injury. They may hold many resources between them which have been somehow 'disabled' by the injury and its circumstances. For this reason, some families benefit from one to two sessions with the therapist through which to 'normalize' their responses to the whole experience and enable them to 'step back' and reflect on their own interactions, such that their shared 'catastrophic reaction' (Goldstein, 1959) to the injury subsides. This may re-activate previously adaptive coping strategies, and allow them to move forward without embarking on more in depth therapeutic work. Initial work with families, therefore, can involve the process of exploring their opinions and supporting them to stop and reflect on how their perspectives are both similar and different.

For some families, the difference between before and after the injury is *too different*, and noticing similarity and difference is insufficient to enable them to problem solve together. It is these families we need to accompany to 'walk around the top of the Y' (as described in chapter 7), but also offer to them support over a longer period of time. To facilitate this there are a number of useful tactics and techniques taken from family therapy, and for the purpose of describing their applicability to the context of brain injury rehabilitation they are organized below under the following headings:

1. Taking a team approach;
2. Mapping the injury and the system, family scripts and life cycles;
3. Introducing curiosity and flexibility into the system and working with difference;
4. Re-positioning, re-membering, re-constructing;
5. Therapeutic documents and witnessing.

Tactic 1: Taking a team approach

Within neuro-rehabilitation and neuropsychology services, there is a strong emphasis on interdisciplinary, multidisciplinary and across agency working and so it is essential to be mindful of team dynamics and taking a team approach. As we have discussed in earlier chapters, a rehabilitation team would usually consist of a team of rehabilitation support staff or therapy assistants, organized by one or more of each of the following clinicians: Occupational Therapist, Speech and Language Therapist, Physiotherapist, Clinical (Neuro) Psychologist, Doctors, Nurses, and possibly family therapists. In addition, but depending on the nature of their client group, some centres would require access to dieticians, engineers, music therapists, and so on. We have already discussed how professional groups each have their own focus and typical mode of intervention (e.g., verbal, physical, drug), even their own codes of conduct, but it is not uncommon for professionals to have to work across boundaries and to experience a degree of blurring of roles. For example, when conducting visits in the community, it may be necessary to ask a broad range of questions and to feedback to the team before a joint decision is made about whether further visits are required perhaps by other team members. There is a need for the team approach to become part of the professional identity of each and every rehabilitation specialism.

Hence, neuro-rehabilitation specialists are no strangers to a team approach and to team discussions in particular. Yet, what may be more unusual is to meet with survivor and family as a team; an approach taken for granted within family therapy (Burnham, 1986; Stratton, Preston-Shoot, & Hanks, 1990).

Certainly, there are no specific reasons from a medical or psychological point of view for why a team approach and joint meetings in particular could not work in neuro-rehabilitation settings. Indeed, it is often more practical considerations that limit the extent to which team appointments can take place, for example, resource and workload issues, constraints due to physical space, wheelchair access, and typical length of sessions being too long for individuals with neurological difficulties because of their difficulties concentrating. However, adjustments can and are made to adapt these techniques to rehabilitation work, and once a setting is created for rehabilitation specialists to meet as a team with families then this opens the door to other more exotic technology and techniques such as one-way screens, reflecting teams, definitional ceremonies, outsider witnessing, using 'experience consultants' ('expert' families), or an 'in room consultant'.

Let us consider these examples of specific techniques that can be employed:

Reflecting teams (Anderson, 1987)
Reflecting teams have been used in family therapy settings routinely, to comment on process and create opportunities for the family to listen to the therapists talking about what they noticed when the family were talking. Within narrative therapy, they have also been likened to definitional ceremony or outsider witnessing (White, 1995). In the context of executive impairments, they can support retrieval of memory for the session so far (through the therapists 'summarizing'), support the whole family to 'stop and think', and so support the family as a whole to hold a meta-position on their own interactions.

In addition, reflecting teams are also a means of translating the language of medicine and neurology for non-professionals, in part because a range of views are offered and the family sees at first hand that there can be disagreement and difference of opinion within the team (thus introducing the possibility of flexibility, even around neurological 'truths'). Indeed, while there is a pressure to specify the precise nature of difficulties in court reports, it is not uncommon for two professionals to offer differing clinical opinion, or view situations from differing perspectives. Reflecting teams open up professional conversations directly to families, so they do not appear to happen behind closed doors.

Reflecting team discussions follow different formats, some invite spontaneous comment and discussion, whereas others are more highly prescribed. The degree to which they follow narrative ideas also varies. Typically team members (three to six members) speak for about 10–15 minutes from a position of curiosity about preferred developments for the family. Team members might comment on some aspect of the session and then ask a question or converse in a 'wondering way' (Hoffman, 1989). Additionally, they would usually 'situate' what they say by maybe connecting it to some aspect of theory, knowledge, experience, personal or professional. In principle, reflecting as a team organizes the family and brings them together rather than have them divided in their own disputes. Questions and comments may reflect the relational themes of this book about the 'space' the injury occupies and how it operates within social situations (instances of 'problem-free talk'), or how to draw family members into the conversation, or comment on the multi-verse of opinion by subverting a pretence of 'expertise'—that there is no right answer, just dilemmas, confusion, and greyness:

- "I noticed we heard a lot about the times when the injury dominates family life, that this really has had a significant impact on everyone's life. But from speaking to other people with different health problems I know that people often talk about the difficult times because it becomes a habit and because they feel they should do this at hospital. So I wonder about the untold stories about moments when the injury brings people closer, when do they occur? And I also wonder about the times when the family are not at hospital and what they do to have fun together?"
- "I noticed that mum was very quiet during the conversation we heard, and looked worried. This makes me wonder what she might have said had she felt able to, or whether it was too painful to say what was on her mind? I also wonder who else might have noticed she was quiet and whether this is perhaps part of the problem that there is so much going on that people do not notice each other?"

- "We as a team of neuro-rehabilitation professionals can't make our minds up—we see how confusing it is for you all.... My colleague thinks that the brain injury has had a devastating effect on Dad's ability to take part in family activities and that he needs specialist rehabilitation away from the family, whereas I think he is already feeling lonely and isolated and that taking him away from his only support could be devastating."

Further discussion about use of reflection is discussed under 'tactic 5'.

Experience consultants

Another way of recognizing the knowledge and power of families themselves is by using 'experience consultants', based on narrative therapy principles. In contrast to outsider-witnessing that could involve anyone, or use of an 'in room consultant' which involves another professional, experience consultants are survivors who have passed through services and are then called on to witness, even celebrate, the achievements of others. This way survivors and their family are given credit for the intimate knowledge they have acquired of their condition.[2] White (2007) describes a method in which certificates are awarded as in ceremonial fashion but there is no one way to use this technique. Generally, the message has greater authenticity if the consultant has passed through the same service and it is important not to underestimate the powerful source of support that can be provided by other families in a similar but perhaps 'more resolved' positions.

Another approach sometimes used is multi-family group interventions, for which there is a rich literature for psychosis (Asen & Schuff, 2006), depression (Lemmens, Eisler, Migerode, Heireman, & Demyttenaere, 2007), and anorexia nervosa (Eisler, 2005), and this has recently been applied to brain injury (Charles, Butera-Prinzi, & Perlesz, 2007).

User-involvement

Finally, survivors are also in a position to advise care providers about gaps in service provision and even join interview panels in order to give a user-perspective. In this way survivors and their families are given

---

[2] This is similar in ethos to the UK initiative called the 'expert patient programme'.

a voice on strategic matters and this is an approach that has grown in popularity and respectability over recent years. Cottrell, Boston, and Walker (2004) highlight that service-user involvement is important more generally in family therapy because of the technical aspects of the treatment and because of ground rules, also because children may have differing perspectives on the nature of therapy, for example, they may find alternative activities to talking like play beneficial.

Tactic 2: Mapping the injury and system, family scripts, and life cycles

In the early days, family therapy placed considerable emphasis on the role of processes of homeostasis, that is, why change is not always possible in human systems. This followed on from observations of how families became stuck, constrained, were rigid in their functioning, and so on. There was a general belief that in order to bring about change the first step was to identify the problem-maintaining patterns, and this is identified as a key component of the composite formulation model outlined by Vetere and Dallos (2003); see above.

Mapping is a method for discovering the terrain in which therapy needs to operate by examining the language that is used to describe a brain injury. By charting this we raise awareness and articulate the patterns, exceptions, and dilemmas thereby gently challenging the problem-maintaining patterns. The types of questions we might ask ourselves include:

- *Who is attending sessions and who is defining who as a problem?*
- *Is this the result of the brain injury or due to him/her as a person?*
- *What other reason might there be? Was this a problem before the injury? How might people have responded then?*
- *What are the differences in problem definitions?*
- *What is the connection between those people who have a similar/different problem definition?*
- *If this is related to the brain injury/some other cause, where does that leave each family member (and others)?*
- *Which services are involved with whom and on what basis?*
- *Who is responding and to what problem?*
- *Who's not involved (e.g., children, spouse)?*
- *Where are the gaps in support?*

(to the family)

• *Who agrees with this explanation? Who disagrees? How does X's description make you feel?*
• *Is this a problem 100% of the time, or are there exceptions? On these occasions what is each person doing? What happens to the brain injury at these times? (i.e., when does Y experience most/least cognitive difficulties?)*

[See also mapping a problem-determined system (Anderson, Goolishian, & Winderman, 1986)].

Mapping the system

In order to understand the system one needs detailed information about the individuals, but also the quality of the relationships, boundaries, hierarchies, alliances, and communication patterns. The composite model by Vetere and Dallos (2003) is a good starting point for thinking about the issues, which can then be represented in written or visual form (see also 'genogram' below). There are a number of distinctions in the family systems literature that may be helpful when trying to map out the system, such as:

• complementary versus symmetrical relationships;
• enmeshed versus disengaged relationships.

The term complementary relationships is used to describe a situation in which someone is the carer and another cared for, whereas symmetrical relationships describes a process of escalation whereby similar verbal exchanges (e.g., compliments, anger) produce a cycle as each responds to the other in the same fashion, a cycle that is virtuous and circular. 'Enmeshment' is a term that was first coined by Minuchin, that unhealthy relationships may occur across generations that are emotionally very close. More recently, this term has been heavily criticized by opponents of the structural model (Green & Werner, 1996), as have notions of triangulation, for being, insensitive to cultural differences (Falicov, 1998) and ignoring the times when these strategies may be used as an appropriate response to insurmountable challenges in society.

One would also be looking out for repeated patterns across generations again particularly in terms of relationships, boundaries, hierarchies, alliances, and communication patterns. Gregory Bateson has theorized extensively about these processes in his book Steps to an Ecology of Mind.

Attachment systems

Another theory of relevance to discussions of both mapping and family work is attachment theory, following John Bowlby (e.g., Bowlby, 1969). This early work was very much led by observation studies of controlled separation between mothers and their infants, later reunited, and concerned with a classification system of the behaviour of the infant (and mother) during this period, hence the parallel with ideas of mapping. The resultant attachment patterns (secure, anxious, avoidant, and disorganized) have since been widely debated, elaborated to include adult attachment, and despite fierce critics of the intention behind the research particularly on political and gender grounds have ultimately stood the test of time (Dallos, 2006). Ways of specifically incorporating attachment ideas into neuro-rehabilitation include:

• Thinking about how the injury can impair the ability to perform attachment behaviours, such as aligning with others, or 'self-soothing';
• Thinking about the effects of separations due to hospitalization on attachments and the family system (e.g., a brain injury can re-organize family interactions and disorganized attachment systems; and children and their parents may need sensitive and supported reintroductions).

This is an area covered in relation to couples work in chapters 4 and 5.

Working with family scripts and life-cycle issues

This is a technique proposed by John Byng-Hall as key to working with families, now extended to the neuro-rehabilitation field by Rolland's Family-Illness-Systems Model (Rolland, 1990; 1994; 1999; Rolland & Willians, 2005; Rolland & Williams, 2006), to include the psychosocial demands of various neurological conditions in relation to life-cycle issues. Byng-Hall defines family scripts as:

> "… a way of thinking about repeated patterns of family interaction. A family script is the family's shared expectations about what roles are to be played in various contexts, so that family members know their roles and enter on cue in unfolding family scenarios. Family stories are linked to scripts through a recursive and evolving process." (Byng-Hall, 1998, p. 136)

Family members are undoubtedly aware of their roles and there are situations and circumstances when this becomes more or less obvious. One moment when this is the case is following a neurological injury or illness. Future-oriented questioning can help couples and family members think beyond the problem. By facilitating conversations about joint hopes for the relationship, the focus of the conversation is removed from 'how *you are* different' to 'how *we, could* be different' and through this, couples and families can be helped to create shared goals and re-connect.

Life-cycle issues are patterns of family interaction that change and evolve through expected and predicted ways, for example, when children leave home and parents start to become frail and more dependent on their children. Events can also work against or run counter to family scripts such as when parents have to continue to care for their children over long periods of time or into adulthood. Hence, to suffer a brain injury is against the typical life-cycle pattern, and challenges families to adapt to unexpected transitions and perhaps reverse the family script about who cares for whom. Recent research has also highlighted the potential issues that surround the term 'carer' (Bowen, MacLehose, & Beaumont, 2010)—how there may be a script about who is to be the 'main carer'—or how someone may in every respect act as a carer, but if this is not in their script they will not identify with the term and consequently could miss out on potential services that are open to carers. Now we discuss some of the techniques that are used when mapping the system, family scripts, and life cycles:

• The use of 'genograms' can be helpful to illustrate patterns across generations. Simple annotation allows quite a lot of detailed information at a quick glance (e.g., Figure 2 below: squares refer

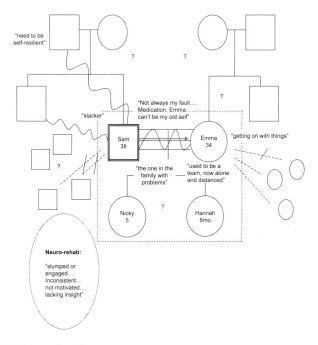

"need to be
self-resilient"

?   ?

"Not always my fault....
Medication, Emma......
can't be my old self"

"slacker"

Sam
38

Emma
34

"getting on with things"

?

"the one in the
family with
problems"

"used to be a
team, now alone
and distanced"

Nicky
5

?

Hannah
8mo

Neuro-rehab:

"slumped or
engaged....
Inconsistent...
not motivated....
lacking insight"

Figure 2. Example of a genogram.

to men, circles to women, ovals to services, straight lines represent close relationships, wavey lines represent conflictual relationships). For further descriptions of symbols typically used, please
see Burnham (1986) Stratton, Preston-Shoot, and Hanks (1990)
and Dallos and Draper (2007). This technique has been extended
into a 'cultural genogram' (Hardy & Laszloffy, 1995).

• Eco-mapping (Hartman, 1995)—this extends the genograms to
include all services and other systems impacting on the family
system (see Figure 3 below: ovals represent involved services, and
several ovals are intentionally left blank to stimulate a consideration of who else needs to be involved).

*Tactic 3: Introducing curiosity and flexibility
into the system and working with difference*

Working with difference is both a tactic and technique. As a tactic,
working with difference is central to work with people after brain inju-

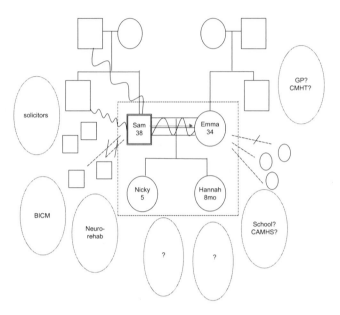

Figure 3. Example of eco-mapping (Hartman, 1995).

ries, due to the likelihood of physical impairments but also because they may have sustained cognitive and emotional changes and have an altered sense of self and identity. In this sense, the field of neuro-rehabilitation has much in common with the holistic approaches taken in services for people with learning disabilities and older adults. This approach emphasizes acceptance, respect and that individual uniqueness is recognized as valid, even special in some way, and a personal resource. A good illustration of this would be how some people following brain injury have re-evaluated their lives in the light of their unusually rich experience and taken this as an opportunity to transform the direction of their life (Nochi, 2000). Others have been granted special talents, for example, it has been documented that some individuals following an ABI become very talented artists (one only needs to use an internet search engine to find many instances of this). Similarly, some individuals with a diagnosis of Autistic spectrum and Asperger's syndrome have specific savant skills, particularly in relation to their visuo-spatial processing skills and some aspects of memory.

As a technique, working with difference entails using a therapeutic style and questions that draw out different perspectives; the multi-verse of opinion on a particular issue, perhaps even the nature of the brain injury itself. Of course, in chapter 6 we have already seen that this can be contested and so here we pick up again on the skills necessary to bring all parties to the table and hold meetings for all members within a system of care, to deconstruct the problem as the system sees it. There is also a need to identify negative cycles and highlight the dilemmas for the family, thereby fostering inter-personal relations and the creation of empathic connections. In this regard, systemic, reflexive, and narrative questions are fit for purpose and specific sample questions that draw out different ways of considering the problem are suggested below:

Systemic/circular questions (Burnham, 1986; Palazzoli, Boscolo, Cecchin, & Prata, 1980)

• Mind reading—for example, 'What do you think Sam would say to that question …? What would the old Sam say to that …? What would Emma think your answer would be? If your mother was alive today, what do you think her opinion would be about the problems you are experiencing?'
• Degree and difference—for example, 'If Sam did not need caring for, who most likely would …? What would Sam be doing then …? When are the moments when Sam is least affected by his injury …? What is happening then …? How does everyone know when the brain injury is back …? Who notices first/is most sure?'
• Relational (also called sequential)—for example, 'Who notices when Sam is having a bad day …? When Sam is most affected, how does everyone react? When they react in such and such a way, how does Sam then respond?'
• Feed-forward—for example, 'How will others in the family know when there is an improvement/this therapy has worked/been helpful …? If the old Sam were to start coming back, who would notice what …? What would it feel like …? What would you be doing? If you woke up tomorrow morning and the problems were gone, how would you know? (also called the 'miracle question')
• Hypothetical—'Let's just say you were able to concentrate at school, you passed your exams, got a place at university, and move away from home. Who would notice your leaving the most, dad or mum?'
• Action—'When you say that she cannot cope, what does she do to make you believe that she cannot cope?'

- Diachronic—'I understand that Emma and your daughter are extremely close, but did they get so close before or after the injury to Sam?'

Reflexive questions (Tomm, 1987)

- Future-oriented—for example, 'How do you imagine your future if things do improve?'
- Observer-perspective—for example, 'When Sam gets upset, what response does that trigger in others'?
- Unexpected context-change—for example, 'When was the last occasion when the two of you had a good time together?'
- Embedded-suggestion—for example, 'If instead of leaving and withdrawing when Emma gets upset, you stayed and put your arm around her, what would happen?'
- Normative-comparison—for example, 'How would you feel if you found out most families in your situation had faced a similar situation?'
- Distinction-clarifying—for example, 'What would need to happen for you to be convinced the situation was not as it appears?'
- Questions introducing hypotheses—for example, 'If Sam gets angry to cover up his vulnerability, how are you able to connect with him?'
- Process-interruption—for example, 'When your parents are at home do they argue as much as here?'

Narrative questions (Payne, 2006; White, 1988)

Many narrative questions grew from the principle of looking for exceptions; times when the outcome is very slightly different and not how the family or the therapist expects it to be. For example:

- Unique outcome—for example, 'Can you identify an incident during which your relationship felt fitter and stronger?'
- Unique account—for example, 'When were you first aware of the need to try something new?'
- Unique re-description—'What does this new direction for the relationship signify?'
- Unique possibility—for example, 'What new possibilities would open up for you as a new couple if you could convince Sam to try something new?'

- Landscape of action—for example, 'Can you recall an occasion when you could have given in to the problem but didn't? Just prior to taking this step, did you nearly turn back? If so, how did you stop yourself from doing so?'
- Landscape of consciousness—for example, 'What does this history of struggle in your life suggest to you?'
- Experience of experience—for example, 'If I had been a spectator to your life when you were younger, could I have anticipated the direction your life has taken?'
- Externalizing—'When did the brain injury start to divide you as a couple …? When are you most effective at reclaiming your husband/wife/relationship from the brain injury?'

Of course, with so many types of questions there is bound to be overlap. We now pick up the last of these questions, namely externalization, as a specific form of reframing and describe this in more detail.

Reframing

Reframing begins already when a referral is made and there is considerable difference between a referral system that identifies the 'patient as the client' versus 'the couple/family as client', in terms of recognizing the shared impact of the injury and disability. The objective is not just to embrace difference but to extend and broaden our common understanding of difference and to be curious about the stories that are told, but also untold, in therapy. Examples of reframing 'problem saturated' thinking that emphasizes change and disability, to more positive or neutral interpretations of events would include the reframe of 'stubborn' to 'determined' as a personal quality described in the case of 'Ben' (described below). In fact, many negative or pejorative descriptions can be reframed if one is willing to entertain the possibility (e.g., to love and care for someone can mean more complaints and demands). The process of reaching a helpful reframe is described extensively in the family therapy literature, but here we highlight a number of specific tactics such as:

- The introduction of continuums to create flexibility within previously polarized characteristics or rigidly held opinions. A useful framework for considering this is the 'problems-possibilities/

restraints-resources' grid described by John Burnham (Burnham, 2006) for helping people generate new possible means for making a situation "less of a problem." Use of this grid involves inviting family members to think about the resources that they have, and focusing on the use of such skills to move 'forwards'.

- Normalizing reactions in terms of the pre-injury relationship or pre-injury coping style broadens the time scale in which comparisons are made, thereby lessening the emphasis of the before/after comparison.
- Changing the topic of conversation to one of joint hopes and aspirations for relationships, including specified relationships such as the couple relationship, rather than problem descriptions.
- 'Thickening' the narrative of the injury by focusing on those stories that are untold in the hope that this gives greater information on context thus allowing more helpful and positive reframes.

Externalization

Externalization is one strategy that can be considered part of the toolkit of therapeutic approaches when working with self and identity. By externalizing a 'problem', it is personalized and delineated and thereby given boundaries, simultaneously making a clear distinction between problem and individual. Externalization also enables members of the family and social network, who may previously have been divided by the problem, to unite against it with a common understanding. Within relational rehabilitation the strategy of externalization can be used to encourage the individual to relate in a new way to the brain injury, through investigating its properties and the ways in which it has impacted on the story told about one's former and current life. As rehabilitation therapists, we notice the idiosyncratic ways in which individuals describe their personal experience of brain injury and the language they use to relate this to others. Sensitivity to this is important in recognition of each individual as the expert on how their brain injury has changed their life. The character of a brain injury reveals itself in the way it impacts on an individual to a greater or lesser degree depending on particular circumstances, for it is not unitary and constant but varies. Nevertheless, it is important to remain mindful that any brain injury places limitations on a person's thinking and memory skills and to talk as if this is not the case may lessen the chances of a therapeutic alliance developing and may be considered disrespectful by the client.

Metaphors for a brain injury are many and among the obvious ones that come to mind are: to imagine it as a block through which one hopes to pass, or a ceiling, or a blanket that stops one seeing things for what they are. To use such terms or to speak about particular times and places when the effects of the brain injury 'took over' or 'were resisted', personalizes the brain injury while at the same time making it feel real, as a dominant force in the life of the person. Indeed, couples may describe times when the brain injury is more or less present in their communications, for example, times when they 'forget' the problems or when they can think of little else other than the brain injury. In this way, the brain injury impacts on communication between people and can be thought to exist in the space between people. Thus, there is a cogent need to help individuals in the process of disentangling the brain injury from this space, and to discover together ways of identifying what is the effect of the brain injury and how this is separate and different to self or personhood; in other words couples and families can be supported to find where the brain injury starts and finishes, which helps to identify ways around it, and also to find a place for the brain injury that does not 'push out' the person or people.

Further techniques have been outlined by Hayward (2009) (adapted here):

1. Nounification: turn neurological/neuro-psychological adjectives into nouns—for example, "the brain injury ... the memory problems" rather than "the brain injured person ... the memory disabled person";
2. Use gerunds—verbs in ending in "ing"—"forgetting in the family" rather than "the forgetful member of the family";
3. Prefix words with "the ..." to render them nouns—for example, "the depression between you, pushing you both down" rather than "your depression";
4. Personify problems to separate them further from the person—for example, "What is the disagreement trying to do to you?" (This attributes intentions and agendas to problems, therefore underlining the common problem for the alliance of all family members);

5. Prefix problematic descriptions with the relationship with the person—for example, "this huge wave of anger that stops you being able to think and use your ideas as a family" rather than "his anger";
6. Externalize positive things too—this prevents the social history of skills or abilities getting dead-ended—for example, "using confidence" is preferable to "being confident."

By changing our language and seeing the 'ability in disability', we can lessen the impact of the secondary social injury on top of the original injury. By reframing and externalizing the injury so that it is seen to occupy social spaces (not just head space) it becomes at least potentially less internal and less stable, and so potentially more controllable.

Hypothesizing

This is a technique that was first proposed as a legitimate thera-peutic activity by the Milan group (Palazzoli, Boscolo, Cecchin, & Prata, 1980), although the term is not unfamiliar to any member of the helping professionals. When used in formal family therapy, team members allocate specific time to meet as a group prior to an appointment, to remember the discussion from the previous meeting and to anticipate issues that may have arisen in the intervening time, also reviewing the session in some detail following its completion. This is of benefit when working in neuro-rehabilitation, especially when as professionals we know and can anticipate the next stage of disease progression (incapacity), or the next level of recovery that might occur. It is one way of forewarning and forearming ourselves for the therapeutic conversation (e.g., thinking of the worst possible scenario) and acknowledging, for example, the 'silent' voice of the carer who may be present in sessions but silent in the presence of the survivor; also a way of recognizing the issues for children who may not yet be able to verbalize their views. Typical issues to watch out for include the impact of brain injury on:

- Social isolation/need for space;
- Social difficulties because it is difficult to hold conversations with more than one person at any one time;
- Stigma (wheelchairs, etc.);

- Relationship role reversal;
- Difficulties setting boundaries for children;
- Insecure child-parent relations;
- Personal care tasks and their impact on relationships.

The odds/evens ritual for shifting rigid problem constructions

In the early days of the Milan school of family therapy, there was a belief that in order to bring about a change, a form of 'family prescription' was required to introduce difference into the family experience. The following is a sequence of instructions to illustrate this technique:

- *'One week/on odd days, Emma you act as if you all need to consider the injury at all times, and take constant responsibility for the children and everything else';*
- *'The next week/on even days Emma act as if there was no injury, and where safe pass on responsibilities to Sam';*
- *'In the third week Sam take responsibility for certain important tasks';*
- *'During each period note down your private experiences and your idea of the other person's perspective. Keep a record of when it feels like the brain injury is more present than the old Sam ...'*
- *'We will meet next session to compare notes ...'*

This sequence of instruction heightens family awareness of flexibility of cognition in social settings but also inconsistencies in the effects of the brain injury. It dovetails well with externalizing conversations that are investigating unique outcomes and primes the family to think of reasons why this may be happening. Over time one would expect for the boundary of what is controllable to be identified and extended by family members. This can be an empowering experience in comparison to previous hospital visits that may have focused solely on diagnosis, pathology, deterioration, and so on.

Tactic 4: Re-positioning, re-membering, re-storying, re-constructing

Within family therapy there is a huge literature now gathering about the active role of the therapist in shaping conversations, and this has mirrored epistemological developments that began with the advent of social constructionism. Once we accept that we are no longer a neutral but an active part of the therapy, then the self of the therapist becomes a resource to draw on (Simon, 2006), as is evident in some of the techniques to be described below. First, we describe one of a class of interventions that Burnham (1986) calls 'direct' interventions, a technique called 'spatial sculpting':

Spatial sculpting (Minuchin, 1974)

The structural approach to family therapy places considerable emphasis on the interpretation of non-verbal behaviour and it is for this reason that therapists may be interested in the physical placing of participants in therapy. With this in mind, and armed with a genogram, the clinical significance of this information then becomes quite obvious (remember to think in terms of boundaries, hierarchies, alliances, communication). Below we show a case example from one clinic in which Minuchin's spatial sculpting allowed a family to explore their proximity and emotional closeness in their inter-relationships before and after intervention in the form of parental role re-negotiation, family problem-solving, education about brain injury for the child relatives, and activity resumption (the stroke survivor returns to work):

Note that Andy finally came out of the toilet!

Enactment

This was originally described by Minuchin and Fishman (1981) as a way of seeing at close quarters the way the family organize around the issues they bring to therapy. In neuro-rehabilitation settings, the technique can be a way of intervening that potentially brings about immediate results and also does not rely on verbal recall (at least if the details are contested this has the potential of being resolved and in any case, this makes for useful clinical material). Burnham (1986) has identified three stages to the process and these are:

1. Selection: the worker selects a particular problematic issue that the family has talked about or demonstrated;

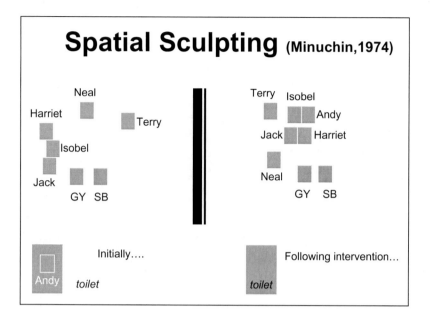

Figure 4. Visual representation of spatial sculpting exercise before and after role renegotiation with a family.

2. Organization: the worker prompts and organizes the family to enact this problem in the session and withdraws to observe and to avoid triangulation;

3. Alternative: after sufficient observation the worker re-enters the scenario to propose alternative ways of dealing with the problem and asks the family to re-enact the scenario using this new strategy. (taken from Burnham, 1986, p. 127–128).

This approach has the potential to be of use with families following a brain injury because of the tendency for family members to interrupt, and act on the basis of their anxiety and desire to keep the injured person safe at the cost of their independence and confidence (see again chapter 7 and further details of the 'y-shaped' model). This is also of relevance to issues related to the self and identity, particularly the ambiguous role of the carer (Gosling & Oddy, 1999; Palmer, 2006).

Co-creating a (new) shared narrative

This is a technique from family and narrative therapy, which can be helpful in the context of a contesting dynamic between family members. It involves engaging individual family members and the family as a whole, in a personally and socially meaningful conversation, to co-create a narrative that makes sense to them and will typically be about the impact or meaning of specific aspects of change to life post-injury. This process involves facilitating the clear expression of thought process leading to each person's opinion regarding the problem, for exploring difference and can further support the family to negotiate a shared and flexible understanding of one another's positions.

Techniques for helping families to re-consider their positions or perspectives include asking the following questions:

• To the person who is emphasizing their solution to a problem that persists: "You may be right, but is it working?" or "what you are suggesting may be true, but is it helpful?"
• To the family who present you, the therapist, with their 'evidence' and ask you to 'make a ruling' about their various suggested solutions: "Therapy is not like the legal system … why do you think I don't do it like that?"
• "I'd like to talk to you a little about what you did and your contribution to the outcome of the situation that you have described."
• "It is possible that you can be right and still handle the situation badly … or [conversely] if you didn't handle the situation as well as you'd like to, that doesn't mean that you're necessarily you did such a bad job … Can you see what I mean?"

From an attachment perspective, we know that constructing a coherent narrative is helpful in an individual sense, but it can help in an inter-personal sense in that it is useful rehearsal or role play for future social situations. This connects back to what we were discussing earlier about taking a longer-term, whole-life perspective that comes quite naturally when working in brain injury because people are immediately faced with before and after comparisons of their self and identity.

Identity reconstruction as a family goal

Making sense of one-self post-injury seems to be such a hugely important issue for so many survivors and this can be helped or hindered by the social and family network. The Y-shaped model (Gracey, Evans & Malley, 2009) indicates that after an injury the individual can experience significant 'discrepancies' in their sense of self (i.e., the differences between what I should be able to do, and what I am doing now). This discrepancy creates a sense of 'self under threat' that the person attempts to alleviate through a number of ways, but often in unhelpful ways, for example, by taking some distance from other people but isolating oneself. Hence, discrepancies sometimes manage degrees of closeness between family members. Moreover, within a system there may be a number of people all trying to reduce an internal discrepancy and all at the same time. Their attempts to reduce the discrepancy could inadvertently increase or maintain the discrepancy of others.

Among the techniques for achieving this reconstruction are:

- Behavioural experiments within a social context to develop an updated and realistic sense of self post-injury. In this way, small changes can be made towards reconstructing one's self-identity. Importantly, the self also can be viewed as independent from the brain injury itself, which operates by getting in between people, leading sometimes to relational 'disconnects' and sometimes to 'connects';
- Narrative 'landscape of action and consciousness' questions as applied to notions of shared identity within the family (e.g., 'What has happened in your family life to help prepare you all for this situation?').

Using reflection and reflexive thinking

Survivors and their families can sometimes become locked into viewing difficulties solely in terms of brain pathology, mirroring the sometimes rigid thought processes of the survivors themselves. Similarly, as rehabilitation specialists we experience a considerable cognitive load because we are challenged to provide executive skills for another person. Hence we monitor not only our own performance but also that of another, organizing and planning their time, sequencing tasks, prompting them, and giving feedback on their performance. The system of care is consequently set up to focus inwards and we therefore need to consciously adhere to the technique of reflecting in order to enable 'de-skulling' (Yeates, 2007) to occur, which is essential when working with the social aspects of the mind-brain-behaviour relationship. Reflection is equally important for therapists as for the family members. The following questions and techniques can support reflection.

- Use colleagues to support reflection on parallels between team/family dynamics, and what each team member might be contributing to the situation, or what action made the difference and made it possible to shift a particular dynamic.
- In sessions, relational risk-taking (Mason, 2005) may help, whereby if a therapist offers a reflection this is mirrored by the client or family, it allows them the space to come forward with their own self-reflection. However, when reflecting, ensure that this is done from a position of strength so as to maintain safety for the client and family within the therapeutic alliance.
- Another technique is to 'take a break' as a planned aspect of a therapy meeting with a family. This is helpful for reasons described in the family therapy literature (Burnham, 1986; Stratton, Preston-Shoot, & Hanks, 1990), but additionally can help manage fatigue for people with ABI.

Tactic 5: Therapeutic documents and witnessing

Documenting change is a technique that grew in stature with the emphasis given in the narrative literature (White, 2007). It is a practice that makes intuitive sense when working with people who have poor memory, concentration, and executive skills to help consolidation of the new story. Not only do therapy sessions need revisiting for survivors to remember the details of what was said, but when there is a paucity of coherence to a narrative about the self or the injury, written documentation can bring some relief and semblance of orientation. Reading is also useful practice as a rehabilitation task in and of itself.

Documents of 'evidence' that we have found helpful in clinical practice include:

1. Summary tables of strategies and examples of when they have helped (Wilson, Bateman, & Evans, 2009);
2. Therapeutic Letters (Moules, 2003);
3. Visual illustrations of relational processes and cartoon drawings with clients to create an image of 'how we would like it to be' (see chapter 8);
4. Cue cards with key words on them which capture the 'new story'.

The tactics and techniques described above are all included in Table 1.

Family 1 revisited

If we return to the case of Julie, given the mapping of the system (Figure 3, see above), what interventions were indicated in this situation? First, due to the community setting, relational approaches had to be essentially non-technical in nature (no one-way screens, ear-bugs, and so on). However, using the 'in room consultant' approach a team approach was simulated using two therapists, one taking a lead and the other observing and acting in a support role only (Vetere & Dallos, 2003). A referral to the organization 'Young Carers' was made because roles within the family had reversed to a degree and so there were issues around protection and boundaries especially for the younger child. There was a difference of opinion between Julie and her children, who clearly did not feel they could leave the family home and their mother would be safe, let alone rely on the mother for support. It was also hoped that because the injury had impacted substantially on the system a referral to Young Carers would also strengthen the sibling sub-system boundary.

In terms of the family life cycle, the events of the past six months had clearly transported this family far into the future, to a time and situation that was not a part of the family script because the children were feeling the need to look after their mother when this is more usually encountered in adult-life, even mid-life. Moreover, the psychosocial demand characteristics when a person suffers a ruptured aneurysm entail huge amounts of anxiety and uncertainty

Table 1. Family therapy approaches and techniques for use in neuro-rehabilitation settings.

Approach	Technique
Taking a team approach	Reflecting teams; Experience consultants; Multi-family group approaches; User involvement.
Mapping	Mapping the injury; Mapping the system (formulation circles); Attachment systems; Working with family scripts and life cycles; Genograms; Eco-mapping.
Introducing curiosity and flexibility into the system	Use of systemic/circular, reflective, and narrative questions, etc.; Reframing; Externalization; Hypothesizing; The odds/evens ritual.
Re-positioning, re-membering, re-storying, re-creating	Spatial sculpting; Enactment; Co-construction of a shared narrative; Identity reconstruction as a family goal; Using reflection and reflexive thinking.
Therapeutic documents and witnessing	Summary tables of strategies; Therapeutic letters; Visual illustrations of relational processes; Cue cards.

about the future, and there was considerable work to be done to reassure Julie that medical professionals would investigate further bleeds. Julie would also ask about the heritability of the condition out of concern for her children, and again it would be difficult to reassure her about this. Therapy involved helping the family recognize the atypical event that had presented itself, how unlucky they had been and the loss of the future they had previously imagined.

There was also a need to support the family to seek and accept support from the wider family and friends, which initially they had been reluctant to do.

A further difficulty was the fact that Julie would repeatedly get stuck in her thinking and it would be hard to introduce some curiosity about alternatives into her mind. That said, with time and therapeutic effort, she was able to feel less guilty about the time she spent in hospital and begin to recognize the tremendous way her children had coped in her absence. For Julie, who felt very different since her injury, the path of recovery also involved facing issues around her new identity and protecting her thoughts from overwhelming anxiety about aneurysms and what further insults could occur. Julie appeared to perseverate on particular issues around the loss of autobiographical detail when remembering events and so therapy involved co-creating a shared narrative around this.

Despite the challenges that were faced, Julie engaged well in the therapy, as did her children, and a therapeutic space was opened up in which to explore new possibilities and ways of looking at the issues. Julie experienced an existential reframe along the lines of 'before I was invincible, now I am not' that helped her adjust to the injury. Attachment work was a significant part of work conducted, providing external support to facilitate a coming together between mother and each of the children, and opportunity for them to confide in their mother as they used to, safe in the knowledge that someone was observing to ensure no further attachment injury could take place.

The following cases illustrate snapshots of relational interventions, intended to illustrate aspects of systemic formulation and the techniques described above.

Family 2

This case was conceptualized as one in which each family member held a slightly different perspective about what was different for Ben since the accident, and how things might be improved. It was important for each family member's point of view to be heard and for them to hear each other's perspectives in order for their concerns to be lessened and drawn together into one 'collective concern'.

Ben

Ben, a 42-year-old British man, sustained a very severe TBI and multiple orthopaedic injuries when his motorcycle crashed into the back of another vehicle while on holiday away from his wife and stepdaughter. Although he made a fast physical recovery, he continued to feel "different" and "not the old me." Assessment 12 months post-injury revealed impairments with executive functioning including attention control, divergent thinking, and cognitive flexibility. He also reported cognitive and physical fatigue. Ben's wife, stepdaughter, brothers, and parents explained that they were concerned about what was happening, and that he needed professional help because he would have 'rages' where he threw items (such as a door) or would 'bang' his fist loudly on the table in a restaurant and shout in response to apparently small triggers. Ben said his family were constantly evaluating whether he was 'still different' or whether he had 'come back' and telling him that he wasn't the "old Ben" anymore, which led him to evaluate himself harshly in return. The narrative among some professionals was that his recovery was "miraculous"; Ben said this was because he worked so hard at recovering and needed to keep on being determined in order to recover 'completely' and be the "old Ben" again. However, the 'rages' continued and so he was referred for holistic rehabilitation.

It was hypothesized that reducing the anxiety within the system and ensuring that family concerns were heard and responded to by a third party, would lessen the 'pressure' that Ben experienced about whether he was 'back yet' (i.e., no longer unacceptably different). It was also conceptualized that Ben's family needed to develop a 'shared understanding' between them (Wilson, Gracey, Malley, Bateman, & Evans, 2009) about what was happening for Ben, which incorporated each of their observations and made sense of their multiple stories. Such a shared narrative could support Ben in developing a more coherent sense of who he is and what has happened, rather than a sense of self as fractionated by numerous narratives about how and why he is 'still different'.

Ben was observed to have many strengths and resources, and he demonstrated an ability to emphasize with other clients in the rehabilitation centre, taking time away from his own tasks to support them with theirs. Another client said that she may not have continued her rehabilitation programme if it was not for Ben's support, encouragement, and 'positive attitude'. While he was at home, however, his ability to emphasize was noted to be completely absent and his opinions were observed to be inflexible. Frequently, Ben had become angry with his family members; shouting at them, banging the table or throwing things. However, he was not reported to throw objects directly at any other person. It was formulated that although Ben had difficulties with flexible thinking, and abstract thought, these difficulties were exacerbated by (a) his strong emotions resulting from his wish to "be better" and subsequent tendency to evaluate himself negatively, as well as the sense he described that others also 'evaluated' him at home. Inflexibility was also thought to be exacerbated by (b) his memory of himself as being 'very opinionated and blunt' before the injury, so in an effort to be judged as 'back' and being more like 'the old Ben' he was expressing his opinions bluntly and inflexibly at home. Ben was not able to share his family's point of view that although he was "blunt" before, he had not been "rude" before, and would have listened to another's point of view.

Interventions were provided within the framework of a 6-month interdisciplinary neuro-psychological rehabilitation (Wilson, Gracey, Malley, Bateman, & Evans, 2009). Specific relational work included working with Ben and his wife to map out a narrative of their relationship and identify characteristics of each of them that were valued within the relationship prior to the injury. This yielded information about the importance of

- time apart
- humour
- clear roles for one another at home: him as the "lead horse; the provider" and she has a "woman; a house keeper and communicator."

These sessions also included a discussion of characteristics that Ben had always held (such as being 'determined' and 'stubborn') and trying to map out, in a measurable way, how they would each know when the 'old Ben' was back; otherwise he would be attempting to reach an indefinable goal. Family sessions then expanded to include discussion of alterations in roles at home, reduction in time apart, and loss of humour in their interactions. At home, Ben's stepdaughter had naturally become increasingly supportive to his wife, and although he had previously recognized their closeness, observing this post-injury created a sense of 'exclusion' for him because of his sensitivity to feeling like he did or did not belong.

At points during the rehabilitation programme, wider family meetings were held, to share views, request feedback, and provide education about brain injury and specific aspects of how cognition and mood can interact. This was intended to challenge the focus of concern in the system and gradually build the shared understanding about similarities and strengths 'in spite of' the brain injury.

After the six-month rehabilitation programme, Ben and his family reported to the rehabilitation centre that he must be "one of your success stories!" They each reported a sense of things being "more peaceful" at home and that 'the old Ben' was almost back. However, his wife, step daughter, and wider family agreed at the final family meeting that they no longer sought the 'old Ben' but liked the 'new Ben', who was rather like the old Ben. They spoke as a group about how their focus was now more about the future together, than it was about their past.

The process that Ben went through during rehabilitation can be mapped onto the Y Shaped model of rehabilitation (Gracey, Evans & Malley, 2009; Wilson, Gracey, Malley, Bateman, & Evans, 2009). In this case, the narratives that his family held about difference and concern could be seen to maintain the whole family system at the 'top of the Y' where they were stuck in thinking about risk and the discrepancy between 'how things are' and 'how things ought to be'. At that point, each individual had a solution in mind, which would resolve part of the problem but not the complete problem. Their solutions often involved highlighting the difficulties to Ben, which paradoxically served to maintain Ben's own sense of 'unacceptable difference', sense of threat to identity that magnified his inflexibility 'blunt' communication, and so continued to create a system organized by concern. Ben's family were therefore also supported to 'take a step back' and 'look at the bigger picture', and this allowed Ben to explore his post-injury changes in a more private forum with his wife. This enabled the family to notice a 'more reflective and less reactive Ben' and further reduce their concern regarding risk. Through this, he and his family followed the process identified within the Y-shaped 'cone' model (see chapter 7) to achieve a position of 'safe uncertainty' (Mason, 1993) for the whole family where although Ben was not 'back', the difference was viewed differently; at worst as 'manageable and understandable' and at best as 'positive, impressive and evidence of his strong, determined and upbeat character'.

Neuropsychology within systemic family work

In chapter 3 we have outlined in more detail ideas for a relational neuro-psychological practice. Here we want to make a connection between those ideas and the approaches we have described within this chapter. Organic brain dysfunction has actually been an exclusion factor for participants in the aforementioned RCT of systemic couples therapy for depression (Leff et al., 2000). Systemic therapy that is not adapted for the survivor's cognitive difficulties is likely to be limited and exclusionary to some degree. We follow Johnson and McGown (1997) and Larøi (2003) in advocating a core integration of neuropsychology and family therapy, but specify a relational orientation in chapter 3 to promote a fit between the two models. From the perspective of the systemic therapist, the formulation and hypothesizing of family arrangements, conversational patterns, and feedback loops would be incomplete without a relational neuro-psychological understanding of how cognitive impairment can amplify and structure these. Similarly interventions aiming to facilitate new helpful, curious conversations of difference between all family members require a neuro-psychological orientation to include and empower the survivor. As discussed in chapter 6, the acceptance of neuro-rehabilitative intervention within the family can be enhanced by formulating the relational meaning of the injury and a particular intervention for different members within a particular family, at a particular point in time.

Summary: Making the shift to working relationally

In the above chapter we have outlined aspects of family therapy theory and technique that can be usefully applied to brain injury and other neuro-rehabilitation work. But it is important to say that this does not entail a whole new way of working or a completely different approach. Equally, there may not be a specific moment when a difference in one's style of working becomes stark, but perhaps like when one learns to drive one thinks about each individual manoeuvre technically, and then only later on, about how these

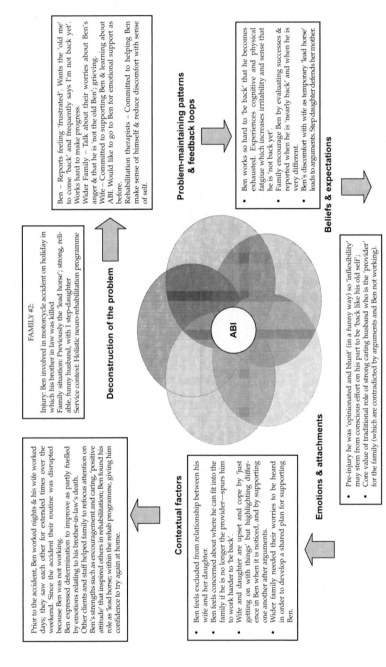

Deconstruction of the problem

FAMILY #2:

Injury: Ben involved in motorcycle accident on holiday in which his brother in law was killed
Family situation: Previously the 'lead horse'; strong, reliable, funny husband, with 1 step-daughter
Service context: Holistic neuro-rehabilitation programme

Problem-maintaining patterns & feedback loops

Ben – Reports feeling 'frustrated'. Wants the 'old me' to come 'back' and frequently says I'm not back yet'. Works hard to make progress.
Wider Family – Talk about their worries about Ben's anger & that he is 'not the old Ben'; grieving.
Wife – Committed to supporting Ben & learning about ABI. Would like to go to Ben for emotional support as before.
Rehabilitation therapists – Committed to helping Ben make sense of himself & reduce discomfort with sense of self.

Beliefs & expectations

- Ben works so hard to 'be back' that he becomes exhausted. Experiences cognitive and physical fatigue which increases irritability and sense that he is 'not back yet'.
- Family encourage Ben by evaluating successes & reported when he is 'nearly back' and when he is very different.
- Ben's discomfort with wife as temporary 'lead horse' leads to arguments. Step daughter defends her mother.

Contextual factors

Prior to the accident, Ben worked nights & his wife worked days; they saw each other for extended times over the weekend. Since the accident their routine was disrupted because Ben was not working.
Ben expressed determination to improve as partly fuelled by emotions relating to his brother-in-law's death.
Other clients and staff helped family to refocus attention on Ben's strengths such as encouragement and caring, 'positive attitude' that inspired others in rehabilitation; Ben found his role as 'lead horse' within the rehab programme, giving him confidence to try again at home.

Emotions & attachments

- Ben feels excluded from relationship between his wife and her daughter.
- Ben feels concerned about where he can fit into the family if he is no longer the provider—spurs him to work harder to 'be back'.
- Wife and daughter are upset and cope by 'just getting on with things' but highlighting difference in Ben when it is noticed, and by supporting one another after arguments.
- Wider family needed their worries to be heard in order to develop a shared plan for supporting Ben.

- Pre-injury he was 'opinionated and blunt' (in a funny way) so 'inflexibility' may stem from conscious effort on his part to be 'back like his old self';
- Core value of traditional role of strong caring husband who is the 'provider' for the family (which are contradicted by arguments and Ben not working).

ABI

Figure 5. A systemic formulation of family 2.

technicalities fit into the whole picture of life on the road. The complexity of the problems faced by people after brain injury is maybe not something to be appreciated fully until later when working as part of a specialist team, with adequate support and supervision. In many ways it is all about working with complexity and which parts of that complexity that you emphasize and draw upon, and how to make decisions about this within your practice.

When working relationally the difference could be explained as one of breadth rather than of depth, also less about the technicalities and more about the breadth of experience that the client brings into the therapy space. When working with people after brain injury one is forced to take a broader more holistic and integrative approach because they bring to therapy the stark dilemma of the 'me before and me after', so therapy necessarily takes a longitudinal perspective on adjustment as the client updates their relationship with themselves. The relational approach to neuro-rehabilitation also represents a shift in therapy to a more intuitive position that comes naturally when thinking about the person's whole life story.

Key to working relationally is the need to engage individuals into the activity of co-creating a new narrative about the self that incorporates the injury. Survivors of ABI have no frame of reference for living life with ABI, and so there is a simultaneous need to find a personal and meaningful language (not one that is pre-determined or imposed from outside) for the emerging narrative. But to make sense of brain injury is no easy task and clinicians need to work with families so they can articulate this experience that is wholly different. Not only is there a lack of preparation for such an experience but also the strong influence of social and media representations that dominate lay understandings. Clinicians on the other hand access a professional discourse about brain injury but have typically never experienced this for themselves so both clinicians and families need each other to come to a shared understanding of the unique impact of brain injury. Formulation in this sense is a social activity, a social encounter, and a meeting of perspectives (a multi-verse), that answers a number of needs including the need for connection and reassurance to make the experience manageable and meaningful. Furthermore, forming a bigger picture takes the person outside of themselves and this can be helpful. Responding to the call for externalization, once we begin to think of the brain injury as outside but impacting in then we see the value of working at the social-family interface.

CHAPTER TEN

Integrating 'doing' and 'meaning' in rehabilitation: A case example

Additional authors: *Jacqui Cooper, Fergus Gracey, Donna Malley, Joseph Deakins and Leyla Prince*

Introduction

This chapter describes an interdisciplinary approach to relational work with a couple, in the context of a holistic neuro-psychological rehabilitation programme. The issues for this couple were conceptualized using the 'Y-shaped' model of change (Gracey, Evans, & Malley, 2009) that highlights threat to self and discrepant social identity as key targets for change after brain injury. In this chapter an activity-based approach to rehabilitation, derived from this model, is illustrated in by using behavioural experiments, as a means of linking 'doing' and 'meaning'.

The holistic model of rehabilitation, described elsewhere (Dewar & Gracey, 2007; Wilson, Evans, Brentnall, Bremner, Keohane, & Williams, 2000; Wilson, Gracey, Malley, Bateman, & Evans, 2009) addresses social, emotional, and functional aspects of brain injury simultaneously (Wilson, Evans, & Keohane, 2002). Specifically, this involves increasing awareness, acceptance, and understanding of what has happened, the provision of strategies to reduce cognitive difficulties, the development of compensatory skills and the provision of vocational counselling. Although the holistic model lends itself to a relational approach, goal setting is commonly an individually-focused part of the rehabilitation. Inclusion of significant others and wider systems in goal setting, as illustrated here, moves this process towards a truly relational approach.

This case will describe work towards cognitive, vocational, and adjustment goals within a relational framework. A characteristic of cognitive rehabilitation is the provision of internal and external aids or strategies to circumnavigate identified cognitive impairments and thus reduce disability and progress in personally meaningful social participation goals. Although there is some debate within the literature about potential gains from restorative approaches, specific compensatory approaches to cognitive rehabilitation are supported by reviews of published evidence (Cicerone et al., 2005; Rohling, Faust, Beverly, & Demakis, 2009). The review authors (Cicerone et al., 2005) advocate for strategy training over restitution training for many cognitive functions. Examples of compensatory cognitive strategies and techniques include attention process training (Sohlberg, McLaughlin, Pavese, Heidrich, & Posner, 2000), goal management training (Levine et al., 2000; Robertson, 1996) and electronic memory aids (Wilson, 2000) such as the NeuroPage (Wilson, Evans, Emslie, & Malinek, 1997) or other systems to provide external alerting. All such interventions would be valid within a relational framework, if approached with consideration of relational principals (see chapter 2). For example, integrating cognitive rehabilitation efforts with the personal and social contexts of the individual is critical since the 'contexts of importance' (personal, physical, and social) influence interactions between impairment and activity, and also influence interactions between activities and social participation (Wade, 2006). Thus, context consideration is arguably central to provision of cognitive rehabilitation. Similarly, addressing emotional and familial or systemic factors is an important aspect of cognitive rehabilitation because it affords the opportunity to influence the personal and social contexts, which in turn influence the individual's capacity to benefit from individual interventions. The contribution of working with the social context, and the important place of systemic family therapy within neuro-rehabilitation is highlighted in other literature (Bowen, 2007). Bringing aspects of the personal and social context into the rehabilitation while also bringing the rehabilitation into these contexts, addresses these interacting factors simultaneously.

Rehabilitation following this 'Y-shaped' model is organized to address sense of threat or inter-personal discrepancy through an activity-based approach using behavioural experiments conducted within a safe therapeutic milieu. A behavioural experiment (Bennett-Levy et al., 2004; McGrath & King, 2004) consists of identification of the client's belief or a client's prediction about the consequences of doing or not doing an identified task (for example; "*if I attempt to cook a meal at home, I will burn everything, become completely overwhelmed and my wife will laugh at me ... and this will mean I cannot contribute at home and am a failure as a husband*"). The second stage of the behavioural experiment is to identify an alternative prediction (e.g., "*If I attempt to cook a meal at home, I don't know if it will be more difficult since my injury, but if I do burn something then it will help me learn where I can use strategies next time ... which will mean I am being brave and exploring my skills*"). The third stage is to plan how to approach the feared/identified task and consider compensatory or coping strategies that could be helpful. The fourth stage is to do the task and the final stage is to reflect on how it went and review which predictions were borne out in practice. Given what was learned from this experiment, the client is then supported to identify the next task and consider their predictions about these. This constitutes one 'cycle' of a behavioural experiment because the learning from one experiment feeds back into the planning of the next experiment. Cycles of 'behavioural experiments' provide information and explore different perspectives in a non-threatening manner. Supporting the injured person to reflect on the meaning of outcomes from experiments is crucial in reducing discrepancy, moving the client towards a realistic self-appraisal and facilitating emotional adjustment. Reflection may be done individually or with significant others from the client's social context. Further behavioural experiments may be organized between therapists and set collaboratively with the client and family to provide a vehicle for change towards social participation goals and reduction of discrepancies within individuals and within the system. Having resolved the core sense of discrepancy and under conditions of reduced or absent sense of threat, further experiments are devised to support the client in consolidating their emerging post-injury sense of self, through meaningful activities and social relationships (Mooney & Padesky, 2000).

We describe a client, James, who experienced a very severe traumatic brain injury. The impact of these difficulties on personally meaningful activities and contexts, particularly the relationship with his wife, Helen, is presented.

Methodology used to evaluate the intervention

Design

In order to illustrate the 'Y-shaped' model, measures of hypothesized processes relating to identity and relationship change were taken. Outcome measures relating to brain injury symptoms and goal attainment were also recorded. All measures were administered at initial assessment and at the end of the six-month programme.

Measures

Measures of emotional adjustment included the Beck Anxiety Inventory (BAI) (Beck, Epstein, Brown, & Steer, 1988) and the Robson Self-Concept Questionnaire (RSQ) (Robson, 1989). In order to explore the notion of self-discrepancy and the identity change process, a novel measure was used based on personal construct ratings of pre-injury, ideal and current selves (Gracey, Palmer, Rous, Psaila, Shaw, O'Dell, Cope, & Mohamed, 2008). Measures of outcome in terms of social participation were also taken. This included ratings of goal attainment and ratings of satisfaction, performance, and ability on the Canadian Occupational Performance Measure (COPM) (Law, Baptise, McColl, Opzoomer, Polaajkom, & Pollock, 1990). Client and relative's ratings of frequency of brain injury symptoms were also included using the European Brain Injury questionnaire (EBIQ) (Teasdale, Christensen, Willmes, Deloche, Braga, Stachowiak, Vendrall, Alexandre, Ritva, & Leclercq, 1997).

James and Helen

James, a white British man, was involved in a motorcycle accident 13 months prior to first assessment at the rehabilitation centre and 17 months prior to starting rehabilitation. His injuries included numerous orthopaedic injuries, closed brain injury with traumatic subarachnoid haemorrhage and frontal contusions. It was reported that he was in a coma for 3 weeks, with an extensive period of PTA, indicating a very severe injury. At the time of starting the programme, James was 54 years old.

James' partner of 30 years was Helen. Helen was a professional gardener and an active member of her local community. Both James and Helen enjoyed socializing with their friends, and hosting dinner parties, but they also enjoyed quiet time working on their home and garden together and walking their dogs over long distances. When asked to 'set the scene' about their lives prior to the accident, they said:

> Helen: It was quite a contented period. The house was just sort of 'bedding in'. We'd just finished the patio the night before the accident. James had gone back to motorcycling after 15 years ... because the traffic was so bad to get into town. You were enjoying the motorcycling, although it was a necessity as well as a pleasure.

Initial assessment and formulation

The interdisciplinary assessment was conducted in accordance with a biopsychosocial-familial model over an eight-day period. Details of brain pathology, impairments (cognition, communication, physical, and emotional), and their functional consequences in the context of individual (physical environment and emotional adjustment) and social factors (family, friends, relationships, and culture) were gathered by the interdisciplinary team. Relationships between these factors were identified through team discussion and collation of information into an interdisciplinary formulation (Gracey, Henwood, Evans, Malley, Psaila, Bateman, & Wilson, 2006). The results of this assessment are summarized in Table 1; James presented with executive impairments apparent in reduced initiation, self-monitoring on task, prospective memory, and goal neglect. He described physical problems with pain and fatigue, and limited movement in his right foot.

Emotionally, James appeared flat, demonstrated poor awareness of the severity of his difficulties, and described his own sense of confusion about why people told him he was different. On items from a personal construct scale (Gracey et al., 2008) he rated a reduced sense of 'knowing himself', feeling 'stable', 'confidence in relationships',

Table 1. Description of impairments, restrictions, and implications for the couple following the WHO framework as described by Wade (2005).

Impairment	Activity and participation restriction	Implication for couple
1. Lowered arousal level, reduced initiation, and impaired attention 2. Decreased ability to detect social inference 3. Decreased fluency of speech and expression	Difficulty initiating conversation and action	Reduced spontaneity and expressions of interest Impacting on ability to complete tasks
4. Reduced speed of processing	Currently unable to return to work	Reduced sense of contribution to the home and financial restrictions to their life style
5. Variable awareness of cognitive impairments	Difficulty following instructions Poor prospective memory	Helen assuming roles that were previously James'
6. Physical impairments including right foot drop	1) Unable to drive	Helen drives everywhere. Loss of spontaneity in activities and relationship
	2) Unable to take dog for a walk	Reduced opportunities for talking and 'being' together
	3) Unable to kneel	Impacts on ability to garden as shared leisure interest
	4) Requires two sticks for walking	Unable to carry items when walking (wine, tea, logs)

and 'knowing my own limitations' compared with both 'pre-injury' and 'ideal' self ratings. See Table 2 for personal construct scale.

James' scores on the RSQ placed him three-fourths of 1 standard deviation below the mean score, taken from a population of healthy controls, indicating slightly low level of self-esteem. On this measure, he strongly disagreed with the statement 'I am a reliable person' and strongly agreed with statements 'I often wonder what other people are thinking about me' and 'when people criticise me, I often feel helpless and second-rate'. James noted that these ratings to be at odds with how he saw himself pre-injury.

At the beginning of rehabilitation, Helen reported significant distress and low mood. She reported feeling emotionally drained ("other people plug into me and drain me ... and I am now a husk") and that her relationship with James was "strained." On the EBIQ James and Helen endorsed several symptoms of brain injury (Table 6), which Helen reported as occurring more frequently than James reported.

Presenting problem described by James

Although unable to recognize the specific changes Helen described, James described a general sense that things were not 'right'. From James' perspective, the problems were 'Helen's unhappiness' and his own sense of 'uncertainty' regarding his skills and abilities. James described his experience post-injury of tasks 'falling out of the sky', which triggered a realization that he had not completed

Table 2. Examples of two personal constructs, where pre-injury is circled, current rating is in bold, ideal rating is underlined.

Construct pole	Rating							Construct pole
Knowing myself	1	(2)	**3**	4	5	6	7	Being unsure of myself
Not confident with relationships	1	2	3	(4)	5	6	7	Feeling confident with relationships, able to trust
Feeling vulnerable to instability	1	**2**	(3)	4	5	6	7	Constantly stable
Not being aware of limitations	1	2	3	4	5	(6)	7	Knowing/understanding your limitations

a task important to the running of the house, or important to his relationship. He described 'not knowing himself' because he often found tasks more difficult than he expected.

Presenting problem as described by the couple

Alongside the completion of standard individually focused assessment, James and Helen were interviewed together, which formed the beginning of the 'relational assessment'. They explained that prior to the accident, they would have described themselves as a 'team'; with no children or close family, they were an independent, self-sufficient couple. They valued fun and spontaneity in their relationship and enjoyed spending time together. The care they took of one another and the ways in which they showed thoughtfulness about each other were important. James and Helen noted that prior to the injury, he had been like a 'hero' to her; strong and caring and looked after Helen. Her role was described as his 'partner' and support. In his role as 'hero', he previously held responsibility for home duties including: laying the fire, mowing the lawn, cooking, driving, and responding to Helen's emotional needs. Describing their experiences in intensive care, they said:

James: So … the waking up was so gradual … so *unlike* the films … it took several weeks, well … it took a couple of years actually … and the point was, that there was no real information about the extent of the damage until the end of those weeks. Even … you could argue, even later … but …

Helen: … but your physical incapacity was the thing that we focussed on first … I remember all James being able to do was squeeze my hand, and that was a *big thing* in intensive care, being able to squeeze my hand … that was an *enormous thing*. But James did … even in intensive care … seem to know and to respond to me, and that was an enormous comfort, because there were a lot of relatives there who did not have that, that 'spark'—and that 'fuelled' me.

James: When I went back to the Intensive Care Unit was part of my rehabilitation, and we went into the relative's room, the coffee room … a strange atmosphere … I started to really appreciate then what Helen had been through …

[pause]

Initially when I was waking up, and people were … I thought being a bit soppy, and saying things like "you're coming back to us, that's wonderful!" and I'm thinking "what the hell are you on about?! I haven't been anywhere!" and Greg showed me that digital photo that you took of me in intensive care, and there I was, framed up and wires and pipes and … I thought … oh sh*t."

They agreed that the injury had substantially affected their 'independence' as a couple and James was not able to fulfil many of his pre-injury roles within the relationship. Specifically, certain household tasks were not achievable because they required physical strength (e.g., turning the mattress). James said that occasions where they could not be independent, caused him to feel guilty for the motorbike accident. He said "I started off just feeling guilty … not just for being such a clot as to have an accident … but for being such a clot as to have a motorcycle at all." Helen reported that these same occasions made her feel guilty for being unable to cope and for not being a 'good enough' wife, carer and support. Helen said she was unhappy because something had led to a reduction in the 'small things' that James did for her, such as ask about her day, or recognize that she needed a drink, a cuddle, time to relax or for him to 'take over' the chores. She said she felt less 'connected' and less cared for by him. James said these were things he intended to do, but seemed to 'miss his moment' every time and by the time he had thought of what he ought to do, the moment has passed. Therefore, since the accident, they defined their roles as 'failure' (James) and 'carer' (Helen).

Goals

James' primary goal for rehabilitation was to return to paid employment. Given concerns about how realistic this was and in line with the exploratory approach to rehabilitation, the following goal was set with James:

1. Identify if he is able to return to his previous work role and have a written realistic vocational action plan for the forthcoming year.

James also said he would like to 'know himself more', be 'less vulnerable to instability' and understand more about his contribution to his wife's distress. Work on developing a shared understanding of himself with clinicians and Helen was subsumed under the following broader 'understanding' goal:

2. To develop a timeline of the injury and significant subsequent events and use this to create a written account of physical, cognitive, mood, and communication consequences including the strategies to manage these.

Through a structured interview using the COPM (reference), James identified areas for potential change relating to DIY tasks, domestic chores, and paperwork:

3. To have a memory and planning system in place to allow planning and initiation of domestic, DIY, social, and work-related tasks more effectively over a specified period.

4. To develop a system for organizing finances and managing correspondence and rate myself as more competent and confident.

Intervention

James participated in the intensive holistic rehabilitation over a six-month period. This was organized to follow the formulation indicated by the 'Y-shaped' model relational formulation.

Collaborative formulations: Reaching a shared understanding

After the assessment, the couple's account was formulated in terms of discrepancy between pre- and post-injury identity. The key discrepancy was between the couple's pre-injury identity (as self-sufficient, spontaneous, caring, and stable) and post-injury identity (as uncertain, confused, requiring support of others, and unstable). The unhappiness and uncertainty were viewed as secondary to the discrepancy.

It was formulated that a combination of slow speed of processing, impairment in initiation (thus preventing spontaneity), and sense of guilt (which led James to withdraw) had led to a reduction in frequency with which James did the 'small things' that had previously indicated he was 'caring' and were a source of 'connection' between them. The absence of these things was creating discrepancy for each of them between 'how things should be' and 'how I think things are'. This discrepancy threatened their identity as a 'team'. Each attempted to resolve the discrepancy in different ways.

James coped with the discrepancy by dismissing the idea that he was different. Consequently, he did not utilize strategies for initiation or problem-solving, which could have helped him to alter his behaviour. Therefore, his coping strategy was inadvertently contributing to maintaining the discrepancy between James and Helen's accounts ("you're different" vs. "I'm not that different ... am I?").

Helen coped with the discrepancy by attempting to do all the tasks at home without asking for help, but this would increase James' guilty feeling when he saw her exhausted. His guilt would further exacerbate his initiation difficulties, so he did not acknowledge her hard work and Helen felt increasingly like a 'carer' and less like a 'partner'. In turn, James felt increasingly like a 'failure' because he was unable to help and be the 'hero'.

James and Helen attended assessment sessions together and they agreed to talk through their experience together. They named their difficult feelings as the 'unspoken fears' that they could not talk about. Systemic approaches of circular questioning (Tomm, 1988), solution-focused questioning, and interviewing the internalized other (Pare, 2001) wleteere used to gently begin a conversation about what might not be said between them since the accident. Their interacting thoughts, feelings, and behaviours were mapped out with the couple together and are illustrated in Figure 1. In this illustration, the alternative formulation of how things could be (hero-partner) was captured together with the problem formulation (failure-carer).

Interventions: Individual

The process of becoming 'strategic'

James was introduced to specific strategies to address executive difficulties, including goal management (Levine et al., 2000, Robertson, 1996) and content-free alerting (Fish, Manly, & Wilson, 2008). Memory and planning systems were also introduced to help stay on top of tasks (e.g., arriving at sessions on time). James

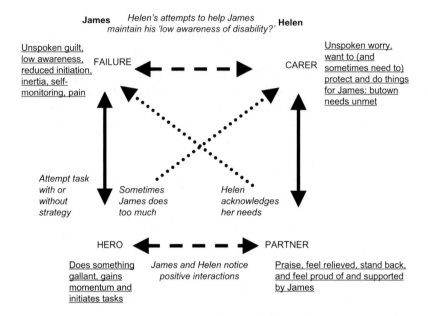

Figure 1. Formulation of interactions between James and Helen that lessened or heightened their discrepant identity. Actions in *italics* are attempts to resolve discrepancies.

identified himself as someone who wouldn't have used supports to help stay on top of tasks before his injury, and demonstrated low levels of motivation to use external aids for memory and planning. The potential 'threat' (to identity) of strategy use was addressed in a number of ways. James was supported to reframe his negative perspective by identifying a 'hero' of his for whom 'being strategic' was acceptable and positive. Furthermore, James developed his own metaphor for executive functioning in familiar and personally relevant terms (specifically in relation to electronic feedback systems that allow a piece of equipment to 'self-regulate' on the basis of sensors picking up a difference between desired state and actual state). The potential 'threat' of strategy use was further addressed through collaboratively identifying opportunities for behavioural experiments to test predictions relating to strategy use initially within the safety of the rehabilitation centre and later in home and work contexts.

Table 3. Examples of behavioural experiments completed with James.

Situation/task	Predication or strategy to test	What happened?	What did you learn about: Strategy use? Yourself post-injury? Your relationship with Helen? What is the meaning in terms of your relationship and your identity?
Need to check oil level at home and order if required	Whether having an alert on my PDA at appropriate time allows me to complete task	Checked and ordered oil	• Having the alert helped to initiate • Helen was pleased that I did it, as she was not confident. • Made me feel like able to fulfil role as husband
Make Sunday roast dinner	Planned out the steps in writing according to timing before preparation	Planned roast and prepared in appropriate timeframe	• That I need to plan in order to remember all parts of the task, e.g., getting things out of the freezer • Made me feel like my old self (was a chef prior to changing career) • Helen enjoyed my cooking

Achievement of functional tasks

Details of some behavioural experiments conducted with James are described in Table 3. This shows how James began to complete significant domestic roles, such as laying the fireplace, checking the oil and making dinner, while utilizing strategies. The reflections James made after these planned tasks illustrate ways in which he was learning about strategy use and in turn reducing his subjective and inter-personal discrepancies.

Couple interventions

As a behavioural experiment in session, James and Helen began to share their 'unspoken fears', and recognized how their efforts to protect each other were maintaining each other's positions as 'failure' and 'carer'. Next, they agreed to keep these ideas in mind and to try to notice these patterns and mention them to each other when they thought it was happening at home, for example, Helen 'mothering' James or James 'allowing' Helen to do tasks he might be able to do himself; which were both inadvertently preventing James 'caring for' Helen. Experiments were designed (see Table 4) to investigate what happened if they talk about their emotions and whether James' use of strategies to achieve tasks, or Helen 'standing back' and doing less might enable them to glimpse their desired positions of 'hero' and 'partner'. This process of reflection between the couple continued throughout the rehabilitation programme, alongside other cognitive and vocational interventions as they became increasingly able to talk about their emotions and the meaning of change and difference to them both individually and in terms of their identity as a 'team'.

Changes in subjective and inter-personal discrepancy

At the end of the programme, James described understanding more about factors contributing to Helen's unhappiness, including his own variable awareness of cognitive impairments and behavioural changes since injury. James' ratings on personal construct measures indicated a move towards his ideal self, in terms of developing his understanding of himself and feeling less vulnerable to instability (Table 5).

Table 4. Examples of couple's experiments.

Situation/experiment	Negative prediction	Alternative prediction	What happened?	What did you learn?
1. Express emotions, and tell each other how you are feeling.	James: If I tell her I am feeling sad, this will irritate Helen and remind her about the accident, and she will be angry with me. Helen: He would be devastated to know how I feel, and I will not be able to support him.	(a) This could be helpful, and enable us to understand each other better as a couple. (b) This could be helpful and mean that it is easier to talk to each other about other things, like planning, and so we will get things done.	James and Helen had a conversation about their feelings in the session, and why they responded in a particular way to a situation at dinnertime.	James: I understand why Helen reacted like she did, and can think of other ways to respond in future. Like 'just say it'. She was not angry. Helen: I understand why James reacted like he did. It was not because he did not care, it was because he was worried about me. He was not devastated.
2. Use keyword to signal when Helen is 'mothering' James (and protecting him from failure).	James: Did not report a potential negative outcome of reducing Helen's 'mothering' behaviour. Helen: If James were to fail he would be devastated and I would not be strong enough to support him.	Both James and Helen said they would like it to be different and have a new way of being together, that is less 'mother'—'child' in role	James and Helen used a keyword to feedback to each other.	James and Helen said it was easier to talk to each other about their emotions now they were working on shared goal of James becoming more independent.

Table 5. Personal construct ratings at the end of the programme, where changes of 'current self' rating are indicated by the arrow (starting at rating at start of programme with tip on end of programme rating), P denotes the 'pre-injury self' and I 'ideal self' ratings, respectively.

Negative construct pole	7-point scale							Positive construct pole
	1	2	3	4	5	6	7	
Feeling vulnerable to instability	1	2	3 (P)	4	5 →	6 (I)	7	Constantly stable
Not having confidence with relationships	1	2	3	4	5	6 → (P)	7 (I)	Feeling confident with relationships, able to trust
Not being aware of limitations	1	2	3	4	5	6 → (PI)	7	Knowing/understanding your limitations

These ratings suggest a reduction in discrepancy between current and ideal selves, consistent with the application of the Y-shaped model in rehabilitation. In support of this, James also reported improved self-esteem and reduced anxiety on the BAI.

The individual work with James led to a shift in completion of some tasks. While there were ongoing difficulties with reliability of completion of tasks, the experiments were sufficient to challenge James and Helen's perception of discrepancy and to identify occasions when the desired 'hero-partner' relationship occurred. Some reframing of strategies by James as 'strategic tools' for attaining this salient goal was also possible. The couple reported a more equal distribution of roles at home. They also reported improved communication and a shared sense that the 'unspoken fears' between them had lessened.

Social participation changes

On the COPM, James rated himself as performing better at work and seemed to have a more realistic appraisal of his ability to follow through on domestic activities through completing the behavioural experiments. James reported feeling more satisfied with domestic and work tasks at the end of the programme (see Figures 2 and 3).

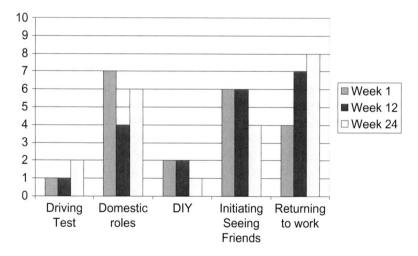

Figure 2. Canadian Occupational Performance Measure satisfaction scores (where rating of satisfaction is 1–10 with 10 indicating greater satisfaction).

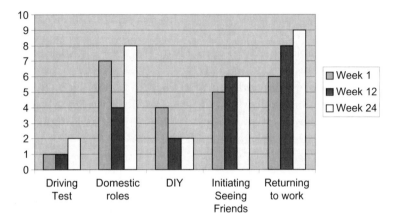

Figure 3. Canadian Occupational Performance Measure performance scores; James rated his sense of how well he was performing in a range of areas, using a scale of 1–10 where 10 is the best performance.

James achieved his primary goal of returning to employment. On the EBIQ, both James and Helen reported a reduction of symptoms since the prior to commencing the programme (Table 6). Further, James was initiating more tasks at home, had a system in place for managing correspondence and had made progress towards the development of an effective memory and planning system.

At one-year post programme, James had returned to his previous work role in a paid capacity on a part-time basis and reported himself to be satisfied with this outcome. He had gradually learnt to accept support from his colleagues and use strategies in the work environment more consistently, such that his performance and productivity was acceptable to his employer. At a review appointment, James described looking back over the past few months and not recognizing himself; he considered this to indicate progress. One personally important event was surrounding the empathy and support James showed Helen following the death of a family member, which enabled them to reflect on the shifts occurring in their relationship towards each caring for the other and being a 'team' again, and in so-doing, moving further away from the 'failure-carer' positions. They described this event as a 'sea change' in their relationship.

Table 6. Changes in reported frequency of symptoms measured using the EBIQ, BAI, and RSQ between start and finish of the programme.

		James	Helen
EBIQ	Prior to programme	126	139
	End programme	97	113
BAI	Prior to programme	10	
	End programme	5	
RSQ	Prior to programme	126	
	End programme	146	

"Life is change": Interview with James and Helen

Approximately two years after a motor cycle accident, and towards the end of a six-month holistic neuro-psychological rehabilitation, James and Helen are interviewed by the treating clinical psychologist about their reflections on their experience of life after brain injury. A section of this interview is transcribed below:

James: I started off when I woke in hospital, just feeling guilty … not just for being such a clot as to have an accident … but for being such a clot as to have a motorcycle at all. When I realised that Helen wasn't going to hold that against me … there was no, not a hint of "I told you so" …

Helen: … well, that would have been a bit pointless. I do think that it would have been utterly pointless to think "why me?" … well … "Why not me?" You just have to look around the world, and bad things happen to good people all the time. Not that we're "good" … but it's *just arbitrary*. I think that both of us have rather gained comfort from that.

James's ability to communicate grew, and I think that was a vital part of "re-forging" and … *making me laugh*; we still had jokes, even in intensive care. It wasn't as if we were making it light-hearted, which

could sound a bit cold hearted really ... but it was a way of us having a 'code against the world'. Our private language was re-established. Our way of talking to each other was re-established quite early on. So I knew that there was a kernel of James "James-ishness" still in there, and our connection was re-established. I mean, it faltered ... I also got very, um, tired of his physical disabilities. I was wearied by his pain. It sounds bad ... "It hurts me more than it hurts you" and all that, but you do ... when someone you love is in pain, you *almost* feel it yourself. I found that incredibly tiring to watch him struggle. I was worried he was in pain. Pushing a not-particularly-heavy man in a wheelchair up a hill was really hard work. That was when I got really close to despair ... that was when I suddenly realised what the reality of this was.
[pause]

Interviewer: lets fast forward a couple of years ... do you know any more about the consequences of the accident have been, for example, do you know about any cognitive changes?

James: No.
Not at all.

I suppose, if pushed, we would come back to the old thing of where I say "I'm fine, there aren't any consequences" and Helen would laugh and say "um ... well actually ... " but as far as I'm concerned, I'm just getting back to normal.

Helen: Also, it sounds quite ridiculous, having known James for so many years before the accident, but you sort of forget what he was like before the accident. I mean, maybe that's my great skill ... having a ...
[pause]

James: ... a lousy memory?
[both laugh]

James: It makes me think of the times when I was in hospital, and I used to phone you up and say "where are you?" because I was *expecting* 'to be visited' ...

Helen: which was a bit irritating because I came every bloody
            day, but you couldn't remember … in the early days,
            almost every day I would say to myself "can I live
            with this?" You know, "he's not going to be able to
            walk … can I live with this? … yes" … "he's not go-
            ing to be able to talk, at one point … [waves hand in-
            dicating uncertainty] … yes, we can live with this …
            we can do it" … and … It has become so I don't say
            that anymore. This is the way we are now … whether
            we have "reached it" (whatever *it* was) but it's just
            the way, the way you live, is how we live.

James: yes, I mean, I think my instinct would be to sort of sit
            there and twiddle my thumbs and wait "for normality
            to descend" just by virtue of time … but that is not the
            way to do anything, and that's not what I'm doing …

Helen: … well, life is change, and it's how you deal those
            changes, with it that's important … because even
            without the accident we're, you know, 2 and a half
            years on … so things might have changed.

Helen: We had the great good fortune that it's happened to
            us when we've been older …

James: … but young enough to recover …

Helen: I mean, we have become much more, well I think
            we've always been quite 'philosophical', but when
            you're in your 30s it must be must tougher.

James: … thinking about the Dorset trip. I recognised that
            before went we went down there, Helen was respon-
            sible for 2 dogs

Helen: We stupidly went and bought another dog.

James: so it was 4 times, not just twice the effort … and also be-
            cause I've normally done the driving on long trips like
            that, Helen hasn't ever driven that distance in one go.

Helen: which was *good* for me!

James: oh absolutely!

Helen: "what doesn't kill you makes you strong." I mean,
            there have been some very positive things … that
            we have both learned that we're 'tough' which is an
            enormous thing …

James: … yes, I said that my self-image was as 'a bit of a wimp' before all this happened … but that was obviously not true … we've learned a great deal.

This section of transcript is included because of the eloquent ways in which this couple have described aspects of their connection, alongside their individual worries, uncertainty, and confusion during the early stages of acute recovery and later. Their experiences are likely to be similar to that of others, and they draw attention to the 'small things' such as the 'joke' and the 'hand squeeze' as important connectors; a 'code against the world', which was important to them before the accident and so 'fuelled' the non-injured relative during her days visiting the hospital. James, meanwhile comments on his amazement that people are so 'soppy' when he emerges from coma, himself having no memory of 'where he has been'. They also draw our attention to their important reflections on the 'meaning of it all' and the constant "struggle" that they felt "wearied" by.

Helen and James describe their coping strategy of looking to the future, rather than looking to 'make sense' of what happened to cause the accident, and they accept it as something that happened 'arbitrarily'. Perhaps it is this absence of blaming that enabled them to talk openly with one another and with the interviewer. At times during their rehabilitation, they spoke about emotions that were difficult to share with each other. For example, James spoke of guilt, and wondering whether Helen was really blaming him for the accident. Helen spoke of feeling exhausted and sometimes feeling frustrated with herself (I must be a better wife) and with James (why does he continue to do that new and irritating habit?) and also with society (why are mattresses designed such that they need two able-bodied people to turn them?). Individual and couples sessions with different members of an interdisciplinary team supported them to make their own sense of these emotions, and how they influenced their communications, and ultimately to be able to talk with each other about the questions or dilemmas that remained important. Their struggle to balance Helen's role between 'carer' and 'partner' is described. Despite significant cognitive and physical impairments following the accident, this couple remained together, and although Helen supports many of his post-injury needs, James re-established a role for himself within the home, and returned to work on a part-time basis, indicating that this case would be viewed as a 'positive outcome' both individually and as a couple. Protective factors for the couple, as identified in the literature that would support such a positive outcome include the length of their relationship pre-injury, their age, and the absence of children in their relationship.

Discussion

This case has been described to illustrate how the proposed 'Y-shaped' model, and associated concept of discrepancies in selves and social identity, was used to guide interdisciplinary interventions using an activity-based relational approach to support achievement of goals. Activities were set up as behavioural experiments, based on functional goals that James was motivated to achieve. The cycle of planning, doing, observing, and reflecting within a safe environment led James and Helen to reappraise their responses to the injury individually and as a couple. It is likely that this method contributed to reduced anxiety and changed behaviour and strategy use observed and reported by James. Furthermore, it is possible that this process operated interpersonally in terms of reducing the 'contesting' dynamic' (Yeates, Henwood, Gracey, & Evans, 2007) with his wife, where they initially reported different perspectives of changes post-injury. See chapter 6 for further discussion of contesting dynamics and awareness.

The behavioural experiments were used to address discrepancy within James' personal identity and within his marriage. Helen had commented on the return of James' ability to empathize with her position, which is noteworthy in light of recent literature identifying empathy as a significant predictor of relationship satisfaction (Burridge, Williams, Yates, Harris, & Ward, 2007). During this process, James increased his awareness and understanding of impairments and began to consider strategy use. It is thought that the shifts in performance ratings on the COPM reflect alterations in awareness. Additionally, James reported improvements in mood and self-esteem.

Both James and Helen reported reduced symptoms of brain injury. Increased initiation at home and successful reintegration to work were significant factors in reconnecting James with his sense of teamwork with Helen. They described situations when they worked together post-injury in a way that was consistent with their pre-injury identity. For example, James brought Helen the glass of wine when she was on the telephone and Helen said this gave her hope because James was a 'hero' in that moment when he considered her needs, initiated the activity, and overcame physical limitations to pour and carry the wine. This provides an example of how a 'loss of self in the eyes of others' (Nochi, 1998a) might be addressed through rehabilitation.

The description of James and Helen's situation post-injury and this rehabilitation process illustrates the significance of considering neuro-rehabilitation and neuro-psychological work within the social context, and the benefit of involving Helen in his rehabilitation. This case extends previous work (Dewar & Gracey, 2007; McGrath & King, 2004; Williams, Evans, & Fleminger, 2003; Ylvisaker & Feeney, 2000) in which rehabilitation efforts have specifically aimed to integrate self and identity-related issues and interpretations of change with activity in meaningful contexts. Secrest and Zeller's qualitative study (Secrest & Zeller, 2003) of experiences in the acute phase after stroke suggested a complex mix of experiences of both continuity and discontinuity of self. Subsequent extension of the study (Secrest & Zeller, 2006) identified control, independence, and connection with others as being central to sense of continuity of self, with loss permeating the theme of discontinuity. Although carried out with a different clinical population, the case we have illustrated here suggests similar issues regarding 'continuity of self' over a year post severe traumatic brain injury. Positive meanings associated with integration of pre- and post-injury selves, noting growth and renewed ways to view the self 'in spite of' or 'because of' the injury' has been highlighted as important in the narratives of those who have adjusted to life post-TBI (Nochi, 2000). We would argue that there is sufficient justification in the literature and from emerging clinical case descriptions to warrant a strong argument for attention to intra- and inter-personal discrepancy in the rehabilitation context and for the linking of 'doing' and 'meaning' to support meaningful change and adjustment post-injury. It may not always be the case that degree of meaning of change (to client and family) is consistent with *amount* of behavioural change as much as what this signifies to the person and those around them in relevant contexts. If it is the case that with regard to self-identity, it is the small things that matter, (at least in part) then this raises questions regarding the ways in which rehabilitation outcome measurement is conceptualized. For example, in this case a highly significant outcome for James and Helen was James' ability to recognize Helen's needs and respond to these. Such an outcome is difficult to capture in standardized outcome measures (e.g., the EBIQ) but might be captured through clinical interview or use of personalized scales such as the 'personal constructs' questionnaire (reference FG) or relational measures such as the Dyadic Adjustment Scale (Spanier, 1976).

The case described here was selected for intensive holistic rehabilitation because of the presence of complex and interacting social, emotional, cognitive, and physical needs. The 'Y-shaped' model presented has been developed to address the needs of this specific subset of people with brain injury and can be applied to relational rehabilitation efforts. Therefore, the limitations of both the model and clinical approach taken with this case must be held in mind.

There are dilemmas for the clinician, which may arise in transferring this model of couples work to other cases. Of note, the approach described may not be possible for many couples because it requires a time commitment from the non-injured relative that may not be feasible. This approach also requires that the couple are able to reflect on links between their emotional experience and activities, which can sometimes be compromised by aspects of emotional adjustment or cognitive functioning.

Conclusion

A clinical case has been described, formulated using the 'Y-shaped' model of rehabilitation, and treatment strategies based on a relational neuro-rehabilitation and neuro-psychological perspective. The process of moving towards resolution of discrepant identity through use of behavioural experiments, linking the essential rehabilitation aspects of 'doing' and 'meaning', has been described, highlighting the significance of addressing everyday 'small things' that individuals do within their social context in addition to larger goals.

The case we have described demonstrated change on a number of different levels of adjustment for this couple. The 'Y-shaped' model can be useful in organizing integrated rehabilitation efforts across professions, and is a means of conceptualizing the change process, which typically incorporates several models and therapeutic approaches.

With special thanks to Joanna Cope and the Oliver Zangwill Centre.

CHAPTER ELEVEN

Neglected subsystems: Siblings, work colleagues, and community members

With additional contribution from Andy Tyerman

Frequently neglected subsystems

It is our aim in this book to make prominent the significant web of social relationships around a survivor of injury. However we are, as others have been, organized by an implicit prioritization of certain kinds of relationship. As with other writers, we have devoted more page space to the romantic, parental, and child familial relationships, alongside rehabilitation relationships within the clinic. In keeping with the literature, certain other groups and relationships are neglected to a lesser extent. We are not proud of this, but we have reached the limits of our scope in this book. We would like to use this chapter to introduce the reader to the existing literature and some new research on the response to injury experienced by siblings, work colleagues, and differing relationships within a community, transient or more enduring. We would welcome future in-depth discussion of these and other marginalized groups within ABI research.

Siblings

This is one of the most under-researched system sub-groups in the adult ABI literature. Waaland and Kreutzer (1988) noted that at that time of the 20 articles they reviewed that explored comprehensive family needs post-injury, only two mentioned the experiences of siblings (at any age). This neglect is often mirrored both within family response to injury and in the clinical service response (Perlesz, Kinsella, & Crowe, 1999): the experience and needs of siblings can be least thought about within family coping, parents and partners often bring the agenda to family sessions at the brain injury service, and it is their addresses that most often feature in clinical notes. Siblings often fade away in the documentation and thinking of the service, despite documented wishes for supportive counselling in this group (Gill, 1998).

Those few studies that have investigated the experiences of siblings have highlighted significant need. It has been noted that at the time by more than one author that parents of an injured child will have less time to spend with other children in the family (O'Hara, Goldfine, Ambrose, Hardgrove, Costello, O'Brien, 1991; Spanbock, 1992). At the same time, themes of parentification and taking on too much responsibility may be pertinent to siblings' experiences as child relatives (Nodell, 1990). Siblings report a sense of responsibility, relied on by parents to help care for their injured relative, to be constantly encouraging and being there for the person with ABI (Maurer, 1991; O'Hara et al., 1991; Spanbock, 1992). In a study by Willer and colleagues (1990), sibling respondents described themselves as 'assistive parents', and cited their increased responsibilities as one of their top five problems experienced since the injury. As adult siblings, this may be an adoption of a parental role to the injured-sibling, despite the fact that the non-injured brother or sister may be the younger of the two.

In a qualitative study, Willer and colleagues (1990) noted that personal and family distress, concern for the future of injured relative, and anticipated changes to balance between the autonomy of the person with injury and the responsibility of the sibling were key themes. A large sample of adult siblings, noted that their future concerns were about the professional services available to their injured relative, together with that person's independence and future social relationships (Degeneffe & Olney, 2008). An unpublished qualitative thesis (Gill, 1998) identified a collective sense by eight siblings of being *forever different*. This was in relation to who they were, the life they had expected for themselves and their family prior to the injury, and the people around them, with change constantly occurring.

This meta-theme comprised four sub-themes: the sense of transition being *initiated by change in the injured sibling* post-ABI, a *mixture of emotions* in their response to injury, a *different 'life-rhythm'* for the way in which they went about their daily lives (including 'doing what it takes' and redefining relationships around them to re-instate predictability or homeostasis), and a *change in self* as a result of these experiences. Emotional experience for siblings include worry (for self, for the injured sibling, for parents, worry about being teased by people outside of the family), other forms of anxiety, depression, anger, feeling trapped or isolated (Lezak, 1978; Maurer, 1991; O'Hara et al., 1991; Spanbock, 1992; Willer, Allen, Durnan, & Ferry, 1990).

Psychological distress of siblings was quantified in a study by Orsillo, McCafney and Fisher (1993), who noted that in a sample of 13 siblings (average of five years post-injury), 83% met the clinical caseness criteria on the Brief Symptom Inventory. However, emotional experience following injury may not be entirely negative for all siblings, however. One study found siblings' ratings of their family functioning as a whole to be no different from that of controls (Orsillo, McCafney, & Fisher, 1993). Gill (1998) highlighted the mixture of positive and difficult emotions in her sample of siblings. It is also worth noting that ambivalent relationships can often characterize sibling relationships in the absence of injury, with positive and challenging dimensions to the relationship (Gustafsson, Engquist, & Karlsson, 1995). Other ABI authors have documented positive growth changes, including increased respect for their relative, experiencing the injury and recovery as a transformative or triumphant, maturing process, feeling more independent and assertive, and increasing their awareness of mortality and appreciation of life itself (Maurer, 1991; O'Hara et al., 1991). Depression and measures of caregiver burden were shown by Degeneffe and Lynch (2006) to have an inverse relationship, suggesting at least that the caring dimension of being a sibling post-ABI is not entirely a depressogenic experience, perhaps even a protective or at least a mediating one.

New research

A hitherto unpublished study on siblings following brain injury is presented here, with thanks to Dr Andy Tyerman for kind permission to report this research.

The impact of severe head injury on siblings—a pilot investigation

Russell, A., Walmsley, J., Tyerman, A., Booth, J., & Fraser, S. (2003). *The impact of head injury on the siblings of head-injured people. A partnership to inform clinical practice.* Unpublished manuscript available from Andy Tyerman: Andy.Tyerman@buckspct.nhs.uk.

Introduction

An exploratory study investigating the impact of severe TBI on siblings was funded by the School of Health and Social Welfare (SHSW, now the Faculty of Health and Social Care) at the Open University and conducted in partnership with the Community Head Injury Service (CHIS), then Vale of Aylesbury, now Buckinghamshire Primary Care Trust. A literature search revealed that little had been published in this area. At the time CHIS provided a range of specialist family services (brain injury educational programme; annual follow-up relatives' workshops; individual carer counselling; and relationship counselling). However, the specific support needs of siblings had been raised at relatives' workshops and CHIS wanted to clarify the needs of siblings after TBI to inform future practice.

Methods

Semi-structured interviews were drafted and refined following comments from client and family representatives on the CHIS Steering Group. Interviews focused on the impact of TBI on siblings and families, facilitated by prompt questions in six areas: life pre-injury (including family relationships); nature of TBI (and early sibling involvement/information provision); return home (early difficulties, impact on siblings); rehabilitation (sibling involvement); long-term effects (ongoing difficulties and impact on siblings and their family relationships); support for siblings. An opportunity was provided for any additional comments about TBI and its effects.

Persons with severe TBI at least two years post-injury whose relatives had attended sessions of the CHIS relatives' educational programme were approached for consent to approach their adult siblings (16+ years) to invite their participation in the study. From

12 subsequent invitation letters to siblings, nine consented and eight interviews were conducted (one consenting sibling was absent). The interviews were conducted by one researcher from SHSW and two from CHIS. (Provision was made for follow-up at CHIS afterwards should any sibling request this). Tapes were transcribed and analysed using a grounded theory approach (Glaser & Strauss, 1965).

Participants

Of the eight siblings interviewed, six had a brother and two a sister with severe TBI. The duration of PTA ranged from two weeks to three months and was over a month for six people. At the time of injury six people with TBI were living in the family home and the other two with spouses (see Table 1 below). They were referred to CHIS between three months and 30 years post-injury. Time post-injury on interviewing siblings ranged from three to 32 years.

Table 1. Person with TBI and interviewed siblings—age/residence at injury.

No.	Person with TBI (age) & residence	Sibling (age) & residence
1	Younger brother (20)—family home	Older sister (24)—left home
2	Older brother (11)—family home	Younger brother (9)—family home
3	Older brother (28)—with spouse	Younger sister (23)—family home
4	Older brother (24)—family home	Younger sister (21)—left home
5	Older brother (17)—family home	Younger sister (14)—family home
6	Younger sister (18)—family home	Older brother (19)—at university
7	Younger brother (11)—family home	Older brother (18)—family home
8	Younger sister (29)—with spouse	Older sister (49)—with spouse

Six of the siblings interviewed were sisters (four younger, two older) and two brothers (one older, one younger). At time of injury four siblings were living in the family home, three had left and one was away at university. (see Table 1 above).

Results

The major themes identified with illustrative quotations from siblings were as follows:

A traumatic experience for siblings

All siblings interviewed commented on the traumatic nature of head injury, both at the time of injury and later. A younger brother in the car at the time of the accident commented, *"We went into the back of a lorry ... and my brother hit his head ... and just kind of like exploded his head kind of thing ... I've never seen so much blood on anything in my life ... like his skull and stuff and his brain, cos it was all in pieces. ..."* On first seeing her brother in hospital a younger sister commented, *"We managed to get up there and I was awful really, because he, he wasn't my big brother any more. He was a baby, you know he was just kinda curled up in a little ball and he was just lying on the bed. And it was quite a shock. ..."* A sister commented as her brother was emerging from coma, *"They sort of, they knew he was coming round and my parents for some reason had to go somewhere and it was just me and it was quite frightening really cos I didn't know what to expect at all."*

Desire for information

Siblings wanted more information to be available to them at all stages—in hospital, on discharge, during rehabilitation, and late post-injury. Sometimes parents did not pass on information and some siblings expressed a need for personal explanations, particularly in the hospital setting. A younger sister commented, *"... Erm me personally, no, I mean sort of by proxy through my Dad and stuff, I was sort of told things but no, not directly."*

Need for involvement

Siblings wanted to be involved and help their injured brother or sister but were often not sure what to do. Some went to great lengths to assist in rehabilitation with associated family role change, while others were much less involved. Some saw their most important role to be that of supporting their parents. A younger sister commented, *"And then he came home and that was probably the turning point of my life then when he came home it was like, like (own name) now you've gotta grow up and look after your brother. It wasn't a case of you go out and party with all your friends and … it was how I felt, I wanted to do it and I knew he needed me so. And that was probably the turning point where we got closer as well."*

Influence on family relationships

The experience of TBI often had a major impact on wider family relationships, sometimes bringing families closer together, with some siblings seeing it as their role to support their injured sibling who often became the centre of attention. However, sometimes the TBI was reported to have contributed to family breakdown in already difficult relationships. An older brother commented, *"Yes it tore it to pieces … It was the final straw … I don't think the parents would have lasted the course anyway … I lost the chance to grow up with a brother that … I'm sure we'd have been a lot closer … Erm I'd say it was down to that that you perhaps had another relationship with (brother's name) that you wouldn't otherwise have had and that's a father figure as well. So not only are you best mate and a big brother and a life-board, you're fulfilling a father's roles … I find that quite an intrusion on my life … I stepped in and became a half-parent even in those days I took on responsibilities. …"*

Perceptions and blame—some turning points

Siblings described how they perceived their brother or sister had changed since the TBI. They found it difficult to understand some behaviours and two people reported a great release when they were able to blame the TBI for their siblings' challenging behaviour. The new understanding that followed the explanations provided by CHIS helped to promote resilience and enabled them to cope and support their injured sibling. However, a degree of sadness often remained that the injured sibling would not be able to enjoy the opportunities they had to find partners and high-status employment. An older sister commented, *"To understand that she wasn't better and she might never get better, back to her old self. She was always, still happy, but it was the didn't care attitude that she never had before, you know that was difficult to understand and if we would have known then that that was all part of the head injury and it just wasn't her couldn't be bothered."*

Need for continuing support

Siblings expressed the need for support to continue to be available to help them to make sense of their experience of the effects of their brother or sister's TBI. They had to live with the uncertainty and unpredictability that accompanies TBI and might need information and help to cope at any time in the future in order to continue to support their sibling. They were very appreciative of the help available for people with TBI and their families at CHIS and a need was identified by some participants for occasional workshops for siblings to share information and experiences. An older sister commented, *"You know it's difficult to think, why is she saying that? Or why is she doing that? And not have an answer on how to deal with it. To have somebody like CHIS explain it and I can't emphasise enough how much CHIS helped us, I really can't... ...they had to discharge my sister... ...but erm they said, "It's always open" ...they've said to us we can contact them at any time if we've got any problems or worries and just knowing that, is a great relief."*

Discussion

The experiences described in these eight interviews illustrated the often major and wide-ranging but also variable impact of TBI on siblings and their family relationships. The following themes were identified: a traumatic experience for siblings; desire for information; need for involvement; influence on family relationships; perceptions and blame—some turning points; need for continuing support.

The research was a successful partnership between a university faculty and a service agency. It informed CHIS about the needs of siblings and provided preliminary evidence on which to develop future clinical practice. The study was enhanced by the involvement of clients and relatives from CHIS Steering Group and provided a rare opportunity for the voice of siblings to be heard. It is vital that TBI services consider the needs of siblings, along with the needs of the person and their parents and/or partner and children.

Siblings' experiences in context

This mixture of both positive and negative experiences suggests that either siblings' experiences are multi-faceted, or this as a researched group is heterogeneous. Both are indeed the case—many readers may be a sibling and can understand how a brain injury occurring in their family with different relatives would have specific meanings at certain times, leading to particular responses for that time. The sibling research that does exist in the ABI literature comprises studies investigating the experiences of both children and adults, all at differing times post-injury (Gill, 1998). As such careful analyses of the literature as a whole have been presented (for overviews see Daisley & Webster, 2008; Gill, 1998; Perlesz, Kinsella, & Crowe, 1999). Family systems theory has been used by one author to frame their interpretation of cross-study findings (Gill, 1998). We will follow suit, applying the organizing constructs of contextual difference and family life cycles.

The experience of the sibling in relation to an injured relative is unique in the family, in that they are the one member who has not consciously chosen to have a relationship with that person pre-injury (Degeneffe & Burcham, 2008). A sibling has been documented as a resource in everyday life and in emotional crises (Lewis & Karen, 1990). The ABI literature supports the notion that the injured-relative receives support from a non-injured sibling. At the same time the non-injured sibling can become isolated and loses the kind of support they received from the survivor of ABI pre-injury.

Age, and age of other siblings, or position in the family has been identified as significant for experience. Daisley and Webster (2008) emphasize the need to consider the context of birth-order to understand the experiences and demands placed upon each child relative post-injury. In the broader literature on siblings' experiences in general and in following chronic illness of any kind, authors identified being older than the ill sibling as associated with greater additional responsibility (Goetting, 1986; McHale & Gamble, 1989; Williams, Lorenzo, & Borja, 1993). This is equally pertinent for adult children and their parents when, following a brain injury in the family, financial and other responsibilities have to be re-assigned and negotiated as parents themselves age, become ill, and less able to manage certain responsibilities. Younger siblings may experience jealousy and rivalry for parental attention, be this in the case of an injured parent or child within the system (Faux, 1993; Peretti & Abderholden, 1995). In contrast other studies have documented sibling reports of decreased rivalry with the injured relative (Johnson, 1995; Willer, Allen, Durnan, & Ferry, 1990). These differences have been interpreted on methodological grounds, and importantly the age of the siblings, with sibling conflict and age having an inverse relationship (Gill, 1998). Daisley and Webster (2008) have noted that in young children, the cognitive developmental abilities of a child at a particular age will determine how flexibly and adaptively they will make sense of the injury and its consequences without professional intervention.

Parental perspectives elicited in one study highlight how siblings become less involved with their injured relative over time (Lezak, 1978), where siblings themselves describe a closer emotional connection, friendship, and concern for their relative. Again, the importance of family life-cycle transitions in general is emphasized to make sense of these apparently contradictory findings (McGoldrick, Gerson, & Petry, 2008). Studies of families without ABI highlight how as siblings enter into adult life, actual face-to-face contact may be less but they experience their relationships as more supportive and based on friendship (Goetting, 1986).

Gender may be a further key factor, with female siblings reporting greater levels of depression and additional responsibilities in both ABI groups and in chronic illness groups generally (Degeneffe & Lynch, 2006; Goetting, 1986; McHale & Gamble, 1989; Williams, Lorenzo, & Borja, 1993). Pre-injury experiences, such as suffering a depressive episode, were shown by Degeneffe and Lynch (2006) also to predict the likelihood of post-injury depression in siblings, alongside perceived restrictions in valued family activities.

Life seems to change for siblings in their relationships outside of the family. Reports of progressive social isolation, less time, and opportunities to socialize with peers, and challenges of managing feelings of embarrassment regarding their injured brother or sister have been noted by several authors (Hardgrove, 1991; Lezak, 1978; O'Hara et al., 1991; Spanbock, 1992). Within sibling groups, decreased access to social support post-injury has been associated with increased levels of depression (Degeneffe & Lynch, 2006). Gill (1998) compared these findings to studies of siblings with brothers or sisters who have chronic illness, but not brain-injuries, who do not report the same levels of embarrassment or decreasing social activity. She suggests that the inter-personal consequences of cognitive and behavioural changes post-injury may be the unique, discriminating factors. It is worth noting that once again we have a close family sub-group that experiences a change in self and identity (Gill, 1998) in parallel with personality changes in the survivor (see partners' experiences, chapter 4 & 5), emphasizing the relational dimension of personhood change post-injury.

It can therefore be inferred that siblings are a heterogeneous group of relatives, and that differences in age, gender, family composition (and the place of the sibling in this), pre- and post-injury experiences all contextually influence the experience of any given sibling. Authors have recommended that future studies use larger and comparative samples to explore the significance of variable such as age, gender (these factors being pertinent to all family members), and time post-injury for siblings' experiences (Gill, 1998; Perlesz, Kinsella, & Crowe, 1999).

Working systemically with siblings

Given these contextual factors, siblings should be approached as a diverse group with differing needs, understood in each case with reference to the broader family and social contexts in which they are situated. Gustafsson, Engquist, and Karlsson (1995) note that differing family therapy models vary in their approach to siblings, with some requiring sibling attendance at sessions as a pre-requisite to their occurrence, and other approaches seeing sibling involvement as optional or peripheral. Within the ABI siblings literature, suggested family interventions include the facilitation of relationships around the sibling that may be ignored or suffer through the increased focus on the family member with injury. This may include the freeing up of parental or older sibling time from caring responsibilities to invest in the non-injured family relationships (Kahn, 1997). Degeneffe and Burcham (2008) highlight a range of both practical and emotional factors that require support in ensuring the well-being of siblings. The involvement of siblings in a family therapy session may be a point of resource for other family members, such as parents (Gustafsson, Engquist, & Karlsson, 1995). This may be via their physical presence in the session or an invitation to consider their perspectives in their absence, via circular questioning. Finally, the formation of siblings-only relative support groups may be a further arena for conversations about the unique qualities of experience that would not feature prominently within whole family sessions. It is worth noting that some of the ABI siblings studies were conducted as group interviews, valued by participants as useful experiences (Johnson, 1995; Willer, Allen, Durnan, & Ferry, 1990).

Few publically available clinical resources exist specifically for siblings. Notable exceptions include detailed fact sheets obtainable at the following URLs:

http://braininjury.org.au/portal/children/siblings-and-acquired-brain-injury-fact-sheet.html

http://www.headwest.asn.au/factsheets/siblings-and-brain-injury.pdf

http://www.braininjurymn.org/library/siblings.pdf

Work colleagues

Vocational rehabilitation is becoming an increasingly recognized and essential component in a brain injury service ideally, if not in routine practice. Supporting a survivor of injury to find a meaningful and sustainable role within a work context (paid, voluntary, supportive, or other) has been advocated by authors for vocational, financial, and psychological gain for the survivor and family (Tyerman, Tyerman, & Viney, 2008). Employment status of the survivor has also been shown to influence the functioning of the family as a whole (Vanderploeg, Curtiss, Duchnick, & Luis, 2003). Good introductions and overviews to vocational brain injury rehabilitation are provided by Carew and Collumb (2008), Johnson and Stoten (2008), Ownsworth and McKenna (2004), and Tyerman, Tyerman and Viney (2008).

Workplace consultation is also an increasingly established context for systemic practice (e.g., Campbell, Coldicott, & Kinsella,

1994). We have briefly in passing, considered ABI and the workplace from a systemic perspective in a previous publication (Bowen et al., 2009) and would like to unpack a particular issue in more detail here. The brain injury vocational rehabilitation literature has considered the workplace from the perspective of the survivor and family, and the employer when framed as a collaborator in rehabilitation (e.g., Johnson & Stoten, 2008). However, it is much harder to find any account of the unique perspective of employers or work colleagues on ABI outside of rehabilitation liaison.

Furthermore, a finding that has been encountered by one author (GY) while working across differing vocational rehabilitation services is that there is often a particular dynamic between a work placement and an ABI service that has never been described in the literature. When certain ABI sequelae are present (particularly executive and social communication difficulties), workplace contacts will often feed back that things are going well with the survivor, up until the eleventh hour. Then suddenly services may receive a flurry of phone calls from the workplace saying that the placement has broken down in an irrecoverable way (although gaining precise feedback and problems definitions from work seems to be difficult, or too late). This can happen despite the most open and collaborative preparation by vocational rehabilitation services in liaison with the workplace. This is indeed a powerful, confusing and not uncommon dynamic, and requires some systemic formulation.

In terms of the injury itself, identified predictors of post-injury employment outcome are often multi-factorial but include some revealing issues: executive dysfunction (Crepeau & Sherzer, 1995; Nybo, Sainio, & Müller, 2004; Vilkki et al., 1994), social communication impairments (Ownsworth & McKenna, 2004; Power & Hershenson, 2003) such as difficulties in turn-taking and regulating quantity of verbal output (Watt & Penn, 2000), difficulties with social contact and interactions with co-workers during and after work (West, 1995), overt inappropriate behaviours such as irritability (Groswasser, Melamed, Agranov, & Keren, 1999; Sale, West, Sherron, & Wehman, 1991; Wehman, Kregel, Sherron, Nguyen, Kreutzer, Fry et al., 1993), insufficient motivation to work (Wehman et al., 1993) and other changes described at the level of personality (Brooks, Campsie, Symington, Beattie, & McKinlay, 1987). In addition, other predictors included mental health status post-injury (Hoofen et al., 2001) and a lack of awareness of disability (e.g., Sherer, Boake, Levine et al., 1998; Watt & Penn, 2000). To someone without ABI knowledge, exposure to these difficulties must be a confusing, frustrating, and at times even a hurtful experience (e.g., a survivor may be functioning inconsistently over time and situations; there might be a disconnect between what a survivor is saying about their performance and what would actually be happening, and colleagues may feel intimidated, uncomfortable, or offended by the comments or behaviour of some survivors during a coffee break). If these issues are present but do not prevent the survivor from accessing a work environment initially, the perspectives and responses to these from line managers and work colleagues working with a survivor need to be mapped and connected with their responses to the work placement process.

Campbell, Coldicott, and Kinsella (1994) advocate the need to understand the responses of one part of the work organization system (e.g., bosses or colleagues) as part of circular processes of influence (feedback) and given meaning through broader contextual influences. Colleagues at work routinely draw upon different discourses and meanings from relatives and clinicians, and these need to be made explicit in a systemic assessment of the workplace. These may include referents to the survivor's self and personality if they have known that person for a while pre-injury, although these may be quite different facets of self than that co-constructed within family contexts. In addition, there may be discourses of productivity and diligence, the right kind of work ethic and attitude, being a team player, trustworthiness, and harassment and prejudice. It would therefore be against these frames of meaning that an issue with the survivor's performance or behaviour would become recognizable or interpreted ("he's lazy ... having us on ... is having a free ride ... is weird/creepy ... can't be bothered with anyone). Dominant managerial and corporate discourses of motivational speaking and autonomy may organize a great deal of the meaning of post-ABI sequelae to others in the workplace. A particular form of agency and deliberate intention may be constructed to position the survivor in quite a malevolent way. In relation to the service-workplace dynamic mentioned above, it may be that certain difficulties cannot be talked about very easily at all, even with the rehabilitation team, in comparison to a practical analysis of task-related performance. The social faux pas during the coffee break may not so easily be

brought to the attention of services, perhaps for fear of embarrassment, slurring of the survivor's character, or making other staff
members vulnerable. However, the vocational rehabilitation literature above indicates that even small social transgressions, built up
repetitively over time are more likely to cost a job status than task-
related problems (Ownsworth & McKenna, 2004).

In addition to these discourses and frames of meaning, employers
respond in relation to two other contextual factors, (a) employment and
disability law and (b) the support of vocational services. With regards
to the former, Johnson and Stoten (2008) note that in the UK the Disability Discrimination Act (DDA, 1995, 2005) is intended to be an infor-
mational resource for employers and employees alike. However, they
also note that physical and sensory disabilities appear at first glance
to be more congruent with the DDA, with few referents to the 'hidden
disabilities' associated with cognitive dysfunction (mental health is
now being more firmly represented, however). It is the authors' experience that employers often assume that ABI is not covered by the
DDA at all. It makes sense, therefore, that the vocational consequences
of injury are not sufficiently visible to employers, if relevant legislation
does not articulate such in an immediate way. This surface inconsid-
eration may even serve to disqualify ABI sequelae as a legitimate set of
needs within the workplace in the minds of employers.

The vocational service in liaison with a workplace is an observing,
influencing system. If the vocational service has a health identity in
any way, this may connote 'otherness' to the employers, people who
do not share the same business concerns, and who will naively suggest
unprofitable courses of action to support the survivor's well-being at
work. Alternatively, the service may be seen with miraculous potential
to solve a confusing issue in an employee's brain, a solution that may
divert curiosity away from environmental factors within the workplace
such as shift/rota patterns, office layout, availability of breaks, etc.

Working systemically with employers and colleagues

Following Campbell, Coldicott, and Kinsella (1994), the dominant
discourses and meanings within the workplace that contextualize
post-injury problems need to be mapped, along with the practices
and interactions that are organized by and reciprocally sustain them.
New ideas do need to be brought in, a knowledge of ABI and its

consequences is required to make sense of confusing experiences. These ideas should be imported in a way that supports the workplace system to seek out exceptions to problems and find a way to ensure more consistent positive outcomes. Roles and responsibilities of each service or individual should ideally be mapped out clearly and collaboratively, with attention paid to power dynamics and ensuring that each is empowered to complete their tasks. A systemic resource can be found in the multiple numbers of employees within an organization—existing employment practices such as 360-degree feedback can be used (via the use of circular questions) to generate rich and diverse accounts of both need and competency, along with differing explanations and judgements. Rehabilitation ideas may be useful in making sense of dilemmas and contradictions brought by work colleagues.

For areas that can't so easily be talked about by colleagues, such as social communication faux pas and their consequences, the onus is on the vocational rehabilitation service to make these explicit in the outset. This would include identifying the behaviours that may be seen, the corresponding emotions and responses that may be elicited in colleagues as a result, and the dilemmas that managers may face when caught in the cross-fire. This conversation needs to be returned to regularly to give employers permission to discuss these issues. Of course, there is a balance here in making such topics visible and not pre-determining the construction of the survivor by their work peers, contributing to stigmatization, etc. The vocational rehabilitation specialist needs to be on the lookout for subtle indications that socially awkward experiences are occurring yet not discussed. In planning for the work placement, selection of a work context appropriate to the survivor's strengths and needs is essential. For example, if there are serious social communication needs, work that involves customer liaison and/or an officious culture of colleague relations may be unrealistic.

A useful approach would be to frame vocational experience post-injury both as a potential for benefiting an organization and a long-term process, requiring frequent liaison with services, and susceptible to changes in personal, practices, and environment (Tyerman, Tyerman, & Viney, 2008). The introduction of the DDA into conversations should be done sensitively if one is trying to create a collaborative relationship, as its legislative dimension risks intimidation and distancing the employer. Finally, one approach to

Case example

Social communication difficulties and a manager's dilemma

Following a TBI at 17 a 34-year-old survivor was left unable to return to long-term work as a result of social communication difficulties. He would have a tendency to call every female work colleague "darling, my lovely, sweetheart etc.," despite their position (boss, line manager, colleague, customer). When shaking someone's hand he would quickly progress to touching their forearm, even kissing their hand or face. He would also swear indiscriminantly and talk about inappropriate topics, while often openly picking his nose in front of colleagues.

A work placement was secured where he would perform administrative duties in a firm of solicitors (photocopying, sorting post, assembling documents). This company worked with clients who have sustained injuries, understood ABI sequelae, and were keen to help in providing a placement. While the senior partners had this knowledge, the office clerks who have immediate contact with the survivor on a day-to-day basis were less prepared, and after a few inappropriate comments and touching began to complain and even call off work on sick-leave. The position of the manager was untenable: despite acknowledging that more time may help get an effective cuing and feedback procedure in place to help the survivor moderate his behaviour, he had to protect the well-being of his staff. The placement was terminated early.

dissolving the conceptual and geographical split between service and employer would be to use support workers in-situ. Funding schemes in the UK such as Jobcentre Plus' Access to Work may permit this in the first instance. A support worker may be useful in modelling practices, mediating between perspectives and creating opportunities for connecting thinking and practice. They may also be well placed to monitor social behaviour and inter-personal processes in the workplace (including the responses of colleagues).

Internet-based resources to use with employers to explain the consequences of ABI for the workplace can be found in the links below:

http://braininjury.org.au/portal/discharge/information-for-employers-fact-sheet.html

http://www.differentstrokes.co.uk/download/InfoPack/WASEmployersGuide-Dec08.pdf

www.jan.wvu.edu/media/brai.htm

www.efd.org.uk

Community members

Within rehabilitation contexts, the importance of community in recovery and well-being has been recognized for some time, through the concept of 'therapeutic social milieu' (Ben-Yishay, 1996; 2000), which has remained a core component of many programmes (Prigatano, 1999; Wilson et al., 2000; Wilson, Gracey, Malley, Bateman, & Evans, 2009). This is the use of empathic connection and collectivity arising from survivors of injury-sharing experiences with other survivors, even if this is only briefly over a cup of coffee between professional sessions. Specific psychotherapy and community groups have been suggested to emphasize the building of community around difficult shared experiences post-injury. An example is the psychological support group (Gracey, Yeates, Palmer, & Psaila, 2009), using a collection of ideas including Bion's (1961; Garland, 1998) group psychoanalytical psychotherapy approach. This aims to bring to the group's awareness both its chosen purpose as a community but also the ways in which such a purpose is undermined by emotional (and/or neuro-psychological) factors.

But what about communities outside of rehabilitation? We know that social isolation is a common and major outcome for both TBI survivors and their relatives (Dawson & Chipwell, 1995; Elsass & Kinsella, 1987; Kinsella, Ford, and Moran, 1989; Prigatano, 1986), and this has been shown to increase over time post-injury (Bond, Brooks, & McKinlay, 1979; Brooks, Campsie, Symington, Beattie, & McKinlay, 1987). At the same time, social relationships and community integration have been highlighted as essential long-term protective factors for survivors post-injury (Yates, 2003). Re-development of identity and self post-injury has been shown to be dependent on wider social and community group membership (Cloute, Mitchell, & Yates, 2008; Haslam et al., 2008; Nochi, 1997; Oddy, 1995; Yeates et al., 2006; 2007; 2008). For example, participating in multiple groups post-stroke has been shown to be a more powerful predictor of post-injury well-being than reported cognitive difficulties or pre-injury group membership (Haslam et al., 2008). In addition, social support has been shown to buffer the effects of a brain injury on relatives (Ergh, Rapport, Coleman, & Hanks, 2002; 2003), as does the successful community participation and social integration of the survivor post-injury (Chan, 2007;

Machamer, Temkin, & Dikem, 2002; Marsh, Kersel, Havill & Sleigh, 1998; Ponsford, Olver, Ponsford, & Nelms, 2003; Winstanley, Simpson, Tate, & Myles, 2006). Social isolation can therefore be seen to be a progressive negative cycle, further undermining or minimizing opportunities for survivors and relatives to cope and adjust. Many communities involving survivors can be viewed as a fragmented and displaced, potentially united through their common experiences but separated through limiting physical, cognitive, psychosocial, and financial difficulties.

Working Systemically with Communities: Community user-group and voluntary sector resources have become increasingly important resources for ABI survivors and their families, mapping more closely the continuity of their experiences across the years post-injury. Over time, between and after professional input, these services provide a neutral meeting place, access to information, the first response to a crises, ongoing family support and community building (cf., Headway Houses around the country). While some of these resources mirror professional trends, others have developed new ways of working, both in response to local and national service gaps and as a result of radically different assumptions of support and personhood.

An example is the organization UK CONNECT, who aim to facilitate effective communication between and for people who experience language difficulties (aphasia) following acquired brain injury. Influenced by narrative theory and community work practices such as community witnessing, (Sarbin, 1986; White & Epston, 1990), UK CONNECT will work within families and services to promote forms of communication to enhance family cohesion and survivors' personhood and identity. They also arrange large-scale, one-off community gatherings via road-shows (in central and remote parts of the UK, where service provision is absent) to bring people who experience similar difficulties together, create empowering new conversations, and consolidate new communities and clusters of social support. In response to physical and financial mobility restrictions that would prevent people from meeting, CONNECT will travel across the country and bring the conversations to them. These community initiatives are also commensurate with a view that families have positive resources following ABI (e.g., Adams, 1996), which can be developed within the right social conditions.

In the modern age community and relationship building is as likely to take place virtually in cyberspace as it is via face-to-face contact. Social networking, blogging, chat rooms, and live messaging permit people to connect without the expense or physical demands of travel. This development offers potential to the social needs of survivors of injury who are geographically isolated, cannot afford to travel, and/or who have mobility difficulties. Research has identified concurrent internet needs of relatives and carers following ABI (Chiu, 2006), including access to information, identifying professional resources, e-correspondence chat and support. However, existing research by CONNECT (Elman, Parr & Moss, 2003; Moss, Parr, Byng, & Petheram, 2004; Parr, Watson, & Woods, 2006; see www.ukconnect.org/research_221.aspx) has shown that while social and community access is potentially offered by the internet, survivors of ABI who have language difficulties are undermined by the vast quantity of unstructured and non-signposted information on the web. The specific advantages of websites such as www.heathtalkonline.org.uk, offering multi-medium material (text, audio, streaming videos of personal narratives that can be paused and played at the pace of the user, together with links to information and forums), may offer new promise, as part of a broader movement to facilitate access to web resources for people with disabilities (e.g., www.ataccess.org).

Conclusions

A relational approach to rehabilitation will follow its curiosities outside of the clinic walls to discover the range of actual or potential relationships in the home, work, or wider community. In our modern age we have seen that this form of connection can occur in both physical and virtual space, with communicative practice being the necessary component. The challenge is always keeping abreast of how is and isn't being involved and included, and being able to keep all possible relationships sufficiently in mind when organized in particular ways of thinking as clinicians. Practices such as eco-mapping (Hartmann, 1995) may be useful in this regard, purposefully prompting the practitioner to consider who they have forgotten when mapping out the conceptual territory.

CHAPTER TWELVE

Relational rehabilitation research

In this book, we have presented many ideas about how to engage with the complexity of difficulties faced by survivors of brain injury and their family and social networks. In this chapter we hope to aide the reader as they navigate the plethora of studies that has emerged over the last 40 years, before we delineate some of the emerging lines of research and methodologies within the field of rehabilitation and to link them to aspects of our approach. We then offer some recommendations for future research with a relational orientation.

To begin, and perhaps before we go further; a word about the variety of meaning systems, models, and theories that have been used to infer the issues for families following brain injury. These overarching frameworks help shape the research that is conducted and as such set the parameters of what is to be discovered. So far in this book we have mentioned a multitude of interventionist approaches and theoretical positions, even some that have been established outside of brain injury, but have in common an emphasis on defining brain injury against a backdrop of differing perspectives within the social context. What follows is a synthesis of the main lines of family research conducted in the brain injury field. This is of course only one interpretation of the literature and many others have been suggested (Blais & Boisvert, 2005; Boschen, Gargaro, Gan, & Gerber, 2007; Camplair, Kreutzer, & Doherty, 1990; Cavallo & Kay, 2005; Florian, Katz, & Lahav, 1989; Kreutzer, Marwitz, & Kepler, 1992; Muir, Rosenthal, & Diehl, 1990; Oddy & Herbert, 2003; Perlesz, Kinsella, & Crowe, 1999; Sander & Kreutzer, 1999; Sander, 2005; Verhaeghe, Defloor, & Grypdonck, 2005).

Complexity of conditions

In the UK, the National Service Framework (NSF) for Long-Term (Neurological) Conditions (2005) has pioneered new thinking about assessing the quality of research for rehabilitation settings:

> *"Randomised controlled trials and other quantitative methodologies are not necessarily best suited to research questions involving long-term outcomes, varied populations with complex needs and assessment of impact on quality of life rather than cure. Existing tools which put a numerical score on 'quality of life' also often bear little relation to an individual's own definition of actual quality of life. Longitudinal studies and well conducted qualitative research are therefore equally likely to be appropriate methods to evaluate the interventions that are recommended as part of this NSF" (p. 87)*

The NSF for Long-Term (Neurological) Conditions goes further by stating that they value the opinions of service users and their families/carers, as well as the views of professionals; that depending on the research context qualitative and mixed methods designs can have equal validity; and that research evidence should be assessed in terms of Design, Quality, and Applicability.

This approach is documented by the World Health Organization and mirrors the general feeling among leading rehabilitation specialists that while the medical model, and randomized controlled studies in particular are highly relevant to assessing new treatments and interventions in which a single drug is administered to a patient with an isolated physical health problem (e.g., insulin to a diabetic patient), the same cannot be said to be true in rehabilitation settings. Hence, rehabilitation specialists are beginning to look broader than just to the so-called 'gold-standard' of treatments. There are a number of reasons for taking such a wider perspective; first, there are significant difficulties conducting any kind of controlled study within a rehabilitation setting because of the complications due to aspects of the long-term conditions themselves (the irreversible effects of many cases of neurological illness and injury and the co-morbidity of conditions, for example, brain injury and epilepsy), so because of the interaction of complex relationships within and between complex conditions. Taking a broader position also reflects the non-medical dominance within the rehabilitation professional groups, that there are speech and language therapists, occupational therapists, physiotherapists, dieticians, social workers, and psychologists, who all potentially have highly relevant roles to play yet operate by using inter-personal skills and techniques to impart knowledge rather than prescribing medications.

Lines of family research with neuro-rehabilitation

(a) Subjective burden studies in the field of brain injury

Studies of the subjective burden of relatives were a feature of very early family research conducted in Glasgow. In particular, this group of researchers used a method of assessing 'subjective burden' whereby participants gave a rating on a 7-point scale ranging from the low point "I feel no strain as a result of changes in my spouse/relative," to the maximum of "I feel severe strain …" These researchers found that relative strain by no means diminished over a 7-year period post-injury, but rather increased, and that it was associated with perceptions of personality change in the patient (Brooks & McKinlay, 1983; Brooks, Campsie, Symington, & Beattie, 1986; McKinlay et al., 1981). Using the Questionnaire on Resources and Stress (QRS-SF) to assess burden, Allen, Linn, Gutierrez, and Wille (1994) found high levels of burden for both spouses and parents, and common to many studies, they found that the presence of social aggression and cognitive disability in the individual with brain injury had a greater association with burden of caregivers than the presence of physical disability or injury severity. Knight, Devereux, and Godfrey (1998) also conducted a similar study of carer burden using the Care Burden Scale (CBS) and found that parents were significantly more worried about the future than spouses and reported more physical burden, but this may be because of the age difference between the two groups. Most recently, Sander et al. (1997) again used this method to assess predictors of psychological health in caregivers and found that subjective burden predicted emotional distress scores on the General Health Questionnaire. In one of the few studies to assess the association between caregiver burden (or strain) and family functioning, Gan, Campbell, Gemeinhardt, and McFadden (2006) found that the two were linked and that higher scores on the Caregiver Strain Index were predictive of poorer scores on the Family Assessment Measure.

Despite an impressive number of studies, research using carer 'burden' as a concept is outdated, derogatory, and overly negative in the view of the authors. Nevertheless, these were some of the very earliest of studies conducted in the field.

(b) Psychological distress in relatives and associated predictor variables

Studies of subjective burden were closely followed by investigations of "negative psychological symptoms" (i.e., symptoms of anxiety and depression) in relatives, and the literature contains numerous examples of such studies. For example, a study by Gervasio and Kreutzer (1997) assessed family members' psychological distress after TBI using the Brief Symptom Inventory in a large sample of 116 relatives and found that 40% had clinically elevated scores particularly on Obsessive Compulsive, Psychoticism, Paranoid Ideation, and Hostility subscales.

With the increase in studies also came an increase in sophistication of design and analysis. In particular, it became common procedure to assess the contributing factors associated with psychological distress and symptom level. Two early examples of research studies using more complex statistical procedures such as stepwise multiple regressions are those by Moore, Stanbrook, and Peters (1993) and Douglas and Spellacy (1996). In the former study some evidence was found for 'centripetal' forces acting to bring the family closer together (family coping style, marital adjustment, and number of years married), also 'centrifugal' forces having the opposite effect (number of children, age of oldest child, and amount of perceived financial strain). In a frequently cited paper, Douglas and

Spellacy (1996) examined the importance of four sets of predictor variables (demographic, injury-related, patient functioning, and caregiver functioning) to long-term family functioning, as measured by the Family Environment Scale. The researchers found that the largest amount of variance (55% or 44% adjusted), was accounted for by the caregivers' self-report variables, including caregiver depression, social support, and coping, as well as caregivers' perceptions of patient competency. While this paper achieved its aim that was to clarify some associations between overall family environment and specific predictor variables, firm conclusions are difficult to make because of the retrospective design used (3.5 years post-injury).

Another interesting line of research has been conducted by Anderson and colleagues (Anderson, Parmenter, & Mok, 2002; Anderson, Simpson, Mok, & Parmenter, 2006; Winstanley, Simpson, Tate, & Myles, 2006) who applied path analysis to family neurorehabilitation research. The aim here was to investigate the role of family functioning as a possible mediating variable between the chronic stress of the impact of brain injury (in particular, neurobehavioural problems) and psychological distress. In the first study (Anderson, Parmenter, & Mok, 2002), the researchers claimed to have found evidence for this conclusion within a sample of spouse/caregivers (N = 64; 47 females; 17 males), on average 43 months post-injury. Interestingly, in a later study (Winstanley, Simpson, Tate, & Myles, 2006) using a larger, mixed sample a different conclusion was offered: that the mediator to psychological distress in relatives was in fact the level of participation of the injured relative, rather than family functioning that was deemed relatively healthy at admission to a rehabilitation unit and at follow-up (median 16 months later). Finally, a further study (Anderson, Simpson, Mok, & Parmenter, 2006) again used a mixed sample but at increased time post-injury (mean 3.3 years) and they found elevated scores on the FAD, as compared with Winstanley, Simpson, Tate, and Myles (2006), concluding again that psychological distress experienced by parents and spouses was "intensified" by neuro-behavioural impairments through family functioning. It seems likely that the path analysis is a simplification of what is a complex and multi-factorial relationship between a number of variables and psychological distress in family members.

Further studies highlighting the complexity of issues and of relationships between variables is provided by studies of children with brain injury. Perhaps because it is more obvious to study family impact for children who sustain brain injury, numerous studies exist, including some well-designed ones examining the interconnectedness and mutual influence of members' reactions. Among those of interest, Taylor, Yeates, Wade, Drotar, Stancin, and Burant (2001) found that higher parent distress at six months predicted more child behaviour problems at 12 months (controlling for earlier behaviour problems); and more behaviour problems at six months predicted poorer family outcomes at 12 months (controlling for earlier family outcomes). Max, Castillo, Robin, Lindgren, Smith, Sato et al. (1998) studied both children and adolescents (children aged 6 to 14) at the time of hospitalization after TBI using assessments of pre-injury factors (psychiatric, family functioning, and family life events), severity of injury, and post-injury factors (coping, development of a "novel" psychiatric disorder). These researchers found the strongest influences on family functioning after childhood TBI were pre-injury family functioning, the development of a novel psychiatric disorder in the child, and pre-injury family life events or stressors. These studies represent the beginnings of empirical backing for reciprocal and circular patterns between the injury and the family, as predicted from a systemic or relational perspective.

Studies looking to account for degrees of variance in psychological coping have also found evidence for the value of social support in moderating distress in adult survivor populations (Ergh, Rapport, Coleman, & Hanks, 2002; Sander et al., 1997) and caregivers (Ergh, Rapport, Coleman, & Hanks, 2002; 2003), and for the importance of the presence of a partner in relation to parental distress following childhood brain injury (Kinsella, Ong, Murtagh, Prior, & Sawyer, 1999). Moreover, Hanks, Rapport, and Vangel (2007) found that perceived social support alone was the strongest predicting factor in one's perception of caregiving mastery and satisfaction with the caregiving relationship. Another relatively common finding for this type of study is a negative correlation between family coping and depression in the injured individual (Leach, Frank, Bouman, & Farmer, 1994), and similarly between coping for the injured person and depression in the caregiver, for example, in stroke studies (Carnwath & Johnson, 1987). Confirming a number of strands of the research, Riley (2007) found higher depression and stress scores were associated with more severe behaviours in the injured person and when there was less available social support.

One must bear in mind a caveat of this type of research, that for each self-report measure used, an assumption is being made that this score maps onto reality, for example, the Beck Depression Inventory is only valid in as far as the concept of depression is thought to exist (Parker et al., 1995). Another limitation of predictor studies that purport to account for degrees of variance is that we can only control for variables we are aware of as impacting on the issues under consideration; important variables could be masked by other variables. More will be said on the topic of quality control later in this chapter; for now we only introduce the issue.

(c) Multiple perspectives on the nature of the injury

Some of the first family studies conducted in the field accessed relative's accounts of the nature of problems and compared them to patients (Oddy & Humphrey, 1980; Prigatano, Fordyce, Zeiner, Roueche, Pepping, & Wood, 1984; Oddy, Coughlan, Tyerman, & Jenkins, 1985). Most commonly, the ratings given by relatives exceeded those given by the patient, who had a tendency to underestimate the extent of difficulties that were typically more severe (Thomsen, 1984). Another early study by Fordyce and Roueche (1986) found that patients could be distinguished according to the degree to which their awareness of neuro-psychological impairments concurred with relatives and staff. Those with more awareness tended to be those with lesser injuries and these patients also showed greater emotional disturbance that reduced over the course of rehabilitation. In contrast, those patients that were less aware showed less emotional disturbance, but this would tend to increase over the course of rehabilitation, as the views of one group became better aligned with staff members and relatives' perspectives at discharge. This line of research is still used today highlighting its continued value and more recent examples of this type of study would include Donnolly, Donnelly, and Grohman (2000), who reported clusters of problems from three perspectives (patient, relative, and staff) and concluded that problems centred on: (in)dependence, intimacy, treatment complications, executive functioning, non-executive cognitive functions, mood, and psychotic symptoms. In addition, Prigatano, Borgaro,

Baker, and Wethe (2005) compared levels of awareness and relative distress for TBI, dementia, and a group of people with memory complaints. They concluded that the presence of brain dysfunction associated with neuro-psychological disturbances appears to influence the magnitude of the relationship between the distress level of family members and their ratings of impaired awareness in the injured person. Finally, Holm, Schönberger, Poulsen, and Caetano (2009) compared the reports of difficulties on the EBIQ as rated by 50 patients in comparison to their relatives (n = 52) at the time of discharge from a post-acute rehabilitation brain injury unit. They found that the most frequent complaints in both groups related to somatic and cognitive problems, and that relatives reported significantly more problems on all subscales. The relationship between different perspectives and distress levels could, of course, be mediated by how the family copes with these contesting dynamics; see chapter 6 for further relational discussion of 'awareness'.

Prigatano (2005) reviewed the research gathered over a twenty year period, confirming that impaired self-awareness is linked to rehabilitation outcome, increased emotional distress of people with the injuries and their relatives (although cause and effect are difficult to determine), and that moderate support has been found for an association between impaired awareness and severity of injury. However, it important to note that there have been studies that have found no correspondence between level of awareness and severity of injury (e.g., Lanham, Weissenburger, Schwab, & Rosner, 2000). As discussed earlier in this book, research comparing perspectives has continually highlighted the complexity of issues when assessing for awareness of problems, as shown by the failure to reach a definite conclusion as to the importance of severity of injury as a causal factor. Rather than investigators expecting to find definitive and consistent findings there is perhaps more mileage in discursive approaches that attempt to unpick the context and motivations behind differing opinions on the nature of problems. To illustrate, Yeates, Henwood, Gracey, and Evans (2007) compared perspectives for a group of people with specific injuries (in executive skills) and from these qualitative reports, concluded that people are limited in their understanding of brain injury by their previous experiences. New approaches to researching this area highlight the importance of subjective opinion on the meaning of difficulties, holding contesting accounts of the difference and routes to resolution of different perspectives, and the impact of social context and investigator variables on findings.

(d) Quality of life, life satisfaction, and positivity in relatives

In terms of studies of carers and relatives, there has been a general bias towards negative (or what are sometimes considered 'pathological') emotions, for example, when investigating distress, sadness, or depression. Reacting to this bias has now become the focus of a new 'Positive Psychology' movement (Seligman & Csikszentmihalyi, 2000), and within the field of brain injury this has stimulated new studies, most notably examining instances of post-traumatic growth (McGrath & Linley, 2006). In fact, generally little is known about positive emotions, resilience, or instances when depression does not occur, and more research is needed in this area (Kendall & Terry, 2008). Yet there are exceptions, and a good example of such research is provided by studies that challenge the stereotype that brain injury will naturally lead to separation and divorce in the family (e.g., Kreutzer, Marwitz, Hsu, Williams, & Riddick, 2007; Wood & Yurdakul, 1997); see also the earlier chapter on 'Connections, closeness and intimacy'.

Some novel studies have also approached the issue from a quality of life perspective, an approach that holds much promise and one that has been widely used with other conditions. Studies that have attempted to assess this concept with family members, include a published study by Koskinen (1998), and one unpublished work by Bull (2000). Interestingly, Koskinen concluded that "The relationship between the quality of life of the injured and strain felt by the relative was not linear." Most recently, Pinto (2008) used a concept mapping exercise and consulted 20 caregivers who brainstormed about the problems and challenges they faced and rated these in terms of impact on quality of life. Of particular significance, relatives took a more pragmatic survival approach to rating their difficulties, whereas professionals emphasized losses. The researcher interpreted the findings in terms of Maslow's hierarchy of needs. Similar to findings of studies related to negative symptoms, Wells, Dywan, and Dumas (2005) also found that the type of neurobehavioural difficulty of the injured person and the approaches taken to cope with the associated stress by caregivers had a specific impact on dimensions of their life satisfaction.

(e) Intervention studies

Interventions for families have been described in the literature, but demonstrations of their efficacy have been few and far between, in part because family measures have tended to be used in an ad-hoc way but another complicating factor is that it is common for relatives to refuse treatment (Foster & Tilseb, 2003). In chapter 7 we have already discussed how we might understand engagement with family members from a relational perspective to prepare a family for therapeutic intervention. One also needs to bear in mind that some studies have shown no effect for interventions (Carnevale, Anselmi, Busichio, & Millis, 2002; Grimm, 2002; Singer, Glang, Nixon, Cooley, Kerns, Williams, & Powers, 1994).

A variety of interventions in the literature that have been suggested (not necessarily supported by outcome data) include the following:

• psycho-education using video materials (Sanguinetti & Catanzaro, 1987),
• crisis intervention (Söderström, Fogelsjöö, Fugl-Meyer, & Stensson, 1988),
• stress management (Singer et al., 1994),
• family cognitive behavioural support (Smith & Godfrey, 1995),
• mentor programme (Blosser & De Pompei, 1995),
• family counselling (Perlesz & O'Loughlan, 1998),
• telephone support (Brown, Pain, Berwald, Hirschi, Delehanty, & Miller, 1999),
• social work liaison programme (Albert, Im, Brenner, Smith, & Waxman, 2002),
• education and behaviour management (Carnevale, Anselmi, Busichio, & Millis, 2002),
• empowerment intervention (Forsyth, Kelly, Wicks, & Walker, 2005),
• web-based interventions (Bergquist, Gehl, Mandrekar, Lepore, Hanna, Osten, & Beaulieu, 2009; Rotondi, Sinkule, & Spring, 2005; Wade, Wolfe, Brown, & Pestian, 2005)

- psycho-education (Sinnakaruppan, Downey, & Morrison, 2005),
- multi-family group intervention (Charles, Butera-Prinzi, & Perlesz, 2007),
- problem-solving groups (Rivera, Elliott, Berry, & Grant, 2008),

Of the approaches described, one of the most compelling is that of Charles, Butera-Prinzi, and Perlesz (2007) who used multiple family groups to foster connections among a diverse group of family members who then use each other as a resource for empathy, support, and comparison. Case study evidence for the effectiveness of this approach was found. In terms of randomized controlled trials, evidence for organizing cognitive and physical interventions and supports for children with TBI around the everyday routines of their lives, with intensive supports for their families has been shown to be effective by Braga, Da Paz Jnr and Ylvisaker (2005). This is a wider issue in that especially in countries of low socio-economic status it is paramount to work with families in their own context and on their terms because of inconsistent access to rehabilitation.

Whole systems research

In terms of early underpinnings of this line of research, Gervasio and Kreutzer (1997) found that following brain injury there was a greater impact for especially live-in spouses (as measured on Brief Symptom Inventory). Perlesz, Kinsella, and Crowe (2000) then went on to examine the differential impact for primary versus secondary versus tertiary caregivers, and unsurprisingly found that the impact lessened the greater the 'distance' of the relative from the injured individual. We have already summarized such findings in relation to awareness but another line of research has extended the literature by examining multiple perspectives on family functioning after brain injury. That said, there are methodological complications to address within the literature, in terms of sampling and design (Thompson, 2009) and reporting. For example often mixed groups of relatives are used, even on occasions a mixed group of family relatives and survivors, or family measures are not incorporated in the design. Due to the fact that an analysis of family impact is not always the primary focus, omissions about crucial details (e.g., relative/survivor characteristics, degree of rehabilitation received and content, duration of relationship with survivor pre- and post-injury) also make it difficult to interpret results. However, research has proceeded along a number of lines and tended to include at least three types of comparison study:

1. before/after the incident/accident (i.e., retrospective design);
2. before/after rehabilitation; and
3. before/after family intervention.

Methodological considerations

As the number of studies and variables of potential interest has increased so has the demand for increasingly sophisticated psychometric instruments. Most family research has been conducted using measures taken from the mental health field, for example, the Family Assessment Device (FAD; Epstein, Baldwin, & Bishop, 1983), the Family Adaptability and Cohesion Evaluation Scales (FACES; Olson, Sprenkle, & Russell, 1979), and the Family Environment Scale (FES; Moos & Moos, 1976). For these measures, questionable assumptions of relevance have been made, particularly with regard to item content and norms[1] (Thompson, 2009). However, this research has been a first step and as we will now explore, some studies have looked to combine these measures in a quite elaborate way and with some success (see Table 10 below for a full list of studies using family functioning measures).

(a) Increasing degrees of sophistication through combining family functioning measures

Some of the most interesting research has been conducted using quantitative methods that employ more than one family measure, for example, the FAD in combination with the FACES-II

---

[1] Other researchers have developed new family measures specific to brain injury/rehabilitation but not necessarily to family functioning such as: Family Involvement Assessment Measure (?) (McNeill, Schuyler, & Ezrachi, 1997), the Family Involvement Questionnaire (Shaw et al, 1997), and the Family Needs Questionnaire (FNQ; Serio, Kreutzer, & Witol, 1997). Other measures recently developed in the family therapy field (the SCORE measure) also may similarly prove to be relevant and valid to brain injury populations (Janes, 2005).

(e.g., Kosciulek, 1996; Kosciulek & Lustig, 1999; Zarski, DePompei, & Zook, 1988), extending an approach first described by Dickerson and Coyne (1987). The FACES measure enables one to differentiate between 'Balanced' and 'Extreme' families (and also 'Mid-range' families), and this was found to be a meaningful distinction to make, given that groups of families could be differentiated in terms of their FAD scores for the General Functioning and Communication subscales. Kosciulek and colleagues found that families were more likely to be identified as 'extreme' if the primary caregiver was of a younger age, and if the injured relative suffered from affective and cognitive difficulties. However, the observed patterns have not always been in the predicted direction. For example, the Circumplex model, which is the overarching framework for interpreting scores on the FACES (or FACES-II), suggests that a curve-linear relationship applies. Hence, the two extremes of the cohesion scale, namely: 'disengaged' and 'enmeshed' should be equally pathological but contrary to this, Zarski, DePompei, and Zook (1988) found that subjects categorized as 'disengaged' on the FACES-II measure generally had more pathological scores on the FAD than those classified as 'enmeshed'. Unfortunately, this type of finding has cast a shadow over many of the studies conducted using measures derived from non-brain-injured populations; namely, that some of the assumptions made about family functioning are culturally biased and that families affected by brain injury represent a unique culture, which questions the validity of this research. Additionally, incorporating and hypothesizing about the interactions between two measures, both with questionable validity when applied to the brain injury field, has implications for the overall level of reliability and validity. Nevertheless, this is an interesting development in terms of future directions for research and moves beyond merely documenting the levels of 'case-ness', of unhealthy family functioning.[2]

*(b) The transferability of measures based
on non-brain-injured populations*

While some of the limitations of family research in the field are due to poor design (e.g., no use of family measures), there is a case for

---

[2] The author knows of a number of other unpublished dissertations that have also used this methodology.

arguing that some measures, such as the FAD, are inappropriate. As demonstrated thus far, the use of such measures is common, for example to show that relatives of people with brain injury are in some way different from some other distinct group; but is this a valid approach? In addition, although revised, many of the models and measures were originally devised in the 1960s and 1970s.

The advantage of using measures based on other populations is that a quick and easy comparison can be made between groups to see if relatives of people with brain injuries are different from another population. For example, the FAD and FAM enable researchers to ascertain how family members solve problems, communicate with each other, and how they organize themselves in terms of roles, and a comparison can be made with a general or normative population. Few would argue that these are not pertinent domains to every family situation, and so such an analysis undoubtedly tells us something of relevance about the impact of brain injury on the family. Yet, one of the disadvantages of using global measures relates to the assumptions that are made; namely, they assume too much in terms of the questions that are asked, the models they are based on, and the norms. Additionally, universal skills are held to be equally valid across cultural and illness contexts. The tendency for questionnaires to be administered by sending them by postal method, in the absence of any face-to-face contact is further problematic since in most cases it is advised that measures are used in conjunction with a clinical interview (ideally a family interview), or accompanied by observations. Consistent standards of reporting all subscale scores would also help improve matters.

In terms of whether a questionnaire is asking pertinent questions, there is sometimes a mismatch in terms of the specificity of questions asked, or gaps in the areas that are covered by domains. To illustrate, the questions asked may not be sufficiently specific in terms of their sensitivity to the actual consequences of brain injury within a particular family context (for example, the gender implications of role changes). Omissions in the content of measures are more likely to occur when measures are developed from traditional models based on 'normal' or psychiatric populations. The fact that in the studies reported, family measures were not always sensitive to the predicament of families following brain injury is evidence that the theories and models on which measures were based may not be appropriate. Psychiatric populations vary greatly with respect to people with brain injuries and the item pool for one group cannot be expected to represent the other without going through a further process of item expansion and refinement. If this is not undertaken then too much is assumed from an outsider perspective, without due consultation with the relatives of people with brain injuries themselves. The item pool from which items for a final questionnaire are selected needs to be representative and include all the issues of concern to families of neuro-rehabilitation patients. With regard to possible gaps in domains, positive dimensions of caregiving are commonly omitted (Adams, 1996; McGrath & Linley, 2006).

Further, item content relates to the level of assessment that is conducted and within some measures there is a blurring of the distinction between assessing individual skills (or capacities) versus family functioning/adaptation[3] although it is acknowledged that some measures include a 'systems' level version (FAM and FACES). In particular, given the common procedure adopted by researchers of asking individuals to complete measures in isolation from other family members, it is interesting to speculate on differences that might be observed if interviews were instead conducted with the family as a group. A truly systemic approach to data collection would most probably require individual members to negotiate and fill in one questionnaire only.

(c) Item content of questionnaires used in family research

In their critical review of psychological and marital adjustment in couples following traumatic brain injury, Blais and Boisvert (2005) highlight three factors that may account for tendencies in the outcomes literature, namely: severity of injury, stage post-injury, and differential impact on spouses versus parents. Blais and Boisvert conclude by saying that the evidence is equivocal, partly because of a lack of consistency in the definition of variables (in relation to the determinants of severity of injury, and in terms such as 'stress', 'burden', 'distress') and consequently also in the measures used. This is a criticism also levelled by Perlesz, Kinsella, and Crowe (1999) in

---

[3] An example of this type of distinction is provided by the Family Strain Questionnaire (FSQ), a generic carer measure that has been usefully applied to relatives of a number of chronic disease populations such as persons with cancer, kidney, respiratory problems, as well as families of people in a vegetative state (Chiambretto, Rossi, Ferrario, & Zotti, 2001). It is described as a family measure, yet primarily assesses individual coping.

their review paper. In light of this critique, it is pertinent to review how family measures are developed.

In terms of the family functioning measures mentioned above, the first issue to be mentioned is problems associated with the labelling of domains. Indeed, there is considerable similarity in the item content for measures but often different labels are used for the scales and the subscales to which they belong. For example, the FAD and FAM originate from the same model and bear a striking resemblance in terms of the domains they cover but the labels sometimes differ as can be seen in items such as, 'We try to think of different ways to solve problems' (taken from 'Problem-solving' on the FAD) versus 'When problems come up, we try different ways of solving them' (taken from 'Task accomplishment' on the FAM). Conversely, item similarity with scale convergence can be seen in the following items, both taken from the 'Communication' domains of the FAD and the FAM: 'You can't tell how a person is feeling from what they are saying' (FAD) versus 'When someone in our family is upset, we don't know if they are angry, sad, scared or what' (FAM).[4]

---

[4] To address the issue of the degree to which item-scale convergence and divergence adds to confusion in the literature one of the authors organized an experimental 'item sort' task to be conducted by three colleagues (Professor of Neuropsychology, Head of Research, and a Research Psychologist). Over a period of an hour, these colleagues randomly selected 78 questionnaire items from a pooled collection of all 255 items taken from the FAD, FACES, FES, and FAM measures (approximately one-third of all items). The only instruction given was to, as a group, take items one at a time and to sort them according to whether they were similar or different to other items and to assign similar items to the same category. Items within each category were regularly reviewed for consistency and each item could be placed into only one category, also the panel gave each category a name that reflected the full range of items in each pile. The category names chosen by the panel showed some, but not complete similarity to the domain names selected by the original authors of the measures. The category names that were chosen by the panel were as follows: 'Emotional Sharing' (18 items), 'Practical Co-operation' (14 items), 'Too Connected' (7 items), 'Negative Independence' (13 items), 'Chaos' (12 items), 'Dissatisfaction' (2 items), 'Autocratic/authoritarian' (10 items), and 'Not Sure' (2 items).

The different emphasis given to the category names chosen by the panel perhaps reflects a changing context; the fact considerable time had passed since the original measures were first devised and domain names may no longer carry the same meaning. In addition, the aforementioned issues to do with directionality and curve-linear interpretations were commented on by the panel, also cultural factors. The panel commented that cultural factors were most blatant for item 78 on the FES: "The Bible is a very important book in our home." The exercise highlights that there is considerable item-scale convergence and divergence in family measures currently used in family neuro-rehabilitation research.

Table 1. Neuro-rehabilitation studies using family functioning measures.

Measure (& latest version)	Domains	Relevant studies
Family Assessment Device (FAD—60 items)[5]	Problem-Solving (PS) Communication (C)	Anderson, Parmenter, & Mok (2002; Anderson, Simpson, Mok, & Parmenter 2006)
	Roles (R)	Brown et al. (1999)
	Affective Responsiveness	Charles, Butera-Prinzi, & Perlesz (2007)
	(AR)	Ergh, Rapport, Coleman, and Hanks (2002)
	Affective Involvement (AI)	Groom, Shaw, O'Connor, Howard, & Pickens (1998)
	Behaviour Control (BC)	Hall et al. (1994)
	General Functioning (GF)	Hanks, Rapport, and Vangel (2007)
		Kosciulek (1994; 1996; 1997); Kosciulek & Lustig (1999)
		Kreutzer, Gervasio, & Camplair, (1994a; 1994b)
		Nabors, Seacat, & Rosenthal (2002)
		Ponsford, Olver, Ponsford, & Nelms (2003)

(continued)

Table 1. Continued

Measure (& latest version)	Domains	Relevant studies
		Sander et al. (2002; 2003)
		Testa, Malec, Moessner, & Brown (2006)
		Tyerman & Booth (2001)
		Winstanley, Simpson, Tate, & Myles (2006)
		Zarski, DePompei, & Zook (1988)
Family Assessment Measure	Task Accomplishment	Gan & Schuller (2002)
(FAM-III)	Role Performance	Gan, Campbell, Gemeinhardt, and
	Communication	McFadden (2006)
	Affective Expression	
	Involvement	
	Control	
	Values & Norms	

Family Adaptability and Cohesion Evaluation Scales (FACES-IV)[6]	Curtiss et al. (2000)
Adaptability	Koscuilek (1996; 1997);
Cohesion	Koscuilek & Lustig (1999)
Family Communication	Zarski, DePompei, & Zook (1988)
Family Satisfaction	
Family Environment Scale	Blankfeld & Holahan (FES)[8] (1999)
The Relationship[7]	Douglas & Spellacy (1996)
Personal Growth[9]	Perlesz & O'Loughlan (1998)
System Maintenance[10]	
The Dyadic Adjustment Scale (Spanier, 1976)	Charles, Butera-Prinzi, Perlesz (2007)
Dyadic Consensus	Moore et al. (2003)
Dyadic Satisfaction	Peters et al., 1992
Affectional Expression	
Dyadic Cohesion	

[5] Further studies conducted with children include Barney & Max (2005); Bragg et al (1992).
[6] Further studies conducted with children include Caminiti, Amore, Sapienza, Premoli, Pietrapiana, Zaina, and Rago (2001); Youngblut and Brooten (2008).
[7] The Relationship domain includes cohesion, expressiveness, and conflict.
[8] Further studies conducted with children include Benn and McColl (2004); and those by Rivera and colleagues (e.g: Rivera, Jaff, Polissar, Fay, Liao, & Martin, 1996).
[9] The Personal Growth domain includes independence, achievement orientation, intellectual cultural orientation, active recreational orientation, and moral religious emphasis.
[10] The System Maintenance domain includes organization and control.

Other questionnaires used in family research (e.g., the Caregiver Strain Index, the Burden Interview, Family Strain Questionnaire) have taken a predominantly negative and pathologizing conceptual frame to the issues and consequently may miss important elements of the phenomenological subjective experience. They also at least implicitly operate on the assumption that there is one 'main caregiver' and that other family relatives will remain unaffected.

(d) Qualitative research approaches

Recent interest in using qualitative methods in the brain injury field has provided new insights on family functioning, family dynamics, or experiences within rehabilitation services. This movement has also paralleled frustrations with questionnaire-based methods, as detailed above. We will now illustrate the range of approaches used and the types of findings produced. Of those studies that has attempted to assess family functioning from a qualitative perspective a good example is a study by Waldrop, Milch, and Skretny (2005) who conducted in-depth interviews with hospice patients with 'life-limiting illnesses' that included neurological conditions and their family members and discovered six modes of family functioning:

1. reactive (for example, heightened sensitivity),
2. advocacy (voicing patients' needs),
3. fused (everything is shared),
4. dissonant (incongruence between patient/family members),
5. resigned (decline and death are anticipated), and
6. closed (matter of fact).

Using general measures of family functioning would not have allowed for such a detailed analysis of patterning of grief in families. Also when interpreting the results researchers need to ensure that relatives are given opportunity to speak in the absence of the injured relative and/or staff members, otherwise data may not be representative of their views.

Some studies have focused specifically on children of parents with traumatic brain injury, for example, Butera-Prinzi and Perlesz (2004) conducted an interesting interview study concluding that children were at risk of emotional and behavioural difficulties. These children displayed a complexity of feelings associated with trauma and multiple losses, including profound grief, social isolation, fear of family disintegration, and violence. With this, however, they were also likely to show resilience and greater independence.

Other studies have focused on particular issues that arise in the rehabilitation setting. For example, one of the authors [GY] used a discourse analysis approach to show that insight into the effects of disability is often contested within the family, and this can be particularly distressing for relatives who observe a lack of awareness in their injured relatives (Yeates, Henwood, Gracey, & Evans, 2007). A further study also conducted by the authors [SP] used Interpretative Phenomenological Analysis or IPA (Smith, Flowers, & Larkin, 2009) to examine successful factors in building the family-therapist alliance (see Chapter 7).

As researchers have become more interested in using qualitative approaches this has brought a refreshing perspective to the field and also stimulated new ideas. Furthermore, studies investigating sensitive issues such as specific aspects of relatives' experience or transition to a hospice setting are thought to require innovative qualitative research methods. Among the qualitative methods that have been used are content/thematic analysis, focus groups, and discourse analysis. The approach of using mixed methods or triangulated approaches may offer one solution to overcome remaining questions about the validity of standardized measures derived from non-brain-injured populations. Some researchers have used mixed methods such as Man (2002) who included a content analysis of long interviews with four selected families and showed that it was not every family that coped well. Possible factors leading to better adjustment, such as clear personal expectations, a desire to master the situation, strong motivation, flexibility to adjust life goals, and awareness of one's own powerless state are proposed. Results indicate that family coping varies with individual families and should be explored further for the development of intervention guidelines.

A dilemma for context-focused, qualitative research is the assumptions of rationality and agency in the survivor and in their co-constructive meaning-making practices with relatives. Patterson and Scott-Finlay (2002) have noted the high likelihood for tangential, contradictory, and inconsistent answers in the qualitative transcripts of this population. This may be a realist dilemma of validity for some, or an invitation for a deeper level of analysis for others. A parallel development is the field of psychosocial studies, where discursive, narrative, and social constructionist ideas are integrated with psychoanalytical accounts to produce readings of contradictory, fragmented social constructions and motivated uptakes of cultural discourses to achieve defensive purposes (e.g., Frosh, Phoenix, & Patman, 2004; Hollway, 1989; Hollway & Jefferson, 2000). This particular qualitative analytical approach has been incorporated by some ABI investigators to produce a rich reading of their data and identify specific conditions associated with contradictions within this (Yeates, Henwood, Gracey, & Evans, 2006; Yeates & Whitehouse-Hart, 2009).

In a similar vein, the general issue of cognitive impairments such as memory difficulties has prompted some researchers (Patterson & Scott-Finlay, 2002; Yeates, Henwood, Gracey, & Evans, 2007) to advocate the use of quite radical qualitative research practices, such as active interviewing (Holstein & Gubrium, 1998), moving away from an assumption of a realist, uncontaminated account of experience independent from researcher. In summary, the use of qualitative research in ABI generally, and in family research in particular, is progressing from a few early thematic studies, some of which have been used by generic qualitative research commentators as examples of bad practice, to be a vibrant, diverse and self-reflexive project.

(f) Case study methodology

Case study approaches have existed since the outset of interest into family adaptation and coping after brain injury. In one of the earliest papers, Romano (1974) described a series of family adaptations to severe brain injury, following coma and described denial as a typical mode of coping, specifically 'common fantasies, verbal refusals, and inappropriate responses'. In this sense, the reactions observed in families at least start out looking like a grief but this cannot take the traditional path. Lezak (1978) also described common patterns of partner response in her clinic, likening it to parenting but that the person you are trying to help cannot remember from moment to moment. Thomsen (1984) conducted longitudinal studies of 40 patients with severe blunt head trauma and their relatives and found that problems related to dependence, personality, and emotional changes were the most difficult for relatives to cope with. Additionally, the parent-child relationships for injured parents typically 'developed badly'.

Watzlawick and Coyne (1980) was one of the first authors to document a systemic approach to neuro-rehabilitation, a paradoxical couple intervention with successful outcome in response to a husband's depression secondary to two strokes. Since then, more case studies have emerged in the literature describing family therapy approaches (Bowen, 2007; Fujii, Schaefer Hanes, & Kokuni, 1996; Johnson, Crane & Tatekawa, 2004; Larøi, 2000; 2003; Maitz & Sachs, 1995), an approach that often requires some restructuring of relationships. In one specific example given by Larøi (2000; 2003) a 22-year-old son was experiencing difficulties relating to and communicating with his parents. These problems were formulated as due to both the son's impairments directly related to the brain injury (e.g., cognitive difficulties in expressing himself, behaviour control, attentional deficits) and secondary effects the injury had on family dynamics (e.g., parents' unwillingness to modify their level of communication with him). Further details of these cases are given in chapter 8.

Relational rehabilitation research

In this book we have outlined a number of principles about relational processes in neuro-psychological neuro-rehabilitation. What follows are our ideas about incorporating and extending these ideas in the field of research, but before we do this let us return briefly to the position statements in chapter 1, which were as follows:

- Injured brains are always in interaction with other brains;
- A shared experience of mind emerges from these interactions;
- The consequences of brain injury are often more apparent when people are with others, than when alone;
- The brain injury can therefore exist in the spaces between people, infiltrating and amplifying distance and disconnection;
- Brain injury and its consequences are socially constructed to a degree.

With these in mind, along with the call for a bi-directional perspective, of looking outwards and inwards in order to understand the effects of brain injury, we now argue that research needs to build on and strengthen understanding of:

- The impact of brain injury on all members of the social-family network;
- The social impact of brain injury (cognitive impairment) and socially mediated brain 'repair';
- Tactics and techniques for supporting and building an alliance with families in response to brain injury;
- Tactics and techniques for gaining a shared understanding of brain injury within the family;
- Communication processes, shared re-membering and the co-construction of coherent and therapeutic narratives;
- Identity mapping and reconstruction within the family;
- The characteristics and attributes of brain injury as described by survivors and their families from a narrative perspective;
- The exploration of cultural and economic diversity within brain injury family research.

These future avenues for research capture something of the nature of brain injury as described in this book. We are still learning about the 'truths' of brain injury, and continue to be humbled by courageous stories of survivors and families achieving recovery and showing cohesion against the odds. Research thus far conducted in the field has revealed very few substantive 'truths' and we have been frustrated in many ways in the pursuit of these, yet ironically this has opened up the necessary space relational approaches now occupy. Principles of relational approaches that highlight the role of family processes in biopsychosocial formulations, also the inconsistency of cognition across different social contexts may hold a key to resolving the lack of consensus of findings in the literature.

In order to examine the effects of brain injury on each and every family member it will be necessary to conduct interviews with each family member, but also to conduct family interviews. We should therefore also expect the contestation of accounts about brain injury and value these observations as giving information on the complexity of brain injury and its socially constructed consequences.

We should use the challenges due to flexibility, inconsistency, and diversity in cognitive abilities and accounting by survivors as an invitation to experiment with novel and diverse qualitative and quantitative epistemological practices, both in obtaining and analysing data. For this we may need to use more sophisticated quantitative analytical techniques such as structural equation modelling to provide evidence, as gross as it is, to support a systemic/relational perspective; yet temper such usage with a plea for a strong, self-reflective conceptual foundation in terms of construct operationalization, measure selection, and conception of constructs. Perhaps more importantly, we need clinicians with relational inclinations to conduct this research.

CHAPTER THIRTEEN

Conclusion

ntonio Damasio (1999) continued a long conceptual tradition within neurology when he described the brain
as "a system of systems" (p. 331). We have extended this
systemic view beyond the skull to situate neural systems within
inter-personal, social, community and cultural systems, alongside
systems and pattern transmissions of ideas and meaning. Our
conceptual heritage and resource in this regard has been related
to traditions of post-Milan systemic family therapy, second-order
cybernetics, communication theory, social constructionism, post-
structuralism, and narratology. Isolated individuals and their damaged brains disappear within this scheme, replaced by brain injury
as a pattern, dynamic, and relationship. Interestingly, in applying
systemic theory for this group of people we are continuing traditions within both brain injury and family therapy literatures. For
example, although hidden behind broader labels such as chronic or
physical illness, survivors of stroke can be found in the case examples of key family therapy publications such as the early work of
John Rolland (1990) and even a contemporary of Gregory Bateson,
Paul Walzlawick (Watzlawick & Coyne, 1980).

We have described the brain injury as existing in the spaces between people, the brain injury as a thief, an intruder, and disrupter. Couples, families, and communities are re-organized within this frame as connected in their distress, struggles, confusion, and triumphs, the latter where the sense of 'us' is reclaimed, if only momentarily from the brain injury as a determinant of family life.

It is to be expected that concluding a manuscript such as this one will be difficult, when a purposeful attempt has been made to broaden conceptions, to add complexity to understanding, to take a meta-position, but ultimately also, to leave some questions unanswered. Another aim has been to highlight subjugated stories within the literature, and then to synthesize these with more mainstream frameworks of knowledge.

However, the idea of a 'relational approach' is not something new. This we know because of the number of 'hits' one finds when searching the literature, but also because of the way people have been open to and offered new interpretations of the term when we have discussed our ideas, most recently at a British Psychological Society Division of Neuropsychology study day in London. We now revisit some of the themes contained in earlier chapters, in the spirit of re-membering, re-positioning, and re-constructing a synthesis of the ideas.

The family therapist John Burnham has articulated a framework for systemic conceptualizations that has three phases, namely: *approach, method,* and *technique.* We originally used this as a guiding principle to navigate the territory we wanted to cover (see also Bateson, 1972). While this was not the final organizing scheme of the book , this tripartite distinction reflects some of the essential elements within the preceding chapters.

A relational *approach* to rehabilitation, as outlined in chapter 1, is one that proceeds outwards, to context, to gain useful understandings of a material brain injury within the interior. It encompasses and utilizes aspects of many approaches, all of which have in common an emphasis on defining brain injury against a backdrop of differing perspectives within the social context. The organizing principles behind the approach have then been articulated in chapters 2 to 5, as applied to neuro-rehabilitation, neuropsychology, and couples therapy. Neuro-rehabilitation and neuropsychology are both distinct fields in their own right and traditionally focused on the interior of the individual's brain. We have made an attempt to present an outward-looking perspective that charts the backdrop against which individuals are situated, the social-family context, including culture and environment, which operates as a contextual force on each social interaction, each episode, and behaviour (Pearce, 2007). We draw a parallel here to the formation of a rock; a rock or a pebble has many layers within it, and distinct markings on the outer layers. Such features can be analysed and quantified and provide information about the particles and connecting fibres from which it is formed. Although we can obtain a great deal of information about the story of the rock's history by looking 'inwards' at its structure and composition, we might also look 'outwards' to the context from which the rock originated. Many of our questions about the history of the rock (or of a person?) can be answered by looking inwards at the fibres and formations, yet by accepting the invitations of our curiosity, we may look at the relational context (looking outwards) which gives meaning beyond what could be obtained from merely looking inwards. The environment helps shape the rock (large and small), and the rock in a small way defines the environment.

Couples therapy automatically takes a broader view, of a brain injury which occupies not just head space but also social space, for it can bring people together and act as a bond, but also distance people and pull them apart. When before there were defences caused from inescapable anxiety getting in the way of connection, now there is something foreign, alien, and unusual, and it attracts attention and will not go away; an intruder of sorts. But it is not just any intruder because it also acts against the traditional family script, which described a smooth transition from birth to later life and finally death at a time when every dream and goal should have been accomplished, our own and also some of our children's aspirations. Therefore, this intruder acts as a thief because it attempts to steal people's history and memories; their intimacy and connection. But injured brains are continually communicating and this is something it cannot steal, if one listens patiently one hears a story of occasional successes, of courage in spite of fear, and sometimes a longing to re-connect. Relational approaches allow the therapist to focus their skills by attending to points of connection and intimacy. This requires skill in attending to the unseen, sometimes reflecting back like a mirror, or focusing like a magnifying glass on the space between, or scattering light outwards like a prism to the sources of support that are hidden from view. A brain injury may also have a degree of power and appear cunning because it takes advantage of insecurity and vulnerability, their need for certainty and answers, or the need for someone to tell them what to do. And it disguises itself when least expected to divert attention and stop people who may be able to help from doing so, such as from rehabilitation professionals who talk of therapeutic relationships. However, as survivors become interested in the idea that a brain injury is always seeking to repair itself they too may see that it is always finding ways to surprise people by re-organising relationships. We live in a myriad of connections, all around a web of relationships (partners, children, brothers, sisters, parents, friends, neighbours, colleagues ...), each relationship a story in itself.

Clinical implications

(a) Relational neuro-rehabilitation
The very latest scientific understanding suggests that for a relatively accurate prognosis following ABI composite and repeated assessment methods are required in most cases, but that no two injuries are the same, and that there are many mediators and moderators impacting on outcome for the survivor (such as biological, psychological, family, social, and environmental factors). Hence, substantial weight is given to the survivors' subjective experience and social and family network, and support services need to be prepared to meet this need. Yet as rehabilitation specialists we rarely have first-hand experience of brain injury, and so this presents a challenge of empathy, related to the subjective-objective divide and ultimately, of therapeutic skill. For family members, there too is a need to connect to the injured family member who has sustained an unusual and atypical life experience and there is little in the way of preparation for this process.

Approaches to neuro-rehabilitation struggle to hold and attend to wider social and family dynamics because of the 'pull' towards understanding the interior functioning of the brain. Yet we know that social support is crucial to achieving the best outcomes in rehabilitation (Ergh, Rapport, Coleman, & Hanks, 2002; Sander et al., 2002). With this tension in mind, it then becomes of paramount importance to adopt a stance that aligns itself with current trends to:

- increase understanding of the overlap between the related medical specialties of neurology, rehabilitation, and palliative care;
- to extend the evidence base on which clinical decisions are made to include studies using qualitative methods and/or that include user representatives;
- to broaden the skill mix within rehabilitation teams
- to broaden the support offered by teams to include family members.

(b) Relational neuropsychology

Traditional neuro-psychological approaches are faced with the temptation to continually look inwards but can be frustrated by spurious findings in the search for biological translations of cognitive processes. In the case of higher-level abilities such as meta-cognition there is a risk of an infinite regress, adding more and more frontal cortex for every new recursive meta-stance on one's thinking, until we eventually hit the material barrier of the skull (Murray & Yeates, in preparation)! Luria's focus on language and social context may provide one way out of the epistemological cul-de-sac, and indeed there has been a recent resurgence of interest in the application of his ideas.

A consideration of difficulties in the domains of language, memory, visuo-spatial perception and praxis, attention, and executive functioning following ABI has led some researchers to investigate conversational and interactional conditions that produce relational successes and failures. Perhaps this is most obvious in the case of attention when disengaging attention and switching can be socially disastrous and lead to major social transgressions (e.g., intruding on others' personal space, cutting over or ignoring others in conversation, or failing to attend to social feedback that their behaviour is problematic). The narrative technique of externalization offers one creative method for extending awareness in survivors, by conversationally approaching the topic of injury from a third-person perspective, an approach that is empirically supported.

(c) Relational couples therapy for ABI
The unit of analysis and work here has to be the couple, the relationship. Not one damaged brain and its effect on a responding partner. We must dissolve these conceptual boundaries to consider the brain-damaged couple, their inter-subjective space infiltrated and progressively undermined by a lesion that exists within their socially situated brain-brain system. We need to take seriously that a partner can experience the subjective consequence of say, an anterior cingulated lesion in the other, because that subjectivity is not parcelled within one head, but is a binding relationship between two or more people. The disturbing extent of the quality of this intrusion needs to be attended to and taken seriously by the clinical and research communities that may have previously even been guilty of shying away from something so awful. Attachment theory, affective neuroscience, psychosexual therapy, and the unique language of psychoanalysis can all contribute here, alongside the dynamic and responsive interviewing toolkit of the systemic therapist. However, the first step is to note when we divide couples ourselves as services, with our historical focus on the survivor in social isolation, splintering the couple's conversation and connection from the initial assessment onwards.

(d) Relational systemic therapy for acquired brain injury
The lenses provided by systemic therapy and the epistemological traditions it draws upon, communication, conversation, narrative, system, observing system, systems and community of ideas and meaning, offer new ways of envisioning and working with brain injury. Certain neuro-psychological trends permit us to working within these framings in considering failures of communicating, remembering, attending, acting and interacting, intending and reflecting, and connecting between people as an end result (but not a linear result) of a biological change in a brain within the system somewhere. A compensatory neuro-rehabilitative approach that works on these levels can increase the potency of systemic questioning and the relationship of therapists and families to promote curiosity, difference, and change.

(e) Relational considerations of ABI within a wider multi-verse of perspectives
We think this is the bonus of this approach, by playing with professional, reductionist certainties, and canvassing opinions from the

web of perspectives and communications in which an ABI is situated, new and richer ideas always emerge. Action, connection an opportunity become possible that hitherto had remained invisible within the boundaries of an acute medical perspective. Each new construction of brain injury, be it lay or professional, offers a new point of accessibility and inclusion for more and more survivors and families stumbling in the dark, grasping for meaning.

Service implications

A relational, community model of brain injury service provision requires different resources. The core team of occupational therapists, physiotherapists, psychologists, rehabilitation consultants, social workers, speech and language therapists remain as essential, although their activities may change, and their professional contacts and networks may widen outwards to include regular liaison with schools, social services, community leaders, employers, solicitors, governmental agencies, and others. It may be that the use of relationship, communication, and self-reflexivity as a product of new combinations of relationships and conversations may inspire new patterns of team working. Co-therapy may become the norm for sessions, with interdisciplinary collaborations formed for the purpose of a communication or relationship goal (e.g., a psychologist and occupational therapist developing new leisure opportunities to increase the connection of a survivor and partner, or working with a speech and language therapist to provide new opportunities within the minutiae of communication for connection and thinking). Within team meetings, it may become regular practice for the team to split into two halves and one half listen to the other's discussion of a case, then offer their reflections upon hearing this from a second-order cybernetics perspective. How has the service become situated and positioned in their thinking about the client? What discourses are at play here and what do they offer and deny? The notion of expertise and certainty can be played with for therapeutic gain (e.g., multi-verse communications in reflecting teams) but it also requires serious thought and respectful consideration. Professional certainty may be the most essential and useful thing in an acute service and the most disabling thing in a community service response several years post-injury.

Johnson and McCown (1997) conclude their work with the suggestion of a new profession, an amalgam of neuropsychology and family therapy. We differ in our recommendations. As we are three UK-trained clinical psychologists, we have valued our parallel emersion in systemic and neuropsychology practice, which we have each nurtured post-qualification. Clinical psychology is a bridging discipline that fosters valuable opportunities for connective thinking, such as in chapter 3. We are aware of colleagues who have trained in family therapy subsequent to a core neuro-rehabilitation professional training (medicine, psychology, occupational therapy), and provide a rich contribution to their respective services. The regular appointment of family therapists to brain injury services would be a welcome new chapter, and there are inspiring exceptional examples of this already in Australia, UK, and USA. But above all, it is the concerns and practices of the service team, an emergent property of each profession's input and the wider professional discourses and conceptual lenses in which the team is situated, which will potently develop relational rehabilitation as a common practice.

Research implications

The above picture is symbiotically related to the emergence of a professional literature that takes seriously circular causal relationships, the over-determining influence of wider and wider levels of social context, and the reflexivity of the researcher. Seriously investigating circularity and non-linear causal relationships requires a broader palette of methodologies. The acceptance of plurality and mixed methodology in brain injury research is essential, as is the inclusion of all key system members as participants. With interest, we await multiple (or even any) publications on groups such as survivors as mothers, male partner experiences, grandparents of survivors, lesbian, gay, bisexual and transgendered relationships post-injury, work colleagues, community relations, and friends.

REFERENCES

Adams, N. (1996). Positive outcomes in families following traumatic brain injury (TBI). *Australia and New Zealand Journal of Family Therapy*, 17: 75–84.

Adolphs, R., Tranel, D., Damasio, H., & Damasio, A.R. (1994). Impaired recognition of emotion in facial expressions following bilateral damage to the human amygdala. *Nature, 372*: 669–672.

Adolphs, R., Tranel, D., & Damasio, A. (2003). Dissociable neural systems for recognizing emotions. *Brain & Cognition, 52*: 61–69.

Albert, S.M., Im, A., Brenner, L., Smith, M., & Waxman, R. (2002). Effect of a social work liaison program on family caregivers to people with brain injury. *Journal of Head Trauma Rehabilitation, 17*: 175–189.

Alderman, N. (2003). Contemporary approaches to the management of irritability and aggression following traumatic brain injury. *Neuropsychological Rehabilitation, 13*: 211–246.

Alderman, N., & Burgess, P. (1994). A comparison of treatment methods for behaviour disorder following herpes simplex encephalitis. *Neuropsychological Rehabilitation, 4*: 31–48.

Alderman, N., Fry, R.K., & Youngson, H.A. (1995). Improvement of self-monitoring skills, reduction of behaviour disturbance and the dysexecutive syndrome: Comparison of response cost and a new programme of self-monitoring training. *Neuropsychological Rehabilitation, 5*: 193–221.

311

Alderman, N., & Ward, A. (1991). Behavioural treatment of the dysexecutive syndrome: Reduction of repetitive speech using response cost and cognitive overlearning. *Neuropsychological Rehabilitation, 1*: 65–80.

Allen, K., Linn, R., Gutierrez, H., & Willer, B. (1994). Family burden following traumatic brain injury. *Rehabilitation Psychology, 39*: 29–48.

Anataki, C., & Lewis, A. (1986). *Metacognition in Social Knowledge and Communication.* London: Sage.

Anderson, T. (1987). The reflecting team: Dialogue and meta-dialogue in clinical work. *Family Process, 26(4)*: 415–428.

Anderson, H., Goolishian, H., & Winderman, L. (1986). Problem determined systems: Towards transformation in family therapy. *Journal of Strategic and Systemic Therapies, 3(4)*: 1–14.

Anderson, M.I., Parmenter, T.R., & Mok, M. (2002). The relationship between neurobehavioural problems of severe traumatic brain injury (TBI), family functioning and the psychological well-being of the spouse/caregiver: path model analysis. *Brain Injury, 16*: 743–757.

Anderson, A.K., & Phelps, E.A. (2000). Expression without recognition: Contributions of the human amygdala to emotional communication. *Psychological Science, 11*: 106–111.

Anderson, M., Simpson, G.K., Mok, M., & Parmenter, T.R. (2006). A contemporary model of stress for understanding family functioning and the psychological distress in relatives of people with severe traumatic brain injury (TBI). In D. Johns (Ed.), *Stress and Its Impact on Society* (pp. 23–56). New York: Nova.

Andrews, J., & Andrews, M. (1993). A family based systemic model for speech-language services. *Seminars in Speech-Language, 7*: 159–165.

Armstrong, D. (1987). Theoretical tensions in biopsychosocial medicine. *Social Science and Medicine, 25*: 1213–1218.

Asen, E., & Schuff, H. (2006). Psychosis and multiple family group therapy. *Journal of Family Therapy, 28*: 58–72.

Aston, M. (2009). *The Asperger Couple's Workbook: Practical Advice for Couples and Counsellors.* London: Jessica Kingsley.

Atkinson, A.P., Heberlein, A.S., & Adolphs, R. (2007). Spared ability to recognise fear from static and moving wholebody cues following bilateral amygala damage. *Neuropsychologia, 45(12)*: 2772–2782.

Avero, P., Corace, K.M., Endler, N.S., & Calvo, M.G. (2003). Coping styles and threat processing. *Personality and Individual Differences, 4(35)*: 843–861.

Babinski, J. (1914). Contribution à l'étude des troubles mantaux dans l'hemiplégie organique cérébale (anosognosie). *Revue Neuroloogique, 27*: 845–848.

Baird, A., Dewar, B.-K., Critchley, H., Dolan, R., Shallice, T., & Cipolotti, L. (2006). Social and emotional functions in three patients with medial frontal lobe damage including the anterior cingulated cortex. *Cognitive Neuropsychiatry, 11*: 369–388.

Bakhtin, M.M., & Holquist, M. (1982). *The Dialogical Imagination: Four Essays*. Austin: University of Texas Press.

Baldwin, C., & Capstick, A. (2007). *Tom Kitwood on Dementia: A Reader and Critical Commentary*. Maidenhead, Berkshire, UK: Open University Press/McGraw-Hill Education.

Balestreri, M., Czosnyka, M., Chatfield, D.A., Steiner, L.A., Schmidt, E.A., Smielewski, P., Matta, B., & Pickard, J.D. (2004). Predictive value of Glasgow coma score after brain trauma: Change in trend over the past ten years. *Journal of Neurology, Neurosurgery & Psychiatry, 75*: 161–162.

Baron-Cohen, S. (1997). *Mindblindness: An Essay on Autism*. Cambridge, MA: MIT Press/Bradford Books.

Bartels, A., & Zeki, S. (2000). The neural basis of romantic love. *Neuro Report, 11*: 3829–3834.

Bartels, A., & Zeki, S. (2004). The neural correlates of maternal and romantic love. *NeuroImage, 21*: 1155–1166.

Bateson, G. (1972). *Steps to an Ecology of Mind*. London: Paladin.

Bateson, G., Jackson, D.D., Haley, J., & Weakland, J. (1956). Toward a theory of schizophrenia. *Behavioral Science, 1*: 251–264.

Bechara, A., Damasio, A.R., Damasio, H., & Anderson, S.W. (1994). Insensitivity to future consequences following damage to human prefrontal cortex. *Cognition, 50*: 7–15.

Benn, K.M., & McColl, M.A. (2004). Parental coping following childhood acquired brain injury. *Brain Injury, 18*: 239–255.

Bennett-Levy, J., Westbrook, G., Fennell, M., Cooper, M., Rouf, K., & Hackman, A. (2004). Behavioural experiments: Historical and conceptual underpinnings. In J. Bennett-Levy, G. Butler, M. Fennell, A. Hackman, M. Mueller, & D. Westbrook (Eds.), *Oxford Guide to Behavioural Experiments in Cognitive Therapy* (pp. 1–20). New York: Oxford University Press.

Ben-Yishay, Y. (1996). Reflections on the evolution of the therapeutic milieu concept. Historical aspects of neuropsychological rehabilitation. *Neuropsychological Rehabilitation, special issue, 6*: 327–343.

Ben-Yishay, Y. (2000). Postacute neuropsychological rehabilitation: A holistic perspective. In A.L. Christensen & B.P. Uzzell (Eds.), *Critical Issues in Neuropsychology, International Handbook of Neuropsychological Rehabilitation* (pp.127–136). The Netherlands: Kluwer Academic.

Ben-Yishay, Y., Silver, S.M., Piasetsky, E., & Rattock, J. (1987). Relationship between employability and vocational outcome after intensive holistic cognitive rehabilitation. *Journal of Head Trauma Rehabilitation,* 2: 35–48.

Bergquist, T., Gehl, C., Mandrekar, J.N., Lepore, S., Hanna, S., Osten, A., & Beaulieu, W. (2009). The effect of internet-based cognitive rehabilitation in persons with memory impairments after severe traumatic brain injury. *Brain Injury, 23(10):* 790–799.

Berrios, G.E., & Markova, I.S. (1998). Insight in the psychoses: A conceptual history. In X. Amadour & A. David (Eds.), *Insight and Psychosis.* New York: Oxford University Press.

Bieman-Copeland, S., & Bywan, J. (2000). Achieving rehabilitative gains in anosognosia after TBI. *Brain and Cognition, 44:* 1–5.

Bigler, E.D. (2001). The lesion(s) in traumatic brain injury: Implications for clinical neuropsychology. *Archives of Clinical Neuropsychology, 16:* 95–131.

Bion, W.R. (1959). Attacks on linking. In W.R. Bion (Ed.), *Second Thoughts* (pp. 93–99). London: Heineman.

Bion, W.R. (1961). *Experiences in Groups.* London: Tavistock.

Bion, W.R. (1962). *Learning from Experience.* London: Heinemann.

Bion, W.R. (1990). *Brazilian Lectures.* London: Karnac.

Bird, C., Castelli, F., Malik, O., Frith, U., & Husain, M. (2004). The impact of extensive medial frontal damage on 'Theory of Mind' and cognition. *Brain, 127:* 914–928.

Blackerby, W.F. (1990). A treatment model for sexuality disturbance following brain injury. *Journal of Head Trauma Rehabilitation, 5:* 73–82.

Blair, R., & Cipolotti, L. (2000). Impaired social response reversal: A case of acquired sociopathy. *Brain, 123:* 1122–1141.

Blais, M.C., & Boisvert, J.-M. (2005). Psychological and marital adjustment in couples following traumatic brain injury (TBI): A critical review. *Brain Injury, 19:* 1223–1235.

Blankfeld, D.F., & Holahan, C.J. (1999). Social support, coping, and psychological adjustment among caregivers of head-injured patients. *Psychology & Health, 14:* 609–624.

Blosser, J., & De Pompei, R. (1995). Fostering effective family involvement through mentoring. *Journal of Head Trauma Rehabilitation, 10:* 46–56.

Blow, A.J., Sprenkle, D.H., & Davis, S.D. (2007). Is who delivers the treatment more important than the treatment itself: The role of the therapist in common factors. *Journal of Marital and Family Therapy, 33:* 298–317.

Boake, C. (1991). Social skills training following head injury. In J.S. Kreutzer & P.H. Wehman (Eds.), *Cognitive Rehabilitation for Persons with Traumatic Brain Injury: A Functional Approach.* Baltimore, MD: Paul H. Brookes.

Bond, M.R., Brooks, D.N., & McKinlay, W.W. (1979). Burdens imposed on the relatives of those with severe brain damage due to injury. *Acta Neurochirurgica, 28*: 124–125.

Bond, J., Corner, L., Lilley, A., & Ellwood, C. (2002). Medicalisation of insight and caregivers' responses to risk in dementia. *Dementia, 1(3)*: 313–328.

Bornhofen, C., & McDonald, S. (2008a). Comparing strategies for treating emotion perception deficits in traumatic brain injury. *Journal of Head Trauma Rehabilitation, 23*: 103–115.

Bornhofen, C., & McDonald, S. (2008b). Emotion perception deficits following traumatic brain injury: A review of the evidence and rationale for intervention. *Journal of the International Neuropsychological Society, 14*: 511–525.

Boschen, K., Gargaro, J., Gan, C., & Gerber, G.B.C. (2007). Family interventions after acquired brain injury and other chronic conditions: A critical appraisal of the quality of the evidence. *NeuroRehabilitation, 22*: 19–41.

Boscolo, L., & Bertrando, P. (1996). *Systemic Therapy with Individuals.* London: Karnac.

Boscolo, L., Cecchin, G., Hoffman, L., & Papp, P. (1987). *Milan Systemic Family Therapy: Conversations in Theory and Practice.* New York: Basic Books.

Bowen, C. (2007). Family therapy and neuro rehabilitation: Forging a link. *International Journal of Therapy and Rehabilitation, 14*: 344–349.

Bowen, C., Hall, T., Newby, G., Walsh, B., Weatherhead, S., & Yeates, G. (2009). The impact of brain injury on relationships across the lifespan and across school, family and work contexts. *Human Systems: The Journal of Consultation and Training, 20*: 65–80.

Bowen, C., & MacLehose, A. (2010) Multiple sclerosis: Long-term care and the 'family care pathway'. *Social Care and Neurodisability, 1(1)*: 31–38.

Bowen, C., MacLehose, A., & Beaumont, J.G. (2010). Advanced multiple sclerosis and the Psychosocial Impact on Families. *Psychology & Health, In Press.*

Bowen, C., Madill, A., & Stratton, P.M. (2002). Parental accounts of blaming within the family: A dialectical model for understanding blame in systemic therapy. *Journal of Marital and Family Therapy, 28(2)*: 129–144.

Bowlby, J. (1969). *Attachment and Loss Volume 1: Attachment.* London: Pimlico.

Braga, L., Da Paz Jnr, A., & Ylvisaker, M. (2005). Direct clinician-delivered versus indirect family-supported rehabilitation of children with traumatic brain injury: A randomized controlled trial. *Brain Injury, 19*: 819–831.

Breunlin, D.C. (1999). Towards a theory of constraints. *Journal of Marital & Family Therapy, 25*: 365–382.

Briggs, M. (1997). *Building Early Intervention Teams: Working Together for Children and Families.* Aspen.

British Broadcasting Corporation (BBC). (25 February, 2007). Recovery. *BBC One Drama starring David Tennant and Sarah Parish.*

British Society of Rehabilitation Medicine. (1998). *Rehabilitation after Traumatic Brain Injury. A Working Party Report of the British Society of Rehabilitation Medicine.* London.

Brooks, N., Campsie, L., Symington, C., & Beattie, A. (1986). The five year outcome of severe blunt head injury: A relative's view. *Journal of Neurology, Neurosurgery & Psychiatry, 49*: 764–770.

Brooks, D.N., Campsie, L., Symington, C., Beattie, A., & McKinlay, W.W. (1987). The effects of severe head injury on patient and relative within seven years of injury. *Journal of Head Trauma Rehabilitation, 2*: 1–13.

Brooks, D.N., & McKinlay, W.W. (1983). Personality and behavioural change after severe blunt head injury: A relative's view. *Journal of Neurology, Neurosurgery & Psychiatry, 46*: 336–344.

Brothers, L. (1997). *Friday's Footprint: How Society Shapes the Human Mind.* Oxford: Oxford University Press.

Brown, G.W., & Harris, T.O. (1978). *The Social Origins of Depression.* London: Tavistock Publications.

Brown, R., Pain, K., Berwald, C., Hirschi, P., Delehanty, R., & Miller, H. (1999). Distance education and caregiver support groups: Comparison of traditional and telephone groups. *Journal of Head Trauma Rehabilitation, 14*: 257–268.

Browne, C.J., & Shlosberg, E. (2005). Attachment behaviours and parent fixation in people with dementia. The role of cognitive functioning and pre-morbid attachment style. *Aging & Mental Health, 9*: 153–161.

Bull, R.C. (1999) Traumatic brain injury and quality of life within family settings. *Dissertation Abstracts International: Section B: The Sciences and Engineering, Aug 1999, 60/2-B (0871)*, 0419–4217.

Burgess, P.W., Quayle, A., & Frith, C.D. (2001). Brain regions involved in prospective memory as determined by positron emission tomography. *Neuropsychologia, 39*: 545–555.

Burgess, P.W., & Wood, R.L. (1990). Neuropsychology of behaviour disorders following brain injury. In R.L.Wood (Ed.), *Neurobehavioural Sequalae of Traumatic Brain Injury* (pp. 110–133). Hove: Lawrence Erlbaum.

Burnham, J.B. (1986). *Family Therapy: First Steps Towards a Systemic Approach.* London: Routledge.

Burnham, J. (1993) Systemic supervision: The evolution of relationships in the context of the supervisory relationship. *Human Systems,* 4: 349–381

Burnham, J.B. (2006). Overcoming problems—creating possibilities through wrestling with restraints and embracing resources. *Conference Proceedings from 'Systemic Interviewing: the therapeutic relationship and the development of therapeutic style'.* Institute of Family Therapy, London.

Burridge, A., Williams, W.H., Yates, P.J., Harris, A., & Ward, C. (2007). Spousal relationship satisfaction following acquired brain injury: The role of insight and socio-emotional skill. *Neuropsychological Rehabilitation, 17:* 95–105.

Butler, R.W., & Light, R. (2003). Late diagnosis of neurodegenerative disease in children: Anosognosia by proxy. *The Clinical Neuropsychologist, 17(3):* 374–382.

Butters, M., Glisky, E., & Schacter, D. (1993). Transfer of new learning in memory-impaired patients. *Journal of Clinical & Experimental Neuropsychology, 15:* 219–230.

Byng-Hall, J. (1998). Evolving ideas about narrative: Re-editing the re-editing of family mythology. *Journal of Family Therapy, 20:* 133–141.

Calder, A.J., Keane, J., Manes, F., Antoun, N., & Young, A.W.E. (2000). Impaired recognition and experience of disgust following brain injury. *Nature Neuroscience, 3:* 1077–1078.

Cameron, L.D., & Leventhal, H. (2002). *The Self-Regulation of Health and Illness Behaviour.* London: Routledge.

Caminiti, E., Amore, M., Sapienza, S., Premoli, B., Pietrapiana, P., Zaina, P., & Rago, R. (2001). Instruments to evaluate behavioral dynamics of the traumatic brain injury patient's family: clinical interview, FACES III and DSSVF. *Revista Espanola de Neuropsicologia, 3(3):* 38–57.

Campbell, D., Coldicott, T., & Kinsella, K. (1994). *Systemic Work with Organisations.* London: Karnac.

Campbell, R., Haywood, C., Cowey, A., Regard, M., & Landis, T. (1990). Sensitivity to eye gaze in prosopagnosic patients and monkeys with superior temporal sulcus ablation. *Neuropsychologia, 28:* 1123–1142.

Camplair, P.S., Kreutzer, J., & Doherty, K. (1990). Family outcome following adult traumatic brain injury: A critical review of the literature. In J. Kreutzer & P. Wehman (Eds.), *Community Integration*

Following Traumatic Brain Injury (pp. 207–224). Sevenoaks (Kent): Edward Arnold.

Cappa, S., Sterzi, R., Vallar, G., & Bisiach E. (1987). Remission of hemineglect during vestibular stimulation. *Neuropsychologia, 25:* 775–782.

Carew, D., & Collumb, S. (2008). Supported employment and job coaching. In A. Tyerman & N. King (Eds.), *Psychological Approaches to Rehabilitation After Traumatic Brain Injury.* Oxford: Blackwell.

Carnevale, G.J., Anselmi, V., Busichio, K., & Millis, S.R. (2002a). Changes in ratings of care giver burden following a community-based behaviour management programme for persons with traumatic brain injury. *Journal of Head Trauma Rehabilitation, 17:* 83–95.

Carnwath, T.C.M., & Johnson, D.A.W. (1987). Psychiatric morbidity among spouses of patients with stroke. *British Medical Journal, 294:* 409–411.

Cavallo, M., & Kay, T. (2005). The family system. In J. Silver, T.W. McAllister, & S.C. Yudofsky (Eds.), *Textbook of Traumatic Brain Injury* (pp. 533–558). London: American Psychiatric Publishing.

Cecchin, G. (1987). Hypothesizing, circularity, and neutrality revisited: An invitation to curiosity. *Family Process, 26:* 405–413.

Chan, J. (2007). Carers' perspective on respite for persons with acquired brain injury. *Journal of Rehabilitation Research, 30:* 137–146.

Channon, S. (2004). Frontal lobe dysfunction and everyday performance: Social and non-social contributions. *Acta Psychologia, 115:* 235–254.

Channon, S., & Crawford, S. (1999). Problem-solving in real-life-type situations: The effects of anterior and posterior lesions on performance. *Neuropsychologia, 37:* 757–770.

Channon, S., & Crawford, S. (2000). The effects of anterior lesions on performance on a story comprehension test: Left anterior impairment on a theory of mind task. *Neuropsychologia, 38:* 1006–1017.

Charles, N., Butera-Prinzi, F., & Perlesz, A. (2007). Families living with acquired brain injury: A multiple family group experience. *NeuroRehabilitation, 22:* 61–76.

Chiambretto, P., Rossi Ferrario, S., & Zotti, A.M. (2001). Patients in a persistent vegetative state: Caregiver attitudes and reactions. *Acta Neurologica Scandinavica, 104(6):* 364–368.

Chiu, T. (2006). Family caregivers' needs of internet-based services: A survey of caregivers of brain injury survivors in Ontario. *Paper presented at the MedNet Congress.*

Christensen, T.M., Skaggs, J.L., & Kleist, D.M. (1997). Traumatic brain injured families: Therapeutic considerations. *The Family Journal, 5:* 317–324.

Chwalisz, K. (1998). Brain injury: A tapestry of loss. In J.H. Harvey (Ed.), *Perspectives on Loss: A Sourcebook*. Philadelphia: Brunner/Mazel.

Cicerone, K.D., Dahlberg, C., Malec, J.F., Langebahn, D.M., Felicetti, T., Kneipp, S., Ellmo, W., Kalmar, K., Giacino, J., Harley, P., Laatsch, L., Morse, P.A., & Catanese, J. (2005). Evidence-based cognitive rehabilitation: Updated review of the literature from 1998 through 2002. *Archives of Physical Medicine and Rehabilitation, 86*: 1681–1692.

Cicerone, K., & Tanenbaum, L. (1997). Disturbances of social cognition after traumatic orbitofrontal brain injury. *Archives of Cognitive Neuropsychology, 12*: 173–188.

Clare, L. (2002). Developing awareness about awareness in early-stage dementia: The role of psychosocial factors. *Dementia, 1(3)*: 295–312.

Clare, L. (2003). Managing threats to self: Awareness in early stage Alzheimer's disease. *Social Science & Medicine, 57(6)*: 1017–1029.

Clare, L. (2004). The construction of awareness in early-stage Alzheimer's disease: A review of concepts and models. *British Journal of Clinical Psychology, 43(2)*: 155–175.

Clarici, A., & Guiliani, R. (2008). Growing up with a brain damaged mother: Anosagnosia by proxy? *Neuro Psychoanalysis, 10*: 59–80.

Cloute, K., Mitchell, A., & Yates, P. (2008). Traumatic brain injury and the construction of identity: A discursive approach. *Neuropsychological Rehabilitation, 18*: 651–670.

Clulow, C. (2001). *Adult Attachment and Couple Psychotherapy: The 'Secure Base' in Practice and Research*. London: Karnac.

Coetzer, R. (2009). *Anxiety and Mood Disorders Following Traumatic Brain Injury: Clinical Assessment and Psychotherapy*. London: Karnac.

Coetzer, B.R. & Corney, M.J.R. (2001). Grief and self-awareness following brain injury and the effect of feedback as an intervention. *Journal of Cognitive Rehabilitation, 19(4)*: 8–14.

Collins, D.L., Baum, A., & Singer, J.E. (1983). Coping with chronic stress at Three Mile Island: Psychological and biological evidence. *Health Psychology, 2*: 149–166.

Conway, M.A., & Tacchi, P.C. (1996). Motivated confabulation. *Neurocase: The Neural Basis of Cognition, 2*: 325–339.

Cotrell, V. (1997). Awareness of deficits in Alzheimer's disease: Issues in assessment and intervention. *Journal of Applied Gerontology, 16(1)*: 71–90.

Cottrell, D., Boston, P., & Walker, D. (2004). Family therapy. In H. Remschmidt, M.L. Belfer, & I. Goodyer (Eds.), *Facilitating Pathways: Care, Treatment and Prevention in Child and Adolescent Mental Health*. Berlin: Springer.

Cowley, N.J., & da Silva, E.J. (2008). Prevention of secondary brain injury following Head Trauma. *Trauma, 10*: 35–42.

Crepeau, F., & Sherzer, P. (1995). Predictors and indicators of work status after traumatic brain injury: A meta-analysis. *Neuropsychological
Rehabilitation, 3*: 5–35.

Croker, V., & McDonald, S. (2005). Recognition of emotion from facial
expression following traumatic brain injury. *Brain Injury, 19*: 787–799.

Cronen, V.E., Johnson, K.L., & Lannamann, J.W. (1982). Paradoxes, double binds and reflexive loops: An alternate theoretical perspective.
Family Process, 20: 91–112.

Curtiss, G., Klemz, S., & Vanderploeg, R.D. (2001). Acute impact of severe
traumatic brain injury on family structure and coping responses.
Journal of Head Trauma Rehabilitation, 15: 1113–1122.

Daisley, A., & Webster, G. (2008). Familial brain injury: Impact on and
interventions with children. In A. Tyerman & N. King (Eds.), *Psychological Approaches to Rehabilitation after Traumatic Brain Injury*
(pp. 475–509). Oxford: Blackwell.

Dallos, R. (2006). *Attachment Narrative Therapy: Integrating Systemic, Narrative and Narrative Perspectives*. Maidenhead, Berkshire, UK: Open
University Press.

Dallos, R., & Draper, R. (2007). *An Introduction to Family Therapy: Systemic Theory and Practice*. (2nd ed.). Maidenhead, Berkshire, UK:
Open University Press.

Dallos, R., & Vetere, A. (2005). *Researching Psychotherapy and Counselling*.
East Sussex, UK: Routledge.

Dallos, R. & Vetere, A. (2009). *Systemic Therapy and Attachment Narratives*. Hove: Routledge.

Damasio, A.R. (1994). *Descartes' Error: Emotion, Reason and the Human
Brain*. New York: Grosset/Putnam.

Damasio, A. (1999). *The Feeling of What Happens*. San Diego, CA: Harcourt.

Damasio, A.R. (2003). *Looking for Spinoza: Joy, Sorrow and the Feeling
Brain*. London: Heinemann.

Damasio, A.R., Grabowoski, T.J., Bechara, A., Damasio, H., Ponto, L.L.B.,
Parvizi, J. & Hichwa, R.D. (2000). Subcortical and cortical brain activity during the feeling of self generated emotions. *Nature Neuroscience,
3*: 1049–1056.

Deaton, A.V. (1986). Denial in the aftermath of traumatic head injury: Its
manifestations, measurement and treatment. *Rehabilitation Psychology, 31*: 231–240.

de Jong, P., & Berg, I.K. (2002). *Interviewing for Solutions*. (2nd Ed.). University of Michigan: Brooks/Cole.

Degeneffe, C.E., & Burcham, C.M. (2008). Adult sibling caregiving
for persons with traumatic brain injury: Predictors of affective and
instrumental support. *Journal of Rehabilitation, 74(3)*: 10–20.

Degeneffe, C.E., & Lynch, R.T. (2006). Correlates of depression in adult siblings of persons with traumatic brain injury. *Rehabilitation Counseling Bulletin, 49*: 130–142.

Degeneffe, C.E., & Olney, M.F. (2008). Future concerns of adult siblings of persons with traumatic brain injury. *Rehabilitation Counseling Bulletin, 51*: 240–250.

DeLuca, J. (2000). A cognitive perspective on confabulation. *Neuro Psychoanalysis, 2*: 119–132.

Dennis, M., O'Rourke, S., Lewis, S., Sharp, M., & Warlow, C. (1998). A quantitative study of the emotional outcome of people caring for stroke survivors. *Stroke, 29*: 1867–1872.

Department of Health. (2005). The National Service Framework for Long-term Conditions. Retrieved from the World Wide Web http://www.dh.gov.uk/en/Publicationsandstatistics/Publications/Publications PolicyAndGuidance/DH_4105361

Department of Health. (2007). Mental Capacity Act 2005. London. Retrieved from the World Wide Web http://www.dh.gov.uk/en/Publicationsandstatistics/Bulletins/theweek/Chiefexecutivebulletin/DH_4108436

DePompei, R., & Williams, J. (1994). Working with families after TBI: A family centered approach. *Topics in Language Disorders, 15*: 68–81.

De Shazer, S. (1982). *Patterns of Brief Family Therapy: An Ecosystemic Approach*. United States of America: The Guilford Press.

Dewar, B.-K., & Gracey, F. (2007). "Am not Was": Cognitive behavioural therapy for adjustment and identity change following herpes simplex encephalitis. *Neuropsychological Rehabilitation, 17*: 602–620.

Dewing, J. (2008). Personhood and dementia: Revisiting Tom Kitwood's ideas. *International Journal of Older People Nursing, 3*: 3–13.

Dickerson, V.C., & Coyne, J.C. (1987). Family cohesion and control: A multitrait-multimethod study. *Journal of Marital & Family Therapy, 13(3)*: 275–285.

Dimitrov, M., Grafman, J., & Hollnagel, C. (1996). The effects of frontal lobe damage on everyday problem solving. *Cortex, 32*: 357–366.

Dinnebeil, L.A., & Rule, S. (1994). Variables that influence collaboration between parents and service coordinators. *Journal of Early Intervention, 18*: 349–361.

Dirette, D. (2002). The development of awareness and use of compensatory strategies for cognitive deficits. *Brain Injury, 16(10)*: 861–871.

Disability Discrimination Act (1995; 2005). London: HMSO.

Ditzen, B., Schaer, M., Gabriel, B., Bodenmann, G., Ehlert, U., & Heinrichs, M. (2009). Intranasal oxytocin increases positive communication and reduces cortisol levels during couple conflict. *Biological Psychiatry, 65*: 728–731.

Dixon, R.A. (1996). Collaborative memory and aging. In D. Herrmann, C. McEvoy, C. Hertzog, P. Hertel, & M.K. Johnson (Eds.), *Basic and Applied Memory Research: Theory in Context*. Mahwah, NJ: Laurence Erlbaum.

Doka, K.J. (1989). *Disenfranchised Grief: Recognizing Hidden Sorrow*. Lexington, MA, UK: Lexington Books/D.C. Heath and Com.

Domes, G., Heinrichs, M., Gläscher, J., Büchel, C., Braus, D.F., & Herperz, S.C. (2007). Oxytocin attenuates amygdala responses to emotional faces regardless of valence. *Biological Psychiatry, 62*: 1187–1190.

Domes, G., Heinrichs, M., Michel, A., Berger, C., & Herperz, S.C. (2007). Oxytocin imprices 'mind reading' in humans. *Biological Psychiatry, 61*: 731–733.

Donnelly, K.Z., Donnelly, J.P., & Grohman, K.J. (2000). Cognitive, emotional, and behavioral problems associated with traumatic brain injury: A concept map of patient, family, and provider perspectives. *Brain and Cognition, 44*: 21–25.

Douglas, J.M., & Spellacy, F.J. (1996). Indicators of long-term family functioning following severe traumatic brain injury in adults. *Brain Injury, 10*: 819–839.

Duncan, J. (1986). Disorganisation of behaviour after frontal lobe damage. *Cognitive Neuropsychology, 3*: 271–290.

Dunn, J., Brown, J., & Beardsall, L. (1991). Family talk about feeling states and children's later understanding of others' emotions. *Developmental Psychology, 27(3)*: 448–455.

Dunn, B.D., Dalgleish, T., & Lawrence, A.D. (2006). Somatic marker hypothesis: A critical evaluation. *Neuroscience & Behavioural Reviews, 30*: 239–271.

Eames, P. (2001). Distinguishing the neuropsychiatric, psychiatric and psychological consequences of acquired brain injury. In R.L. Wood & T. MacMillan (Eds.), *Neurobehavioural Disability and Social Handicap following Traumatic Brain Injury* (pp. 29–45). Hove: Psychology Press.

Eisler, I. (2005). The empirical and theoretical base of family therapy and multiple family day therapy for adolescent anorexia nervosa. *Journal of Family Therapy, 27*: 104–131.

Elliot, J., & Remenyi, A. (1982). Perceptions of the sequel of head injury of rehabilitation staff members and family members of clients. *Australian Rehabilitation Review, 6*: 50–56.

Elman, R.J., Parr, S., & Moss, B. (2003). The internet and aphasia: Crossing the digital divide. In S. Parr, J. Duchan, & C. Pound (Eds.), *Apha-*

sia *Inside Out: Reflections on Communication Disability.* Maidenhead: Open University Press.

Endler, N.S., & Parker, J.D.A. (1994). Assessment of multidimensional coping: Task, emotion, and avoidance strategies. *Psychological Assessment, 6:* 50–60.

Endler, N.S., & Parker, J.D.A. (1999). *Coping Inventory for Stressful Situations (CISS). Manual (second Edition).* New York: Multi-Health Systems.

Engel, G.L. (1980). The clinical application of the biopsychosocial model. *American Journal of Psychiatry, 137:* 535–544.

Epstein, N., Baldwin, L., & Bishop, D. (1983). The McMaster Family Assessment Device. *Journal of Martial Family Therapy, 9:* 171–180.

Ergh, T.C., Hanks, R.A., Rapport, L.J. & Coleman, R.D. (2003). Social support moderates caregiver life satisfaction following traumatic brain injury. *Journal of Clinical and Experimental Neuropsychology, 25(8):* 1090–1101.

Ergh, T.C., Rapport, L.J., Coleman, R.D., & Hanks, R.A. (2002). Predictors of caregiver and family functioning following traumatic brain injury: Social support moderates caregiver distress. *Journal of Head Trauma Rehabilitation, 17:* 155–174.

Eslinger, P.J. (1998). Neurological and neuropsychological bases of empathy. *European Neurology, 39:* 193–199.

Falicov, C.J. (1998). The cultural meaning of family triangles. In M. McGoldrick (Ed.), *Re-Visioning Family Therapy: Race, Culture, and Gender in Clinical Practice* (pp. 37–49). London: The Guilford Press.

Faux, S.A. (1993). Siblings of children with chronic physical and cognitive disabilities. *Journal of Pediatric Nursing, 8:* 305–317.

Feinberg, T.E. & Roane, D.M. (1997). Anosognosia, completion and confabulation: the neutral-personal dichotomy. *Neurocase, 3,* 73–85.

Feinberg, T.E., & Roane, D.M. (2003a). Misidentification syndromes. In T.E. Feinberg & D.M. Roane, (Eds.), *Behavioral Neurology and Neuropsychology* (2nd *Edition).* New York: McGraw-Hill Professional.

Feinberg, T.E. & Roane, D.M. (2003b). Anosognosia. In T.E. Feinberg & D.M. Roane, (Eds.), *Behavioral Neurology and Neuropsychology* (2nd *Edition).* New York: McGraw-Hill Professional.

Feldman, M. (1994). Projective identification in phantasy and enactment. *Psychoanalytic Inquiry, 14:* 423–440.

Fiegelson, C. (1993). Personality death, object loss and the uncanny. *International Journal of Psycho-analysis, 74:* 331–345.

Fischer, S., Trexler, L.E., & Gauggel, S. (2004). Awareness of activity limitations and prediction of performance in patients with brain injuries and orthopedic disorders. *Journal of the International Neuropsychological Society, 10(2):* 190–199.

Fish, J., Manly, T., & Wilson, B.A. (2008). Long-term compensatory treatment of organizational deficits in a patient with bilateral frontal lobe damage 14. *Journal of the International Neuropsychological Society, 14*: 154–163.

Fivush, R., & Fromhoff, F.A. (1988). Style and structure in mother-child conversations about the past. *Discourse Processes, 11*: 337–355.

Florian, V., Katz, S., & Lahav, V. (1989). Impact of traumatic brain damage on family dynamics and functioning: A review. *Brain Injury, 3*: 219–233.

Fordyce, D., & Roueche, J.R. (1986). Changes in perspectives of disability among patients, staff and relatives during rehabilitation of brain injury. *Rehabilitation Psychology, 31*: 217–229.

Forsyth, R.J., Kelly, T.P., Wicks, B., & Walker, S. (2005). 'Must try harder?': A family empowerment intervention for acquired brain injury. *Pediatric Rehabilitation, 8*: 140–143.

Foster, M., & Tilseb, C. (2003) Referral to rehabilitation following traumatic brain injury: A model for understanding inequities in access. *Social Science & Medicine, 56(10)*: 2201–2210.

Fotopoulou, A., Conway, M.A., & Solms, M. (2007). Confabulation: Motivated reality monitoring. *Neuropsychologia, 45*: 2180–2190.

Fotopoulou, A., Rudd, A., Holmes, P., & Kopelman, M. (2009). Self-observation reinstates motor awareness in anosognosia for hemiplegia. *Neuropsychologia, 47*: 1256–1260.

Fotopoulou, A., Solms, M., & Turnbull, O. (2004). Wishful reality distortions in confabulation: A case report. *Neuropsychologia, 42*: 727–744.

Freud, S. (1891/1953). *On Aphasia: A Critical Study.* Translated by E. Strengel. Oxford: International Universities Press.

Freud, S. (1915). Mourning and Melancholia. *Standard Edition, 4*: 237.

Freud, S. (1919). *The Uncanny. Standard Edition, 17.* London: The Hogarth Press.

Freud, S. (1957). Mourning and Melancholia. In J. Strachey (Ed.), *The Standard Edition of the Complete Psychological Works of Sigmund Freud* (Vol. 14, pp. 237–259). London: The Hogarth Press (Original work published in 1917).

Freud, S. (1961). The ego and the id. In J. Strachey (Ed.), *The Standard Edition of the Complete Psychological Works of Sigmund Freud* (Vol. 19, pp. 3–66) London: The Hogarth Press (Original work published in 1923).

Frith, C.D. (2003). *Neural Hermeneutics: How Brains Interpret Minds.* Keynote Lecture, 9th Annual Meeting of the Organization of Human Brain Mapping New York.

Frith, C.D., and Frith, U. (2006) The neural basis of mentalizing. *Neuron, 50*: 531–534.

Frith, C.D., & Wolpert, D.M. (2004). *The Neuroscience of Social Interaction: Decoding, Imitating and Influencing the Actions of Others*. Oxford, UK: Oxford University Press.

Frith, U., & Frith, C.D. (2003). Development and neurophysiology of mentalizing. *Philosophical Transactions of the Royal Society, London B, 358*: 459–473.

Frith, U., & Frith, C.D. (2004). Development and neurophysiology of mentalising. In C.D. Frith & D.M. Wolpert (Eds.), *The Neuroscience of Social Interaction: Decoding, Imitating and Influencing the Actions of Others* (pp. 45–76). Oxford: Oxford University Press.

Frosh, S., Phoenix, A., & Pattman, R. (2003). Taking a stand: Using psychoanalysis to explore the positioning of subjects in discourse. *British Journal of Social Psychology, 42(1)*: 39–53.

Funnell, E., & Sheridan, J. (1992). Categories of knowledge: Unfamiliar aspects of living and nonliving things. *Cognitive Neuropsychology, 9*: 135–154.

Gagnon, J., Bouchard, M.A., Rainville, C., Lecours, S., & St Amand, J. (2006). Inhibition and object relations in borderline personality traits after traumatic brain injury. *Brain Injury, 20*: 67–81.

Gainotti, G. (1975). Confabulation of denial in senile dementia: An experimental study. *Psychiatric Clinics, 8*: 99–108.

Gainotti, G. (1993). Emotional and psychosocial problems after brain injury. *Neuropsychological Rehabilitation, 3*: 259–277.

Gallese, V. (1999). From grasping to language: Mirror neurons and the origin of social communication. In A. Hameroff & D. Chalmers (Eds.), *Towards a Science of Consciousness* (pp. 165–178). Cambridge, MA: MIT Press.

Gallese, V. (2006). Intentional attunement: A neurophysiological perspective on social cognition and its disruption in autism. *Cognitive Brain Research, 1079*: 15–24.

Gallese, V., Keysers, C., & Rizzolatti, G. (2004). A unifying view of the basis of social cognition. *Trends in Cognitive Science, 8*: 396–403.

Gallese, V., & Lakoff, G. (2005). The brain's concepts: The role of the sensory-motor system in conceptual knowledge. *Cognitive Neuropsychology, 22*: 455–479.

Gambescia, N., & Weeks, G. (2006). Sexual dysfunction. In N. Kazantis & L. L'Abate (Eds.), *Handbook of Homework Assignments in Psychotherapy* (pp. 351–358). New York: Springer US.

Gan, C., Campbell, K.A., Gemeinhardt, M., & McFadden, G.T. (2006). Predictors of family functioning after brain injury. *Brain Injury, 20*: 587–600.

Gan, C., & Schuller, R. (2002). Family system outcome following acquired brain injury: Clinical and research perspectives. *Brain Injury,* *16*: 311–322.

Garland, C. (1998). Working with traumatised groups. In C. Garland (Ed.), *Understanding Trauma: A Psychoanalytical Approach.* London: Karnac.

Gaston, L. (1990). The concept of the alliance and its role in psychotherapy: Theoretical and empirical considerations. *Psychotherapy: Theory, Research, Practice, Training, 27*: 143–153.

Gasquoine, P.G. (1992). Affective state and awareness of sensory and cognitive effects after closed head injury. *Neuropsychology, 3*: 187–196.

Gasquoine, P.G., & Gibbons, T.A. (1994). Lack of awareness of impairments in institutionalized, severely and chronically disabled survivors of traumatic brain injury: A preliminary investigation. *Journal of Head Trauma Rehabilitation, 9(4)*: 7–17.

Gervasio, A.H., & Kreutzer, J.S. (1997). Kinship and family members' psychological distress after traumatic brain injury: A large sample study. *Journal of Head Trauma Rehabilitation, 12*: 14–26.

Gibson, E.J. (1977). The theory of affordances. In R.E. Shaw & J. Bransford (Eds.), *Perceiving, Acting, and Knowing.* London: Erlbaum.

Gibson, J.J. (1979). *The Ecological Approach to Visual Perception.* Boston: Houghton Mufflin.

Gill, D.J. (1998). *Forever Different: Siblings' Experience of Living with a Brother or Sister Who has a Traumatic Brain Injury.* Unpublished Doctoral Thesis University of Toronto.

Gillen, R.H., Tennen, H., Affleck, G., & Steinpreis, R. (1998). Distress, depressive symptoms and depressive disorder among caregivers of patients with brain injury. *Journal of Head Trauma Rehabilitation, 13*: 14–26.

Glaser, B., & Strauss, A. (1965). *Awareness of Dying.* New York: Aldine.

Godfrey, H.P.D., Knight, R.B., & Bishara, S.N. (1991). The relationship between social skill and family problem solving following very severe closed head injury. *Brain Injury, 5*: 207–211.

Goetting, A. (1986). The developmental tasks of siblingship over the life cycle. *Journal of Marriage and the Family, 48*: 703–714.

Gold, D.A., & Park, N.W. (2009). The effects of dividing attention on the encoding and performance of novel naturalistic actions. *Psychological Research, 73(3)*: 336–349.

Goldberg, E., & Barr, W. (1991). Three possible mechanisms of unawareness of deficit. In G.P. Prigatano & D.L. Schacter (Eds.). *Awareness of Deficit After Brain Injury: Clinical and Theoretical Issues* (pp. 152–175). New York: Oxford University Press.

Goldner, V., Penn, P., Sheinberg, M.S.W., & Walker, G. (1990). Love and violence: Gender paradoxes in volatile attachments. *Family Process,* *29*: 343–364.

Goldstein, K. (1939). *The Organism.* New York: American Book Company.

Goldstein, K. (1942). *After Effects of Brain Injuries in War.* New York: Grune & Stratton.

Goldstein, K. (1959). Notes on the development of my concepts. *Journal of Individual Psychology, 15*: 5–14.

Gosling, J., & Oddy, M. (1999). Rearranged marriages: Marital relationships after head injury. *Brain Injury, 13*: 785–796.

Gouvier, W.D., Prestholdt, P.H., & Warner, M.S. (1988). A survey of common misconceptions about head injury and recovery. *Archives of Clinical Neuropsychology, 3*: 331–343.

Gracey, F., Evans, J., & Malley, D. (2009). Capturing process and outcome in complex rehabilitative interventions: A "Y-shaped" model. *Neuropsychological Rehabilitation, 19(6)*: 1–24.

Gracey, F., & Onsworth, T.E. (2008). Neuropsychological rehabilitation: Identity special issue. *Neuropsychological Rehabilitation, 18(5/6)*: 513–783.

Gracey, F., Palmer, S., Rous, B., Psaila, K., Shaw, K., O'Dell, J., Cope, J. & Mohamed, S. (2008). "Feeling part of things": Personal construction of self after brain injury. *Neuropsychological Rehabilitation, 18*: 627–650.

Gracey, F., Henwood, K., Evans, J., Malley, D., Psaila, K., Bateman, A. & Wilson, B.A. (2006). There was a big meeting ... and then everybody seemed to pull together: Clinical difficulty, team functioning and the role of interdisciplinary formulation. *Journal of the International Neuropsychological Society, 12(S2)*: 5.

Gracey, F., Yeates, G., Palmer, S., & Psaila, K. (2009). The Psychological Support Group. In B.A. Wilson, F. Gracey, J.J. Evans, & A. Bateman (Eds.), *Neuropsychological Rehabilitation: Theory, Models, Therapy and Outcome* (pp. 123–137). Cambridge: Cambridge University Press.

Grafman, J. (1994). Alternative frameworks for the conceptualisation of prefrontal lobe functions. In F. Boller & J. Grafman (Eds.), *Handbook of Neuropsychology, Vol. 9* (pp. 187–202). Amsterdam: Elsevier.

Grafman, J., Schwab, K., Warden, D., Pridgen, B.S., Brown, H.R., & Salazar, A.M. (1996). Frontal lobe injuries, violence and aggression: A report of the Vietnam Head Injury Study. *Neurology, 46*: 1231–1238.

Graham, K.S. (1999). Semantic dementia: A challenge to the multiple trace theory? *Trends in Cognitive Sciences, 3*: 85–87.

Graham, K.S., Becker, J.T., & Hodges, J.R. (1997). On the relationship between knowledge and memory for pictures: Evidence from the study of patients with semantic dementia and Alzheimer's disease. *Journal of the International Neuropsychological Society, 3*: 534–544.

Grattan, L., & Eslinger, P. (1989). Higher cognition and social behaviour. Changes in cognitive flexibility and empathy after cerebral lesions. *Neuropsychology, 3*: 175–185.

Greatrex, T.S. (2002). Projective identification: How does it work? *Neuro Psychoanalysis, 4*: 187–198.

Green, R.J., & Werner, P.D. (1996). Intrusiveness and closeness-caregiving: Rethinking the concept of family "enmeshment". *Family Process, 35*: 115–136.

Greene, J.D.W. (2005). Apraxia, agnosias, and higher visual function abnormalities. *Journal of Neurology, Neurosurgery & Psychiatry, 76*: 25–34.

Greenson, R. (1971). The real relationship between the patient and the psychoanalyst. In M. Kanzer (Ed.), *The Unconscious Today* (pp. 213–232). New York: International Universities Press.

Gregory, R.J. (1998). Neuro-talk: An intervention to enhance communication. *Journal of Psychosocial Nursing, 36*: 28–31.

Grimm, G.C. (2002) Brain injury survivors: Effects of targeted family counseling. Dissertation Abstracts International: Section B: *The Sciences and Engineering, 62(7)-B*(3377): 0419–4217.

Groom, K.N., Shaw, T.G., O'Connor, M.E., Howard, N.I., & Pickens, A. (1998). Neurobehavioral symptoms and family functioning in traumatically brain-injured adults. *Archives of Clinical Neuropsychology, 13*: 695–711.

Groswasser, Z., Melamed, S., Agranov, E., & Keren, O. (1999). Return to work as an integrative outcome measure following traumatic brain injury. *Neuropsychological Rehabilitation, 9*: 493–504.

Guastella, A.J., Mitchell, P.B., & Dadds, M.R. (2008). Oxytocin increases gaze to the eye region of human faces. *Biological Psychiatry, 63*: 3–5.

Gustafsson, P.A., Engquist, M.L., & Karlsson, B. (1995). Siblings in family therapy. *Journal of Family Therapy, 17*: 317–327.

Guthrie, T.C., & Grossman, E.M. (1952). A study of the syndromes of denial. *Archives of Neurology and Psychiatry, 68*: 362–371.

Haley, J. (1978). *Problem-Solving Therapy.* New York: Harper & Row.

Hall, K., Karzmark, P., Stevens, M., Englander, J., O'Hare, P., & Wright, J. (1994). Family stressors in traumatic brain injury: A two-year follow up. *Archives of Physical Medicine and Rehabilitation, 75*: 876–884.

Hammond, R. (2007). *On the Edge: My Story.* London: Weidenfeld & Nicolson.

Hanks, R.A., Rapport, L.J., & Vangel, S. (2007). Caregiving appraisal after traumatic brain injury: The effects of functional status, coping style, social support and family functioning. *NeuroRehabilitation*, *22*: 43–52.

Happé, F., Brownell, H., & Winnder, E. (1999). Acquired 'theory of mind' impairments following stroke. *Cognition*, *70*: 211–240.

Happé, F., Malhi, G., & Checkley, S. (2001). Acquired mind-blindness following frontal lobe surgery? A single case study of impaired 'theory of mind' in a patient treated with stereotactic anterior capsulotomy. *Neuropsychologia*, *39*: 83–90.

Hardgrove, H. (1991). Special issues for a child. In J.M. Williams & T. Kay (Eds.), *Head Injury: A Family Matter*. Toronto: Paul H. Brookes Publishing.

Hardham, V. (2006). Bridges to safe uncertainty: An Interview with Barry Mason. *Australia and New Zealand Journal of Family Therapy*, *27*: 16–21.

Hardy, K.V., & Laszloffy, T.A. (1995). The cultural genogram: Key to training culturally competent family therapists. *Journal of Marital & Family Therapy*, *21*: 227–237.

Harré, R. (2002). *Cognitive Science: A Philosophical Introduction*. London: Sage.

Hartman, A. (1995). Diagrammatic assessment of family relationships. *Families in Society*, *76*: 111–122.

Haslam, C., Holme, A., Haslam, S.A., Lyer, A., Jetten, J., & Williams, W.H. (2008). Maintaining group memberships: Social identity continuity predicts well-being after stroke. *Neuropsychological Rehabilitation*, *18*: 671–691.

Hatfield, E., Cacioppo, J., & Rapson, R.L. (1994). *Emotional Contagion*. New York: Cambridge University Press.

Havet-Thomassin, V., Gardey, A.M., Aubin, G., Legall, D. (2004). Several factors to distinguish anosognosia from denial after a brain injury. *Encephale*, *30(2)*: 171–181.

Hawton, K. (1985). Sex therapy. *Behavioural and Cognitive Psychotherapy*, *19*: 131–136.

Haxby, J.V., Hoffman, E.A., & Gobbini, M.I. (2000). The distributed human neural system for face perception. *Trends in Cognitive Sciences*, *4*: 223–233.

Haxby, J.V., Hoffman, E.A., & Gobbini, M.I. (2002). Human neural systems for face recognition and social communication. *Biological Psychiatry*, *51*: 59–67.

Hayes, N., & Coetzer, R. (2003). Developing a brain injury service information booklet based on service users' perceived needs. *Clinical Psychology*, *21*: 36–39.

Hayward, M. (2009). Is narrative therapy systemic? *Context, 105*: 15–18.

Health Select Committee. (2001). *Head Injury: Rehabilitation (Third Report)*. HMSO: House of Commons.

Heilman, K. (1991). Anosognosia: possible neuropsychological mechanisms. In G.P. Prigatano & D.L. Schacter (Eds.). *Awareness of Deficit After Brain Injury: Clinical and Theoretical Issues* (pp. 53–64). New York: Oxford University Press.

Hof, L., & Berman, E. (1986). The sexual genogram. *Journal of Marital & Family Therapy, 12*: 39–47.

Hoffman, L. (1989). Reflecting teams: An imaginary dialogue. *See: http:// users.california.com/~rathbone/reflecting.htm.*

Hollander, E., Bartz, J., Chaplin, W., Phillips, A., Sumner, J., Soorya, L. Anagnostou, E., & Wasserman, S. (2007). Oxytocin increases retention of social cognition in autism. *Biological Psychiatry, 61*: 498–503.

Hollander, E., Novotny, S., Hanratty, M., Yaffe, R., DeCaria, C.M., Aronowitz, B.R., & Mosovich, S. (2003). Oxytocin infusion reduces repetitive behaviours in adults with autistic and Asperger's disorders. *Neuropsychopharmacology, 28*: 193–198.

Hollway, W. (1989). *Subjectivity and Method in Psychology: Gender, Meaning and Science*. London: Sage.

Hollway, W., & Jefferson, T. (2000). *Doing Qualitative Research Differently: Free Association, Narrative and the Interview Method*. London: Sage.

Holm, S., Schönberger, M., Poulsen, I., & Caetano, C. (2008). Patients' and relatives' experience of difficulties following severe traumatic brain injury: The sub-acute stage. *Neuropsychological Rehabilitation, 19*: 444–460.

Holstein, J.A., & Gubrium, J.F. (1998). Active interviewing. In D. Silverman (Ed.), *Qualitative Research-Theory, Method and Practice* (pp. 113–129). London and New York: Routledge.

Hornak, J., Rolls, E.T., & Wade, D. (1996). Face and voice expression identification in patients with emotional and behavioural changes following ventral frontal lobe damage. *Neuropsychologia, 34*: 247–261.

Horwitz, R., Horwitz, S., Orsini, J., Antoine, R., & Hill, D. (1998). Including families in collaborative care: Impact on recovery? *Family Systems Health, 16*: 71–83.

House, A., & Hodges, J. (1988). Persistent denial of handicap after infarction of the right basal ganglia: A case study. *Journal of Neurology, Neurosurgery, & Psychiatry, 51*: 112–115.

Humphrey, G.W., Donnelly, N., & Riddoch, M.J. (1993). Expression is computed separately from facial identity and is computed separately for moving and static faces: Neuropsychological evidence. *Neuropsychologia, 31*: 173–181.

Hutchinson, S.A., Leger-Krall, S.L., & Skodol Wilson, H. (1997). Early probable Alzheimer's disease and Awareness Context Theory. *Social Science and Medicine, 45(9)*: 1399–1409.

Hutto, D.H. (2004). The limits of spectatorial folk psychology. *Mind & Language, 19*: 548–573.

Hynes, C.A., Baird, A.A., & Grafton, S.T. (2006). Differential role of the orbital frontal lobe in the emotional versus cognitive perspective-taking. *Neuropsychologia, 44*: 374–383.

Institute of Family Therapy. (2005). Sexualities and sexual relationships: What can systemic approaches offer? In One Day Workshop, IFT London.

Iriki, A., Tanaka, M., & Iwamura, Y., 1996. Coding of modified body schema during tool use by macaque postcentral neurons. *Neuroreport, 7*: 2325–2330.

Iriki, A., Tanaka, M., Obayashi, S., et al. (2001). Selfimages in the video monitor coded by monkey intraparietal neurons. *Neuroscience Research, 40*: 163–173.

Jackson, H., & Moffat, N. (1987). Impaired emotional recognition following severe head injury. *Cortex, 23*: 293–300.

Jacobs, H. (1991). Family and behavioral issues. In J. Williams & T. Kay (Eds.), *Head Injury: A Family Matter*. Baltimore: Brookes.

Jacobson, N.S., Christensen, A., Prince, S.E., Cordova, J., & Eldridge, K. (2000). Integrative behavioural couple therapy: An acceptance-based, promising new treatment for couple discord. *Journal of Consulting and Clinical Psychology, 68*: 351–355.

Jaffe, J., & Slote, W.H. (1958). Interpersonal factors in denial of illness. *Archives of Neurology & Psychiatry, 80*, 653–656.

Janksepp, J., Fuchs, T., Garcia, V.A., & Lesiak, A. (2007). Does any aspect of mind survive brain damage that typically leads to a persistent vegetative state? Ethical considerations. *Philosophy, Ethics, and Humanities in Medicine*. Published 17 December 2007. Accessed November 21, 2009 from http://www.peh-med.com/content/2/1/32.

Janoff-Bulman, R. (1992). *Shattered Assumptions: Towards a New Psychology of Trauma*. New York: Free Press.

Johnson, B.P. (1995). One family's experience with head injury: A phenomenological study. *Journal of Neuroscience Nursing, 27*: 118.

Johnson, M.L. (1997). Source monitoring and memory distortion. *Philosophical Transactions: Biological Sciences, 352*: 1733–1745.

Johnson, S. (2004). *The Practice of Emotionally-Focussed Couples Therapy: Creating Connection*. New York: Other Press.

Johnson, B.D., Crane, S.C.M., & Tatekawa, L. (2004). Communication on both sides of the mirror: Helping a family cope with a traumatic brain injury. *The Family Journal, 12*: 178–183.

Johnson, J., & McCown, W. (1997). *Family Therapy of Neurobehavioral Disorders: Intergrating Neuropsychology and Family Therapy.* New York: The Hawthorn Press.

Johnson, R., & Stoten, S. (2008). Return to previous employment. In A. Tyerman & N. King (Eds.), *Psychological Approaches to Rehabilitation after Traumatic Brain Injury* (pp. 351–375). Oxford: Blackwell.

Jones, E., & Asen, E. (2000). *Systemic Couples Therapy and Depression.* London: Karnac.

Jones, S., Nyberg, L., Sandblom, J., Neely, A.S., Ingvar, M., Petersson, K.M., & Bäckman, L. (2006). Cognitive and neural plasticity in aging: General and task-specific limitations. *Neuroscience & Biobehavioral Reviews, 30(6),* 864–871.

Jorge, R., & Robinson, R.G. (2002). Mood disorders following traumatic brain injury. *NeuroRehabilitation, 17*: 311–324.

Jorge, R.E., Robinson, R.G., Moser, D.M., Tateno, A., Crespo-Facorro, B., & Arndt, S. (2004). Major depression following traumatic brain injury. *Archives of General Psychiatry, 61*: 42–50.

Jorgensen, M., & Togher, L. (2009). Narrative after traumatic brain injury: A comparison of monologic and jointly-produced discourse. *Brain Injury, 23(9)*: 727–740.

Joseph, B. (1987). Projective identification: Some clinical aspects. In E.B. Spillius & M. Feldman (Eds.), *Psychic Equilibrium and Psychic Change: Selected Papers of Betty Joseph.* (pp. 168–180). London: Routledge.

Judd, T. (1999). *Neuropsychotherapy and Community Integration. Brain Illness, Emotions, and Behavior.* New York: Plenum.

Kahn, P. (1997). Siblings of children with brain injuries. *Rehab Update, Winter*: 1–4.

Kaplan-Solms, K., & Solms, M. (2000). *Clinical Studies in Neuro-Psychoanalysis: An Introduction to a Depth Neuropsychology.* London: Karnack.

Karpman, T., Wolfe, S.J., & Vargo, J.W. (1986). The psychological adjustment of adult clients & their parents following closed-head injury. *Journal of Applied Rehabilitation Counseling, 17*: 28–33.

Kausar, R., & Powell, G.E. (1999). Coping and psychological distress in carers of patients with neurological disorders. *Asia Pacific Disability Rehabilitation Journal, 10*: 64–68.

Kay, T., & Cavallo, M. (1994). The family system: Impact, assessment and intervention. In R. Hales, J. Silver, & S. Fudofsky (Eds.),

Neuropsychiatry of Traumatic Brain Injury (pp. 533–567). Washington, DC: American Psychiatric Press.

Kendall, E., & Terry, D.J. (2008) Understanding adjustment following traumatic brain injury: Is the goodness-of-fit coping hypothesis useful? *Social Science & Medicine, 67(8)*: 1217–1224.

Kesler, S.R., Adams, H.F., & Bigler, E.D. (2000). SPECT, MR and quantitative MR imaging: Correlates with neuropsychological and psychological outcome in traumatic brain injury. *Brain Injury, 14*: 851–857.

Khan, F., Turner-Stokes, L., Ng, L., & Kilpatrick, T. (2007). *Multidisciplinary Rehabilitation for Adults with Multiple Sclerosis (Full Review).* (April 18, ed.). (Vols. 2:CD006036). Oxford: Update Software.

Kihlstrom, J.F., & Tobias, B.A. (1991). Anosognosia, consciousness, and the self. In G.P. Prigatano & D.L. Schacter (Eds.), *Awareness of Deficit After Brain Injury: Clinical and Theoretical Issues* (pp. 198–222). New York: Oxford University Press.

Kinsbourne, M., & Wood, F. (1975). Short-term memory processes and the amnesic syndrome. In D. Deutsch & J.A. Deutsch (Eds.), *Short-Term Memory* (pp. 256–291). New York: Academic Press.

Kinsella, G., Ford, B., and Moran, C. (1989). Survival of social relationships following head injury. *International Disability Studies, 11(1)*: 9–14.

Kinsella, G., Ong, B., Murtagh, D., Prior, M., & Sawyer, M. (1999). The role of the family for behavioral outcome in children and adolescents following traumatic brain injury. *Journal of Consulting and Clinical Psychology, 67*: 116–123.

Kirmayer, L.J., & Corin, E. (1998). Inside knowledge: Cultural considerations of insight in psychosis. In X. Amadour & A. David (Eds.), *Insight and Psychosis*. New York: Oxford University Press.

Kirsch, P., Esslinger, C., Chen, Q., Mier, D., Lis, S., Siddhanti, S., Gruppe, H., Mattay, V.S., Gallhofer, B., & Meyer-Lindenberg, A. (2005). Oxytocin modulates neural circuitry for social cognition and fear in humans. *Journal of Neuroscience, 25*: 11489–11493.

Kitwood, T. (1997). *Dementia Reconsidered: The Person Comes First*. Buckingham: Open University Press.

Klein, M. (1946). Notes on some schizoid mechanisms. In M. Klein (Ed.), *The Writings of Melanie Klein (Volume III)* (pp. 1–24). London: The Hogarth Press.

Knight, R.G., Devereux, R., & Godfrey, H.P.D. (1998). Caring for a family member with a traumatic brain injury. *Brain Injury, 12*: 467–481.

Knight, C., Rutterford, N., Alderman, N., & Swan, L. (2002). Is accurate self-monitoring necessary for people with acquired neurological problems to benefit from the use of differential reinforcement methods? *Brain Injury, 16*: 75–87.

Kosciulek, J.F. (1996). The circumplex model and head injury family types: A test of the balanced versus extreme hypotheses. *Journal of Rehabilitation, 62*: 49–54.

Kosciulek, J.F. (1997a). Relationship of family schema to family adaptation to brain injury. *Brain Injury, 11*: 821–830.

Kosciulek, J.F. (1997b). Dimensions of family coping with head injury: A replication and extension. *Rehabilitation Counseling Bulletin, 41*, 43.

Kosciulek, J.F., & Lustig, D.C. (1999). Differentiation of three brain injury family types. *Brain Injury, 13*: 245–254.

Kotila, M., Numminen, H., Waltimo, O., & Kaste, M. (1998). Depression after stroke: Results of the FINNSTROKE study. *Stroke, 29*: 368–372.

Krefting, L. (1990). Double bind and disability: The case of traumatic head injury. *Social Sciences & Medicine, 30(8)*: 859–865.

Kreutzer, J.S., Gervasio, A.H., & Camplair, P.S. (1994a). Patient correlates of caregivers' distress and family functioning after traumatic brain injury. *Brain Injury, 8*: 211–230.

Kreutzer, J.S., Gervasio, A.H., & Camplair, P.S. (1994b). Primary caregivers' psychological status and family functioning after traumatic brain injury. *Brain Injury, 8(3)*: 197–210.

Kreutzer, J.S., Kolakowsky-Hayner, S.A., Demm, S.R., & Meade, M.A. (2002). A structured approach to family intervention after brain injury. *Journal of Head Trauma Rehabilitation, 17*: 349–367.

Kreutzer, J., Marwitz, J., Hsu, N., Williams, K., & Riddick, A. (2007). Martial stability after brain injury: An investigation and analysis. *NeuroRehabilitation, 22*: 53–59.

Kreutzer, J.S., Marwitz, J., & Kepler, K. (1992). Traumatic brain injury: Family response and outcome. *Archives of Physical Medicine and Rehabilitation, 73*: 771–777.

Kreutzer, J.S., Serio, C.D., & Bergquist, S. (1994). Family needs after brain injury: A quantitative analysis. *Journal of Head Trauma Rehabilitation, 9*: 104–115.

LaBaw, W.L. (1966). Cerebral concussion with concomitant acute brain syndrome: A subjective report. *Medical Times, 94(4)*: 407–414.

LaBaw, W.L. (1967). *Res Physician, 3*: 149–160.

LaBaw, W.L. (1968a). Closed brain injury: Thirty-three months of recovery from trauma, a subjective report. *Medical Times, 96(8)*: 821–829.

LaBaw, W.L. (1968b). Thirty-five months months of recovery from trauma, a subjective report: Closed brain injury. In N. Kapur (Ed.), *Injured Brains of Medical Minds: Views from Within* (pp. 298–304). Oxford: Oxford University Press.

LaBaw, W.L. (1969). Denial Inside out: Subjective experience with anosognosia in closed head injury. *Psychiatry, 32(1)*: 174–191.

Lacan, J. (1949). The mirror stage as formative of the I as revealed in psychoanalytic experience. In J. Lacan (Ed.), *Écrits: A Selection*. London: Tavistock Publications.

Lacan, J. (1953). The function and field of speech and language in psychoanalysis. In J. Lacan (Ed.), *Écrits: A Selection*. London: Tavistock Publications.

Lacan, J. (1958). The meaning of the phallus. In J. Mitchell & J. Rose (Eds.), *Feminine Sexuality*. London: Macmillan.

Lacan, J. (1977). *Écrits: A Selection*. Bristol: Routledge.

Langer, K.G. (1992). Psychotherapy with the neuropsychologically impaired adult. *American Journal of Psychotherapy, 46*: 620–639.

Langer, K.G. (1994). Depression and denial in psychotherapy of persons with disabilities. *American Journal of Psychotherapy, 48*: 181–194.

Langer, K.G., & Padrone, F.J. (1992). Psychotherapeutic treatment of awareness in acute rehabilitation of traumatic brain injury. *Neuropsychological Rehabilitation, 2*: 59–70.

Lanham, R.A.J., Weissenburger, J.E., Schwab, K.A., & Rosner, M.M. (2000). A longitudinal investigation of the concordance between individuals with traumatic brain injury and family or friend ratings on the Katz Adjustment Scale. *The Journal of Head Trauma Rehabilitation, 15(5)*: 1123–1138.

Laroi, F. (2003). The family systems approach to treating families of persons with brain injury: A potential collaboration between family therapist and brain injury professional. *Brain Injury, 17*: 175–187.

Law, M., Baptise, S., McColl, M.A., Opzoomer, A., Polatajko, H., & Pollock, N. (1990). The Canadian occupational performance measure: An outcome measure for occupational therapy. *Canadian Journal of Occupational Therapy, 57*: 82–87.

Laws, K.R. (2004). Sex differences in lexical size across semantic categories. *Personality and Individual Differences, 36*: 23–32.

Laws, K.R. (2005). Illusions of normality: A methodological critique of category specific naming. *Cortex, 41*: 842–851.

Lazarus, R.S., & Folkman, S. (1984). *Stress, Appraisal and Coping*. New York: Springer.

Leach, L.R., Frank, R.G., Bouman, D.E., & Farmer, J. (1994). Family functioning, social support and depression after traumatic brain injury. *Brain Injury, 8*: 599–606.

Lederach, J.P. (2003). *The Little Book of Conflict Transformation. Intercourse*. Intercourse, PA: Good Books.

Lefebvre, H., & Levert, M.J. (2006). Breaking the news of traumatic brain injury and incapacities. *Brain Injury, 20*: 711–718.

Lefebvre, H., Pelchat, D., & Levert, M.J. (2007). Interdisciplinary family intervention program: A partnership among health professionals, traumatic brain injury patients and caregiving relatives. *Journal of Trauma Nursing, 14*: 100–113.

Lefebvre, H., Pelchat, D., Swaine, B., Gelinas, I., & Levert, M.J. (2005). The experiences of people with a traumatic brain injury, familes, physicians and health care professionals regarding care provided throughout the continuum. *Brain Injury, 19*: 585–597.

Leff, J.L., Vearnals, S., Wolfe, G., & Alexander, B. (2000). The London Depression Intervention Trial: Randomised controlled trial of antidepressants vs couple therapy in the treatment and maintenance of people with depression living with a partner: clinical outcome and costs. *British Journal of Psychiatry, 177*: 95–100.

Lemmens,G.M.D.,Eisler,I.,Migerode,L.,Heireman,M.,&Demyttenaere,K. (2007). Family discussion group therapy for major depression: A brief systemic multi-family group intervention for hospitalized patients and their family members. *Journal of Family Therapy, 29*: 49–68.

Levack, W.M.M., Siegert, R.J., Dean, S.G., & McPherson, K.M. (2009). Goal planning for adults with acquired brain injury—how clinicians talk about involving family. *Brain Injury, 23*: 192–202.

Levine, B., Robertson, I.H., Clare, L., Carter, G., Hong, J., & Wilson, B.A. (2000). Rehabilitation of executive functioning: An experimental-clinical validation of goal management training. *Journal of International Neuropsychological Society, 6*: 299–312.

Levine, J., & Zigler, E. (1975). Denial and self-image in stroke, lung cancer and heart disease patients. *Journal of Consulting and Clinical Psychology, 43*: 751–757.

Lewis, L. (1989). Individual psychotherapy with patients having combined psychological and neurological disorders. *Bulletin of the Menninger Clinic, 50*: 75–87.

Lewis, L. (1991). Role of psychological factors in disordered awareness. In G.P. Prigatano & D.L. Schacter (Eds.), *Awareness of Deficit After Brain Injury: Clinical and Theoretical Issues* (pp. 223–239). New York: Oxford University Press.

Lewis, L. (1999). Transference and counter-transference in psychotherapy with adults having traumatic brain injury. In K.G. Langer, L. Laatsch, & L. Lewis (Eds.), *Psychotherapeutic Interventions for Adults with Brain Injury or Stroke: A Clinician's Treatment Resource* (pp. 113–130). Madison, CT: Psychological Press.

Lewis, K., & Karen, G. (1990). Siblings: A hidden resource in therapy. *Journal of Strategic and Systemic Therapies, 9*: 39–49.

Lewis, L., & Rosenberg, S.J. (1990). Psychoanalytical psychotherapy with brain-injured adult psychiatric patients. *Journal of Nervous & Mental Disease, 176*: 69–77.

Lezak, M.D. (1978). Living with the characterologically altered brain injured patient. *Journal of Clinical Psychiatry, 39*: 592–598.

Lezak, M.D. (1986). Psychological implications of traumatic brain damage for the patient's family. *Rehabilitation Psychology, 31*: 241–250.

Lezak, M.D. (1988). Brain damage is a family affair. *Journal of Clinical and Experimental Neuropsychology, 10*: 111–123.

Lezak, M.D. (1995). Family perceptions and family reactions: Reconsidering 'denial'. In H.S. Levin, A.L. Benton, J.P. Muizelaar, & H.M. Eisenberg, (Eds.), *Catastrophic Brain Injury* (pp. 175–181). New York, NY: Oxford University Press.

Livingston, M.G., & Brooks, D.N. (1988). The burden on families of the brain injured: A review. *Journal of Head Trauma Rehabilitation, 3*: 6–15.

Llewellyn, C.D., McGurk, M., & Weinman, J. (2005). Striking the right balance: A qualitative pilot study examining the role of information on the development of expectations in patients treated for head and neck cancer. *Psychology, Health & Medicine, 10*: 180–193.

Luria, A.R. (1961). *The Role of Speech in the Regulation of Normal and Abnormal Behaviour.* Oxford: Liveright.

Luria, A.R. (1968). The directive function of speech in development and dissolution. I: Development of the directive function of speech in childhood. II: Dissolution of the regulative functions of speech in pathology of the brain. In E. Millar (Ed.), *Foundations of Child Psychiatry* (pp. 273–282, 282–284). Oxford & New York: Pergamon Press.

Luria, A.R. (1976). *Cognitive Development: Its Cultural and Social foundations.* Oxford: Oxford: University Press.

Madanes, C. (1981). *Strategic Family Therapy.* Jossey-Bass.

Maegele, M., Engel, D., Bouillon, B., Lefering, R., Fach, H., Raum, M. et al. (2007). Incidence and outcome of traumatic brain injury in an urban area in Western Europe over 10 years. *European Surgical Research, 39*: 372–379.

Maia, T.V., & McClelland, J.L. (2004). A reexamination of the evidence for the somatic marker hypothesis: What participants really known in the Iowa Gambling Task. *Proceeding of the National Academy for Science USA, 101*, 16075–16080.

Maitz, E.A., & Sachs, P.R. (1995). Treating families of individuals with traumatic brain injury from a family systems perspective. *Journal of Head Trauma Rehabilitation, 10*: 1–11.

Malec, J., Brown, A.W., Leibson, C.L., Flaada, J.T., Mandrekar, J.N., Diehl, N.N., & Perkins, P.K. (2007). The Mayo classification system for traumatic brain injury severity. *Journal of Neurotrauma, 24*: 1417–1424.

Malec, J.F., Brown, A.W., & Moessner, A.M. (2004). Personality factors and injury severity in the prediction of early and late traumatic brain injury outcomes. *Rehabilitation Psychology, 49*: 55–61.

Malec, J.F., Machulda, M.M., & Moessner, A.M. (1997). Differing problem perceptions of staff, survivors and significant others after brain injury. *Journal of Head Trauma Rehabilitation, 12(3)*: 1–13.

Malia, K. (1997). Insight after brain injury: What does it mean? *The Journal of Cognitive Rehabilitation, 10*: 10–16.

Man, D.W.K. (2002). Family caregivers' reactions and coping for persons with brain injury. *Brain Injury, 16*: 1025–1037.

Marcel, A.J., Tegnér, R., & Nimmo-Smith, I. (2004). Anosognosia for plegia: Specificity, extension, partiality and disunity of bodily unawareness. *Cortex, 20*: 19–40.

Marsh, N.V., & Martinovich, W.M. (2006). Executive dysfunction and domestic violence. *Brain Injury, 20*: 61–66.

Martin, R., & MacDonald, S. (2003). Weak coherence, no theory of mind, or executive dysfunction? Solving the puzzle of pragmatic language disorders. *Brain and Language, 85*: 451–466.

Mason, B. (1993). Towards positions of safe uncertainty. *Human Systems, 4*: 189–200.

Mason, B. (2005) Relational risk taking and the therapeutic relationship. In C. Flaskas, B. Mason, & A. Perlesz, (Eds.), *The Space Between: Experience, Context and Process in the Therapeutic Relationship.* London: Karnac.

Masters, W.H., & Johnson, V.E. (1976). Principles of the new sex therapy. *American Journal of Psychiatry, 133*: 548–554.

Maurer, J. (1991). Special issues for a sibling. In J.M. Williams & T. Kay (Eds.), *Head Injury: A Family Matter.* Toronto: Paul H. Brookes Publishing.

Mauss, N., & Ryan, M. (1981). Brain injury and the family. *Journal of Neurosurgical Nursing, 13*: 165–169.

Max, J.E., Castillo, C.S., Robin, D.A., Lindgren, S.D., Smith, W.L.J., Sato, Y., et al. (1998). Predictors of family functioning after traumatic brain injury in children and adolescents. *Journal of the American Academy of Child & Adolescent Psychiatry, 37*: 83–90.

Mazaux, J.M., Masson, F., Levin, H.S., Alaoui, P., Maurette, P., & Barat, M. (1997). Long-term neuropsychological outcome and loss of social autonomy after traumatic brain injury. *Archives of Physical Medicine and Rehabilitation, 78*: 1316–1320.

Mazzucchi, A., Cattelani R., Cavatorta, S., Parma, M., Veneri, A., et al. (2000). Traumatic brain injury rehabilitation as an integrated task of clinicians and families: Local and national experiences. In A.L. Christensen & B. Uzzell (Eds.), *International Handbook of Neuropsychological Rehabilitation* (pp. 299–314). Dordrecht, Netherlands: Kluwer Academic.

McDonald, S. (2000). Putting communication disorders in context after traumatic brain injury. *Aphasiology, 14*: 339–347.

McDonald, S. (2004). Who Am I Now? BBC Four StoryVille television production by Shena McDonald.

McDonald, S., Bornhofen, C., & Hunt, C. (2009). Addressing deficits in emotion recognition after severe traumatic brain injury: The role of focussed attention and mimicry. *Neuropsychological Rehabilitation, 19*: 321–329.

McDonald, S., & Flanagan, J. (2004). Social perception deficits after traumatic brain injury: Interaction between emotion recognition, mentalising ability and social communication. *Neuropsychology, 3*: 572–579.

McDonald, S., & Saunders, J.C. (2005). Differential impairment in recognition of emotion across different media in people with severe traumatic brain injury. *Journal of the International Neuropsychological Society, 11*: 392–399.

McDonald, S., Tate, R., Togher, L., Bornhofen, C., Long, E., Gertler, P., & Bowen, R. (2008). Social skills treatment for people with severe, chronic acquired brain injuries: A multicenter trial. *Archives of Physical Medicine & Rehabilitation, 89*: 1648–1659.

McGlynn, S.M., & Kaszniak, A.W. (1991). Unawareness of deficits in dementia and schizophrenia. In G.P. Prigatano & D.L. Schacter (Eds.), Awareness of deficit after brain injury: Clinical and theoretical issues (pp. 84–110). New York: Oxford University Press.

McGlynn, A.M., & Schacter, D.L. (1989). Unawareness of deficits in neuropsychological syndromes. *Journal of Clinical and Experimental Neuropsychology, 11*: 143–205.

McGlynn, S.M., Schacter, D.L., & Glisky, E.L. (1989). Unpublished observations.

McGoldrick, M., Gerson, R., & Petry, S. (2008). Tracking individuals and families through the life cycle. In M. McGoldrick, R. Gerson, & S. Petry (Eds.), *Genograms: Assessment and Intervention* (3rd ed., pp. 189–224). New York: Norton.

McGrath, J. (1997). Cognitive impairment associated with post-traumatic stress disorder and minor head injury: A case report. *Neuropsychological Rehabilitation, 7(3)*, 231–239.

McGrath, J. (2004). Beyond restoration to transformation: Positive outcomes in the rehabilitation of acquired brain injury. *Clinical Rehabilitation.*

McGrath, J., & King, N. (2004). Acquired Brain Injury. In J. Bennett-Levy, G. Butler, M. Fennell, A. Hackman, M. Mueller, & D. Westbrook (Eds.), *Oxford Guide to behavioural experiments in Cognitive Therapy* (pp. 331–350). New York: Oxford University Press.

McGrath, J.C., & Linley, P.A. (2006). Post-traumatic growth in acquired brain injury: A preliminary small-scale study. *Brain injury, 20*: 767–773.

McHale, S.M., & Gamble, W.C. (1989). Sibling relationships of children disabled and nondisabled brothers and sisters. *Developmental Psychology, 25*: 14–29.

McKinlay, W.W., Brooks, D.N., Bond, M.R., Martinage, D.P., & Marshall, M.M. (1981). The short-term outcome of severe blunt head injury as reported by relatives of the injured persons. *Journal of Neurology, Neurosurgery & Psychiatry, 44*: 527–533.

McNeill, D.E., Schuyler, B.A., & Ezrachi, O. (1997). Assessing family involvement in traumatic brain injury rehabilitation: The development of a new instrument. *Archives of Clinical Neuropsychology, 12*: 645–660.

Meeter, M., & Murre, J.M.J. (2004). Consolidation of long-term memory: Evidence and alternatives. *Psychological Bulletin, 130*: 843–857.

Mesulam, M.M. (1981). A cortical network for directed attention and unilateral neglect. *Annals of Neurology, 10*: 309–325.

Miesen, B. (1992). Attachment theory and dementia. In G. Jones & B. Miesen (Eds.), *Care-Giving in Dementia.* (Vol. 1, pp. 38–56). London: Routledge.

Miesen, B. (1993). Alzheimer's disease, the phenomenon of parent fixation and Bowlby's attachment theory. *International Journal of Geriatric Psychiatry, 8*: 147–153.

Miesen, B. (1999). *Dementia in Close-Up. Understanding and Caring for People with Dementia.* London & New York: Routledge.

Miesen, B., & Jones, G. (1997). Psychic pain resurfacing in dementia. From new to past trauma? In L. Hunt, M. Marshall, & C. Rowlings (Eds.), *Past Trauma in Late Life. European Perspectives on Therapeutic Work with Older People* (pp. 142–154). London: Jessica Kingsley.

Milders, M., Fuchs, S., & Crawford, J.R. (2003). Neuropsychological impairments and change in emotional and social behaviour following severe traumatic brain injury. *Journal of Clinical and Experimental Neuropsychology, 25*: 157–172.

Milders, M., Letswaart, M., Crawford, J.R., & Currie, D. (2008). Social behaviour following traumatic brain injury and its association with emotion recognition, understanding of intentions and cognitive flexibility. *Journal of the International Neuropsychological Society, 14*: 318–326.

Miller, S.M., McDaniel, S.H., Rolland, J.S., & Feetham, S.L. (2006). *Individuals, Families, and the New Era of Genetics: Biopsychosocial Perspectives*. London: W.W. Norton & Company.

Milner, A., & Goodale, M.A. (1995). *The Visual Brain in Action*. Oxford: Oxford University Press.

Minuchin, S. (1974). *Families and Family Therapy*. Harvard: Harvard University Press.

Minuchin, S., & Fishman, H.C. (1981). *Family Therapy Techniques*. Cambridge, MA: Harvard University Press.

Mitchell, C. (2003). Problem-solving exercises and theories of conflict resolution. In D. Sandole & H. van der Merwe (Eds.), *Conflict Resolution Theory and Practice: Integration and Application*. Manchester: Manchester University Press.

Monahan, K., & O'Leary, D. (1999). Head injury and battered women: An initial inquiry. *Health and Social Work, 24*: 269–278.

Moore, A.D., Stambrook, M., & Peters, L.C. (1989). Coping strategies and adjustment after closed head injury: A cluster analytical approach. *Brain Injury, 3*: 171–175.

Moore, A., Stanbrook, M., & Peters, L. (1993). Centripetal and centrifugal family life cycle factors in long-term outcome following traumatic brain injury. *Brain Injury, 7(3)*: 247–255.

Moos, R.H., & Moos, B.S. (1976). A typology of family social environments. *Family Process, 15*: 357–372.

Morgan, M. (1995). Projective gridlock: A form of projective identification in couples relationships. In S. Ruszczynski & J.V. Fisher (Eds.), *Intrusiveness and Intimacy in the Couple* (pp. 33–48). London: Karnac.

Morin, C. (2004). *'Daughter-Somatoparaphrenia' in Women with Right Hemisphere Syndrome: A Psychoanalytical Perspective of Neurological Body Knowledge Disorders*. Paper presented at the 4th International Neuropsychoanalysis Congress, Rome, Italy.

Morin, C., Thibierge, S., Bruguiere, P., Pradat-Diehl, P., & Mazavet, D. (2005). "Daughtersomatoparaphrenia" in women with right hemisphere syndrome: A psychoanalytic perspective on neurological body knowledge disorders. *Neuropsychoanalysis, 7*: 171–184.

Moritz, S., & Woodward, T.S. (2007). Metacognitive training in schizophrenia: From basic research to knowledge translation and intervention. *Current Opinion in Psychiatry, 20(6)*: 619–625.

Morris, K.C. (2001). Psychological distress in carers of head injured individuals: The provision of written information. *Brain Injury, 15*: 239–254.

Morris, P., Prior, L., Deb, S., Lewis, G., Mayle, W., Burrow, C., et al. (2005). Patients' views on outcome following head injury: A qualitative study. *BMC Family Practice, 6*: 30.

Morris, R.G., Pullen, E., Kerr, S., Bullock, P.R., & Selway, R.P. (2006). Exploration of social rule violation in patients with focal prefrontal neurosurgical lesions. *Proceedings of the 6th International Conference of Disability, Virtual Reality & Associated Technology, Esbjerg, Denmark.*

Moss, B., Parr, S., Byng, S., & Petheram, B. (2004). 'Pick me up and not a down down, up up': How are the identities of people with aphasia represented in aphasia, stroke and disability websites. *Disability and Society, 19*: 753–768.

Moss, A.D., & Turnbull, O.H. (1996). Hatred of the hemiparetic limbs (misoplegia) in a 10 year-old child. *Journal of Neurology, Neurosurgery & Psychiatry, 61*: 210–211.

Moules, N.J. (2003). Therapy on paper: Therapeutic letters and the tone of relationship. *Journal of Systemic Therapies, 22*: 33–49.

Moules, S., & Chandler, B.J. (1999). A study of the health and social needs of carers of traumatically brain injured individuals served by one community rehabilitation team. *Brain Injury, 13*: 983–993.

Muir, C., Rosenthal, M., & Diehl, L. (1990). Methods of family intervention. In M. Rosenthal, E.R. Griffen, & J.D. Miller (Eds.), *Rehabilitation of the Adult and Child with Traumatic Brain Injury* (2nd ed., pp. 433–448). Philadelphia: F.A. Davis Company.

Murray, C. & Yeates, G.N. (in preparation). Metacognition after acquired brain injury: In the head or the conversation?

Murre, J.M.J. (1996). A model of amnesia and consolidation of memory. *Hippocampus, 6*: 675–684.

Murre, J.M.J., Graham, K.S., & Hodges, J.R. (2001). Semantic dementia: New constraints on connectionist models of long-term memory. *Brain, 124*: 647–675.

Myerhoff, B. (1982). Life history among the elderly: Performance, visibility and remembering. In J. Ruby (Ed.), *A Crack in the Mirror: Reflexive Perspectives in Anthropology.* Philadelphia: University of Philadelphia Press.

Nabors, N., Seacat, J., & Rosenthal, M. (2002). Predictors of caregiver burden following traumatic brain injury. *Brain Injury, 16*: 1039–1050.

Nadel, M., & Moscovitch, M. (1997). Memory consolidation, retrograde amnesia and the hippocampal cortex. *Cognitive Neuroscience, 7*: 217–227.

Neely, A.S., Vikström, S., & Josephsson, S. (2009). Collaborative memory intervention in dementia: Caregiver participation matters. *Neuropsychological Rehabilitation, 19(5)*: 696–715.

Newnes, C. (2006). Reflecting on recovery after head injury. *Clinical Psychology Forum, 159*: 45–49.

Nochi, M. (1997). Dealing with the 'void': Traumatic brain injury as a story. *Disability and Society, 12(4)*: 533–555.

Nochi, M. (1998a). Struggling with the labelled self: People with traumatic brain injuries in social settings. *Qualitative Health Research, 8(5)*: 665–681.

Nochi, M. (1998b). "Loss of self" in the narratives of people with traumatic brain injuries: A qualitative analysis. *Dissertation Abstracts International: Section B: The Sciences & Engineering, 58(12-B): 6871.*

Nochi, M. (2000). Reconstructing self-narratives in coping with traumatic brain injury. *Social Science and Medicine, 51*: 1795–1804.

Nodell, S. (1990). The forgotten feeling, fears and family: Sibling issues from a parent's perspective. *Cognitive Rehabilitation, 8*: 6–7.

Nolan, M., & Lundh, U. (1999). Satisfactions and coping strategies of family carers. *British Journal of Community Nursing, 4*: 470–475.

Novack, T.A., Bergquist, T.F., Bennett, G., & Gouvier, W.D. (1991). Primary caregiver distress following severe head injury. *Journal of Head Trauma Rehabilitation, 6*: 69–77.

Nybo, T., Sainio, M., & Müller, K. (2004). Stability of vocational outcome in adulthood after moderate to severe preschool brain injury. *Journal of the International Neuropsychological Society, 10*: 719–723.

Obonsawin, M., Jefferis, S., Lowe, R.A., Crawford, J.R., Fernandes, J., Holland, L.M., Woldt, K.E., Worthington, E. & Bowie, G. (2007). A model of personality change after traumatic brain injury and the development of the Brain Injury Personality Scales (BIPS). *Journal of Neurology, Neurosurgery & Psychiatry, 78*: 239–1247.

O'Connor, C., Manly, T., Robertson, I.H., Hevenor, S.J., & Levine, B. (2004). An fMRI study of sustained attention with endogenous and exogenous engagement. *Brain & Cognition, 54*: 133–135.

Oddy, M. (1995). He's no longer the same person: How families adjust to personality change after head injury. Ion N.V.T. Chamberlain (Ed.), *Traumatic Brain Injury Rehabilitation* (pp. 197–180). London: Chapman and Hall.

Oddy, M. (2001). Sexual relationships following brain injury. *Sexual Relationship Therapy, 16*: 247–259.

Oddy, M., Coughlan, T., Tyerman, A., & Jenkins, D. (1985) Social adjustment after closed head injury: A further follow-up seven years after injury. *Journal of Neurology, Neurosurgery & Psychiatry, 48*: 564–568.

Oddy, M., & Herbert, C. (2003). Interventions with families following brain injury: Evidence based practice. *Neuropsychological Rehabilitation, 3*: 259–273.

Oddy, M., & Humphrey, M. (1980). Social recovery during the year following severe head injury. *Journal of Neurology Neurosurgery & Psychiatry*, *43(9)*: 798–802.

Oddy, M., Humphrey, M., & Uttley, D. (1978). Stresses upon the relatives of head-injured patients. *British Journal of Psychiatry*, *133*: 507–513.

Odent, M. (2001). *The Scientification of Love (Second Edition)*. London: Free Association Books.

O'Hanlon, S., & Bertolino, B. (1999). *Evolving Possibilities: Selected Papers of Bill O'Hanlon*. London: Brunner/Mazel.

O'Hara, C., Goldfine, J., Ambrose, S., Hardgrove, H., Costello, R., O'Brien, D., et al. (1991). Meeting the needs of siblings and children of traumatic brain injury survivors. *Cognitive Rehabilitation*, 8–14.

Olson, D., Sprenkle, D., & Russell, D. (1979). Circumplex model of marriage and family systems I. Cohesion and adaptability dimensions, family types and clinical applications. *Family Process*, *18*: 3–28.

Orsillo, S.M., McCafney, R.J., & Fisher, J.M. (1993). Siblings of head-injured individuals: A population at risk. *Journal of Head Trauma Rehabilitation*, *8*: 102–115.

Owen, A. (2008). Using neuroimaging to detect awareness in disorders of consciousness. *Functional Neurology*, *23*: 189–194.

Ownsworth, T.L. (2005). The impact of defensive denial upon adjustment following traumatic brain injury. *Neuro-Psychoanalysis*, *7(1)*: 83–94.

Ownsworth, T., Clare, L., & Morris, R. (2006). An integrated biopsychosocial approach to understanding awareness deficits in Alzheimer's disease and brain injury. *Neuropsychological Rehabilitation*.

Ownsworth, T., & Fleming, J. (2005). The relative importance of metacognitive skills, emotional status, and executive function in psychosocial adjustment following acquired brain injury. *Journal of Head Trauma Rehabilitation*, *20(4)*: 315–332.

Ownsworth, T.L., McFarland, K., & Young, R. (2002). The investigation of factors underlying deficits in self-awareness and self regulation. *Brain Injury*, *16(4)*: 291–309.

Padrone, F.J. (1999). Psychotherapeutic issues in treating family members. In K.G. Langer, L. Laatsch, & L. Lewis (Eds.), *Psychotherapeutic Interventions for Adults with Brain Injury or Stroke: A Clinician's Treatment Resource* (pp. 191–209). Madison, CT: Psychosocial Press.

Palazzoli, M.S., Boscolo, L., Cecchin, G., & Prata, G. (1978). *Paradox and Counterparadox: A New Model in the Therapy of the Family in Schizophrenic Transaction*. London: Jason Aronson.

Palazzoli, M.S., Boscolo, L., Cecchin, G., & Prata, G. (1980). "Hypothesizing-cicularity neutrality: Three guidelines for the conductor of the session." *Family Process*, *19*: 3–12.

Palmer, S. (2005). *Understanding and Coping: An Exploration of the Family's Experience of Services and Health-Care Professionals When Someone in the Family Suffers a Brain Injury.* Doctoral Thesis University of Surrey.

Palmer, S. (2006). Understanding and coping: Family members' experience of rehabilitation services. *Brain Impairment, 7(2),* 162.

Palmer, S., & Gracey, F. (2008). A journey through the dilemmas of family working. *Presented at 12th Annual Conference 'Innovations in Rehabilitation' at the HUH RNRU.*

Palmer, S., Herbert, C., & Vetere, A. What do families want? Hopes and expectations for working with professionals after acquired brain injury. *In preparation.*

Palmer, S., Psaila, K., & Yeates, G. (2009). Simon: Brain injury and the family—the inclusion of children, family members and wider systems in the rehabilitation process. In B.A. Wilson, F. Gracey, J. Evans, & A. Bateman (Eds.), *Neuropsychological Rehabilitation: Theory, Models, Therapy and Outcome.* Cambridge: Cambridge University Press (pp. 272–291).

Panksepp, J. (1998). *Affective Neuroscience: The Foundations of Human and Animal Emotions.* Oxford: Oxford University Press.

Panting, A. & Merry, P. (1972). The long-term rehabilitation of severe head injuries with particular reference to the need for social and medical support for the patient's family. *Rehabilitation, 38:* 33–37.

Park, N.W., Conrod, B., Rewilak, D., Kwon, C., Gao, F., & Black, S. (2001). Automatic activation of positive but not negative attitudes after traumatic brain injury. *Neuropsychologia, 39:* 7–24.

Parr, S., Watson, N., & Woods, B. (2006). Access, agency and normality. In A. Webster (Ed.), *Innovative Health Technologies: New Perspectives, Challenge and Change.* Palgrave Macmillan.

Patterson, B., & Scott-Findlay, S. (2002). Critical issues in interviewing people with traumatic brain injury. *Qualitative Health Research, 12:* 399–409.

Patten, S.B. (1991). Are the Brown and Harris "vulnerability factors" risk factors for depression? *Journal of Psychiatry and Neuroscience, 16:* 267–271.

Payne, M. (2006). *Narrative Therapy: An Introduction for Cunsellors.* (2nd ed.). London: Sage.

Pearce, W.B. (2007). *Making Social Worlds: A Communication Perspective.* London: Wiley-Blackwell.

Pearce, W.B., & Cronen, V.E. (1980). *Communication, Action, and Meaning: The Creation of Social realities.* New York: Praeger.

Pelletier, P.M., & Alfano, D.P. (2000). Depression, social support, and family coping following traumatic brain injury. *Brain and Cognition, 44:* 45–49.

Peretti, P.O., & Abderholden, P. (1995). Effect of imputed or implied loss of parental affection due to the brain-damaged child in the family on sibling rivalry. *The Indian Journal of Clinical Psychology, 22*: 23–26.

Perlesz, A., Kinsella, G., & Crowe, S. (1999). The impact of traumatic brain injury on the family: A critical review. *Rehabilitation Psychology, 44*: 6–35.

Perlesz, A., Kinsella, G., & Crowe, S. (2000). Psychological distress and family satisfaction following traumatic brain injury: Injured individuals and their primary, secondary, and tertiary carers. *Journal of Head Trauma Rehabilitation, 15*: 909–929.

Perlesz, A., & O'Loughlan, M. (1998). Changes in stress and burden in families seeking therapy following traumatic brain injury: A follow-up study. *International Journal of Rehabilitation Research, 21*: 339–354.

Perrett, D., Mistlin, A., Hietanen, J., Benson, P., Bevan, R., Thomas, S., et al. (1990). Social signals analysed at the single cell level: Someone is looking at me, something touched me, something moved! *International Journal of Comparative Psychology, 4*: 25–55.

Perrett, D., Smith, P., Potter, D., Mistlin, A., Head, A., Milner, A. & Jeeves, M.A. (1985). Visual cells in the temporal cortex sensitice to face view and gaze direction. *Proceeding of the Royal Society of London B, 223*: 293–317.

Pessar, L.F., Coad, M.L., Linn, R.T., & Willer, B.S. (1993). The effects of parental traumatic brain injury on the behaviour of parents and children. *Brain Injury, 7*: 231–240.

Peters, L.C. (1989). *Psychosocial Impact of Head Injury in Families: The Wife's Perspective.* ProQuest Information & Learning.

Peters, L.C., Stambrook, M., Moore, A.D., & Esses, L. (1990). Psychosocial sequelae of closed brain injury: Effects on the marital relationship. *Brain Injury, 4*(1): 39–47.

Peters, L.C., Stambrook, M., Moore, A.D., Zubek, E., Dubo, H., & Blumenschein, S. (1992). Differential effects of spinal cord injury and head injury on marital adjustment. *Brain Injury, 6*: 461–467.

Pettersen, L. (1991). Sensitivity to emotional cues and social behaviour in children and adolescents after head injury. *Perception and Motor Skills, 73*: 1139–1150.

Pinto, P.E. (2008). Impact of brain injury on caregiver outcomes and on family quality of life. *Dissertation Abstracts International Section A: Humanities and Social Sciences, 69*: 1285.

Ponsford, J. (2003). Sexual changes associated with traumatic brain injury. *Neuropsychological Rehabilitation, 13*: 275–289.

Ponsford, J., Olver, J., Ponsford, M., & Nelms, R. (2003). Long-term adjustment of families following traumatic brain injury where comprehensive rehabilitation has been provided. *Brain Injury,* *17*: 453.

Posner, M.I., & Peterson, S.E. (1990). The attention system of the human brain. *Annual Review of Neuroscience, 13*: 25–42.

Power, P.W., & Hershenson, D.B. (2003). Work adjustment and readjustment of persons with mid-career onset traumatic brain injury. *Brain Injury, 17*: 1021–1034.

Prentiss, D. (1999). *Paediatric Brain Injury and Families: The Parental Experience.* ProQuest Information & Learning.

Prigatano, G. (1986). *Neuropsychological Rehabilitation after Brain Injury.* Baltimore, MD: John Hopkins University Press.

Prigatano, G.P. (1991). Disturbances of self-awareness of deficit after traumatic brain injury III. In G.P. Prigatano & D.L. Schacter (Eds.), *Awareness of Deficit After Brain Injury: Clinical and Theoretical Issues* (pp. 111–126). New York: Oxford University Press.

Prigatano, G. (1999). *The Principals of Neuropsychological Rehabilitation.* New York: Oxford University Press.

Prigatano, G.P. (2002). Awareness of deficit and psychological interventions after brain injury. *Proceedings of the Third World Congress of Neurological Rehabilitation, Venice, Italy* (pp. 395–398).

Prigatano, G.P. (2005). Disturbances of self-awareness and rehabilitation of patients with traumatic brain injury: A 20-year perspective. *Journal of Head Trauma Rehabilitation*, 20(1): 19–29.

Prigatano, G.P., Altman, I.M., & O'Brien, K.P. (1990).Behavioral limitations that brain injured patients tend to underestimate. *Clinical Neuropsychologist*, 193–176.

Prigatano, G.P., Borgaro, S., Baker, J., & Wethe, J. Awareness and distress after traumatic brain injury: A relative's perspective. *Journal of Head Trauma Rehabilitation*, 20(4): 359–67.

Prigatano, G.P., & Fordyce, D.J. (1986). The neuropsychological rehabilitation program at Presbyterian Hospital. In G.P. Prigatano, D.J. Fordyce, H.K. Zeiner, J.R. Roueche, M. Pepping, & B.C. Wood (Eds.), *Neuropsychological Rehabilitation After Brain Injury* (pp. 96–118). Baltimore: John Hopkins University Press.

Prigatano, G., Fordyce, D., Zeiner, H. Roueche, J.S., Pepping, M., & Wood, B.C. (1984). Neuropsychological rehabilitation after closed head injury in young adults. *Journal of Neurology, Neurosurgery, and Psychiatry*, 47: 505–513.

Prigatano, G.P., & Johnson, S.C. (2003). The three vectors of consciousness and their disturbances after brain injury. *Neuropsychological Rehabilitation, 13(1–2)*: 13–29.

Prigatano, G., & Klonoff, P.S. (1998). A clinician's rating scale for evaluating impaired self-awareness and denial of disability after brain injury. *The Clinical Neuropsychologist, 12*: 56–67.

Prigatano, G.P., & Leathem, J.M. (1993). Awareness of behavioural limitations after traumatic brain injury: A cross cultural study of New Zealand Maoris and non-Maoris. *Clinical Neuropsychologist, 7(2)*: 123–135.

Prigatano, G., Ogano, M., & Amakusa, B. (1997). A cross-cultural study on impaired awareness in Japanese patients with brain dysfunction. *Neuropsychiatry, Neuropsychology, and Behavioural Neurology, 10*: 135–143.

Prigatano, G.P., & Weinstein, E.A. (1996). Edwin A. Weinstein's contribution to neuropsychological rehabilitation. *Neuropsychological Rehabilitation, 6(4)*: 305–326.

Proulx, G. (1999). Family education and family partnership in cognitive rehabilitation. In G. Winocur & D. Stuss (Eds.), *Cognitive Neurorehabilitation* (pp. 252–259). New York: Cambridge University Press.

Pullen, E., Morris, R.G., Kerr, S., Bullock, P.R., & Selway, R.P. (2006). Exploration of social rule violation in patients with focal prefrontal neurosurgical lesions using a virtual reality simulation. *International Journal of Disabilities and Human Development, 5*: 141–146.

Ramachandran, V.S. (1994). Phantom limbs, neglect syndromes, repressed memories and Freudian psychology. *International Review of Neurobiology, 27*: 291–333.

Ramachandran, V.S. (2004). Anosognosia: The interface between neurology, psychiatry and psychoanalysis. *Paper presented at the 5th International Neuropsychoanalysis Congress, Rome.*

Rath, J.F., Hennessey, J.J., & Diller, L. (2003). Social problem solving and community integration in postacute rehabilitation outpatients with traumatic brain injury. *Rehabilitation Psychology, 48*: 137–144.

Read, J. (2005). The bio-bio-bio model of madness. *The Psychologist, 18(10)*: 596–597.

Reisberg, B., Gordon, B., McCarthy, M., & Ferris, S.H. (1985). Clinical symptoms accompanying progressive cognitive decline and Alzheimer's disease. In V.L. Melnick & N.N. Duber (Eds.), *Alzheimer's Dementia*. Clifton: Humana Press.

Riley, G.A. (2007). Stress and depression in family carers following traumatic brain injury. Clinical Rehabilitation, 21: 82–88.

Rivera, P., Elliott, T., Berry, J., & Grant, J. (2008). Problem-solving training for family caregivers of persons with traumatic brain injuries: A randomized controlled trial. *Archives of Physical Medicine and Rehabilitation, 89*: 931–941.

Rivera, P., Elliott, T., Berry, J., Grant, J., & Oswald, K. (2007). Predictors of caregiver depression among community-residing families living with traumatic brain injury. *NeuroRehabilitation, 22*: 3–8.

Rivera, J.B., Jaff, K.M., Polissar, N.L., Fay, G.C., Liao, S., & Martin, K.M. (1996). Predictors of family functioning and change 3 years after traumatic brain injury in children. *Archives of Physical Medicine & Rehabilitation, 77*: 754–764.

Rizzolatti, G., Berti, A., & Gallese, V. (2000a). Spatial neglect: Neurophysiological bases, cortical circuits and theories. In F. Boller, J. Grafman, & G. Rizzolatti (Eds.), *Handbook of Neuropsychology, Vol. I* (pp. 503–537, 2nd ed.). Amsterdam: Elsevier.

Rizzolatti, G., Fabbri-Destro, M., & Cattaneo, L. (2009). Mirror neurons and their clinical relevance. *Natal Clinical Practice of Neurology, 5*: 24–34.

Rizzolatti, G., Fadiga, L., Galles, G., & Fogassi, L. (1996). Premotor cortex and the recognition of motor actions. *Cognitive Brain Research, 3*: 131–141.

Rizzolatti, G., & Matelli, M. (2003). Two different streams form the dorsal visual system: Anatomy and functions. *Experimental Brain Research, 153*: 146–157.

Robson, P. (1989). Development of a new self-report questionnaire to measure self-esteem. *Psychological Medicine, 19*: 513–518.

Robson, C. (2002). *Real World Research: A Resource for Social Scientists and Practioner-Researchers*. (2nd ed.). Oxford: Blackwell Publishing.

Robertson, I. (1996). *Goal Management Training: A Clinical Manual*. Cambridge, UK. PsyConsult.

Rode, G., Perenin, M.T., Honore, J., & Boisson, D. (1998). Improvement of the motor deficit of neglect patients through vestibular stimulation: Evidence for a motor neglect component. *Cortex, 34*: 253–261.

Roeckerath, K. (2002). Projective identification: A neuro-psychoanalytical perspective. *Neuropsychoanalysis, 4*: 177–186.

Rohling, M.L., Faust, M.E., Beverly, B., & Demakis, G. (2009). Effectiveness of cognitive rehabilitation following acquired brain injury: A meta-analytic re-examination of Cicerone et al.'s (2000, 2005) systematic reviews. *Neuropsychology, 23*: 20–39.

Rolland, J.S. (1990). Anticipatory loss: A family-systems developmental framework. *Family Process, 29*: 229–244.

Rolland, J.S. (1994). *Families, Illness, & Disability: An Integrative Treatment Model*. New York: Basic Books.

Rolland, J.S. (1999). Parental illness and disability: A family systems framework. *Journal of Family Therapy, 21*: 242–266.

Rolland, J.S., & Willians, J.K. (2005). Toward a biopsychosocial model for 21st century genetics. *Family Process, 44*: 3–24.

Rolland, J.S., & Williams, J.K. (2006). Toward a psychosocial model for the new era of genetics. In S.M. Miller, S.H. McDaniel, J.S. Rolland, & S.L. Feetham (Eds.), *Individuals, Families, and the New Era of Genetics: Biopsychosocial Perspectives* (pp. 36–78). London: W.W. Norton & Company.

Romano, M. (1974). Family response to traumatic head injury. *Journal of Rehabilitation Medicine, 6*: 1–4.

Rosenbaum, A., & Hoge, S.K. (1989). Head injury and marital aggression. *American Journal of Psychiatry, 146*: 1048–1051.

Rosenbaum, A., Hoge, S.K., Adelman, S.A., Warnken, W.J., Fletcher, K.E., & Kane, R.L.. (1994). Head injury in partner-abusive men. *Journal of Consulting and Clinical Psychology, 62*: 1187–1193.

Rosenbaum, M., & Najenson, T. (1976). Change in patterns and symptoms of low mood as reported by wives of severely brain-injured soldiers. *Journal of Consulting and Clinical Psychology, 44*: 881–888.

Rosenbaum, R.S., Priselac, S., Köhler, S., Black, S.E., Gao, F., Nadel, L., & Moscovitch, M. (2000). Remote spatial memory in an amnesic person with extensive bilateral hippocampal lesions. *Nature Neuroscience, 3(10)*: 1044–1048.

Rosenbaum, R.S., Winocur, G., & Moscovitch, M. (2001). New views on old memories: Re-evaluating the role of the hippocampal complex. *Behaviour Brain Research, 127*: 183–197.

Rosenfeld, H. (1964). On the psychopathology of narcissism: A clinical approach. *International Journal of Psycho-analysis, 45*: 169–179.

Rosenfeld, H. (1971). A clinical approach to the psycho-analytical theory of life and death instincts: the investigation into aggressive aspects of narcissism. *International Journal of Psycho-analysis, 52*: 169–178.

Rosenthal, M. (1983). Behavioural sequelae. In M. Rosenthal, E.R. Griffith, M.R. Bond, & J.D. Miller, (Eds.), *Rehabilitation of the Head Injured Adult* (pp. 197–207). Philadelphia: F.A. Davis.

Rotondi, A., Sinkule, J., & Spring, M. (2005). An interactive web-based intervention for persons with TBI and their families: Use and evaluation by female significant others. *Journal of Head Trauma Rehabilitation, 20*: 173–185.

Rowe, A., Bullock, P.R., Polkey, C.E., & Morris, R.G. (2001). 'Theory of mind' impairments and their relationship to executive functioning following frontal lobe excisions. *Brain, 124*: 600–616.

Royal College of Physicians (2008). *Neurological Long-Term Conditions: Management at the Interface Between Neurology, Rehabilitation and Palliative Care.* Accessed from http://www.bgs.org.uk/PDF%20 Downloads/rcp_long_term_neuro.pdf.

Ruszczynski, S. (1995). Narcissistic object relating. In S. Ruszczynski & J.V. Fisher (Eds.), *Intrusiveness and Intimacy in the Couple* (pp. 13–32). London: Karnac.

Ruszczynski, S., & Fisher, J.V. (1995). *Intrusiveness and Intimacy in the Couple*. London: Karnac.

Sabat, S.R., & Harre, R. (1992). The construction and deconstruction of self in Alzheimer's disease. *Ageing and Society, 12*: 443–461.

Safran, J.D., & Muran, J.C. (2000). Resolving therapeutic alliance ruptures: Diversity and integration. *Journal of Clinical Psychology, 56*: 233–243.

Sale, P., West, M., Sherron, P., & Wehman, P.H. (1991). Exploratory analysis of job separation from supported employment of persons with traumatic brain injury. *Journal of Head Trauma Rehabilitation,6*: 1–11.

Sander, A. (2005). Interventions for caregivers. In W. High, A. Sander, M. Struchen, & K.A. Hart (Eds.), *Rehabilitation for Traumatic Brain Injury* (pp. 156–175). Oxford: Oxford University Press.

Sander, A., Caroselli, J., High, W., Becker, C., Neese, L., & Scheibel, R. (2002). Relationship of family functioning to progress in a post-acute rehabilitation programme following traumatic brain injury. *Brain Injury, 16*: 649–657.

Sander, A., Hibbard, M.R., Hannay, H.J., & Sherer, M. (1997). Predictors of psychological health in caregivers of patients with closed head injury. *Brain Injury, 11*: 235–249.

Sander, A.M., High, W.J., Hannay, H.J., & Sherer, M. (1997). Predictors of psychological health in caregivers of patients with closed head injury. *Brain Injury, 11*: 235–250.

Sander, A.M., & Kreutzer, J. (1999). A holistic approach to family assessment after brain injury. In M. Rosenthal, E.R. Griffen, & J. Kreutzer (Eds.), *Rehabilitation of the Adult & Child with Traumatic Brain Injury* (pp. 199–215). Philadelphia: F.A. Davies.

Sander, A., Sherer, M., Malec, J., High, W., Thompson, R., & Moessner, A. (2003). Preinjury emotional and family functioning in caregivers of persons with traumatic brain injury. *Archives of Physical Medicine and Rehabilitation, 84*: 197–203.

Sarbin, T.R. (1986). *Narrative Psychology: The Storied Nature of Human Conduct*. New York: Chicago.

Saunders, J.C., McDonald, S., & Richardson, R. (2006). Loss of emotional experience after traumatic brain injury: Findings with the startle probe procedure. *Neuropsychology, 20*: 224–231.

Saver, J.L., & Damasio, A.R. (1991). Preserved access and processing of social knowledge in a patient with acquired sociopathy due to ventromedial frontal damage. *Neuropsychologia, 39*: 1241–1249.

Scharff, D.E., & Savege-Scharff, J.S. (1991). *Object Relations Family Therapy*. Lanham, MD: Jason Aronson.

Schnider, A. (2003). Spontaneous confabulation and the adaptation of thought to ongoing reality. *Nature Reviews Neuroscience, 4*: 671.

Schonberger, M., Humle, F., & Teasdale, T. (2006a). The development of the therapeutic working alliance, patients' awareness and their compliance during the process of brain injury rehabilitation. *Brain Injury, 20*: 445–454.

Schonberger, M., Hulme, F., & Teasdate, T.W. (2006b). Subjective outcome of brain injury rehabilitation in relation to the therapeutic working alliance, client compliance and awareness. *Brain Injury, 20*: 1271–1282.

Schore, A.N. (2002). Clinical implications of a psychoneurobiological model of projective identification. In S. Alhanadti (Ed.), *Primitive Mental States, Vol. lll: Pre- and Peri-Natal Influences on Personality Development* (pp. 58–107). New York: Karnac.

Schulte-Ruther, M., Markowitsch, H.J., Fink, G.R., & Piefke, M. (2007). Mirror neuron and theory of mind mechanisms involving face to face interactions: A functional magnetic resonance imaging approach to empathy. *Journal of Cognitive Neuroscience, 8*: 1354–1372.

Schwentor, D., & Brown, P. (1989). Assessment of families with a traumatically brain injured relative. *Cognitive Rehabilitation, 7*: 8–20.

Secrest, J., & Zeller, R. (2003). Measuring continuity and discontinuity following stroke. *Journal of Nursing Scholarship, 29*: 367.

Secrest, J., & Zeller, R. (2006). Replication and extension of the Continuity and Discontinuity of Self Scale (CDSS). *Journal of Nursing Scholarship, 38*: 154–158.

Seligman, M.E.P., & Csikszentmihalyi, M. (2000). Positive psychology: An introduction. *American Psychologist, 55*: 5–14.

Serio, C.D., Kreutzer, J.S., & Gervasio, A.H. (1995). Predicting family needs after brain injury: Implications for intervention. *Journal of Head Trauma Rehabilitation, 10*: 32–45.

Serio, C.D., Kreutzer, J.S., & Witol, A.D. (1997). Family needs after traumatic brain injury: A factor analytic study of the Family Needs Questionnaire. *Brain Injury, 11*: 1–9.

Serotin, Y.B., & Das, A. (2009). Anticipatory haemodynamic signals in sensory cortex not predicted by local neuronal activity. *Nature, 457*: 475–479.

Sexton, T., & Whiston, S. (1994). The status of the counselling relationship: an empirical review, theoretical implications and research directions. *The Counselling Psychologist, 22*: 6–78.

Shallice, T., & Burgess, P.W. (1996). The domain of the supervisory process and temporal organisation of behaviour. *Philosophical Transactions: Biological Sciences, 351*: 1405–1412.

Shamay-Tsoory, S., Tomer, R., Berger, B.D., & Aharon-Peretz, J. (2003). Characterisation of empathy deficits following prefrontal brain damage: The role of the right ventromedial prefrontal cortex. *Journal of Cognitive Neuroscience, 15*: 324–337.

Sheil, A., Horn, S., Wilson, B.A., McLellan, D.L., Watson, M., & Campbell, M. (2000). The Wessex Head Injury Matrix main scale: A preliminary report on a scale to assess and monitor patients recovery after severe head injury. *Clinical Rehabilitation, 14*: 408–416.

Sherer, M., Boake, C., Levin, E., Silver, B., Ringholz, G., & High, W. (1998). Characteristics of impaired awareness after traumatic brain injury. *Journal of the International Neuropsychological Society, 4(4)*: 380–387.

Simon, G.M. (2006). The heart of the matter: A proposal for placing the self of the therapist at the center of family therapy research and training. *Family Process, 45*: 331–344.

Simpson, G. (2001). Addressing the sexual concerns of persons with traumatic brain injury in rehabilitation settings: a framework for action. *Brain Impairment, 2*: 97–108.

Singer, G., Glang, A., Nixon, C., Cooley, E., Kerns, K., Williams, D., & Powers, L. (1994). A comparison of two psychosocial interventions for parents of children with acquired brain injury: An exploratory study. *Journal of Head Trauma Rehabilitation, 9*: 38–49.

Singer, T., Seymour, B., O'Doherty, J., Kaube, H., Dolan, R., & Frith, C.D. (2004). Empathy for pain involves the affective but not sensory components of pain. *Science, 303*: 1157–1162.

Sinnakaruppan, I., Downey, B., & Morrison, S. (2005). Head injury and family carers: A pilot study to investigate an innovative community-based educational programme for family carers and patients. *Brain Injury, 19*: 283–308.

Skinner, H., Steinhauer, P., & Santa-Barbara, J. (1984). *The Family Assessment Measure (3rd ed.).* New York: MultiHealth Systems.

Smith, J.A. (1996). Beyond the divide between cognition and discourse: Using interpretative phenomenological analysis in health psychology. *Psychology & Health, 11*: 261–271.

Smith, J.A, Flowers, P., and Larkin, M. (2009). *Interpretative Phenomenological Analysis: Theory, Method, Research.* London: Sage.

Smith, L.M., & Godfrey, H.P.D. (1995). *Family Support Programs and Rehabilitation: A Cognitive-Behavioural Approach to Traumatic Brain Injury.* London: Plenum Press.

Snowden, J.S., Griffiths, H.L., & Neary, D. (1996). Semantic-episodic memory interactions in semantic dementia: Implications for retrograde memory function. *Cognitive Neuropsychology, 13*: 1101–1139.

Social Services Inspectorate. (1997). *"A Hidden Disability": Report of the SSI Traumatic Brain Injury Rehabilitation Project*. Wetherby: Department of Health.

Söderström, S., Fogelsjöö, A., Fugl-Meyer, K.S., & Stensson, S. (1988). A program for crisis-intervention after traumatic brain injury. *Scandinavian Journal of Rehabilitation Medicine. Supplement, 17*: 47–49.

Sohlberg, M., Mateer, C., Penman, L., Ginny, A., & Todis, B. (1998). Awareness intervention: Who needs it? *Journal of Head Trauma Rehabilitation, 13(5)*: 62–78.

Sohlberg, M.M., McLaughlin, K.A., Pavese, A., Heidrich, A., & Posner, M.I. (2000). Evaluation of attention process training and brain injury education in persons with acquired brain injury. *Journal of Clinical and Experimental Neuropsychology, 22(5)*, 656–676

Sohlberg, M.M., McLaughlin, K.A., Todis, B., Larsen, J., & Glang, A. (2001). What does it take to collaborate with families affected by brain injury? A preliminary model. *Journal of Head Trauma Rehabilitation, 16*: 498–511.

Solomon, M., Goodlin-Jones, B.L., & Anders, T.F. (2004). A social adjustment enhancement intervention for high functioning utism, Asperger's syndrome, and pervasive developmental disorder NOS. *Journal of Autism and Developmental Disorders, 34*: 649–668.

Spanbock, P. (1992). Children and siblings of head injury survivors: A need to be understood. *Journal of Cognitive Rehabilitation, 14*: 8–9.

Spanier, G.B. (1976). Measuring dyadic adjustment: New Scales for assessing the quality of marriage and similar dyads. *Journal of Marriage and the Family, 38*: 15–28.

Spillius, E.B. (1994). Developments in Klenian thought: Overview and personal view. *Psychoanalytic Inquiry, 14*: 324–364.

Stebbins, P., & Pakenham, K. (2001). Irrational schematic beliefs and psychological distress in caregivers of people with traumatic brain injury. *Rehabilitation Psychology, 46*: 178–194.

Steel, R.T., Kreutzer, J.S., & Sander, A.M. (1997). Concordance of patient's and family member's ratings of neurobehavioural functioning after traumatic brain injury. *Archives of Physical Medicine & Rehabilitation, 78*: 1254–1259.

Stiell, K., Naaman, S.C., & Lee, A. (2007). Couples and chronic illness: An attachment perspective and emotionally-focused interventions. *Journal of Systemic Therapies, 26*: 59–74.

Stone, V., Baron-Cohen, S., & Knight, R. (1998). Frontal lobe contributions to theory of mind. *Journal of Cognitive Neuroscience, 10*: 640–656.

Stratton, P., Preston-Shoot, M., & Hanks, H. (1990). *Family Therapy: Training and Practice.* Birmingham: Venture.

Stuss, D. (2007). New approaches to prefrontal lobe testing. In B.L. Miller & J.L. Cummings (Eds.), *The Human Frontal Lobes: Functions and Disorders.* New York: The Guilford Press.

Stuss, D.T. (2007). Stroke and "executive dysfunction: Impact of the type and location of stroke. *Brain & Cognition, 63(2)*: 194.

Stuss, D.T., & Benson, D.F. (1986). *The Frontal Lobes.* New York: Raven Press.

Stuss, D., Gallup, G.G.J., & Alexander, M.P. (2001). The frontal lobes are necessary for 'theory of mind'. *Brain, 124*: 279–286.

Stuss, D.T., & Knight, R.T. (2002). *Principles of Frontal Lobe Function.* Oxford: Oxford University Press.

Sunderland, A., Harris, J.E., & Gleave, J. (1984). Memory failures in everyday life following severe head injury. *Journal of Clinical Neuropsychology, 6*: 127–142.

Swift, T.L., & Wilson, S.L. (2001). Misconceptions about brain injury among the general public and non-expert health professionals: An exploratory study. *Brain Injury, 15*: 149–165.

Szekeres, S.F., Ylvisaker, M., & Cohen, S.B. (1987). A framework for cognitive rehabilitation therapy. In M. Ylvisaker & E.M.R. Gobble (Eds.). *Community Re-entry for Head Injured Adults* (pp. 87–136). Boston, MA: Little Brown.

Tate, R. (2003). Impact of pre-injury factors on outcome after severe traumatic brain injury: Does post-traumatic personality change represent an exacerbation of premorbid traits? *Neuropsychological Réhabilitation, 13*: 43–64.

Tate, R.L. (1999). Executive dysfunction and characterological changes after traumatic brain injury: Two sides of the same coin? *Cortex, 35*: 39–55.

Tate, R.L., McDonald, S., & Lulham, J.M. (1998). Incidence of hospital-treated traumatic brain injury in an Australian community. *Australian and New Zealand Journal of Public Health, 22*: 419–423.

Taylor, G.H., Yeates, K.O., Wade, S.L., Drotar, D., Stancin, T., & Burant, C. (2001) Bidirectional child-family influences on outcomes of traumatic brain injury in children. *Journal of the International Neuropsychological Society, 7*: 755–767.

Teasdale, T.W., Christensen, A.L., Willmes, K., Deloche, G., Braga, L., Stachowiak, F., Vendrall, J.M., Alexandre, C.-C., Ritva, K.L., &

Leclercq, M. (1997). Subjective experience in brain-injured patients and their close relatives: A European Brain Injury Questionnaire study. *Brain Injury, 11*: 543–563.

Teasdale, T.W., Emslie, H. Quirk, K., Evans, J., Fish, J., & Wilson, B. (2009). Alleviation of carer strain during the use of the Neuropage device by people with acquired brain injury. *Journal of Neurology, Neurosurgery & Psychiatry, published online 25 February*.

Teasdale, G., & Jennett, B. (1974). Assessment of coma and impaired consciousness. A practical scale. *The Lancet, 2*: 81–84.

Testa, J., Malec, J., Moessner, A., & Brown, A. (2006). Predicting family functioning after TBI: Impact of neurobehavioral factors. *Journal of Head Trauma Rehabilitation, 21*: 236–247.

The Royal College of Physicians and British Society for Rehabilitation Medicine. (2003). *Rehabilitation Following Acquired Brain Injury: National Clinical Guidelines*. London: RCP, BSRM.

The Royal College of Physicians, N.C.f.P.C.a.B.S.o.R.M. (2008). *Long-Term Neurological Conditions: Management at the Interface between Neurology, Rehabilitation and Palliative Care. National Guidelines, March 2008. Accessed November 21, 2009, from http://www.bgs.org.uk/ PDF%20Downloads/rcp_long_term_neuro.pdf*.

Thomsen, I.V. (1974). The patient with severe head injury and his family. *Scandinavian Journal of Rehabilitation Medicine, 6*: 180–183.

Thomsen, I.V. (1984). Late outcome of very severe blunt head trauma: A 10–15 year second follow-up. *Journal of Neurology, Neurosurgery & Psychiatry, 47*: 260–268.

Thomsen, I.V. (1992). Late psychosocial outcome in severe traumatic brain injury. Preliminary results of a third follow-up study after 20 years. *Scandinavian Journal of Rehabilitation Medicine, 26*: 142–152.

Togher, L., McDonald, S., Tate, R., Power, E., & Rietdijk, R. (2009). Training communication partners of people with traumatic brain injury:Reporting the protocol for a clinical trial. *Brain Impairment, 10*: 188–204.

Toglia, J., & Kirk, U. (2000). Understanding awareness deficits following brain injury. *Neurorehabilitation, 15*: 57–70.

Tomm, K. (1987). Interventive interviewing: Part II. Reflexive questioning as a means to enable self-healing. *Family Process, 26*: 167–183.

Tomm, K. (1988). Inventive Interviewing: III. Intending to ask, circular, strategic or reflexive questions? *Family Process, 27*: 1–15.

Trahan, E., Pepin, M., & Hopps, S. (2006). Impaired awareness of deficits and treatment adherence among people with traumatic brain injury or spinal cord injury. *Journal of Head Trauma Rehabilitation, 21*: 226–235.

Trudel, T.M., Tryon, W.W. & Purdum, C.M. (1998). Awareness of disability and long-term outcome after traumatic brain injury. *Rehabilitation Psychology, 43*: 26–281.

Turnbull, O. (2002). Implicit awareness of deficit in anosognosia? An emotion-based account of denial of deficit. *Neuro-Psychoanalysis, 4(1)*: 69–87.

Turnbull, O. (2004). *Personal Communication*.

Turnbull, O., Evans, C.E.Y., & Owen, V. (2005). Negative emotions and anosagnosia. *Cortex, 41*: 67–75.

Turnball, O.H., & Laws, K.R. (2000). Loss of stored knowledge of object structure: implications for category specific deficits. *Cognitive Neuropsychology, 17*: 365–389.

Turner-Stokes, L. (1999). The effectiveness of rehabilitation: A critical review of the evidence. *Clinical Rehabilitation, 13*: 3–6.

Turner-Stokes, L., Nair, A., Disler, P., & Wade, D. (2005). *Cochrane Review: Multi-Disciplinary Rehabilitation for Acquired Brain Injury in Adults of Working Age*. (Vols. 3) Oxford: Update Software.

Turner, S.A., & Street, H.P. (1999). Assessing carers' training needs: A pilot inquiry. *Aging & Mental Health, 3*: 173–178.

Tyerman, A. (1999). Outcome measurement in a community head injury service. *Neuropsychological Rehabilitation, 9*: 481–491.

Tyerman, A., & Booth, J. (2001). Family interventions after brain injury: A service example. *NeuroRehabilitation, 16*: 59–66.

Tyerman, A., & Humphrey, M. (1984). Changes in self-concept following severe head injury. *International Journal of Rehabilitation Research, 7*: 11–23.

Tyerman, A., & King, N. (2008). *Psychological Approaches to Rehabilitation after Traumatic Brain Injury*. Oxford: Blackwell.

Tyerman, A., Tyerman, R., & Viney, P. (2008). Vocational Rehabilitation Programmes. In A. Tyerman & N. King (Eds.), *Psychological Approaches to Rehabilitation after Traumatic Brain Injury* (pp. 376–402). Oxford: Blackwell.

Ungerleider, L., & Mishkin, M. (1982). Two cortical visual systems. In D.J. Ingle, R.J.W. Mansfield, & M.S. oodale (Eds.), *The Analysis of Visual Behaviour*. (pp. 549–586). Cambridge, MA: MIT Press.

Vanderploeg, R.D., Curtiss, G., Duchnick, G.C., & Luis, C.A. (2003). Demographic, medical, and psychiatric factors in work and marital status after mild head injury. *Journal of Head Trauma Rehabilitation, 18*: 148–163.

Vecera, S.P., & Rizzo, M. (2006). Eye gaze does not produce reflexive shifts if visual attention: Evidence from frontal lobe damage. *Neuropsychologia, 44*: 150–159.

Verhaeghe, S., Defloor, T., & Grypdonck, M. (2005). Stress and coping among families of patients with traumatic brain injury: a review of the literature. *Journal of Clinical Nursing, 14*: 1004–1012.

Vetere, A., & Cooper, J. (2001). Working systemically with family violence: Risk, responsibility and collaboration. *Journal of Family Therapy, 23*: 378–396.

Vetere, A., & Cooper, J. (2003). Masculinity and mens violence: A systemic response. *Context, 69*: 9–10.

Vetere, A. (2007). Dynamic systems: Couples, emotions and attachments. Presented at the 'working with couples after brain injury' Oliver Zangwill Centre workshop.

Vetere, A., & Dallos, R. (2003). *Working Systemically with Families: Formulation, Intervention and Evaluation*. London: Karnac.

Vetere, A. & Dallos, R. (2009). *Systemic Therapy and Attachment Narratives: Applications in a Range of Clinical Settings*. Sussex: Taylor & Francis.

Villki, J., Ahola, K., Holst, P., Ohman, J., Servo, A., & Heiskanen, O. (1994). Prediction of psychosocial recovery after head injury with cognitive test and neurobehavioural ratings. *Journal of Clinical Experimental Neuropsychology, 16*: 325–338.

Viskontas, I.V., McAndrews, M.P., & Moscovitch, M. (2000). Remote Episodic Memory Deficits in Patients with Unilateral Temporal Lobe Epilepsy and Excisions. *Journal of Neuroscience, 20*: 5853–5857.

von Cramon, D., Matthes-von Cramon, G., & Mai, N. (1991). Problem solving deficits in brain injured patients: A therapeutic approach. *Neuropsychological Rehabilitation, 1*: 45–64.

Von Foerster, H. (1982). *Observing Systems*. Seaside, CA: Intersystems Publications.

Vuilleumier, P. (2004). Anosognosia: The neurology of beliefs and uncertainties. *Cortex, 40*: 9–17.

Vuilleumier, P., Chicherio, C., Assal, F., Schwartz, S., Slosman, D., & Landis, T. (2001). Functional neuroanatomical correlates of hysterical sensorimotor loss. *Brain, 124*: 1077–1090.

Vulliamy, E. (2007). Waking the dead. *The Observer Magazine*, pp. 23–33.

Waaland, P.K., & Kreutzer, J.S. (1998). Family response to childhood traumatic brain injury. *Journal of Head Trauma Rehabilitation, 3*: 51–63.

Wachter, J.F., Fawber, H.L., & Scott, M.B. (1987). Treatment aspects of vocational evaluation and placement for traumatically brain injured adults. In M. Ylvisaker & E.M.R. Gobble (Eds.), *Community Re-entry for Head Injured Adults* (pp. 220–240). Boston, MA: Little Brown.

Wade, D.T. (2006). Applying the WHO ICF framework to the rehabilitation of patients with cognitive deficits. In P.W. Halligan & D.T. Wade

(Eds.), *Effectiveness of Rehabilitation for Cognitive Deficits* (pp. 31–42). New York: Oxford University Press.

Wade, D.T. (2009). Control in rehabilitation research. *Clinical Rehabilitation, 23*: 675–680.

Wade, D.T., Legh-Smith, J., & Hewer, R.L. (1986). Effects of living with and looking after survivors of a stroke. *British Medical Journal, 293*: 418–420.

Wade, S.L., Carey, J., & Wolfe, C.R. (2006). An online intervention to reduce parental distress following paediatric brain injury. *Journal of consulting and clinical psychology, 74*: 445–454.

Wade, S.L., Wolfe, C.R., Brown, T.M., & Pestian, J.P. (2005). Can a web-based family problem-solving intervention work for children with traumatic brain injury? *Rehabilitation Psychology, 50*: 337–345.

Waldrop, D.P., Milch, R.A., & Skretny, J.A. (2005). Understanding family responses to life-limiting illness: In-depth interviews with hospice patients and their family members. *Journal of Palliative Care, 21*: 88–96.

Walker, A. (1972). Long-term evaluation of the social and family adjustment to head injuries. *Scandinavian Journal of Rehabilitation Medicine, 4*: 5–8.

Walker, G., & Goldner, V. (1995). The wounded prince and the women who love him. In C. Burck & B. Speed (Eds.), *Gender, Power and Relationships* (pp.24–45). London: Routledge.

Walzlawick, P., & Coyne, J.C. (1980). Depression following stroke: Brief, problem-focused family treatment. *Family Process, 19*: 23–38.

Wantanabe, Y., Shiel, A., Asami, T., Taki, K., & Tabuchi, K. (2000). An evaluation of neurobehavioural problems as perceived by family members and levels of family stress 1–3 years following traumatic brain injury in Japan. *Clinical Rehabilitation, 14*: 172–177.

Wantanabe, Y., Shiel, A., McLellan, D.L., Kurihara, M., & Hayashi, K. (2001). The impact of traumatic brain injury on family members living with patients: A preliminary study in Japan and the UK. *Disability and Rehabilitation: An International, Multidisciplinary Journal, 23*: 370–378.

Warrington, E.K., & Shallice, T. (1984). Category specific semantic impairments. *Brain, 107*: 829–854.

Watanabe, Y., Shiel, A., McLellan, D.L., Kurihara, M., & Hayashi, K. (2001). The impact of traumatic brain injury on family members living with patients: A preliminary study in Japan and the UK. *Disability & Rehabilitation, 23*: 370–378.

Watson, J.C., & Greenburg, L.S. (1995). Alliance ruptures and repairs in experiential therapy. *In Session: Psychotherapy in Practice, 1*: 19–31.

Watt, D. (2007). Towards a neuroscience of empathy: Integrating affective and cognitive perspectives. *Neuropsychoanalysis, 9*: 119–140.

Watt, D.F. (1986). Transference—a right hemisphere event? The boundary between psychoanalytic metapsychology and neuropsychology. *Psychoanalysis & Contemporary Thought, 9*: 43–77.

Watt, N., & Penn, C. (2000). Predictors and indicators of return to work following traumatic brain injury in South Africa: Findings from a preliminary experimental database. *South African Journal of Psychology, 30*: 27–37.

Watzlawick, P., & Coyne, J.C. (1980). Depression following stroke: Brief, problem-focussed family treatment. *Family Process, 19*: 23–38.

Weddell, R., & Leggett, J.A. (2006). Factors triggering relatives' judgements of personality change after traumatic brain injury. *Brain Injury, 20*: 1221–1234.

Weddell, R., Oddy, M., & Jenkins, D. (1980). Social adjustment after rehabilitation: A two year follow-up of patients with severe head injury. *Psychological Medicine, 10*: 257–263.

Wehman, P.H., Kregel, J., Sherron, P.D., Nguyen, S., Kreutzer, J.S., Fry, R. & Zasler, N. (1993). Critical factors associated with the successful supported employment placement of patients with severe traumatic brain injury. *Brain Injury, 7*: 31–44.

Weinstein, E.A. (1991). Anosognosia and denial of illness. In G.P. Prigatano & D.L. Schacter (Eds.), *Awareness of Deficit after Brain Injury: Clinical and Theoretical Issues* (pp. 240–257). New York: Oxford University Press.

Weinstein, E.A., Cole, M., Mitchell, M.S., & Lyerly, O.G. (1964). Anosognosia and aphasia. *Archives of Neurology, 10*: 376–386.

Weinstein, E.A., Friedland, R.P., & Wagner, E.E. (1994). Denial/unawareness of impairment and symbolic behavior in Alzheimer's disease. *Neuropsychiatry, Neuropsychology & Behavioral Neurology, 7*: 176–184.

Weinstein, E.A., & Kahn, R.L. (1955). *Denial of Illness: Symbolic and Physiological Aspects.* Springfield's, IL: Charles C Thomas.

Wells, A. (2008). *Metacognitive therapy for anxiety and depression.* New York: The Guilford Press.

Wells, R., Dywan, J., & Dumas, J. (2005). Life satisfaction and distress in family caregivers as related to specific behavioural changes after traumatic brain injury. *Brain Injury, 19*: 1105–1115.

West, M.D. (1995). Aspects of the workplace and return to work for persons with brain injury in supported employment. *Brain Injury, 9*: 301–313.

White, M. (1988). The process of questioning: A therapy of literary merit? *Dulwich Centre Newsletter,* pp. 8–14.

White, M. (1995). 'Reflecting teamwork as definitional ceremony'. In M. White (Ed.), *Re-Authoring Lives: Interviews & Essays*. Dulwich Centre Books.

White, M. (2007). *Maps of Narrative Practice*. New York: Norton.

White, M., & Epston, D. (1990). *Narrative Means to Therapeutic Ends*. Adelaide: Dulwich.

Whittaker, R., Kemp, S., & House, A. (2007). Illness perceptions and outcome in mild head injury: A Longitudinal study. *Journal of Neurology, Neurosurgery & Psychiatry, 78*: 644–646.

Wilkinson, M. (1992). How do we understand empathy systemically? *Journal of Family Therapy, 14*: 193–205.

Willer, B., Allen, K., Durnan, M.C., & Ferry, A. (1990). Problems and coping strategies of mothers, siblings and young adult males with traumatic brain injury. *Canadian Journal of Rehabilitation, 3*: 167–173.

Williams, P.D., Lorenzo, F.D., & Borja, M. (1993). Pediatric chronic illness: Effects on siblings and mothers. *Maternal-Child Nursing Journal, 21*: 111–121.

Williams, W.H., Evans, J.J., & Fleminger, S. (2003). Neurorehabiliation and cognitive-behaviour therapy of anxiety disorders after brain injury: An overview and case illustration of obsessive-compulsive disorder. *Neuropsychological Rehabilitation, 13*: 133–148.

Wilson, B.A. (1987). *The Rehabilitation of Memory*. New York: The Guilford Press.

Wilson, B.A. (2000). Compensating for cognitive deficits following brain injury. *Neuropsychology Review, 10*: 233–243.

Wilson, B.A. (2002). Towards a comprehensive model of cognitive rehabilitation. *Neuropsychological Rehabilitation, 12*: 97–110.

Wilson, B.A. (2005). The effective treatment of memory-related disabilities. In P.W. Halligan & D. Wade (Eds.), *The Effectiveness of Rehabilitation for Cognitive Deficits* (pp. 143–151). Oxford: Oxford University Press.

Wilson, B.A., Bateman, A., & Evans, J.J. (2009). The understanding brain injury (UBI) group. In B.A. Wilson, F. Gracey, J.J. Evans, & A. Bateman (Eds.), *Neuropsychological Rehabilitation: Theory, Models, Therapy and Outcome* (pp. 68–80). Cambridge: Cambridge University Press.

Wilson, B.A., Coleman, M.R., & Pickard, J.D. (2008). Neuropsychological assessment and management of people in states of impaired consciousness: An overview of some recent studies. *Brain Impairment, 9*: 28–35.

Wilson,B.A.,Evans,J.J.,Brentnall,S.,Bremner,S.,Keohane,C.,&Williams,H. (2000). The Oliver Zangwill Centre for neuropsychological rehabilitation: A partnership between healthcare and rehabilitation research. In A.L. Christensen & B.P. Uzzell (Eds.), *International Handbook of*

Neuropsychological Rehabilitation (pp. 231–246). New York: Kluwer Academic/Plenum.

Wilson, B.A., Evans, J.J., Emslie, H.C., & Malinek, V. (1997). Evaluation of NeuroPage: A new memory aid. *Journal of Neurology, Neurosurgery and Psychiatry, 63*: 113–115.

Wilson, B.A., Evans, J.J., & Keohane, C. (2002). Cognitive rehabilitation: A goal-planning approach. *Journal of Head Trauma Rehabilitation, 17*: 542–555.

Wilson, B.A., Gracey, F., Malley, D., Bateman, A., & Evans, J. (2009). The Oliver Zangwill Centre approach to neuropsychological rehabilitation. In B.A. Wilson, F. Gracey, J.J. Evans, & A. Bateman (Eds.), *Neuropsychological Rehabilitation: Theory, Models, Therapy and Outcome* (pp. 47–67). Cambridge: Cambridge University Press.

Winocur, G., Moscovitch, M., & Sekeres, M. (2007). Memory consolidation or transformation: context manipulation and hippocampal representations of memory. *Nature neuroscience, 10*(5): 555–557.

Winslade, W.J. (1998). *Confronting Traumatic Brain Injury: Devastation, Hope and Healing.* New Haven and London.

Winstanley, J., Simpson, G., Tate, R., & Myles, B. (2006). Early indicators and contributors to psychological distress in relatives during rehabilitation following severe traumatic brain injury: findings from the Brain Injury Outcomes Study. *The Journal of Head Trauma Rehabilitation, 21*: 453–466.

Wong, T.M. (1998). Ethical issues in the evaluation and treatment of traumatic brain injury. In *Avoiding Ethical Misconduct in Psychology Specialty Areas* (pp. 187–200). Springfield, IL: Charles C. Thomas.

Wood, R.L. (1987). *Brain Injury Rehabilitation: A Neurobehavioural Approach.* London: Croom Helm.

Wood, R.L. (2005). Waking up next to a stranger. *The Psychologist, 18*: 138–140.

Wood, D., Bruner, J., & Ross, G. (1976). The role of tutoring in problem-solving. *Journal of Child Psychology & Psychiatry, 17*: 89–100.

Wood, R.L., & Yurdakul, L.K. (1997). Change in relationship status following traumatic brain injury. *Brain Injury, 11*: 491–502.

Yardley, L. (1996). Reconciling discurcive and materialist perspectives on health and illness: A reconstruction of the biopsychosocial approach. *Theory and Psychology, 6*: 485–508.

Yates, P.J. (2003). Psychological adjustment, social enablement and community integration following traumatic brain injury. *Neuropsychological Rehabilitation, 12*: 291–306.

Yeates, G.N. (2007). Avoiding the skull seduction in post-acute acquired brain injury (ABI) services: Individualist invitations and systemic responses. *Clinical Psychology Forum, 175*: 33–36.

Yeates, G.N. (2009). Working with families in neuropsychological rehabilitation. In B.A.Wilson, F. Gracey, J.J. Evans, & A. Bateman (Eds.), *Neuropsychological Rehabilitation: Theory, Models, Therapy & Outcome.* Cambridge: Cambridge University Press.

Yeates, G.N. (in preparation). *Injuries to Intimacy: Personality Change, Love and Couples Relationships Following Acquired Brain Injury.* London: Karnac.

Yeates, G., Gracey, F., & McGrath, J.C. (2008). A biopsychosocial deconstruction of "personality change" following acquired brain injury. *Neuropsychological Rehabilitation, 18*: 566–589.

Yeates, G., Hamill, M., Sutton, L., Psaila, K., Gracey, F., Mohamed, S., & O'Dell, J. (2008). Dysexecutive problems and interpersonal relating following frontal brain injury: Reformulation and compensation in Cognitive-Analytic Therapy (CAT). *Neuropsychoanalysis, 10*: 43–58.

Yeates, G., Henwood, K., Gracey, F., & Evans, J.J. (2006). Awareness of disability after acquired brain injury (ABI): Subjectivity within the psychosocial context. *Neuro Psychoanalysis, 8*: 175–189.

Yeates, G., Henwood, K., Gracey, F., & Evans, J.J. (2007). Awareness of disability after acquired brain injury (ABI) and the family context. *Neuropsychological Rehabilitation, 17*: 151–173.

Yeates, G., Luckie, M., DeBeer, Z., & Khela (2010). Elucidating the psychosocial context of post-concussional syndrome (PCS): A case study from post-Milan systemic family therapy. *Journal of Family Therapy, 32*: 186–202.

Yeates, G., & Whitehouse-Hart, J. (2009). Socio-emotional communication impairments following acquired brain injury and couples' inter-subjective experiences of intimacy. *Paper Presented at the 9th Neuropsychoanalysis Congress, Paris, France.*

Ylvisaker, M., & Feeney, T.J. (1998). *Collaborative Brain Injury Intervention.* San Diego: Singular Publishing Group.

Ylvisaker, M., & Feeney, T. (2000). Reconstruction of identity following brain injury. *Brain Impairment, 1*: 12–28.

Ylvisaker, M., & Szekeres, S.F. (1989). Metacognitive and executive impairments in head-injured children and adults. *Topics in language Disorders, 9*: 34–49.

Ylvisaker, M., Szekeres, S.F., Henry, K., Sullivan, D.M., & Wheeler, P. (1987). Topics in cognitive rehabilitation therapy. In M. Ylvisaker &

E.M.R. Gobble (Eds.), *Community Re-entry for Head Injured Adults* (pp. 137–220). Boston, MA: Little Brown.

Youngjohn, J., & Altman, I. (1989). A performance-based group approach to the treatment of anosognosia and denial. *Rehabilitation Psychology, 34*: 217–222.

Youngblut, J., & Brooten, D. (2008). Mother's mental health, mother-child relationship, and family functioning 3 months after a preschooler's head injury. *Journal of Head Trauma Rehabilitation, 23(2)*: 92–102.

Zarski, J.J., DePompei, R., & Zook, A. (1988). Traumatic head injury: Dimensions of family responsivity. *Journal of Head Trauma Rehabilitation, 3*: 31–41.

Zarski, J.J., West, J.D., DePompei, R., & Hall, D.E. (1988). Chronic illness: Stressors, the adjustment process, and family-focused interventions. *Journal of Mental Health Counseling, 10*: 145–158.

Zuercher, M., Ummenhofer, W., Baltussen, A., & Walder, B. (2009). The use of Glasgow Coma Scale in injury assessment: a critical review. *Brain Injury, 23*: 371–184.

Zihl, J., von Cramon, D., & Mai, N. (1983). Selective disturbance of movement vision after bilateral brain damage. *Brain, 106*: 313–340.

INDEX

Marital dissatisfaction, 72
Marital therapy, 148
Mayo traumatic brain injury
  severity classification
  system, 15
McDonald, Skye, 97
Mediation, 132–137
Memory, 44
  rehabilitation targets, 6
Mental Capacity Act 2005, 30
Mental health
  issues, 96, 97
  protective functions, 127
  status post-injury, 269
Mental Research Institute, 189
Mentor programme, 286
Meta-cognition, 62
Meta-cognitive
  abilities, 63
  process, 63
Mentalizing, 63
  activity, 68
Milan model, 190
Mind and brain, 39–41
Mind-brain-behaviour
  relationship, 220
Minimally conscious state (MCS), 17
Mirror neuron theorists, 68
Multidisciplinary team, role, 27, 28
Multi-factorial relationship, 281
Multi-family group
  interventions, 202, 287
Multiple trace theory (MIT), 46

Narrative means to
  therapeutic ends, 191
Narrative therapy, 3, 135
National Service Framework
  (NSF), 278
  for neurological, 3, 152
  long-term (neurological)
  conditions, 278

Negative construct pole, 246
Negative emotional
  responses, 141
Neglected subsystems, 257
  frequently, 257
Neocortical involvement, 84
Neural mechanisms, 107
Neuro-anatomical module, 64
Neuro-cognitive
  accounts, 123
  error, 136
  expectation, 135
Neuro-disability, 122, 129
Neuro-imaging
  modality, 14
Neurology, 3, 4, 26
Neuropathology, threats
  to intimacy from, 80, 81
Neuro-peptide, 102
Neuro-psychological
  alteration, 59
  assessment at five years
    post-injury stage, 175
  assessment reports, 40, 80
  authors, 120, 124
  deficit, 93
  evidence, 64
  impairments, 283
  perspectives, 41
  process, 58, 68, 107
  rehabilitation, 4, 133,
    149, 225
  typologies of attention, 58
Neuro-psychological rehabilitation
  case descriptions, 171–186
  changes and disputes, 180, 181
  holistic, 249
  simple genogram, 177
  sketching out a shared
    language, case example,
    175–179
  Y-shaped model of, 164, 166